D1477279

GREAT BRITAIN'S
RAILWAYS

GREAT BRITAIN'S
RAILWAYS
A NEW HISTORY

COLIN MAGGS

AMBERLEY

Jacket images, courtesy Gordon Edgar.

Above: 46115 *Scots Guardsman* climbing from Dillicar, Kendal Parish, Westmoreland.
Built in 1927, *Scots Guardsman* featured in the 1936 film *Night Mail*.

Below: Direct Rail Services 57310 *Pride of Cumbria* stands with the sleeper stock of the
1C99 23:45 London Paddington to Penzance, alongside First Great Western 'HST' 43018,
the 1A94 15:59 from Penzance on Friday 22 September 2017.

First published 2018

Amberley Publishing
The Hill, Stroud
Gloucestershire, GL5 4EP

www.amberley-books.com

British Library Cataloguing in Publication Data.
A catalogue record for this book is available from the British Library.

ISBN 978 1 4456 7029 4 (hardback)
ISBN 978 1 4456 7030 0 (ebook)

Typesetting and Origination by Amberley Publishing.
Printed in the UK.

Contents

Note to the Reader

Although this book is generally in chronological order, sometimes to avoid multiple short entries it has been deemed more useful to the reader to include subsequent history of certain subjects.

Train times in this book are those as given in official timetables, the twelve-hour clock being used previous to June 1963 and the twenty-four-hour clock subsequently.

Acknowledgements

Especial thanks are due to Colin Roberts for checking and improving the text and also Graham Bryant for additional help. And a thank you to Gordon Edgar for his splendid jacket photographs.

1

Early British Railways

Which was the first railway in Great Britain? No one knows the answer because railways stretch back into the mists of time. It could have been the maker of the first two-wheeled cart who, when he or she came to a muddy stretch of path, laid down two tree trunks to prevent the wheels sticking – so, hey presto, the railway had been invented. It was economic too, because it was not necessary to build a smooth surface over the whole width of the road, just two narrow paths sufficed.

One of the first railways as we know them was opened in 1604 – note the date, which is well before George Stephenson was born on 9 June 1781 – the 4 foot 6 inch gauge railway was opened at Wollaton, near Nottingham, for the purpose of carrying coal 2 miles from the pithead to navigable water. As the contemporary roads were in such a poor condition that they were unsuited to carrying heavy loads, water transport had proved the most economic method. Supervised by Huntingdon Beaumont, a mining engineer, this line was easy to build: the cross sleepers were oak logs split in half, while the running rails were strips of timber about 4¼ inches square attached to the sleepers with wooden pegs. They were known as 'rails' due to the similarity to rail-and-post fencing. The sleepers were covered with earth or ashes to protect them from wear by the horses' shoes and also to prevent the animals from tripping.

Mines in Northumberland and Durham copied this railway, sometimes adding the improvement of thin iron plates on top of the wooden rails to prevent them from being quickly worn out by the cast-iron wheels. It was not unknown for timber rails to need replacing annually.

Railways proved an economic method of transport as on a railway a horse could draw four or five wagons, but on a road with its much greater friction it was limited to just one cart. The carrying capacity of wagons varied from 33 cwt to 53 cwt. These early lines were confined to collieries and ironworks, often moving the load from a higher to a lower level, the only earthworks being for easing abrupt descents.

South Wales was not slow in adopting this economic method of transport and in 1695 at Neath, Sir Humphrey Mackworth ran 'the said Waggon-way on Wooden Railes from the face of each Wall of Coal twelve hundred yards under Ground quite down to the Water-side about three-quarters of a mile from the mouth of the Coal-pit'.

Sheffield certainly had a wagonway by 1729, which ran from the Sheffield Park Colliery to a yard in the town. It was the cause of at least one fatal accident for it is recorded 'Pd for the Woman that was killed with the Waggon 0.10.6'. The line closed by 1770; it was replaced in 1774 with a 2-mile-long wagonway into the centre of Sheffield – which caused a riot. Although the line had reduced the cost of cartage from 2s 8d to 1s 2d per ton, the colliery owners ceased selling coal at a low price at the pithead. This so annoyed the townsfolk that 'they assembled in a prodigious number, and destroyed several of their [the proprietors'] carriages, totally pulled down a watch-house and compting-house in their new coal yard, and set fire to all the timber machinery erected for discharging their loading, brought one carriage through the town, afterwards kindled fire in, and sent it flaming into the river'. John Curr who laid the line was forced to hide in a wood for three days and three nights 'to escape the fury of the populace'. This line was rebuilt, but closed by 1800.

Another example could be found in Bath. In the eighteenth century the city was developing as a fashionable spa, people were flocking to the city and new houses were required. Ralph Allen owned quarries on a hill above the town. In 1731 he laid a railway on a gradient of 1 in 10 down to the River Avon. Loaded wagons descended economically by gravity and when empty were drawn up the hill by two horses. Stone could be loaded into boats for transport to Bristol, either for use there, or for export, while for use in Bath the wagons were carried across the river on barges – Ralph Allen had invented the train ferry. When constructing the Palladian Bridge below his home, to carry the construction materials, he built a self-acting incline forming a branch line, a descending loaded wagon drawing up an empty one.

Scotland had examples of early railways, one being the Tranent Waggonway of 3 feet 3 inch gauge with wooden rails set on stone blocks. The 2-mile long line opened in 1742 and carried coal to the port of Cockenzie with gravity taking wagons down, and a man running alongside to sprag the wheels to keep the wagons under control. Horses were used for the return journey.

It was the first railway to be used strategically in battle. In 1745 when Sir John Cope with 2,000 English troops was facing Charles Edward Stuart and 5,000 Scots, Cope selected a defensive position at Prestonpans and mounted his artillery on 'a narrow cart road' which in fact was the Tranent Waggonway. The next day one of the Jacobite divisions marched down the wagonway to attack the English cannons.

Another early Scottish line was the Alloa Railway from Sauchie colliery to Alloa harbour. It was opened in 1768 by John, Earl of Mar. With a gauge of 3 feet 3 inches, the first rails were 4-inch sections of Scots fir, but by 1785 a bar of malleable iron was fixed to the upper surface of the fir. The rails were fixed to granite or whinstone blocks but, in due course, after wheel and track breakages, it was realised that timber sleepers provided a smoother ride and less damage. This improved track enabled a horse to draw three 30 cwt wagons compared to just one previously, or just 6 cwt in a road cart before the railway was laid. When cast-iron rails appeared in 1810, a horse could haul up to 10 one-ton wagons.

Early British railways generally used flanged wheels running on plain rails, but later edged rails were used to enable existing carts with plain wheels to run on the track. Practice proved that this was unsatisfactory because the vertical flange was prone to breakage and in addition the flat plate collected dirt and stones, causing friction which impeded the horse. The vertical flange also proved a problem to road users at level crossings, whereas an edged rail could be sunk into grooves when it crossed a road. The first iron edge rails were made at Coalbrookdale, Shropshire, on 13 November 1767 and the Carron Railway, Falkirk, was the first to use them.

Another problem with an L-section plateway was it could not be bent to form a curve. This meant a curved line necessarily had to be a series of tangents thus causing a jerking motion, which was not too serious with the slow speed of horse traction but highly unsatisfactory with the higher speed of steam haulage. The shape of the I-section edge rail permitted it to be bent to a continuous curve, thus allowing rolling stock to pass round it smoothly. In 1820 John Birkinshaw of the Bedlington Iron Works patented rails in wrought iron, which proved less brittle and less liable to fracture, and as they could be rolled in lengths of 15 feet there were far fewer joints and it was at joints that rails tended to fracture.

The rails were wedged by wooden keys into chairs, and, as with the timber rails, were initially carried on stone blocks. Unless these were set very accurately they gave a rough ride and because they were so heavy, adjustment was difficult, so later track was held to gauge by transverse wooden beams. These wooden sleepers were much better as their lightness was preferable when laid on soft ground and any differences in level could simply be adjusted by packing stones beneath the timbers. This type of track was found to be more resilient and offered smoother running.

Charles Blacker Vignoles believed rails should have a broad base so that they could be fixed directly to sleepers and these were widely adopted, except in Britain. British railways preferred the Joseph Locke rail, which was held in a chair and so could be easily lifted. Locke originally had the idea that if the top and bottom of the rail were identical, it could be turned over and the other side used. In the event, it was found that a rail resting in a chair became battered on the underside and thus gave an uneven running surface. The cross section of Locke's rail was eventually modified to offer a larger head, providing for an increased amount of wear so that when a rail was worn too much for main-line service it could be used for lighter traffic on branch lines.

How was the width between the rails decided? A horse drawing a cart was placed between shafts and the width between the shafts was determined by the width of the animal's hindquarters. In turn, the width between the shafts determined the distance the wheels were placed apart and this approximated to 4 feet 8½ inches.

The name for railways varied. Those having plain rails using flanged wheels were generally known as railways or railroads, while those using edged rails and plain wheels were usually referred to as tramways or plateways.

For cheapness, the track was usually single with passing loops within sight of each other, the rule being that if a train was approaching on a single line, the first one to reach a passing loop waited to let the other go by. If two trains happened to meet head-on, it was the custom for the drivers to fight to determine which should go back to a loop.

The Lake Lock Rail Road, built under the Wakefield Inclosure Act of 1793, opened in 1798. With a gauge of 3 feet 4 inches its principal traffic was coal, with lime and road stone carried as subsidiary traffic. As the rail road could be used by anyone with a suitable vehicle, it could be said to be the world's first public railway, rather than the Surrey Iron Railway. The Lake Lock line closed in December 1836.

On the opposite bank of the Calder & Hebble Navigation, a tramway ran from Stanley to St John's Colliery, Normanton, and provided the only example of the Tom Pudding iron compartment boats, which were normally coupled together and drawn by a barge, but in this instance were craned out of the water onto dedicated 12-wheeled two-bogie wagons, this method being used from 1891 until the autumn of 1949.

Another curiosity was that in 1800 the eccentric William Fenton opened a tramway between Wakefield Bridge and New Park Collieries with bullocks, rather than horses, donkeys or mules drawing the wagons.

Early railways were built for carrying the trade of its owner, that is, either coal or stone; they were not available for general traffic.

Most of the early railways were built entirely on property belonging to the owner of the railway. If you wished to construct a line on someone else's land, you had to seek a way leave, and pay a rate of so much on each wagon passing over the line. As building the Surrey Iron Railway demanded right of way through land owned by many individuals, it needed an Act of Parliament to give the railway right of purchase. This marked a new phase in railway history – the presentation of a private bill to Parliament.

Parliamentary legislation for railways was either by a private act, or local & personal act, and getting one was generally a long and costly business. The measure had to come before committees of both Houses as bills and then might be rejected by either House. If it passed these hurdles, the bill had to be passed by both Houses, and the Act then received royal assent. An Act allowed the railway's promoters to acquire land by compulsory purchase, and to raise or borrow, within stated limits, the capital required. In the event of dispute between the railway and property owners, the case would go to arbitration.

Arguably the first public railway in the world was the Surrey Iron Railway. The Act for building it received royal assent on 21 May 1801 and on 26 July 1803 the 9-mile long Surrey Iron Railway opened between Croydon and Wandsworth. On payment of a toll it could be used by anyone who had a cart that could run on its rails – in other words, it was the rail form of the contemporary turnpike road. Competition between the various carriers ensured cheap rates available to the public. Notice the word 'Iron' in the title, no old-fashioned timber rails were used on this double-tracked modern line. Horses, donkeys and mules provided the motive power, or 'lean and half-starved horses' as a contemporary writer described them. It carried principally chalk, fuller's earth, agricultural produce, stone and timber to London, returning with coal and manure. Interestingly parts of the route are used today by the London Tramlink. The Surrey Iron Railway failed to fulfil its proprietors' expectations, traffic declined and the railway closed on 31 August 1846.

The Croydon line's engineer was William Jessop. Double track was laid on stone blocks and the gauge was 5 feet from centre to centre of the stone sleepers and 4 feet 8 inches between the outer faces of the rails. An extension, the Croydon, Merstham & Godstone Railway, opened on 24 July 1805. Traffic seriously declined when the competing Croydon Canal opened in 1809 and shrank even further when the Croydon, Merstham & Godstone closed in 1838, both lines being abandoned in 1846.

Although these early railways may have unofficially carried passengers from time to time, they were solely intended for goods and mineral traffic. The very first railway for passenger use opened in 1807 to carry people from Oystermouth to Swansea, a distance of 5½ miles. Its subsequent history was interesting. Passenger services were withdrawn in the 1820s when a competing turnpike road opened. It was resurrected in 1842 as a standard-gauge, horse-worked, coal-carrying line; horse-drawn passenger services were restored in 1860 and steam power introduced in 1877. In 1929 the line was electrified using the overhead system, passengers carried in large double-deck trams, each seating 106 passengers, two trams sometimes being coupled to form a train. The local bus company purchased the line in 1958 and closed it in 1960.

In 1758 Charles Brandling was unable to get permission to build a 3½-mile-long line from Middleton Colliery across Hunslet Moor to Leeds. He overcame the problem by obtaining an Act of Parliament, the very first Railway Act granted by Parliament. It stated where the railway was to run and what compensation was to be paid to landowners. His horse wagonway was unusual in having double track rather than single with passing loops. The presence of the line encouraged local industry to develop and Leeds' population grew from an estimated 16,380 in 1771 to 30,669 in 1801. In 1881 the gauge of 4 feet 1 inch was altered to standard gauge. When closure seemed likely in 1958 the Middleton Railway Preservation Society took over and ran its first train on 20 June 1960. This preservation society was unusual in that it operated goods, rather than passenger, trains.

The first Scottish railway to obtain an Act of Parliament was the Kilmarnock & Troon Railway, this being granted 27 May 1808. It was for a 10-mile-long double-track goods and the passenger plateway opened on 6 July 1812 with horse traction. It could boast of having the first railway bridge in Scotland as it crossed the River Irvine between Gateshead and Drybridge. The line also carried some of the first seaside trippers – taking Kilmarnock weavers to Troon. Its wooden rails were replaced by iron ones in 1815. Around 1817 a George Stephenson locomotive was tried, but its weight broke the cast-iron plates. Its iron wheels were replaced with wood and it worked mineral, goods and passenger trains until 1848. The line's engineer was William Jessop, who had been responsible for the Surrey Iron Railway.

2

The Early Development of the Steam Locomotive: 1804–1825

When James Watt and Matthew Boulton invented the steam engine, it was different from the engines with which we are accustomed. Due to the primitive state of the metal industry being unable to make a strong boiler, it worked not by high steam pressure moving a piston but by condensing steam creating a vacuum in a cylinder and the piston being forced down by air pressure. Although this type of engine was suitable for pumping water from a mine, it was far too clumsy to power a mobile machine as the design offered a low power-to-weight ratio and was too heavy to be able to move itself, let alone draw a load.

The very first locomotive ran on ordinary roads rather than on a railway and was made by William Murdock, born in Ayrshire on 21 August 1754. Employed by Boulton & Watt, in 1779 he was in Cornwall superintending the erection of James Watt's pumping engines. He turned his thoughts to producing a steam engine capable of moving along. For economy, rather than build a full-sized machine, initially he made a model.

A spirit-fired lamp raised high-pressure steam in a boiler, which provided power to move a cylinder in a piston that moved up and down, thus driving the road wheels via a crank. The initial test indoors proved successful, so he decided to hold a longer test outside. Believing it might frighten residents if they saw it moving in daylight, he resolved to try it at night in a country lane.

It accelerated rapidly, William chased after it and was amused to see that the rector, scared by the puffing and hissing, at first believed it to be a manifestation of the devil!

Murdoch, pleased with his invention, set off to London intending to patent it. Matthew Boulton, alarmed at the possibility of the firm losing its best engineer, persuaded him to return to Cornwall. James Watt, probably thinking that it would be impossible to make a sufficiently strong large boiler, poured scorn on the idea, so Murdock developed it no further.

Richard Trevithick, son of a Cornish mine manager, eager to break Watt's stationary steam engine monopoly and produce another kind of steam engine, developed a stationary engine worked by high-pressure steam. He used a double-acting cylinder with steam admitted through a four-way valve and exhausted not through Watt's condenser but through a chimney. Trevithick's next development was to use a boiler pressed to 45 lb/sq inch, not the 14.7 lb/sq inch of Newcomen & Watt. His principle worked and saved coal – particularly important in Cornwall where there were no locally available supplies. The next development was to build a steam carriage and this first ran on Christmas Eve 1801, travelling faster than walking pace. Between 1801 and 1803, he built three vehicles but the poor surface of the roads prohibited further development.

The obvious advance was to run one on an ultra-smooth surface – a railway. On 21 February 1804, Trevithick ran the very first locomotive in the world, a 0-4-0, on the line between Penydarren Ironworks, near Merthyr Tydfil, to Abercynon. It made the journey of 9½ miles in 4 hours and 5 minutes, at an average speed of 2.4 mph. In addition to hauling 10 tons of bar iron, it also drew a load of seventy sightseers and won a wager of 500 guineas.

As the road was a plateway, the engine would have had flangeless wheels. Its boiler was about 5 feet in length, the single cylinder probably horizontal and set on top of the boiler. With only one cylinder it was believed a flywheel was essential and the running wheels were driven via a set of gears. One of the excellent features of the design was that the exhaust steam was turned up the chimney, thus creating a forced draught and consequently produced a better fire, leading to more steam being created. This feature was copied in all subsequent locomotives. Although a mechanical success, the locomotive's weight of 4 tons fractured so many cast-iron plates that horse traction had to continue.

Trevithick's second locomotive was built in 1805 for Wylam Colliery, Northumberland, but in the event, the poor wooden track prevented its use. This engine had flanged wheels.

Trevithick's third engine, the 2-2-0 *Catch Me Who Can*, was really a fairground venture. In 1808 it offered rides on a circular track near the site of the present Euston station. Reaching speeds of up to 15 mph, its vertical cylinder drove the wheels without the use of a flywheel.

At this point, Whyte's notation should be explained. F. M. Whyte, engineer of the New York Central Railroad, devised a useful system of explaining simply, in shorthand, what a particular locomotive looks like. Three figures indicate the wheels on one side of a locomotive starting from the front and indicating the numbers of leading, coupled and trailing wheels. In the event of no wheels appearing in a particular category, this is indicated by a nought – thus an engine with a four-wheeled bogie in front of six driving wheels is shown as a 4-6-0. Side tank engines are shown by the suffix 'T', with a sub-division of 'PT' for 'pannier tank', 'ST' for 'saddle tank' and 'WT' for 'well tank'. Thus a six-wheeled coupled shunting tank could be classified as 0-6-0T.

Returning to the history of early engines, the Napoleonic wars had caused the price of horses and fodder to increase so John Blenkinsop of the Middleton Colliery experimented with a locomotive. With the aim of avoiding the problem of broken cast-iron rails and to improve haulage, on 10 April 1811 he patented a cogged driving wheel engaging in a rack on one of the rails. Matthew Murray turned Blenkinsop's idea into reality and 0-6-0 *Prince Regent* was tested on 24 June 1812. His two engines cost £350 each, replaced 14 horses, saved one-sixth of the transport cost and hauled 27 wagons on the level at 3½ mph. They were the first locomotives in commercial use and ran successfully for thirty years.

Two more engines were placed in service in 1813. An early fatality occurred in 1818, George Stephenson reporting: 'The driver had been in liquor and had put a considerable load on the safety valve, so that upon going forward the engine blew up and the man was killed.' By 1835 the locomotives were worn out and as the price of fodder had fallen, horse traction was reinstated.

A colliery at Wigan ran a Blenkinsop engine which was described thus:

> The people of the neighbourhood emphatically call it 'The Walking Horse' and certainly it bears no little resemblance to a living animal. The superabundant steam is emitted at each stroke with a noise something similar to the hard breathing or snorting of a horse – the escaping steam representing the breath of its nostrils, and the deception aided by the regular motion of the engine-beam.

The rack rail was found an unnecessary complication and was abandoned in subsequent machines.

Having seen Trevithick's engine, Wylam Colliery's chief engineer William Hedley, and his foreman Timothy Hackworth, converted the wooden track to a plateway. In 1811 Christopher Blackett, owner of the colliery, built a locomotive under the supervision of Hedley, but to economise on costs it had only one cylinder. It proved a case of 'cheap proving dear' and was a failure. In 1812 Hedley, Hackworth and Jonathan Foster, the latter being an enginewright at the colliery, built a two-cylinder locomotive. Although a mechanical success, it broke the tram plates but the difficulty was solved by placing it on two four-wheeled bogies to spread the weight; it then successfully hauled 50-ton loads.

Hedley's next engines for the colliery were the 0-4-0s *Puffing Billy* and *Wylam Dilly*. These ran on edge rails as it was realised that there was little call for running ordinary road vehicles along a plateway. They ran until 1862 when these, the oldest steam locomotives in the world, were preserved: *Puffing Billy* in the Science Museum, London, and *Wylam Dilly* in the Royal Museum, Edinburgh.

George Stephenson, born in a cottage beside the Wylam Colliery railway, was appointed enginewright to Killingsworth Colliery in 1812. He would have seen Hedley's engines and wanted to build one for his own colliery.

In 1814 George Stephenson built his first engine, *Blucher*, named after a Prussian general and also a local colliery. Erected in the colliery workshop behind his house, it used a single-flue boiler rather than Trevithick's better return-flue design which drew more heat from the fuel. It was similar to Blenkinsop's engine but its flanged wheels ran on plain edge rails. It could draw a load of 30 tons up a gradient of 1 in 450 at 4 mph, but was rather prone to breakdown and could be difficult to start. On one occasion George had to ask his sister-in-law to put her shoulder to the wheel. Nevertheless, he built more of the type for various collieries and a six-wheeled version for the Kilmarnock & Troon Railway, but the latter proved too heavy for the cast-iron rails.

In 1820 Stephenson was appointed engineer to build a line from Hetton Colliery to the staithes on the River Wear. The 8-mile line, with a combination of gravity inclines and locomotive-worked sections, was the first railway in the world to avoid horsepower. With a gauge of 4 feet 8 inches, it opened in 1822 and was worked until 1959.

Despite its faults, *Blucher* impressed Edward Pease who was planning the 13-mile-long Stockton & Darlington Railway. George Stephenson was appointed the line's chief engineer in 1822 and with Edward Pease, jointly founded a locomotive works, installing his son Robert Stephenson as managing director. Edward Pease was one of the many members of the Society of Friends who subscribed to early railways.

Devon's first permanent railway was the Haytor Tramway, which opened on 16 September 1820, carrying granite from Haytor to a canal from where it was carried to a sea-going vessel at Teignmouth. The rarity of the line was that its rails were granite, with a flange on the inside, set at a gauge of 4 feet 3 inches. The wagons' wheels were loose on the axles and had treads 3 inches wide. The line descended 1,200 feet in 9 miles. Haytor granite was used for building London Bridge, the British Museum and the National Gallery. Parts of the line can still be seen today and are designated an Ancient Monument. In due course, granite could be obtained from cheaper sources and in 1858 the line fell into disuse.

A somewhat similar line could be found at Conisbrough, Yorkshire, where limestone quarries were connected with the kilns by a ¼-mile line of stone blocks chiselled to form parallel grooves, but unlike the Haytor line the flanges were on the outside of the blocks. The gauge of the Yorkshire line was about 3 feet and it fell out of use about 1902.

Apart from the Barmen-Elberfeld Railway in Germany, the development of suspension lines has been confined to the cableway, but the first proposal for a suspended railway was made by Henry Robinson Palmer, engineer to the London Dock Company, who secured a patent for his system on 22 November 1821. The first line built in 1824 used horse traction in the Royal Victualling Yard, Deptford, for transporting stores from the Thames through the yard to the warehouses. The second, built in 1825, was at Cheshunt, Hertfordshire, for conveying bricks and lime across the Cheshunt marshes to the River Lea for shipment.

Each carriage was suspended from a single rail by two cast-iron wheels 26 inches in diameter, with double ¼-inch flanges. The wagons were divided into two compartments, each with a capacity of 20 cubic feet, one suspended on each side of the rail. Wooden posts of old ships' timber, supporting the rail, were 4 inches by 7½ inches in section and placed about 10 feet apart. They varied in height according to the undulation of the ground from 2 to 5 feet. The rail itself was 3-inch deal planks, 12 inches wide and placed endways in the posts. The upper surface of the rail was covered with a bar of iron. The weight of a train of seven pairs of carriages was 14 tons and this was drawn by one horse by means of a tow rope attached to the first carriage. The opening took place on 25 June 1825, the first carriage being 'elegantly constructed in the barouche style' to carry passengers, though this was not a regular occurrence.

In January 1824, Luke Herbert proposed a Palmer railway between Brighton and London for the rapid conveyance of fresh fish, using sail power as an auxiliary. The project proved abortive. It is interesting that Palmer exhibited a model railway at Elberfeld in 1826 and a company was formed with the object of linking Barmen and Elberfeld with a line for the conveyance of coal, but this too came to naught until the present line was opened three-quarters of a century later.

Thomas Meynell, chairman of the Stockton & Darlington, laid the first rail on 23 May 1822. Shortly after the ceremony a boy with papers shouted in the streets of Stockton, 'Speech of Mr T. Meynell, one penny!' A man bought one and was furious to discover it was a blank sheet of paper and exclaimed, 'You little rascal, there's nought here!' 'No, sir,' said the lad, 'because he said naught.'

The Stockton & Darlington opened on 27 September 1825 as the world's first public railway authorised by Parliament to use steam locomotives as all previous steam-worked lines had been for specialised traffic. George Stephenson drove the 0-4-0 *Locomotion* which he had designed and Hackworth had improved, its wheels being coupled by side rods rather than chains. It hauled six loaded wagons, a passenger carriage, 21 trucks fitted with seats and six wagons filled with coal, making the total weight of the train about 90 tons. It travelled at approximately 12 mph. Only goods trains were regularly steam-hauled, passengers travelling in *Experiment*, a horse-drawn carriage designed by Stephenson which covered the distance of 12 miles in 2 hours, travelling faster than a four-in-hand on the turnpike road. The company did not actually own any passenger carriages, but was allowed by the Act to charge a maximum mileage of 'sixpence upon every coach, chariot, car, gig, waggon, landau, cart or other carriage drawn or used upon their line'.

The line's main income came from the carriage of coal, and its commitment to steam was precarious until 1828 when Timothy Hackworth, its locomotive superintendent, developed reliable locomotives by using a return-flue boiler and developing the blast pipe that drew the exhaust through the boiler tubes. Both these ideas increased the heating surface and enabled coal to be used more economically. In 1828 the company carried 22,442 tons for 22 miles by horse for £998, whereas the same load was carried over the same distance by the 0-6-0 *Royal George* for only £466.

In 1828 the Stockton & Darlington extended to Middlesbrough in order to exploit the coastal coal trade. In 1833 all haulage was performed by steam. The Stockton & Darlington was absorbed by the North Eastern Railway in 1863 but, within 40 years of its founding, the Stockton & Darlington had enabled Teesside to become the most important iron-producing district in the world.

On 17 May 1824 the Monkland & Kirkintilloch Railway obtained an Act to build lines to exploit the coal, iron, limestone and fire clay found in that area. It was the very first British Act to authorise just locomotives, the Act for the Stockton & Darlington Railway having also specified horse traction. The Monkland & Kirkintilloch eventually became the North British Railway, the largest in Scotland, and owning Waverley, Edinburgh, the largest Scottish station. The Monkland & Kirkintilloch was the very first

Scottish railway to build its own locomotives, the work actually taking place in a workshop rented from the Ballochney Railway as William Dodds, engineer of the Monkland, was also manager of the Ballochney.

An Act of Parliament allowing a railway to be built sensibly also required the company's share capital to be equal to its estimated construction costs. In addition to share capital, borrowing powers were standardised at one-third of the authorised share capital. In the early days of a company, usually only part of a share was needed to be paid to cover, say, the legal expenses and land purchase, further 'calls' being made when sums were required to pay construction expenses.

Shares were in specific amounts and numbered, their owners being paid a dividend if the railway made a profit and so the value of a share could rise or fall. Loans were entitled to a fixed rate of interest, thus a loan was safer but might not secure such a good return.

The Canterbury & Whitstable Railway was the first steam-powered passenger and goods line in the south of England, though due to inclines, the greater part of it was worked by cables and stationary engines. With George Stephenson as engineer, it opened on 3 May 1830, almost four months before the Liverpool & Manchester Railway. On the opening day, the 0-4-0 *Invicta* was driven by Edward Fletcher who later became locomotive superintendent to the North Eastern Railway. *Invicta*, built by Stephenson's son Robert at their new locomotive works, was the first engine to have outside cylinders at the front end and therefore the direct ancestor of most subsequent locomotives. Robert took over the position of Canterbury & Whitstable engineer from his father and was anxious to do so because London, easily accessible from Canterbury, was where his girlfriend and future wife, Fanny Sanderson, lived.

The official journey time of 40 minutes for the 6 miles was about the same as that by stagecoach but, from 1831 when the fare was reduced from 9*d* to 6*d*, the railway won on price. As the railway ran a train at a reduced fare on 19 March 1832, it could be considered the first company to run an excursion train; it also had the first tunnel in the world through which ran passenger trains. It was also the first railway to issue season tickets, these being available from 25 March 1834. In 1832 the company built and opened Whitstable Harbour, the first example of a railway building and operating a port.

The Cromford & High Peak Railway opened the 15½ miles from Cromford Wharf to Hurdlow on 29 May 1830 and the remaining 17½ miles to Whaley Bridge on 6 July 1831. It was the first railway of any length in the Midlands and was unusual in that its greatest elevation was 990 ft above the level of the Cromford Canal, this height being maintained for 12½ miles. It had several inclined planes worked by stationary engines.

It was found that the thrust of a locomotive's wheels, being stronger than that of horse-drawn wagons, tended to force the stone blocks out of gauge, so wooden cross sleepers were substituted to hold the rails firmly to gauge. In due course the rail joints were held together with fishplates, 'fish' being a nautical term for 'splint'.

Most of the early engineers preferred cast-iron rails to wrought iron because they corroded less easily and, furthermore, wrought-iron rails tended to contain laminations due to impurities in the metal. Engineers underestimated the sizes of a rail needed for locomotive propulsion, and as they appreciated the problem the 30 lb/yd rails of 1830 increased to 75 lb/yd by 1842.

The men building the railways were often those who a few years before had been engaged on building canals, or navigations, hence the term 'navvy'. Railway contractors based their price estimates for building a line on the ability of a navvy to dig and throw into a wagon 20 tons of spoil daily. The navvies' heavy work produced a heavy thirst. Approximately a third of them were Irish and when they, with others from various parts of England, Scotland and Wales, were together, there were plenty of opportunities for disputes. Local inhabitants dreaded the invasion of the countryside by the navvies and heaved a sigh of relief when their work was complete, though those who had earned an income from providing board and lodging were sad to see them go. Sometimes a contractor paid for police to control the navvies, while do-gooders paid for a railway chaplain and perhaps provided a reading and tea room, thus offering a non-alcoholic alternative to an inn. There was not always enough local accommodation for the navvies, so they built huts and tents in makeshift camps. Pay was generally good – some 15s a week compared with a farm labourer's wage of 10s – but their trade was dangerous and they were uninsured against injury. Some navvies were paid by the truck system whereby they had to purchase food in shops run by the railway contractors where prices were 10 per cent above the market rate. It was under the Truck Act that British Rail employees could claim to be paid in cash rather than by bank transfer and it was not until the mid-1990s that bank transfer became the only method of payment.

As early steam locomotives were poor at climbing gradients, an engineer designed a line to be as flat as possible. To avoid a hill he might make a cutting or tunnel, while to cross a depression he would use an embankment or viaduct. To save labour it was desirable when making a cutting to have somewhere close at hand to deposit the spoil – in other words, an embankment.

Cuttings were usually opened up by first removing the surface soil and forming a gully wide enough to take the wagons that carried the soil to the embankments. Loose subsoil, sand and gravel was removed by pick and shovel, and thrown into wagons. A wagon full of spoil was drawn from a cutting by a horse and then that horse was replaced by a specially trained tipping horse, which galloped to the end of the temporary track before stepping smartly out of the way before the wagon struck a baulk at the end of the track, where its contents shot out to lengthen the embankment.

If the spoil was not required for an embankment it would be dumped at the top of the cutting. It was taken up in a large wheelbarrow, drawn by a horse at the top turning a wheel. To make it easier, the wheelbarrow ran on a plank rather than the earth of the cutting slope. This was fine in dry weather, but imagine having to do this when the narrow plank was wet and slippery and with the danger that if you fell, the wheelbarrow with its load would fall on top of you.

Accidents and fatalities were all too common in railway construction, whether due to falling rock and earth, moving wagons or people smoking near open gunpowder barrels (or storing those barrels in a blacksmith's shop), not to mention the perils of travelling in a large bucket when riding up a shaft out of a tunnel. When Windsor Hill Tunnel was being cut on the Somerset & Dorset Railway, a rock weighing several tons fell and killed four navvies. And what happened to that stone which caused the fatality? It was made into a memorial marking the grave in Shepton Mallet cemetery, and the gruesome reminder can still be seen today.

The railway builders were certainly tough. Again on the Somerset & Dorset, three men were standing on the arch of a viaduct when one of them, observing an opening in the bricks, put his foot in it. Just as he did so the entire arch collapsed. Two of the masons tumbled through the hole and were killed while the third mason had the foresight to jump into the canal as the brickwork collapsed, and this leap saved his life. Although he was injured, this did not prevent him walking 4 miles to his lodgings.

Although of necessity navvies' weekday clothes were not smart, on Sundays and holidays many were 'resplendent in scarlet or yellow or blue plush waistcoats and knee breeches'.

3

The Railway Develops as a Long-distance Link

The merchants of Liverpool and Manchester realised that to keep up-to-date they needed a rail link between the two cities, as the Bridgewater Canal had become inadequate for the traffic it was carrying and charged high tolls. It was said that it took less time to carry goods from America to Liverpool than to transport them by canal from Liverpool to Manchester!

The Liverpool & Manchester Railway was arguably the first major railway, with double track, steam haulage for both passengers and goods and provision for first-, second- and third-class passengers. Problems the engineer, George Stephenson, faced were the very deep cutting at Olive Mount, the 1¼-mile long tunnel at Liverpool and crossing Chat Moss. The latter was a 30-foot-deep bog, eventually crossed by floating the railway on a raft of hurdles, brushwood and heather. Tar barrels were recycled as drains; 67 cubic feet of raw moss became, when dried, 27 cubic feet of embankment. Crossing the 1½ miles of Parr Moss was achieved by dumping clay, stone and shale from a nearby cutting. As on the Stockton & Darlington, the Liverpool & Manchester Railway used wrought-iron rails laid on stone blocks, although for lightness, wooden sleepers were employed over Chat Moss.

Despite Stephenson being a locomotive enthusiast, some Liverpool & Manchester directors believed a stationary engine and cable haulage to be more reliable. A competition was held for finding the best locomotive, a £500 prize being offered for an engine weighing less than 4½ tons that could haul three times its own weight for 35 miles (the distance between Liverpool and Manchester) at an average speed of not less than 10 mph and to cost no more than £550.

In the competition engines were required to travel to and fro at Rainhill over a trial length of 1¾ miles until they had covered the requisite distance. Although ten locomotives were entered, only five began the test on 6 October 1829. The three main contestants were Robert Stephenson's 0-2-2 *Rocket*, the 2-2-0 *Novelty* built by Braithwaite & Ericsson and the 0-4-0 *Sans Pareil* of Timothy Hackworth. The other engines were *Perseverance*, built by Timothy Burstall, which had to be disqualified as it only reached 5 mph, and *The Cycloped* powered by a horse. *Rocket* and *Novelty* reached a speed of 30 mph and caused great excitement among the crowd of at least 10,000. Braithwaite & Ericsson's *Novelty* performed well on 6 October, but then suffered a broken pipe on the 10th. The trial was spread over seven days.

The winner was Stephenson's *Rocket*, painted in a livery of canary yellow and white, and was the only machine to complete the course successfully. It had averaged 16 mph and was capable of exceeding 30 mph. Part of its success could be attributed to the fact that instead of having one large flue through the boiler, it had 25 small copper tubes. This improvement considerably increased the heating area, making the engine more efficient. Another development was that the pipe exhausting steam from the cylinders was designed to draw heat through these tubes. This idea was discovered one night when making a surreptitious inspection of Hackworth's rival locomotive the 0-4-0 *Sans Pareil*.

It is necessary to record the fact that during the Rainhill Trials, *Sans Pareil* burst a cylinder due to the faulty workmanship of its builders – Messrs Stephenson. The cylinder wall was only a sixteenth of an inch thick instead of seven-eighths! Ironically, when *Sans Pareil* was repaired following the trials, she proved superior to the *Rocket*. *Sans Pareil* was sold to the Bolton & Leigh Railway and for some years covered 120 miles daily.

Hackworth's *Globe* was the first engine to have a dome in order to collect dry steam, which made an engine more efficient. Timothy Hackworth deserves far more fame than he currently receives. Stephenson gets all the praise due to Samuel Smiles enjoying making him rise from obscurity to a household name.

The opening of the Liverpool & Manchester Railway on 15 September 1830 marked the first railway fatality other than to workmen. William Huskisson, leader of the progressive wing of the Tories, was killed. The engine, *Northumbrian*, had stopped to take water at Parkside and Huskisson took this opportunity to get out and stretch his legs. *Rocket* approached, and when returning to his carriage he fell and his leg was crushed beneath *Rocket*'s wheels. *Northumbrian* was coupled to a single coach and Huskisson rushed to Eccles at 36 mph, but he died there at the vicarage. The inaugural train carried on to Manchester where the Duke of Wellington, riding in the train, was pelted with cabbages and potatoes by a drunken crowd, angry at the death of a popular MP. The duke, at that time, was the Prime Minister and strongly opposed to parliamentary reform and so was generally unpopular with the working population.

Lesser contenders for being the first major railway were the Bolton & Leigh Railway, opened on 1 August 1828, and the Canterbury & Whitstable, opened on 3 May 1830, four months before the Liverpool & Manchester. The Bolton & Leigh was really simply a feeder to the Leeds & Liverpool Canal and worked by horse and steam, while the Canterbury & Whitstable was worked by stationary engines for two-thirds of its length.

The Liverpool & Manchester achieved quite a number of firsts: the world's first intercity train; the first to run cheap excursion trains; the first to carry road-rail containers for Messrs Pickford; and the first to carry mail. The first mail pouch by train was carried on 11 November 1830, halving the time of letter transit between the two cities and signifying the death of the mail coach. The excursion trains were quite a contrast in the make-up of passengers: one was a Sunday School party in June 1831 from Manchester to Liverpool, while another was for punters heading to the horse races.

The Liverpool & Manchester was the first railway to win a contract to deliver newspapers. Stagecoaches were slow at distributing news, but railways enabled newspapers to be delivered quickly and inexpensively, the companies treating papers as parcels rather than goods and so could offer fast 'ex-press' transport. Between 1820 and 1850 sales of newspapers increased by more than 400 per cent.

Initially porters ran bookstalls as a perk and by 1839 two men and four children were selling newspapers on the platform at

Liverpool Lime Street, but the first platform bookstall was opened by William Marshall at the London & Blackwall's Fenchurch Street station in 1841. His son Horace set up others in the Midlands and South Wales, while Walkley & Son held the bookstall contract on the Bristol & Exeter. Newspaper sales at other stations was either by local newsagents, or by retired or disabled railwaymen. When the London & Birmingham became part of the London & North Western, the general manager Captain Mark Huish discovered that one disabled railwayman, Gibb, was making a profit of £1,200 on a bookstall with an annual rent of £60. The contract for stalls on all the company's stations was put out to tender and won by W. H. Smith & Son for £1,500. Gibb was given notice to leave on 1 November 1848, but refused to go and had to be forcibly ejected by the police.

In mid-November 1848, W. H. Smith secured the Midland Railway contract for station bookstalls and by 1850 owned more than thirty. H. B. Marshall & Sons ran Great Western bookstalls and in 1857 W. H. Smith agreed with John R. Menzies that the latter could operate the stalls north of the border. In addition to selling newspapers, magazines and books, the stalls of the various owners also sorted and distributed books and newspapers to the surrounding towns and villages. They also diversified by selling food, drink, confectionery and candles on spikes to stick into the upholstery for reading in dim compartments. W. H. Smith's outlets were the world's first chain store.

Some of the literature sold by W. H. Smith came close to pornography, *The Times* stating: 'There is poison in the literary refreshment rooms ... stuff whose deleterious effects 20 doctors would not be sufficient to eradicate.' The London & North Western was asked to improve matters and W. H. Smith did so with such zeal that when he entered Parliament in 1868 he was called 'Old Morality'.

Apart from its speed, the railway greatly reduced the cost of travel. Coach fares between Liverpool and Manchester were 5s 0d outside and 10s 0d inside, but the railway reduced this to only 3s 6d outside and 5s 0d inside. Before the opening of the line, goods transported between the two cities were charged at about 18s a ton, but the railway reduced this to less than 10s.

Railway travel brought in the distinction of classes. Covered accommodation was provided for first- and second-class passengers but the third class travelled in open wagon,s which were run in goods trains and left from a goods yard, rather than a passenger station. Basically the third class travelled in what was just a goods wagon, sometimes with the luxury of holes in the floor to let the water drain out, but with the disadvantage that they let the draught in. Although to us today it seems dreadful that the third class should be so segregated, it must be remembered that third-class passengers in those days probably did not have a bathroom at home and may well have been highly odorous. As for travelling in the open air, well that is what those who had paid the cheapest fares on stagecoaches had experienced.

First- and second-class carriages were based on the stagecoach design of an oak or teak underframe, with stout vertical members with teak or mahogany panelling between. Some panels were of *papier mâché*. The roof comprised oak or deal boards covered in canvas. First-class coaches had upholstery, and glass in the windows, while second class initially had hard seats and windows that were simply an open space. Some second-class compartments had seats thinly padded and covered with corded velveteen or American cloth and often two compartments shared an oil lamp. Windows were generally shaped on the stage coach pattern, the centre window of each compartment rectangular with those on either side shaped at the bottom with rounded curves on the partition side. Coaches were protected with several coats of paint and varnish. The Great Western had some very cosy coaches seating 59 passengers in a space only 20 feet 9 inches by 8 feet 6 inches, the 60th seat occupied by the brakesman. As the door was only 18 inches wide, portly passengers perforce had to enter sideways.

By about 1850, spoked iron wheels had been replaced by those of Mansell design with a cast-iron centre and rim bolted to wooden segments.

One of the early locomotives on the Liverpool & Manchester was the 0-4-2 *Lion*, made famous in 1953 in the film *The Titfield Thunderbolt*. Built in 1837 by James Kitson of Hunslet, Leeds, it is reputed that a wall had to be pulled down to extract *Lion* from the mill in which it had been built.

The opening of the Liverpool & Manchester led to the first Railway Mania, which occurred between 1835 and 1837 when 50 new lines with a total of approximately 1,600 miles gained Parliamentary approval.

When questioned as to what would be a suitable gauge for the Leicester & Swannington Railway, George Stephenson made the perceptive reply: 'Make them [i.e. the Leicester & Swannington and the Canterbury & Whitstable] the same width; though they may be a long way apart now, depend upon it they will be joined together some day.'

The Leicester & Swannington opened on 17 July 1832 when the first train, drawn by *Comet*, driven by George Stephenson, ran from Leicester to the foot of Bagworth Incline. When the line opened only one passenger class was available and travelling meant having to stand in a high-sided goods wagon without roof, seats or spring buffers. The tickets were octagonal brass discs collected by the guard at the end of the journey, ready to be used again. August 1832 saw an improvement when a first-class carriage was built, passengers using it being issued with a paper ticket with the name of the station and the passenger being written by hand.

A mishap occurred on New Year's Day 1833 when *Samson* collided with a horse and cart at the Stag & Castle Inn crossing. It happened because the driver was unable to attract the farmer's attention. Mr Bagster, the railway's manager, reported the accident to George Stephenson, suggesting that a steam-operated whistle be fitted to the engine. Stephenson agreed and a local instrument maker produced a whistle, which 10 days later was fitted to *Samson*.

The next major railway to open was the Grand Junction Railway, a link between the Liverpool & Manchester from Newton, later called Earlestown, through Warrington to Birmingham, where it formed a junction with the London & Birmingham. At Warrington it joined the Warrington & Newton. Thus a rail link was formed from London to Manchester and Liverpool.

George Stephenson was appointed the Grand Junction's engineer, though Joseph Locke, his deputy, did most of the work. The directors noticed this, and in 1834, a year after work started, placed him in charge. Locke has not become as famous as he deserves.

Born in Sheffield on 9 August 1805, Joseph Locke was the youngest son of a colliery manager. Articled to George Stephenson, he worked with him on the Liverpool & Manchester Railway and spotted errors in the Edge Hill Tunnel survey, which led to Locke's estrangement and eventual resignation, though on the opening day of the Liverpool & Manchester Locke was the driver of the *Rocket* when it killed the MP William Huskisson.

Locke was responsible for several major railways beside the Grand Junction: the London & Southampton; Sheffield to Manchester; Lancaster & Preston; Lancaster & Carlisle; the East Lancashire; Scottish Central; the Caledonian; the Scottish Midland; and Aberdeen, quite apart from several lines on the Continent. Locke's policy was to plan lines that were easy to build and so involved the minimum of bridges and tunnels, though this had the disadvantage that they could be expensive to operate – such as the gradients at Shap and Beattock. In 1847 he was elected Liberal MP for Honiton, Devon. He died at Moffat, Dumfriesshire, on 18 September 1860.

When George Stephenson was building the Sankey Viaduct on the Liverpool & Manchester, he went to Stourton Quarry for stone and met its owner, Thomas Brassey. When building the Grand Junction, Stephenson decided that it would be wise to put it out to tender. One of those tendering was Brassey; his offer was accepted, and the Grand Junction became his first work.

The two major constructions were viaducts over the River Weaver: Vale Royal and Dutton. The Grand Junction was unusual in that it opened on time – 4 July 1837 for passengers and January 1838 for goods – and was also within its financial estimate. The Grand Junction absorbed the Warrington & Newton in February 1835. On 8 August 1845 the Liverpool & Manchester, together with the Bolton & Leigh, was amalgamated with the Grand Junction. In turn, on 16 July 1846 the Grand Junction was merged with the London & Birmingham and the Manchester & Birmingham to form the London & North Western Railway.

The first major railway to appoint George's son Robert Stephenson as engineer was the London & Birmingham. This 112-mile-long line was originally planned to have Camden as its southern terminus in order to avoid an incline of 1 in 70, but then it was decided to bring it nearer the City and have Euston as the terminus. The boring of Kilsby Tunnel proved difficult; for eight months water was pumped continuously at 1,800 gallons a minute.

Too large an undertaking to be opened as an entity, it opened in stages: from Camden Town to Boxmoor on 20 July 1837; Euston to Tring on 16 October 1837; and, with the completion of Kilsby Tunnel, from Euston to Birmingham on 24 June 1838. To give early railway travellers confidence in this new form of transport, a great Doric portico designed by Philip Hardwick was built at Euston, giving clear indication that it was the Gateway to the North and that the railway was the road of the future. Birmingham had its Ionic counterpart alongside the Grand Junction Railway's terminus. Behind the Euston arch was the original train shed designed by Robert Stephenson and it served as a pattern for subsequent London & North Western roofs.

The line had eight tunnels, of which Kilby, south of Rugby, proved the most difficult due to the problem of dealing with running sand. Deep cuttings were made at Tring and Roade to enable the line northwards of Camden to have a ruling gradient of 1 in 300. Until 1844 when locomotives had developed sufficiently to tackle steeper gradients, the 1¼-mile-long incline at 1 in 70 between Euston and Camden was operated by cable and stationary winding engines. Before leaving Euston, a thin rope called a messenger was hitched on the cable and a double turn made round the coupling hook. As a locomotive passed the summit at Camden the fireman jerked the messenger, thus releasing the train from the cable and avoiding the need to stop.

A method needed to be devised for announcing to the operator of the stationary engine at the head of the incline when a train at Euston was ready to depart. Although Cooke & Wheatstone's electric telegraph was available, it was not adopted and a whistle worked by an airtight pipe was preferred.

Railways were particularly suitable for carrying coal – indeed, it was a product carried by the earliest ones – so it was very surprising that when coal was offered as freight to the London & Birmingham its superintendent, H. P. Bruyeres, exclaimed: 'What, coal by railway, they'll be asking us to carry dung next!' When George Stephenson heard of this he said: 'Tell Bruyeres that when we carry him we do carry dung!' Eventually Bruyeres agreed to carry coal 7½ miles to the Grand Union Canal but stipulated a limit of no more than six wagons of coal in a train and covered with tarpaulins to prevent it being seen.

It will have been noticed by now that Britain's railway network was not planned as an entity but grew piecemeal, and it was only as different railway companies joined together that today's trunk routes were set up. The construction of tunnels, viaducts and bridges were often major undertakings, the like of which had never before seen in Britain; the whole landscape was changing.

A relatively minor line, the Leeds & Selby Railway, opened on 22 September 1834, to carry coal from the Garforth mines to the navigable Ouse at Selby. The line's most notable feature was the 700-yard-long Richmond Hill Tunnel, the second in the world through which passengers were drawn by a locomotive. To encourage nervous passengers to use the line, the tunnel's interior was whitewashed and copper plates fixed at the foot of the air shafts to reflect light. These efforts were so effective that it was claimed that a newspaper could be read in the tunnel. The optimistic railway built all its bridges and earthworks of sufficient width for quadruple tracks.

Some of the passengers arrived at Selby by water, tide times determining the arrival of the connecting boat, so train times necessarily also varied. In its first year the line carried an average of 3,500 passengers weekly, compared with the former average of 400 by stagecoach. The railway operated one of the first excursions in August 1835 from Leeds to Selby by rail and then coaches onwards to the York Festival.

In Scotland the Garnkirk & Glasgow had opened on 1 June 1831, using steam and horse haulage, but it was a mere local line. Its two engines, not the latest design, were supplied by George Stephenson. When the originally horse-drawn Monkland & Kirkintilloch Railway changed from horse to locomotive power on 10 May 1831, a low tunnel offered insufficient headroom, so the temporary expedient was adopted of one engine working north of the tunnel and the other to the south, horses drawing trains through the tunnel.

In due course, the Monkland & Kirkintilloch doubled its line. A problem then arose due to 1½ miles of its line being used by the Garnkirk & Glasgow, which still used much horse traction; careless horse drivers detached horses and allowed wagons to run into and damage Monkland & Kirkintilloch locomotives. The problem was solved by working the double line as two single lines – one for horse-drawn traffic and the other for steam traction.

In 1833 the Monkland & Kirkintilloch operated a wagon ferry on the Forth & Clyde Canal. Loaded wagons were run onto the ferry, which was equipped with rails and a turn plate. The barge was then towed to its destination and the wagons run ashore. Thus the time and trouble of double transshipment of the goods or minerals was avoided, as was the risk of breakage.

A remarkable Scottish railway was the Dundee & Newtyle, opened 16 December 1831 using a gauge of 4 feet 6½ inches. The three inclines were worked by stationary engines, horses drawing wagons on the other sections, and by the end of the decade a train from Newtyle to Dundee harbour, a trip of less than 11 miles, used three stationary engines, two locomotives and a horse. The poverty-stricken line had no money for extensions to Coupar Angus and Glamis, so these were built by separate companies, also poverty-stricken. Horse power was used on these and the solitary passenger vehicle had a canvas sail, which could speed it to 20 mph at times, with the horse ready to take over when the wind dropped.

Another early Scottish railway was the Edinburgh & Dalkeith, opened to exploit the Lothian coalfield. It opened from St Leonards, on the south side of the city, to Craighall on 4 July 1831, reaching Dalkeith in the autumn of 1838. Built to the Scottish gauge of 4 feet 6 inches, the main line was double track.

The Edinburgh & Dalkeith played its part in preventing the citizens from being cheated. Some coal merchants were dishonest so a customer never knew whether he was getting the quality and quantity of coal for which he had paid. The Edinburgh & Dalkeith installed a weighbridge at St Leonards and a certificate was issued with every cart of coal that left the depot showing the weight, quality and time of departure, customers being told to refuse delivery if 'you find that more time than enough has been spent on the journey'.

On 2 June 1832 the railway began a passenger service using a horse-drawn stagecoach fitted for railway use. In the first full month of operation 14,392 passengers had travelled on it, and 20,615 the succeeding month. By 1838 the Edinburgh & Dalkeith was carrying 469 passengers per mile of track, while passenger density on the steam-operated Liverpool & Manchester was only 378, and the

Stockton & Darlington 105. Due to the Edinburgh & Dalkeith's accident-free record, it was known as 'The Innocent Railway'.

From its Edinburgh terminus the line rose through a tunnel on a gradient of 1 in 30, this section being cable worked. But how could the man in charge of the winding engine be notified when a train was ready to start? The canny Scots laid a tube beside the line and when all was ready for the winding engine to be placed in motion, bellows pumped air up the pipe to operate a bell signal.

John Miller, who became an important railway engineer, believed that 5 feet 6 inches was the ideal gauge for safety, and, thinking that his railway would never be connected to another line, adopted this gauge for the Dundee & Arbroath Railway, which opened in October 1838. Its rails were laid on stone blocks, and because the gauge was wider it was expected that its engines would be more powerful, but they were, in fact, simply converted standard-gauge engines. Another oddity was that the line adopted right-hand running.

The first railway journal published in England was the *Railway Gazette*, which published a few issues in 1835, the year a much longer-lived journal, the *Railway Magazine and Annals of Science*, also appeared. In 1839 it became the *Railway Journal* and was edited by John Herapath, often being referred to as '*Herapath's Journal*'. A man of strong views, Herapath detested express and excursion trains and was not reluctant to air his opinions. Another organ, the *Railway Times*, appeared in 1837. By October 1845, no fewer than 16 journals were being published.

One of the oldest railways in Britain has one of the smallest gauges. The Festiniog Railway obtained its Act on 25 May 1832 to lay a 2-foot gauge line (actually 1 foot 11½ inches) 13¼ miles in length from slate quarries at Blaenau Festiniog down to the harbour at Portmadoc where slate could be shipped to its destination. Narrow gauge proved useful as it could traverse sharper curves, used less land and was cheaper to build, thus enabling a railway to be constructed where one to the standard gauge would have been uneconomic. It was the first major narrow gauge railway in the world.

As its terminus was 700 feet above sea level, it descended on a ruling gradient of 1 in 80, loaded wagons coming down by gravity and being drawn back to Blaenau by horses. The line opened on 20 April 1836. It was highly successful; slate production rose from

18,000 tons in 1835 to about 90,000 tons in 1865. To cope with this traffic and to try to prevent another railway seizing some of the trade, the Festiniog needed a more efficient way of working, so steam locomotives were introduced on 6 January 1865. To be even more efficient, the double-boilered *Little Wonder* appeared in the autumn of 1869. A patent of Robert Francis Fairlie, it had a central cab with a boiler on each side, with two powered bogies. This was the first successful application of an articulated steam locomotive. Another peculiarity of the Festiniog Railway was the engineer's inspection car which had a sail, mast and a ship-type prow, the latter for automatically opening level crossing gates when freewheeling downhill. Due to road competition, passenger services were withdrawn in October 1930 for the winter, the summer ones were withdrawn in September 1939 and the line completely closed 1 August 1946. Fortunately this was not the end of the story and preservationists succeeded in bringing it back to life.

Thomas Edmondson, born at Lancaster in 1792, was taught knitting by his mother to keep him out of mischief. In due course he was apprenticed to Gillow, a cabinetmaker. Edmondson was inventive and designed an apparatus that enabled a mother to simultaneously rock a cradle and churn butter. He set up his own furniture business, but it failed.

He then joined the Newcastle & Carlisle Railway and was appointed stationmaster at Milton. Frustrated by the clumsy and time-consuming booking system that had been derived from stagecoach days when every ticket had to be written by hand, torn from a book and a counterfoil filled in, Edmondson felt there must be a simpler and more efficient way. In 1838 he devised the system of using pre-printed tickets measuring 1½₂ of an inch by 2¼ inches and having a thickness of ³⁄₁₆ of an inch, serially numbered. This was done by four wheels, which bore ten digits, and every time the unit wheel moved round once, a stud on it came into contact with a projection on the tens wheel and advanced it one figure. The tens wheel similarly moved the hundreds wheel, and the hundreds the thousands, so that 10,000 tickets from 0000 to 9999 inclusive could be printed from one setting of the machine. Edmondson's system meant that a ticket could be issued to a passenger immediately and no time was wasted.

Edmondson also invented the date stamp, whereby the simple action of inserting a ticket into a press caused the date to be printed on the ticket by an inked ribbon. Using his woodworking skills, the first dating presses were of wood, but later, with John Blaylock, Carlisle clockmaker and iron-founder, they were produced in metal.

Initially tickets were taken as needed from the top of the packets that rested on springs, which pressed them upwards. Later it was found more convenient to place them in tubes with the highest number on top and then abstract them from a gap at the bottom, just large enough for one ticket to be withdrawn. The ticket tube provided the basic idea for the invention of a chocolate-issuing machine.

At the beginning of the day the numbers of the bottom tickets were taken, and as each was withdrawn the next was drawn far enough forward to show its number. At the end of the day the number showing was deducted from the morning number to show the numbers sold, the amount of cash entered in the Train Book and then the Summary Book for the day's takings. Cash was placed in a travelling safe or paid into a bank. The monthly start and closing numbers were entered in a book for the audit office, while collected tickets were sent to the audit office and then to the Railway Clearing House.

The Newcastle & Carlisle failed to recognise Edmundson's genius, and in 1839, when his invention became known to Captain Lawes of the Manchester & Leeds Railway, he was offered the post of chief booking clerk at Manchester Oldham Road at double his former salary. In 1841 he left to establish his own ticket business, trading under the name of his son, John B. Edmondson. From the 1840s, urged by the Railway Clearing House, most British railways adopted his system and paid an annual royalty of 10s a mile. Many foreign railways and those in the colonies adopted his tickets, so he became wealthy and invested in railways. In 1910 more than 1 billion tickets were printed; the card used was enough to cover 500 acres. BR (British Railways) only replaced his system in February 1990.

In 1864 the system of punching tickets was introduced so that the Railway Clearing House would know on a through ticket used over lines of more than one company how much a company would have to pay others for use of the track and rolling stock. Some railways sold the space on the back of the ticket for advertising, while the North Eastern had the original idea of issuing a duplicate ticket for passengers with a bicycle, the duplicate being tied to the cycle so that at the end of the journey it could be checked with the passenger's ticket to avoid theft.

The North Eastern sold coupons for 1,000 miles of first-class travel, each coupon worth 1 mile. The booklet sold for £5 5s 0d which worked out at 1¼d a mile; 4,200 booklets were sold in the first year.

In 1842 William Owen, a thrifty regular traveller on the Liverpool & Manchester, requested a discount for purchasing tickets in bulk and was given a discount of a third. The company developed the idea and offered season tickets generally from 1845.

The first line in the London area was the London & Greenwich. 3¾ miles in length, it was set on a viaduct of 878 brick arches, using 60 million bricks in total. It holds the record of being the longest listed structure in Britain. The first experimental trip, which was free, was on 8 June 1835 when *Royal William* covered 1 mile in 4 minutes. In November 1835, *John Bull* recorded: 'One of the carriages in which a party of noodles ventured themselves was thrown off the rail, but although it ran a vast number of yards no serious accident occurred.' The company's engineer, Lieut-Col G. T. Landmann, observed that the derailment showed how safe accidents were. This statement was, in fact, true because in addition to the 4-foot-6-inch-high parapet walls, the carriages had an unusually low centre of gravity, only 4 inches above the rails. As an additional safety measure, gas lamps illuminated the viaduct at night.

The line was formally opened by the Lord Mayor on 14 December 1836, though trains had been running from a temporary station at Spa Road to Deptford since 8 February 1836. When approaching a temporary terminus, fly shunting was used to allow the engine to get to the other end of the train ready for the return journey. On approaching a terminus, the driver would slow his engine to enable the couplings to go slack and thus permit the front guard to lift the coupling off the hook by means of a rope. When the engine was thus released, the driver would accelerate while the train was being braked by the guards to allow the engine to get ahead and cross a set of points, which could then be quickly changed to allow the coaches to enter a different road. The line was completed from Deptford to Greenwich and opened on 24 December 1838. It crossed Deptford Creek by a manually-operated lifting bridge. It is interesting that initially trains used the right-hand road, rather than the left, and that it was one of the first railways in the country to use tank engines. The London & Greenwich was probably the first in the world to offer Park & Ride facilities. Gentlemen could ride their horses to stables provided under the viaduct at Greenwich and then continue to London Bridge by train.

Wealthier men were moving from their residences within the City to pleasanter areas outside, one of those chosen being Croydon. An Act was obtained on 12 June 1835 to build a line from West Croydon to Corbett's Lane where the London & Croydon Railway would have running powers over the London & Greenwich for the final 1¾ miles to London Bridge where the Croydon company would have its own station. The line was opened formally on 1 June 1839 and public traffic began on 5 June 1839 with a service of 12 trains daily almost on a regular interval basis – then a new concept. The London & Croydon cleverly developed commuter traffic by encouraging those who worked in London to live in Croydon by just charging them the fare from London to Penge, thus offering Croydon passengers 4 miles of free travel.

When the London & Brighton Railway received its Act on 15 July 1837, it was the view of Parliament that London should have only one rail entrance from the south. This meant that the South Eastern Railway's start to Dover was roundabout. It had to run over 1¾ miles of the London & Greenwich between London Bridge and Corbett's Lane; 7¾ miles of the London & Croydon from Corbett's Lane to the Jolly Sailor; 5 miles of the London & Brighton from the Jolly Sailor to Stoat's Nest and then 6½ miles over its own line from Stoat's Nest to Earlswood Common, (Redhill). The most noticeable feature of this roundabout route was that the 46 miles to Ashford were practically straight and dead level and that extensive cuttings and embankments were not required to achieve this. Its engineer was William Cubitt, who, in 1817, had invented the treadmill, installed almost immediately in most English prisons.

Although Sunday was generally observed as a day of rest, bricklayers had to be employed at the 1,327-yard Bletchingley Tunnel on that day because it was essential that excavations made on Saturdays were supported as soon as possible. Construction of the tunnel was unusual in that bricks for lining it were actually made at the top of each working shaft, rather than being brought in from elsewhere.

Two Scottish lines also received Acts on 17 May 1837: the Glasgow, Paisley, Kilmarnock & Ayr and the Glasgow, Paisley & Greenock, opened in 1840 and 1841 respectively. Each railway tried to establish a pier railhead seaward of its competitor for steamers running to the Clyde resorts. The services were most efficient, steamers leaving within 2 minutes of the arrival of the boat train.

A fishing village, Ballantrae, 13 miles south of Girvan, never received a railway and the Glasgow & South Western carted Ballantrae fish by road to Girvan. At this date the Midland route via Settle was open and fish for London should have travelled via the Glasgow & South Western and the Midland, but the London & North Western Railway had a canvasser at Girvan persuading merchants to use the West Coast route. In March 1877 this London & North Western agent found a Midland man changing the 'Via LNWR' labels on the herring barrels to 'Via MR'. When he complained to the stationmaster he was called 'an LNWR prig' and ejected from the station.

The London & Blackwall Railway opened on 6 July 1840 was built almost entirely on arches. Stationary engines and an endless rope was used as a source of power, contemporary belief being that it was unsafe to use locomotives in such a densely populated area as the East End. For the quarter-mile extension from the Minories to Fenchurch Street, incoming coaches coasted by gravity. When locomotives eventually took over in 1849, portions of the line were provided with a light iron roof to prevent sparks from the engines igniting shipping in the nearby docks. The London & Blackwall had a regular interval timetable that was thus easy to remember; trains left every quarter of an hour.

The first main line towards the West of England was the London & Southampton. Its initial engineer, Francis Giles, proved a failure and in 1837 was replaced by Joseph Locke, famous for his work on the Stockton & Darlington and Liverpool & Manchester lines. Nine Elms to Woking opened on 21 May 1838; to Winchfield on 24 September 1838 and to Basingstoke on 10 June 1839, Southampton to Winchester also opening on this date. The gap between Winchester and Basingstoke was closed on 11 May 1840.

The nautical towns of Southampton and Portsmouth were rivals and when the London & Southampton planned a branch to Portsmouth, to avoid the use of 'Southampton' – a word hated by the people of Portsmouth – in 1839 the name of the company was changed to the London & South Western Railway.

The other principal line in the south of England was the Great Western Railway. The use of 'Great' in the title was brilliant as it gave confidence to investors, passengers and those seeking the carriage of goods, so quite a few other railways adopted the word in their titles. The post of engineer was given to the 27-year-old Isambard Kingdom Brunel, well known in Bristol for his improvements to the harbour and for having submitted designs for the Clifton Suspension Bridge. His concept of a railway was a straight, level line. This was achievable from London to Swindon, but westwards required two gradients of 1 in 100 to be worked by stationary steam power. In the event, between the line's planning and opening, locomotives had been improved to such an extent that they proved capable of climbing such a gradient.

Not all were in favour of the GWR – for instance Eton College was against it as the school practised giving as much freedom to the boys as possible and feared that a railway would encourage them to go to the dangers of London. The GWR cunningly evaded the restriction of not being permitted to construct a station within 3 miles of the school by the simple expedient of stopping trains at Slough, 2 miles from Eton, and selling train tickets at the Crown Inn. Interestingly, not long after the opening to Maidenhead on 4 June 1838, the college chartered a special train to convey its pupils to London for Queen Victoria's Coronation.

The Corporation of London was another group that disliked railways and tried to keep them out of the city, so that is the reason that today the main railway stations form a ring round it.

The original intention was for the Great Western to share the London & Birmingham's terminus at Euston, but negotiations failed when that company refused to grant the Great Western permanent use of its land. In order not to delay the line's opening, the Great Western decided to have a temporary station, Bishop's Road Bridge forming the station facade, the rest of the makeshift station being constructed of timber. The section from Maidenhead to Twyford, opened 1 July 1839, required a bridge over the Thames. Brunel used two very flat brick arches of 128-foot span and many people were convinced that when the supporting centring was removed they would collapse. One night in the autumn of 1839 a violent storm blew down the centrings but left the arches quite secure.

The greatest feat was the cutting of Box Tunnel, which at 1 mile and 1,452 yards was 800 yards longer than any other cut prior to the 1840. It was driven using eight shafts, the first and last being enlarged into cuttings. Work started in 1836 and more than 1,000 men and 100 horses were employed. Approximately 5,500 bricks were required for every foot advanced. A ton of gunpowder and a ton of candles, the latter made at Box, were used every week. F. S. Williams recorded in *Our Iron Roads:*

> On one occasion some of the directors of the Great Western Railway were inspecting the works at the Box tunnel, and several of them resolved to descend a shaft with Mr Brunel and one or two of the other engineers, who mentioned the incident to the writer. Accordingly all but one ensconced themselves in the tub provided for the purpose – he declined to accompany them. His friends rallied him for a want of courage, and one slyly suggested, 'Did your wife forbid you before you started?' A quiet nod in response intimated that the right nail had been struck, and the revelation was received with a merry laugh. But as the pilgrims found themselves slipping about a greasy, muddy tub, jolting and shaking as the horses stopped – by whose aid they were lowered – and how at length they were suspended some hundred and fifty feet from the bottom, till the blastings that had been prepared roared and reverberated through the 'long-drawn caverns', more than one of the party who had laughed before, wished that they had received a similar prohibition to that of their friend above, and that they had manifested an equal amount of marital docility.

Until the coming of railways, people used the sun to determine the time. This meant that noon at Exeter was 14 minutes later than at London, while Pembrokeshire noon was 20 minutes later than at London. This caused no problem until the coming of the railway and its faster transport. In November 1840 the GWR announced that London time would be kept at all its stations, and by 1847 all railway companies had agreed that Greenwich Mean Time be adopted, though it was not until 1880 that a royal decree finally established GMT across the country, while four years later GMT became the world's standard basis for timekeeping when 25 nations agreed to it at the Prime Meridian Conference held in Washington.

The Chippenham to Bath section containing Box Tunnel was the last section of the Bristol–London line to be opened, this occurring on 30 June 1841.

Brunel, not content to adopt the ideas of others, used fresh thinking. Most previous lines had chosen the gauge of 4 feet 8½ inches, which had been determined by the plateways on which ordinary carts could travel and the distance between the wheels of these carts, which was approximately 4 feet 8½ inches. Brunel realised that a wider gauge would offer larger and more comfortable coaches, as well as allowing more space to build faster and more powerful locomotives with greater stability, which meant they were safer in the event of an accident. He chose the gauge of 7 feet, with an extra quarter of an inch to give a little play.

Unfortunately he did not look far enough into the future. When the GWR was in isolation the fact that its gauge was incompatible with those of most other lines was of no consequence; problems only arose when stations were opened where two different gauges met.

Brunel was a superb architect and designed tunnel mouths and stations to blend in with the landscape. Many of his station buildings included a large umbrella awning in complete unity with the whole design.

An important publication inaugurated in 1839 was *Bradshaw's Railway Time Tables and Assistant to Railway Travelling.* As railways had grown up independently of each other, each produced its own timetable, but a national one to plan a journey covering several lines was not in existence until Bradshaw filled the gap. George Bradshaw was born at Pendleton, Salford, on 29 July 1801. On leaving school he was apprenticed to an engraver and in 1820 moved to Belfast with his parents and set up an engraving business. Unsuccessful, he returned to Manchester in 1821 and set up a business there, soon specialising in map engraving. In 1830 he published *Map of Canals, Navigable Rivers, Rail Roads, &c in the Midland Counties of England from Actual Survey.* In 1838 he added letter-press printing to his activities and soon after William T. Blacklock became a partner, the firm being known as Bradshaw & Blacklock.

Bradshaw's first general timetable for northern railways was issued in October 1839 and dated '10th Mo. 19th, 1839'; thus he avoided actually writing the name of the month. Bradshaw was a member of the Society of Friends and objected to the adoption of the names of heathen gods in the calendar. The second issue comprised railways in the southern part of the United Kingdom. The third volume, a compilation of both volumes, was the first to show the railway timetables of the whole country. Curiously, although *Bradshaw's Railway Time Tables* appeared on the title page, the cover bore the words *Bradshaw's Railway Companion*. Another of Bradshaw's quirks was that the cover bore an inch measure.

Bradshaw's Railway Guide, with a yellow wrapper as compared to the hardback *Companion*, first became a regular monthly publication in December 1841. A curiosity in the numbering was that the March 1845 edition of the Guide was No. 40, but the April 1845 edition jumped in error to No. 141, successive issues continuing from this number, though Canon Reginald B. Fellows in the *Railway Magazine* for June 1935 claims it was not a mistake, but made deliberately in order to make the *Guide* appear longer-established than was actually the case.

In 1917 railway companies were dropping the issue of their own timetables and in April that year the Great Western arranged for the relevant section of *Bradshaw* to be reprinted for use by its staff. Other railway companies soon followed suit. The last *Bradshaw's Guide* was for May 1961. Subsequently BR did not provide a one-volume replacement as it continued to issue individual timetables for each of the regions until 1974, when a single volume was produced covering the whole of BR. Network Rail ceased publication of timetables in book form in 2007 as they were available electronically.

Although Bradshaw is most well known for his timetables and the *Bradshaw's Handbook* of 1863 made famous by Michael Portillo, he also published a *Continental Railway Guide* monthly from 1847 till 1939 and the *Railway Manual, Shareholders' Guide, and Official Directory*, an annual publication from 1847 till 1922, which proved invaluable to contemporary investors and to today's railway historians. In 1853 Bradshaw visited Christiana, now Oslo, at a time when cholera was raging. Unfortunately he succumbed and died on 8 September. He is buried in the grounds of Oslo Cathedral.

Thomas Edmondson's brother George opened a school and introduced the study of Bradshaw's timetables into its curriculum. Pupils worked out cross-country routes and connections, with George believing this to be better mental gymnastics than studying Greek or Latin.

The opening of the Glasgow, Paisley, Kilmarnock & Ayr Railway was on 5 August 1839. It proved outstandingly successful, the number of passengers carried in the first year being 137,117, compared with an estimate of 21,350. It had been expected that there would be 23,980 local passengers between Glasgow and Paisley in July 1840, whereas the actual figure was 52,696. Glaswegians flocked to the Ayrshire seaside and country folk made trips to Glasgow. That same year, the two railways carried between them 24,000 passengers from Glasgow to Paisley and back during the two days of horse racing.

The stations were just crude ash heaps with simple buildings, and moving trains stirred up clouds of dust from the sand or ash ballast. The early third-class carriages had seats, but these were imaginatively removed to offer more standing room. These open vehicles were divided into four sections by waist-high partitions and nicknamed 'bughts' (sheep pens).

By the end of the century, in a survey of boat train services the *Daily News* wrote regarding those of the Clyde:

> Each of the three services with its minor ramifications is worked with a smartness almost beyond description; within two minutes of the arrival of the boat train the passengers are on board and the steamer is gliding off. The fares are ridiculously low and overcrowding is reduced to a minimum, thanks to the liberal supply of railway trains always forthcoming. The whole, in fact, is an eye-opener to the southerner. Would that we could have something approaching it between London and the South coast.

The resorts continued to be popular and in 1938, the LMS carried between 40,000 and 50,000 passengers to the Ayrshire resorts on a Saturday afternoon. 'Evening breather' trains were run from Glasgow and other stations on weekday evenings to give a few hours on the beach for as little as 1s 3d return.

In 1839 the Glasgow, Paisley & Johnstone Canal ran a rival passenger service, its 'swift' boats offering third-class passengers roofed seats. Fare wars between the competing companies lasted for a year when, in return for a guaranteed annual payment by the railway of £1,358, the canal company said it would sell all its 'swifts'. Passengers suffered: three days after signing the agreement the railway doubled its third-class fare from Glasgow to Paisley and three months later increased it by another 50 per cent.

On 20 August 1840 the Glasgow, Paisley, Kilmarnock & Ayr inaugurated a steamer service between Ardrossan and Liverpool, announcing that Glasgow would be brought within 24 hours of London. The boat train left Glasgow at 2.00 p.m., the steamer leaving at 4.00 p.m. and arriving at 5.00 a.m. The connecting trains were allowed 9 hours to reach London, but in practice the steamer was often late arriving at Liverpool so passengers missed their connection. The service was poorly patronised and on 30 April 1841 was re-organised as a ferry from Ardrossan to Fleetwood. Passengers stayed overnight in the North Euston Hotel before taking the ferry to Ardrossan for a train to Glasgow. A direct line to Scotland opened in 1848.

The Glasgow, Paisley & Greenock Railway opened 29 March 1841. The Greenock Railway proved highly popular and one day in August 1841 the company carried a total of 8,200 passengers and could have carried more had it the locomotives to do so. It speeded passengers to the lower Clyde resorts as the rail journey from Glasgow to Greenock was less than an hour compared with the 2½–3½ hours needed by the paddle boats. Steamers to the resorts left from Custom House Quay, Greenock, and luggage was carried free from the station, while women and children were offered a conveyance, but men had to walk or run to the steamer, the railway urging passengers to use 'all expedition' to reach the pier for a quick departure.

Steamship operators responded to railway competition by cutting Glasgow–Greenock fares to sixpence steerage and 1s 0d cabin, undercutting the railway's 1s 6d third class and 2s 6d first class. The railway replied by reducing its fares and increasing services, which led to overcrowding at times.

The Clyde steamers also carried goods traffic to and from the railway and this grew to such an extent that the paddlers could not wait until all the freight had been transshipped and it had to be sent by the train previous to the advertised steamer connection.

The Eastern Counties Railway opened from Dog Row, Mile End Road, London, to Romford on 18 June 1839. Its official opening was unusual. Instead of one inaugural train there were two, each with an engine at both ends and each train having a brass band. They ran side by side on the Up and Down roads, the bands playing different tunes. Public traffic began on 20 June 1839, and the following day an engine became derailed between Bow and Stratford, killing its crew.

When the Eastern Counties Railway was incorporated in 1836, the 126-mile line from London to Great Yarmouth via Norwich was the longest to that date authorised by Parliament. The 5-foot gauge was adopted because the directors desired a broad gauge line to rival the Great Western, but the line's engineer, John Braithwaite, saw no need, but having originality of thought, when designing a locomotive he believed:

> With a little more space between the tubes we should have a more quiet action of the water in the boiler and consequently less ebullition, and therefore my diagram and my section of my engine, I added all its different bearings, and I added what I considered sufficient additional space to the tubes, the sum of which gave me four feet, eleven and three-quarters inches, and upon that I assumed that five feet would be about the thing.

His locomotive, built on such meticulous calculation, had a heating surface of only 428 square feet in a boiler of less diameter than the *Rocket* and so was less efficient. Between Shoreditch and Bow, Braithwaite encountered the same problem as Stephenson had at Chat Moss: the line's foundations sank. When it ceased to sink, it spread out – so Braithwaite resorted to piling. He was the first British engineer to adopt the American steam pile driver and for making cuttings he used the American mechanical excavator. The line was converted to standard gauge in September and October 1844, the first gauge conversion on an English railway. Traffic was maintained by resorting to single-line working, first one and then the other road converted.

The GWR had the honour of operating the first royal train. The *Illustrated London News* reported on Queen Victoria's first railway journey, which took place on 1 June 1840: 'Queen Victoria abundantly attended by fashionably dressed ladies, took the special train from Slough to Paddington Station on the Great Western Railway line, the whole journey having taken a mere 25 minutes.' Travelling in a specially built coach, she was driven by Daniel Gooch, the locomotive superintendent, with Brunel also on the footplate. The queen enjoyed the experience of railway travel and on 23 July returned from Paddington to Slough with Prince Albert, the Princess Royal and the eight-month-old Prince of Wales. The spread of the railway system was important to the monarchy as it meant that for the very first time the monarch could travel easily all over Britain and be seen by many of her subjects. It also enabled her to have homes in different parts of the kingdom – before the advent of railways it is unlikely that Queen Victoria would have bought Balmoral because of the number of days' travel required to reach it. She was also able to purchase and access rural retreats at Sandringham and Osborne House. Great precautions were taken to ensure that the queen was safe on her rail journeys. Fifteen minutes in front of her train, a pilot engine ran over the track; no train was allowed to proceed or cross the line for half-an-hour before her train, and all shunting work had to cease on adjacent lines. All facing points had to be locked and no engine or train was to leave a station or siding until 15 minutes after the royal train had passed.

An important railway company was the North Midland Railway which ran from Derby through Chesterfield to Leeds. It opened from Derby to Rotherham on 11 May 1840 and to Leeds on 30 June 1840. On 10 May 1844 it amalgamated with the Midland Counties Railway and the Birmingham & Derby Junction Railway to form the Midland Railway. (*See* page 69.)

The Regulation of Railways Act of 1840 gave the Board of Trade power to appoint inspectors to check that new railways were safe for the transport of passengers. These inspectors were officers of the Royal Engineers, who knew something of the problems of building and operating railways but had to learn about the mechanical equipment.

The 31 miles of the Bromsgrove to Cheltenham section of the Birmingham & Gloucester Railway opened on 24 June 1840, some two weeks earlier than expected – an unusual occurrence, as many railways tended to open late due to 'unforeseen difficulties'. The extension from Cheltenham to Gloucester was opened on

4 November 1840 and went through to Camp Hill, Birmingham, on 17 December 1840. This section included the formidable Lickey Incline of 1 in 37.7. Both Brunel and George Stephenson had declared locomotives impracticable on such a steep gradient, but the company's engineer, Captain William Scarth Moorsom, had seen engines in the USA tackling such gradients and placed an order with Norris, locomotive builders of Philadelphia. A tunnel was out of the question because the gentle dip slope beyond the summit would have required its length to be excessive. In the event, operation by steam locomotives proved feasible, though it was not until the advent of diesel-electric locomotives that this gradient ceased to be a bugbear.

On 17 August 1841 an extension was opened from Camp Hill to the London & Birmingham's Curzon Street station. This meant that there was now a continuous line of railway between York, Hull, Leeds, Sheffield, Derby, Nottingham, Leicester, London, Liverpool, Manchester and Gloucester.

The opening of railways had an effect on the economy of an area – innkeepers dependent on stagecoach traffic lost much of their income, as did forage merchants and blacksmiths. In July 1841, it was reported that traffic on the Gloucester to Cheltenham turnpike had so decreased following the opening of the railway, that tolls were insufficient to maintain the road in good repair.

The first important Welsh railway was the Taff Vale, incorporated on 21 June 1836. Running from Cardiff to Merthyr Tydfil, it was the only system in South Wales to have any significant stretch of quadruple track and of its route mileage of 124½, more than 22 miles were four-tracked. Like many other railways in South Wales, it later favoured the 0-6-2T and at least one GWR engineer was told that a Class A Taff Vale 0-6-2T was superior to the newer GWR 56XX design with the same wheel arrangement.

The 16 miles from Cardiff to Abercynon were opened on 8 October 1840. It became the oldest and largest of the Welsh constituent companies of the Great Western Railway and was only a year younger than the GWR itself. Like the GWR, its engineer was Brunel, though due to the line's curvature he favoured the standard, rather than broad gauge.

4

Some Impacts of the Railways on Life in Britain

Boiler explosions were not unknown in the early days of railways. In 1836 the 0-2-2T *Surprise* had been designed by Dr William Church. A curiosity, it had a vertical boiler and its footplate was set at the front between its two cylinders, the crew having no protection from the weather. It had languished unloved in a siding for so long that rain had entered the uncapped chimney and rusted away some of the boiler plating. Rather foolishly, the Birmingham & Gloucester agreed to find fuel for a month's test. On 10 November 1840, following several short trips, it lived up to its name when the thin boiler plates burst with a tremendous explosion, killing the driver and causing fatal injuries to the locomotive foreman. This was the very first boiler explosion investigated by the Railway Inspectorate. At the inquest the coroner imposed a deodand of £60 on the engine. In medieval law any object that killed a human was forfeited to the Crown, but later it became acceptable instead for the coroner's jury to set a price. Steam locomotives causing fatal accidents came within this law, but deodands were abolished in 1846.

The locomotive foreman had left a widow and three small children. A subscription was raised by his colleagues at the station so that she could keep a shop and thus earn a living.

Repaired and renamed *Eclipse*, the locomotive was offered for trial on 30 August 1842, but not surprisingly the proposal was declined. Two years later, the offer was repeated and this time accepted. In the early 1850s it was purchased by a colliery owner near Swansea. In 1857 it was dismantled in the workshops of the Swansea Vale Railway, its lengthened boiler being used in a new small-wheel 0-6-0T designed for hauling heavy mineral trains over sharply curved tracks. It came into Midland Railway ownership when the company was taken over in 1874.

When an important line was projected, people in towns which it did not serve often thought of building a connecting line. The Cheltenham & Great Western Union Railway was a broad gauge line planned to link Cheltenham and Gloucester with the GWR at Swindon. The company's resident engineer was Charles Richardson, later to design and make the first cricket bat with a spliced cane handle, though being first and foremost famous as chief engineer on the Severn Tunnel project.

Unfortunately for the Cheltenham & Great Western, investors were reluctant to invest in the scheme, which involved the costly Sapperton Tunnel just over a mile in length beneath the Cotswold Hills. As the railway was unable to be constructed as a whole, initially the section between Swindon and Cirencester was concentrated on. This length opened on 31 May 1841 and Cirencester, instead of being at the end of a branch off the Cheltenham line, possessed the company's main station. Connection with Gloucester and Cheltenham was temporarily by road.

Like many relatively small companies, the Cheltenham & Great Western Union was worked by a larger concern, in this case the Great Western. It was a case of economics. Although perhaps one engine and one set of coaches would suffice for normal working, a spare locomotive had to be available in the event of engine failure, repair, or heavy traffic requiring extra trains. It was hopelessly uneconomic for a small company to keep reserve stock only used occasionally, but a large company could more readily cope with fluctuations in traffic. Although the Great Western terminated at Bristol, there were those who believed it should be extended westwards. To do this they formed the Bristol & Exeter Railway, another broad gauge line with Brunel as engineer. Like the Great Western, the whole length was not opened at once, but in stages – the section from Bristol to Bridgwater on 14 June 1841. Like the Cheltenham & Great Western, it was worked by the Great Western Railway.

A railway accident at Bridgwater on 11 September 1841 proved fatal to someone who was just an innocent standing by. Following the arrival of the 4.00 p.m. from Bristol, after its passengers left, the engine drew forward with some coaches for about 150 yards to a crossover and then backed them to the Up platform. Between the station and crossover was a level crossing. As the engine was returning on the Down line, tender-first to collect the remaining stock, it struck a stagecoach laden with passengers for Exeter. The front part of the coach was smashed to pieces and freed the horses, which were unhurt. The passengers were thrown off and six injured, one having his head jammed under a wheel of the tender and impossible to extricate until the engine reversed. Unfortunately a lady fruit seller who had just crossed the railway on foot was struck by the toppling coach and received fatal injuries. The engine driver was blameless.

In 1808 Thomas Cook was born at Melbourne, Derbyshire. Trained as a woodturner, he opened his own business at Market Harborough in 1831 and became interested in the temperance movement. On 5 July 1841 a temperance fête was being held in Loughborough, and to encourage attendance Cook arranged with the Midland Counties Railway to carry passengers at special reduced rates from Leicester to Loughborough. Cook himself undertook to sell the tickets, which he did most successfully, managing to get about a thousand passengers. The fare for 11 miles return, including sandwiches, tea, dancing and games, was one shilling. Although this venture was certainly one of the first excursions, it was certainly not the very first. The scheme proving successful, Cook moved into Leicester, set up business as a printer and organised excursions every summer, in 1845–6 to North Wales and Scotland. He went bankrupt in 1846 but then recovered and in 1851 became agent for the Midland Railway's excursion trains to London to see the Great Exhibition, arranging for 165,000 people to see this event. Extending his activities, he arranged trips to France, including hotel stays – he had invented the package holiday.

The Manchester & Leeds Railway opened between Normanton and Hebden Bridge on 5 October 1840, engineered by George Stephenson. Faced with the Pennines, he was forced to abandon his ideal of keeping gradients no steeper than 1 in 330. The opening day must have been memorable with passengers riding on carriage roofs and ducking when they came to an overbridge or tunnel, in fact, the train was so crowded that in order to prevent even more passengers boarding the driver did not stop at stations. When the Summit Tunnel – 1 mile 1,125 yards in length – had been completed, the line was opened throughout on 1 March 1841. It was then the longest railway tunnel in the world, but lost this honour three months later when Box Tunnel inaugurated.

The Manchester & Leeds reduced travelling time between the two places from 6½ to 2¾ hours, yet the rival coaches did not cease immediately as the first-class fare by rail was 15s compared with 12s inside a coach and 8s outside. In July 1844 when the Manchester & Leeds desired to run a cheap excursion from Dewsbury to Leeds, the railway found it did not have a sufficient number of open wagons to accommodate the passengers, so solved this problem by commandeering all the Midland Railway wagons on its system. The Midland Company, annoyed by this affront, responded by seizing all Manchester & Leeds wagons on its lines and took them to Derby, which resulted in a complete stoppage of goods trains between Leeds, Manchester and Liverpool.

The first accident on the Great Western had occurred on 25 October 1840. Faringdon Road station was the temporary terminus and that night the Down goods train approached, sped through the station, and burst through the closed doors of the engine shed beyond. The driver was killed together with four passengers – in the early days, third-class passengers were carried by goods train in open wagons. The accident was caused by the driver falling asleep.

On Christmas Eve 1841 an accident occurred on the Great Western that had far-reaching effects for all the British railway companies. The 4.30 a.m. Down goods train from Paddington consisted of the 2-4-0 *Hecla*, new that April, two open-wagon-type third-class coaches, a station truck conveying parcels for various stations, while in the rear were seventeen goods wagons. In the centre of Sonning cutting, east of Reading, it ran into a slip, which covered the track to a depth of 4 feet. The slip had been caused by excessive rain. The sudden stop when the train ran into obstruction caused the momentum of the goods wagons at the rear of the train to crush the passenger wagons against the tender, smashing one and seriously damaging the other. Of the 38 passengers, eight were killed outright and 17 seriously injured.

The subsequent Board of Trade report stated:

> The third class carriages have seats 18 inches high, but the sides and ends are only two feet above the floor, so that a person standing up, either when the train is unexpectedly put in motion or stopped is, if near the side or end, in great danger of being thrown out of the carriage and those sitting near the sides are also in great danger of falling; besides which, the exposure to the cutting winds of the winter must be very injurious to the traveller, who, if proceeding from London to Bristol, often remains exposed for ten or twelve hours, a great part of which is in the night-time.

This accident caused the Board of Trade to investigate the conditions of third-class passengers on the various railways and resulted in Gladstone's Railway Act of 1844, which required all railways that received at least one-third of their income from passenger traffic to run a minimum of one daily Parliamentary train, including Sundays, calling at every station, and travelling at not less than 12 mph, including stops, in enclosed coaches with seats at a fare of 1*d* a mile including 56 lb of luggage. If those requirements were met, that railway company was exempt from paying the five per cent passenger tax on those fares. Duty remained payable on other tickets until abolished in 1929. Although the speed of a Parliamentary train seems slow to us today, we must remember that it was a lot faster than a stagecoach.

The railway directors objected to the expense of providing better accommodation for the third class, and to try and encourage them to travel by a higher class made the coaches just enclosed boxes with the smallest windows, set high up so you had to stand to see out, and covered with a few slats to allow ventilation. Another ploy to deter third-class travel was to run the Parliamentary trains at night.

Unfortunately the knowledge that an enclosed carriage was available for third-class passengers was not disseminated due to people either being illiterate or unable to afford a newspaper, which would have given them this information. This had fatal results for John Jonathan.

On 14 March 1845, wearing two pairs of trousers, two waistcoats, two body coats and a woollen scarf, he caught a third-class train from Bristol to Bath. On arrival, porter John Fennell found him so frozen that he was unable to leave the open third-class coach. He was assisted out and then down the stairs to street level. Medical assistance was sought, but he died before the doctor arrived. It was ironic that a closed third-class carriage was included in the rake of coaches, but John Jonathan's son said that his father was unaware that a closed vehicle had been available.

Open wagons continued to be used on cheap excursion trains, while on the Sheffield Ashton & Manchester Railway the first cattle trucks, ordered in 1845, were 'to be fitted with spring buffers and drawbars, to answer occasionally for passengers'. A great improvement in passenger comfort had come in the early 1830s when Henry Booth, a Liverpool corn merchant who became a director of the London & North Western Railway, invented the screw coupling, enabling the buffers to be drawn together and thus eradicate most of the bumps and jerks each time a train stopped or started and the links loosened or tightened. Early coaches had their solebars extended and padded with leather or horsehair to form buffers, but by 1835 these had been replaced by spring buffers.

In the early days of passenger railways there were generally four classes of travel: what could be called premium, where passengers travelled in their own coach placed on a flat wagon; first class, where a compartment was enclosed with glass in the windows and whose occupants enjoyed padded seats; second class, enclosed with open windows and more thinly padded seats; and third class, an open wagon offering plenty of fresh air, smoke and steam.

In most of the early coaches, a moderately tall man could not stand in a railway carriage with his hat on. He could nurse it on his knees if sitting down, or in later years, insert it, inverted, in a pair of cords stretched on the ceiling above his seat. Heavy luggage was stowed on the roof, while hand luggage was supposed to be placed under the seat opposite that of its owner.

This could lead to embarrassment, as Hamilton Ellis wrote in *British Railway History 1830–1876*.

> One can only imagine the predicament of the shy, polite young man, travelling to Rugby anxious to recover his carpet bag from behind the massive and most virginal petticoats of the lady opposite, who was going through to Birmingham, and who advised him that if he attempted to enter into conversation with her she would inform the station police.

Third-class passengers being equivalent to those who travelled on the outside of a stagecoach, and thus being used to plenty of fresh air, travelled in open wagons. The more affluent third-class passengers, and those of the second class with open windows, sometimes invested in gauze goggles to guard their eyes from smuts.

Apart from having a less comfortable journey, third-class passengers could be longer in transit. Around 1850 the London & North Western Railway ran a third-class train from London to Liverpool. It left between six and seven in the morning and, travelling at an average speed of 15 mph, arrived at Liverpool, Manchester and Leeds that same evening. It took so long because on arrival at Blisworth, it was always detained for an hour and a half, ostensibly to allow the mail and three other fast trains to overtake, whereas the true reason was to encourage passengers to use a better class in order to secure a faster journey. Thirty-minute stops were also allowed at Birmingham and Derby to offer passengers an opportunity to use the station toilet and refreshment facilities. Even with these breaks, the journey was faster than a few years before when travelling third class took two days to travel from London to Liverpool.

Interestingly, the Liverpool & Manchester Railway used the word 'class' to describe *trains*, a 'first-class' train being the fastest, but the Grand Junction Railway referred to first-class or second-class *passengers*. Until the coming of railways, first and second class had only been used as a term for performance in university examinations. Railways were really obsessed with class: first- and second-class passengers used separate booking offices and waiting rooms, while third-class passengers used goods stations for the practical reason that they travelled by goods trains, which did not normally call at passenger stations.

Each early first-class compartment usually had a rape-oil lamp to itself, whereas those in third class, if they had a light at all, had to share, sometimes just one to a whole carriage. These oil lamps were smoky and the oil was prone to leak out, filling the glass globe with a dirty, dark-coloured liquid that impeded light, making reading almost impossible. Lamp men at the larger stations could earn a tip by installing a newly trimmed lamp into a compartment where passengers were eager to read. Delinquent boys thought it fun to try to head one of these lamps up out of its hole in the roof. To guard against the risk of fire, a lamp room was usually placed in a remote part of the station. Iron-framed tables with slate tops were placed in these rooms and a lamp inserted into a hole so that it could be easily held without slipping when rubbed. The lamp vessels held approximately a pint of oil, which was sufficient to burn for 24 hours. When a train required lamping, lamp barrows were wheeled along the platform. If the lamps already on the train were unused, the lamp man on the roof lit them with a torch. If it had no lamps, or they were dirty and needed changing, fresh lamps were hauled up on a hooked pole, while the used lamps were dexterously dropped into the hand of a lamp man on the platform. These lamps weighed between 15 and 18 lb each. Some passengers wishing to augment the rather feeble slight provided by the railways, provided their own consisting of a candle in a holder with a spike that could be thrust into the upholstery above and behind them. Although improving the level of illumination, it did nothing to improve the upholstery and added to the fire risk.

One very useful, but rather lesser known railway institution set up on 2 January 1842, was the Railway Clearing House. In the early days of railways each line was self-contained, but with their development and the need for a passenger or freight to use more than one railway to reach a destination, some form of unification was required and some managers were reluctant to accept the running of other companies' rolling stock over their lines, or perhaps would bar third-class passengers. There were disputes over the apportioning of receipts as no standard mileage tables were available. There was no common signalling system: on the Great Western two red discs indicated 'All Clear', whereas on the London & Birmingham they indicted 'Clear' – obviously such practices were fraught with danger. Buffers on vehicles were set in different positions so this could lead to interlocking and derailment.

The chief officers of the London & Birmingham were the catalyst and following an invitation to other companies, nine met on 2 January 1842 for the inaugural meeting of the Railway Clearing House (RCH) and five objectives were set out:

1. To organise the through booking of passengers.
2. To organise the through booking of personally-owned carriages and horses.
3. To divide passenger receipts on a mileage basis.
4. To encourage through transport of goods on a rate per mile basis.
5. To settle all inter-company debts.

Initially with a staff of six clerks in a small house in Drummond Street, near Euston, the RCH eventually moved to nearby Seymour Street. Running costs were financed by an annual £5 levy on each station, plus additional levies proportional to receipts. Membership of the RCH was voluntary and the Great Western, the London, Chatham & Dover and the London, Brighton & South Coast did not join until the 1860s. At the meeting in September 1847, it was decided that members would adopt Greenwich Mean Time as standard, and not local time. For instance in 1841 the railway between Leeds and Rugby used Greenwich, but the London & Birmingham adopted local time, hence the confusion when transferring from one system to another at Rugby. Tickets too were standardised. Due to its lack of legal powers the RCH found difficulty in carrying out some of its objectives due to its lack of legal powers, but this was solved by the passing of the Railway Clearing Act of 25 June 1850, which made it easier for the RCH to enforce debt collection.

The RCH set up debtor and creditor accounts with all the railways and the balance due to each was paid at the end of every month. Freight charges could be quite complex. First came the terminal charges, credited equally to the terminus of collection or reception and the terminus of delivery, the rest of the sum divided between the companies according to mileage. The company in ownership of the wagon, which may or may not have been the originating company, was also entitled to a share. If a consignment or wagon became damaged, then costs needed to be apportioned. From 1847 the RCH employed number takers to check the numbers and contents of wagons travelling on 'foreign' lines.

To complete the story, in 1914 the RCH employed a staff in excess of 3,000, but the simplification caused by the 1923 Grouping caused employment to fall to 1,800 by September 1939. Nationalisation in 1948 simplified matters even more and the RCH was disbanded on 31 March 1963.

As the railway system developed, it was obvious that the cities of Edinburgh and Glasgow should be linked. In 1838 John Miller, age 33, was appointed engineer to the Edinburgh & Glasgow Railway, its Act receiving royal assent 4 July 1838. The route selected via Falkirk was virtually flat, except at its western end where it descended the 1½-mile-long Cowlairs Incline on a gradient of 1 in 41 through a 1,040-yard-long tunnel below a canal to the terminus at Queen Street. There were several important engineering features, the largest being Robert Telford's Ratho Viaduct across the Almond Valley. Divided into two sections, there are 36 arches on the Edinburgh side, then an embankment followed by seven arches at its western end. There are six other viaducts and three tunnels, one near Falkirk solely to conceal the railway from a local landowner. In due course the Edinburgh & Glasgow was absorbed by the North British Railway.

Meanwhile, with the opening of the Slamannan Railway on 5 August 1840, a rather complicated railway-plus-canal route had become available between Glasgow and Edinburgh:

	Miles	*Minutes*
Garnkirk & Glasgow	8	20
Monkland & Kirkintilloch	1½	5
Ballochney	3¾	23
Slamannan	12½	40
Union Canal	24	150
Total	49¾	238

The direct line opened on 21 February 1842, the cost of the 46 miles being only £1,200,000 compared with £1,407,172 for the 30½ miles between Liverpool and Manchester. It had been estimated that the line would carry about 340,000 passengers annually, but this proved an underestimate, the actual figures being 666,206 in 1845, 877,902 in 1846 and 1,021,659 in 1846. The reason was that in the pre-railway era people travelled because they *had* to, whereas in the railway age, because travel was relatively cheap and easy, they travelled because they *wanted* to. Nevertheless, early travel was not exactly luxurious as third-class passengers on the Edinburgh & Glasgow had to stand in open wagons, and although the second-class coaches were roofed, there was no glass in the windows.

In 1843 a passenger described the trip between Edinburgh and Glasgow:

In a second class carriage a few weeks ago the cold draught not only pierced me to the very bone, but I was literally covered with clouds of dust swept through and through by the force of the wind, and the misery of this miserable conveyance was completed by a smart shower effectually battering in the dust upon me, and indeed it would be punishment enough to compel the directors to take a similar trip and thus most effectively have them to consider the sufferings of others.

Another serious criticism was that at Queen Street station, the second- and third-class coaches were well inside the tunnel and to reach their seats the unfortunate passengers had to squeeze through a narrow gap between the sooty tunnel wall and the carriages.

The Edinburgh & Glasgow Railway experienced problems at Linlithgow. Ancient charters and Acts of Parliament had allowed the council to levy a duty on vehicles crossing Linlithgow Bridge and passing into or through the town. On 4 February 1842 the provost, bailies and council of Linlithgow announced that this duty would be required on carriages and wagons crossing the railway bridge and passing through the station. Unsurprisingly the railway refused to pay and so was taken to court. The case began in January 1843 and progressed through various courts with the town winning until, in 1853, the House of Lords found in favour of the railway.

In September 1842 Robert Davidson designed for the Edinburgh & Glasgow a four-wheeled electro-magnetic locomotive which could travel at 4 mph. It was powered by current from batteries but proved too expensive to use for everyday working.

To encourage regular traffic, the Edinburgh & Glasgow offered 'villa tickets', that is, free season tickets to those who built homes at any undeveloped site on the line. They were valid for a minimum of five years, with an extra year for every additional £100 spent on the house above £1,000. Although the master of the house travelled free, other members of the family were required to pay and the railway also benefited from the extra freight attracted to the station. The Edinburgh & Glasgow encouraged passengers to go shopping. Railway labels could be bought for ½d each from shopkeepers. Parcels with these labels attached were collected from shops by carters and conveyed to the station where they were recovered by the passengers before boarding their train home. Curiously, excursions were framed as though a favour was being done to the excursionists rather than being seen as a chance for the railway company to make more money. For example, the advertisement for an excursion in August 1842 from Edinburgh to Ayr said that those who travelled on an excursion train took 'advantage of the generosity of the Railway Directors'.

Locomotives and their trains were assisted up the 1 in 42 gradient from Glasgow, Queen Street, by a hemp rope and stationary steam engine. The dexterity with which a locomotive slipped the cable at Cowlairs without stopping was one of the sights of Glasgow. This happened because as the gradient eased the locomotive had sufficient speed to overtake the cable and the inverted coupling fell away. The hemp rope was a constant source of trouble, and in 1844 locomotive superintendent William Paton designed four special six-coupled banking engines, which at the time were the most powerful in the country. Unfortunately they damaged the track, so in 1847 rope haulage was used again, this time using wire rope – but even so, the cables only lasted for 12–18 months before needing replacement, which took a whole weekend.

Paton seems to have been unlucky; following a boiler explosion on one of his locomotives, he received a year's prison sentence for culpable homicide.

Going down to Queen Street, trains descended engineless, with special brake wagons attached. A passenger travelling to Edinburgh in a long excursion train on 7 July 1847 had an exciting moment on the incline.

> The immense weight on the engine caused certain hooks or chains by which the train was attached to the tender and engine to break. At this time the consternation was very great, particularly when it was seen that the engine had left the train. We were ultimately got out of the tunnel, but two other efforts were unsuccessfully made and each time more were brought out more dead than alive with terror and suffocation; and when we did at last get to the top of the incline, it was found that many of the females had fainted. There were at least 1,200 to 1,400 persons stowed into somewhere about forty carriages.

On at least one occasion the 1.05 p.m. express from Edinburgh to Glasgow in charge of 4-4-0 No. 595 ran out of control on Cowlairs incline and demolished the station bar, fortunately not causing serious injury. Forever after, No. 595 was known as 'Carrie Nation', the name of a contemporary American temperance enthusiast. The entertainment on Cowlairs Bank ceased in 1908 when the stationary engine was pensioned off and replaced by a steam engine banking a train in the rear.

At various places along its line, the Edinburgh & Glasgow crossed kirk roads provided to allow the inhabitants of isolated farms and cottages to attend church. Where the railway crossed these paths the company was obliged to provide stiles to allow pedestrians to cross the line, but only for the purpose of attending public worship.

Cowlairs and Euston–Camden were not the only passenger lines in Britain to have a rope-worked incline. On 1 January 1844 a railway was opened from Manchester Victoria to Miles Platting. The 1¼ miles involved gradients as steep as 1 in 30. Trains descending to Victoria did so by gravity headed by a brake wagon. Trains leaving Victoria did so with a locomotive in front and the brake wagon connected to a rope *behind* the train, thus offering rear banking assistance.

The Manchester & Leeds was the first company to run a combined railway and steamboat excursion. This happened at Whitsun 1843, the train working from Manchester over on to the North Midland, the York & North Midland and then the Hull & Selby Railway to Hull from where a steamer carried the passengers to Leith for Edinburgh. In 1847 the Manchester & Leeds changed its name to the Lancashire & Yorkshire Railway and it became one of the most important pre-grouping companies. The Manchester & Leeds was a scenic railway and catered for first-class sightseers by providing two special carriages: the *Gondola*, an enclosed body with open compartments at each end, and *Tourist*, an open carriage capable of being covered with wire gauze or cloth when necessary. An astonishing sight was seen on 12 September 1844 when four trains involving a total of 10 engines and 240 carriages carried 6,600 passengers from Leeds to Hull.

On 7 February 1844 the South Eastern Railway was extended from Folkestone to Dover, thus opening another cross-channel ferry route to the Continent. An unusual feature of the line was that it actually cost less than expected. Between Folkestone and Dover were four significant tunnels: Martello, 530 yards; Abbot's Cliff, 1,933 yards; Shakespeare, 1,392 yards; and the short Archcliffe tunnel, just west of Dover. Between Abbot's Cliff and Shakespeare tunnels was a seawall 30 feet wide at the base and 50 to 70 feet high. The temporary station at Dover consisted of wood and tarpaulin and the cash-strapped South Eastern Railway transferred it physically to Maidstone for that opening on 25 September 1844.

The first excursion run by the London & Brighton Railway was on Easter Monday 1844 when a train of thirty-five carriages hauled by four locomotives left London Bridge at 8.30 a.m. and arrived at Brighton 12.20 instead of the scheduled time of 11.00 a.m. It is interesting to contemplate how its passengers would have been disgorged as the train would have been far too lengthy for the platform. A total of 5,468 passengers were carried to Brighton that

Monday. On one Sunday in August 1844, the Brighton company carried to the seaside 1,710 passengers in forty-six carriages, 300 more passengers having to be turned aside through lack of room.

In May 1844 the South Eastern ran an excursion to France, taking 300 passengers to Boulogne, and as it proved so successful a further six trips were run in the late summer. On 1 June 1844 the *Railway Chronicle* noted that railway excursions were now 'becoming our chief national amusement'.

On the Bristol & Exeter the 22¼ miles from Beambridge to Exeter were completed on 1 May 1844. The special train that had brought dignitaries to Exeter returned, leaving Exeter at 5.20 p.m., and arrived at Paddington at 10.00 p.m. Sir Thomas Acland MP, who had been on the train, immediately went to the House of Commons and by 10.30 p.m. stood up and proudly informed the House that he had been in Exeter at 5.20 p.m.

The first special train for Kent hop pickers ran in 1844 and these became a regular summer feature. A farmer would notify hop-picking families, giving details of date, train time and destination. Up to 30,000 people worked in the fields for several weeks and this required luggage vans to be added to the train. Men normally left at the end of the first weekend to return to their regular jobs, leaving the women and children to continue picking. Due to poor financial circumstances, fewer hoppers' specials ran to Kent than returned, as some people were unable to afford the fare down and had to walk. For instance, in 1880 nearly 19,000 were carried down, but more than 22,600 returned. Hoppers' trains were notorious for violence and drunkenness and in 1863 the mayoress of Maidstone was assaulted on the platform. The South Eastern wisely used its oldest stock on such trains. Special trains were run at weekends for the hop pickers' friends and these visitors could number 40,000. The traffic ended in 1960 when some hops were imported and the demand for Kent hops decreased.

A short but important line opened on 27 May 1844. This was the West London Railway, which connected the London & Birmingham Railway with the Kensington Canal and crossed the GWR on the level. Its principal traffic was freight, and because it was used by so few passengers it was ridiculed by *Punch*. After only six months it closed, but reopened in 1862 as part of the West London Extension

Railway. Leased jointly by the Great Western and the London & North Western Railway, it linked these two companies with the London & South Western, the London, Chatham & Dover and the London, Brighton & South Coast at Clapham Junction.

The Bristol & Gloucester Railway opened on 8 July 1844. Based on an extension of a horse-worked mineral line from collieries at Coalpit Heath, north of Bristol, it was broad gauge. One of the heaviest works on the line was Wickwar Tunnel. On 27 December 1841, the inhabitants of Wickwar heard a noise like thunder, their homes shook and beds appeared to be lifted. An explosion had occurred at the tunnel. Three men were killed outright and five others, seriously injured, were taken to Bristol Infirmary, where one died.

The previous Saturday, more than half a hundredweight of damp gunpowder had been placed in the blacksmith's shop adjoining the tunnel works in the hope that it would dry out. Resuming work on 27 December, the blacksmith was ordered to sharpen workmen's tools. Quite unaware of the presence of the gunpowder, he carried out his task. Sparks from his anvil ignited the powder, which exploded, destroying the shop and part of the tunnel.

5

The Railway Mania

1844

An infamous railway promoter was George Hudson, born in 1800 to an East Yorkshire farmer. In 1827 Hudson inherited a fortune of £30,000, which he invested in early railway schemes. Active in local politics, he became leader of the Tories on York City Council and in due course chairman of the York & North Midland Railway. Under his guidance the company prospered to such an extent that he was able to gain control of other railways, who welcomed him with open arms. In 1844 he started his empire by uniting three railways: the Midland Counties (MCR), the Birmingham & Derby Junction (B&DJR) and the North Midland (NMR).

The earliest of these lines was the MCR, opened between Derby and Nottingham on 4 June 1839. It was extended from Trent Junction to meet the London & Birmingham at Rugby on 30 June 1840. The B&DJR ran from Derby through Burton-upon-Trent to a junction with the London & Birmingham at Hampton-in-Arden, thus offering a competitive route from Derby to London and an inevitable price war as ticket prices and goods rates were reduced. It was never as prosperous as the MCR. The largest engineering feature on the B&DJR was the 20-arch viaduct at Tamworth.

The NMR ran for 73 miles between Derby and Leeds. It opened between Derby and Rotherham on 11 May 1840 and extended to Leeds on 30 June 1840. Works were both extensive and expensive as it required 200 bridges, an aqueduct and seven tunnels, that at Clay Cross being a mile in length. Its building costs were almost twice the estimated amount and when opened its revenue was disappointingly low. In 1842 protesting shareholders, led by George Hudson, investigated the accounts and adopted severe economies by closing some stations, reducing services, dismissing employees and reducing salaries and wages of those remaining.

The lack of success for the NMR allowed George Hudson to expand his empire by persuading the company's shareholders to vote for amalgamation with the B&DJR and the MCR, thus on 10 May 1844 the Midland Railway (MR) was created, the first large-scale railway amalgamation in Britain.

So 1844 was the year the Railway Mania began. Britain's economy was recovering and money was available for investment and the up-and-coming thing to invest in was that wonderful new method of transport – the railway. For some weeks in 1845, the *Morning Post* issued a supplement just dealing with the subject of railways.

Some railways paid excellent dividends, 15 per cent in the case of the Stockton & Darlington, and 10 per cent by the London & Birmingham and Grand Junction. It was obvious that if you had some spare cash, investing in a railway would increase it. Forty-nine Railway Acts were passed in 1844, but 581 in the following three years, such was the Railway Mania. Some lines proved a wise investment, but others offered either a poor return or none at all.

Certain jobs and professions benefited from the Mania: prospectuses had to be printed, engineers appointed and the route surveyed, and the legal profession was required to prepare Parliamentary bills.

The government announced that Sunday 30 November 1845 would be the last day for depositing plans for new railways at the Board of Trade, the offices closing at noon. In those final days, men were rushing to London with plans. Some railway companies refused to carry people whose projects rivalled their own schemes, so imagination was used to disguise the plans as ordinary luggage. One prospective company placed their plans in a coffin attended by mourners and this enabled the coffin to be reverently conveyed by the company that had originally refused to carry the plans.

Many of the schemes proposed were sensible, but others were quite unrealistic. One of the temptations was that when a share was purchased only a fraction needed to be paid initially, the rest of the money being paid in 'calls' as the railway progressed and cash was required to pay the contractor. Some people paid the first call, hoping that their shares would dramatically rise in price and that they would be able to sell them at a substantial profit before another call was made. However, the shares did not always rise in price and some of the purchasers were unable to pay further calls and so lost their money. Giving an example, Lord Clanricarde stated in the House of Lords that a broker's clerk named Guernsey had his name down as a subscriber for London & York shares for £52,000. The problem of non-payment of calls also meant that the company itself may have had problems finding enough finance to complete its line. More than a third of the mileage authorised to be built between 1844 and 1847 was never completed.

The Railway Mania bubble burst at the end of 1847, partly due to investors being unable to pay calls and partly due to the fact that George Hudson's empire had been founded on sand. A committee of investigation found that he had bribed MPs to pass his projects, used insider information to manipulate share prices, sold land he did not own and paid dividends from capital. He was in such disgrace that his waxwork at Madame Tussauds was destroyed. (*See also* page 81.)

The opening of the Cheltenham & Great Western Union Railway between Kemble and Gloucester took place on 12 May 1845. Apart from paving the way from London to Gloucester, it prepared the way to and from South Wales with its mining and metal industries. Kemble was a junction station formed a short distance before Cirencester. Kemble was literally just a junction platform for changing trains and possessed no road access because the local landowner, Squire Gordon, would not permit a public station to be built on his property. The station, which can still be seen today, was the outcome of a Great Western director having a cold wait at this junction. Six acres of land were purchased in 1881, thirty-six years after the line opened, and an agreement was made with Miss Gordon that no intoxicating liquor would be sold on the premises and the only houses built would be for railway employees.

Kemble station had an important well. At first water was raised by a horse-worked pump, but in 1872 locomotive superintendent Joseph Armstrong replaced it with one driven by steam. As Swindon Works, 14 miles distant, was short of water, Armstrong organised trains of rectangular water tanks on wagon frames and modified old tenders to carry this commodity to Swindon. In the early 1900s, the demand for water at the works outstripped the supply by train so a pipeline was laid. Foreseeing the danger of a burst main washing an embankment from under the track, a 'Burst Pipe' indicator was fitted in Kemble signal box.

On the Gloucester side of Sapperton Tunnel were several timber viaducts. When the 129-yard-long Frampton viaduct began to deteriorate, as it would have been difficult to replace without closing the line, the timbering was enclosed in brick. A radar search in recent years revealed that some timbers were certainly left within.

At Gloucester the GWR worked into a platform added to the north side of the Birmingham & Gloucester Railway terminus and which had been used by Bristol & Gloucester trains since 8 July 1844. This brought to light a serious problem created by the Great Western adopting the broad gauge of 7 foot ¼ inches as it meant there could not be through trains from the broad gauge Cheltenham & Great Western Union and Bristol & Gloucester to the standard gauge Birmingham & Gloucester.

On 30 January 1845 the Midland Railway agreed to lease the line from Birmingham to Bristol, this throwing a spotlight on the break of gauge at Gloucester as it was very much in its interest to do so. Although the Great Western's locomotive, carriage and wagon superintendent Daniel Gooch had designed methods of transferring goods between the two gauges, including the idea of having wheels sliding on their axles and standard gauge wagons being carried on broad gauge transporter wagons, neither of these ideas were put into practice. Although Brunel was informed that the transfer shed only held three wagons of each gauge and that this was quite inadequate, he did nothing to alleviate the situation.

An 'Old Carrier's Petition to the Directors of the Great Western Railway against the Break of Gauge', supposedly written by an old carrier, was actually a disguised argument against the broad gauge. It reasoned:

A train would probably consist of thirty-five wagons on the Narrow Gauge line and despatch would require four men at least to each wagon to remove articles and one clerk to every four wagons to mark off goods; thus altogether the expense would be tantamount to 2*s* 6*d* per ton; for to transship one such train with anything like despatch, would require one hundred and forty porters and nine clerks. It is found at Gloucester that to transship the contents of one wagon full of miscellaneous merchandise from one gauge to the other, takes about an hour, with all the force of porters you can put to work upon it!

In the hurry the bricks are miscounted, the slates chipped at the edges, the cheese cracked, the ripe fruit and vegetables crushed and spoiled, the chairs, furniture and oil cake, cast-iron pots, grates and ovens all more or less broken, the coals turned into slack, the salt short of weight, sundry bottles of wine deficient and the fish late for market.

The break of gauge was particularly serious in the case of livestock and it was claimed that the change from one wagon to another deteriorated the quality of the meat 'very greatly' and it was found impossible 'to compel animals taken from one carriage to enter another until an interval of repose in the field or stable has allayed their tremor and alarm'.

A royal commission was appointed to investigate the gauge question on 11 July 1845. When the Parliamentary Gauge Committee visited Gloucester to assess the situation for themselves, J. D. Payne, the Birmingham & Gloucester goods manager, craftily arranged for two trains already dealt with to be unloaded to add to the work and confusion, so that the chaos the break of gauge caused would be the more impressive.

G. P. Neale wrote in *Railway Reminiscences*, 'When the members came to the scene, they were appalled by the clamour arising for the well-arranged confusion of shouting out address of consignments, the chucking of packages across from truck to truck, the enquiries for missing articles, the loading, unloading and reloading, which his clever device had bought into operation.'

In the week ending 25 October 1845, almost 700 tons were transshipped at Gloucester, but the weekly average was 200–300 tons. Despite the claims of the 'Old Carrier', the transfer of goods at Gloucester took an average of 50 minutes for a 5-ton wagon and cost the maximum of 3*d* a ton. Nineteen extra porters had to be employed for the transshipment and the Bristol & Birmingham estimated that the break of gauge cost the company £2,000 a year.

The Croydon Railway, also used by the Brighton and the South Eastern companies, was congested and asked its engineer, William Cubitt, to report on the possibility of using atmospheric traction, which had been tried in the summer of 1840 on a section of the West London Railway. Instead of a locomotive, a pipe ran between the running rails. Into this pipe a piston slung under a special carriage was fitted and when air was withdrawn from the head of the piston by means of stationary engines set at intervals of 3 miles along the line, atmospheric pressure from behind would propel the special carriage and likewise the train to which it was attached.

An atmospherically worked relief line was laid between New Cross and West Croydon and during trials in the second half of 1845, a speed of 70 mph was reached. Regular traffic began on 27 October 1845 and a flyover near the present site of Norwood Junction, probably the world's first flyover, eliminated interference with longer-distance steam-worked trains.

Although in theory the atmospheric railway was excellent, apart from the problem of not being able to have a through pipe at junctions, in actual practice the stationary engines broke their cranks, and the pipe seal failed to do its job properly and leaked. Another disadvantage was that shunting had to be performed by horses or steam locomotives. Atmospheric working ceased on 4 May 1847 after almost half a million pounds had been spent on the project. The aim of the atmospheric railway – saving fuel by using central power stations coupled with rapid acceleration of trains – was answered about sixty years later by the electric railway.

The Woodhead Tunnel opened on 23 December 1845 and at 3 miles 22 yards was the longest in the country at the time. Its construction, begun in October 1838, cost 26 lives while 140 navvies were seriously injured. The single bore rose to a summit of 1,010 feet above sea level at its eastern portal. To avoid a head-on collision on the single line, a pilot engine was required to be coupled to every train that passed through the tunnel. Events proved that a single bore was quite insufficient for the amount of traffic and the contract for an Up line tunnel followed in February 1847. May 1849 saw an outbreak of cholera at the works and when the navvies saw a large load of coffins arrive at Woodhead many rapidly left; four days after the outbreak, only 100 out of the 750 remained. The epidemic caused 28 deaths. This second tunnel opened 2 February 1852. As gradients through this tunnel necessitated low speeds, in an attempt to increase line capacity a signal box was opened in 1899, actually within the tunnel, but due to the choking fumes it was difficult to find men willing to operate it even with the inducement of a shift of only 6 hours, so the box closed about 1909. The corrosive fumes reduced the life of track in the tunnel from the standard 15–17 years in the open to just 3–3½ years.

1846

An outcome of the Railway Mania of 1845, when there was a rush to deposit plans for consideration by Parliament, was that Parliament passed 240 Acts for new railway lines in 1846.

On 10 May 1846 the Midland Railway was formed by the amalgamation of the North Midland, Midland Counties and the Birmingham & Derby Junction. (*See* page 69.) The first sections opened by the newly incorporated company were Nottingham to Lincoln on 4 August, Syston to Melton Mowbray on 1 September and Stamford to Peterborough on 2 October.

The South Eastern Railway opened several sections in 1846: Ashford to Canterbury on 6 February, Canterbury to Ramsgate on 13 April, Tunbridge Wells to Mount Pleasant on 25 November and Ramsgate Town to Margate Sands on 1 December.

The London & Brighton Railway also opened several sections in 1846: Worthing to Littlehampton on 16 March, Littlehampton to Chichester and Brighton to Lewes on 8 June, and Lewes to St Leonards on 27 June. On this latter date the London & Brighton was amalgamated with the London & Croydon to form the London, Brighton & South Coast Railway.

The South Devon Railway, a continuation of the Bristol & Exeter, which itself was a continuation of the Great Western, opened from Exeter to Teignmouth 30 May 1846, a considerable length of this line being beside the sea and most picturesque, but a nightmare to maintain in rough weather. The line was extended to Newton Abbot on 30 December 1846. This line was the first of any length to adopt the atmospheric system of propulsion.

When Messrs Samuda contacted Brunel suggesting that their patent idea should be used, the novelty appealed to Brunel. Due to the cost of the pipe Brunel recommended a single line, and because a head-on collision using atmospheric working was well-nigh impossible there would be no danger. Atmospheric traction was inaugurated on 13 September 1847 when passengers were carried between Exeter and Teignmouth. Brunel's biographer, his son I. Brunel, recorded in *The Life of Isambard Kingdom Brunel*,

> ... except when occasional mishaps caused delay, the new mode of traction was almost universally approved of. The motion of the train, relieved of the impulsive action of the locomotive, was singularly smooth and agreeable; and passengers were freed from the annoyance of coke dust and the sulphurous smell from the engine chimney.

Restarting a train from an intermediate station was not quite as simple as with a steam locomotive. As an atmospheric train approached a station, the piston left the pipe by means of a self-acting valve. Brunel the younger continued:

> An arrangement for starting the train rapidly from the station, without help of horses or locomotives, had been brought practically into operation this consisted of a short auxiliary vacuum tube containing a piston which would be connected with the train by means of a tow-rope and thus draw it along till the piston of the piston-carriage entered the main atmospheric tube. Some accidents at first occurred in using this apparatus, but its defects were after a time removed. The highest speed recorded for an atmospheric train was 68 mph.

Atmospheric working continued for eight months until problems grew too great and steam traction was introduced on 10 September

1848. The leather seal caused difficulties: this seal at the top of the pipe between the rails was difficult to keep supple as the natural oil was sucked out by the pipe's inlet and outlet valves. Another problem was that the pumping engines frequently failed. The cost of installing atmospheric traction had been nine times the estimate, while the working cost was 3s 1d per mile compared with just 1s 4d by steam locomotive. The consequence was that the South Devon Railway had 40 miles of single line, which otherwise would have been made double, and steeper gradients than if designed for locomotive working.

The Eastern Union Railway opened the 17 miles from Colchester to Ipswich on 15 June 1846 and the Ipswich, Bury & Norwich Railway opened to goods traffic on 7 December 1846, passenger traffic commencing on Christmas Eve 1846. From 1 January 1847, the two railways were worked as one and formally united by an Act of 9 July 1847.

On 22 June 1846 the North British Railway was the first line to cross the border when it opened from Edinburgh to Berwick, with the branch from Longniddry to Haddington. This left just the gap between the Tyne and Tweed to be covered by road coach. The North British, initially part of the Hudson empire, was the major Scottish railway company and, at the end of its existence, reached from Glasgow in the west, Fort Augustus and Mallaig in the north-west, Stirling, Perth and Dundee in the north and Bervie and Kinnaber Junction in the north-east. The North British had other claims to fame: it had the Forth and Tay bridges, the largest station in Scotland – Waverley; in 1871 it became the first to introduce the ubiquitous 4-4-0 with inside frames and inside cylinders; in 1873 it pioneered the first British sleeping car and in 1919 its 12-wheeled dining cars were among the first examples of steel passenger rolling stock in Britain.

An important Act passed on 26 June 1846 was that of the Great Northern Railway, which was 30 miles shorter from London to York than Hudson's route. The Great Northern Railway became the southern part of the East Coast route to Scotland. Doncaster was selected as the site of the company's locomotive and carriage works, always known as 'The Plant'. Opened at the end of June 1853 it was fully opened by 9 August. The company spent £1,000 building schools for its workers' children. By 1900 the

Plant covered 200 acres and employed 4,500 men. By this date the St Leger brought 150 or so trains to Doncaster. In order to accommodate them the Plant closed for a week and goods services were suspended to provide vacant sidings for stabling the trains.

The Leeds & Bradford Railway opened, with its Hunslet branch, on 1 July 1846.

On 16 July 1846 the London & Birmingham, Grand Junction and the Manchester & Birmingham were amalgamated to become the London & North Western Railway. It had a total route mileage of 420 and so was then the largest network under single ownership. The first line opened by the new company was Bletchley to Bedford, on 18 November 1846.

Railways were particularly useful for transporting heavy but relatively low-value goods, such as coal and stone. On 6 August 1846 the Aberdare Railway opened a 9½-mile-long line from a junction with the Taff Vale Railway at Abercynon to Aberdare.

What was to become part of the West Coast Line was opened by the Lancaster & Carlisle Railway on 22 September 1846 when the 20 miles from Lancaster to Oxenholme were inaugurated. This was followed by the remaining 50 miles to Carlisle on 17 December. With Locke as engineer and Brassey as contractor, it was the largest single railway contract placed to date and was completed in the short time of two and a half years. At one time almost 10,000 navvies were employed. As was not infrequently the case, the different ethnic groups of navvies quarrelled and in 1846 the military had to be called to quell a fight between English and Irish groups. The line was famous for the Shap Incline with a 31-mile climb culminating in 4 miles of 1 in 75, most trains requiring banking assistance up the gradient.

On 27 October 1846 the Lynn & Ely Railway opened the 10¼ miles from King's Lynn to Downham and the branch to King's Lynn Harbour.

On 17 November 1846 the 16-mile-long Bedford & London & Birmingham Railway was opened linking Bedford with Bletchley on the London & Birmingham Railway and was worked by this latter company.

The 28½ miles of the Eastern Counties Railway opened from Ely North Junction to Peterborough for freight and cattle on 10 December 1846, passengers having to wait until 14 January 1847.

1847

On 27 January 1847 the London & South Western opened the 22 miles from Eastleigh to Salisbury to goods traffic and to passengers on 1 March 1847. The line was an excellent example of cheap proving dear. Landowners had proved obstructive and prices offered for their properties had to go to arbitration. Then, instead of employing the reliable Thomas Brassey, the tender of the delightfully named Hoof & Hill was accepted since it was £18,000 below that of its competitors.

Delay in obtaining land had delayed the contractors in turn, so Joseph Locke, the London & South Western's engineer, offered Hoof & Hill an extra £1,000 if the line could be opened by 10 August 1846. This they were unable to do because farmers gathering in the harvest were able to offer higher wages than the contractor. Opening was postponed until October and then, due to bad weather, November, then to December. When the first goods train arrived on 27 January 1847 it was in the charge of Driver Naylor who usually drove the royal train. Sixteen tons of coal were earmarked for 'distressed persons'. One of the chief benefits the line brought was cheaper coal, advantageous to both households and industry and thus helping to raise living standards.

The Norfolk Railway opened its line between Wymondham and Dereham on 15 February 1847.

In 1847 the London, Brighton & South Coast opened a line from Chichester to Havant on 15 March and Havant to Portsmouth on 14 June.

The Newcastle & Berwick opened from Heaton Junction to Morpeth on 1 March 1847, Chathill to Tweedmouth on 29 March, North Shields to Tynemouth on 31 March and Morpeth to Chathill on 1 July.

On 16 March 1847 the Leeds & Bradford opened a line from Shipley to Keighley, extending it to Skipton on 8 September 1847. Initially stations between Shipley and Keighley were mere temporary structures, though that at Bingley lasted at least two years, for in November 1849 the *Leeds Intelligencer* commented:

A wooden station of the most wretched and disgraceful description ... It consists of a clerk's room, about three yards square at one end, a small open shed in the middle, and at the other end a room similar to the clerk's dignified with the name of the 'Ladies' waiting room'. During wet weather the clerks transact business with an umbrella over their heads, to protect themselves from the rain dropping through the roof. In the open shed are huddled together first, second and third class male and female passengers, sometimes for nearly an hour, exposed to all kinds of weather, as the trains are frequently this period behind time. 'The ladies' waiting room' is avoided from the dread of cholera, for the stench arising from the conveniences, only separated by thin boards, is dreadful. It is expected that the Improvement Commissioners intend to indict the station as a public nuisance, and that the inhabitants will take steps to compel the directors to provide them with proper and civilised accommodation.

The Eastern Counties Railway opened sections in 1847: Wisbech to March on 3 May and Cambridge to St Ives on 17 August, while on 3 May 1847 the 11½ miles from Lowestoft to Reedham was opened to goods, passenger traffic starting on 1 July 1847.

24 May 1847 was the date of a serious bridge failure. The Shrewsbury & Chester Railway had opened in the autumn of 1846 and, with Robert Stephenson as engineer, included a bridge over the Dee. It consisted of three 98-foot spans of cast-iron girders supported on stone piers. On 24 May, as the 6.15 p.m. train from Chester to Shrewsbury passed over the third span of the bridge, its driver heard an odd noise accompanied by unusual vibration. Quickly realising that something serious was amiss, he opened his regulator to get his train clear before the bridge collapsed. The engine managed to reach solid ground before the outer of the two girders broke into three pieces causing the bridge to fall, but the tender was derailed and detached causing his fireman, who was on it engaged in breaking coal, to fall into the river to his death. A guard and two coachmen in the leading van were also killed and one passenger later died of his injuries. Sixteen passengers were hurt, but the casualties were remarkably few considering that the whole train fell with the girder. The driver continued with his engine, minus its tender, to Saltney Junction where he raised the alarm before crossing over the Down road and returning to Chester, bravely re-crossing the bridge using the remaining girders in order to stop Up traffic from plunging into the waters and to secure help from Chester.

Captain Simmons investigated the accident on behalf of the Board of Trade. He condemned the bridge girders as too weak and the design as unsound. Repeated flexing had weakened the girder, with witnesses stating that they had seen the spans deflect by several inches every time a train passed across. At the inquest Robert Stephenson was pale and haggard, for although normally very careful, his design was faulty as the wrought-iron truss-rods actually weakened the cast-iron girders rather than strengthening them, and a charge of manslaughter was a real possibility. Robert Stephenson was extricated from the difficult situation by the fact that eminent engineers saved his face by claiming that the girder could only have snapped as a result of a heavy blow such as would have been caused by the derailment of a tender following the breakage of a wheel. The accident resulted in the Railway Commissioners circularising all British railways for details about their cast-iron bridges, many of which were in due course strengthened, while new construction was generally of wrought iron.

The Southampton & Dorchester, known as 'Castleman's Corkscrew' due to its many curves, opened on 1 June. The previous month the company had been involved in a court case. The Southampton residents were peeved because when the London & South Western arrived in the town, passengers to or from ships, instead of using accommodation in the town and patronising its shops, immediately went aboard ship or train. In order to avoid this problem happening with the Southampton & Dorchester, its Act obliged the company to build a station at Bletchynden Terrace near the town centre and stop most of its trains there. Then when the Southampton & Dorchester started to build a station at Bletchynden, the landowner was upset because the company erected it in view of King John's Pond, instead of at the end of Bletchynden Terrace out of sight of his home at King's Bridge House. The directors, not to be outdone, only two days before the line was to be opened, solved the problem by renting Ivy House, a dwelling in Bletchynden Terrace, and used it as a station until 1850 when a permanent station could be built just east of where Southampton Central station stands today.

The station at Bletchynden, instead of being the penultimate station on the line, for some time became its terminus. This was because on 30 May 1847, the tunnel between the two Southampton stations had collapsed. The fall happened because the disused Andover & Southampton Canal tunnel crossed below the railway tunnel, and Peto, the contractor, in order to appease owners of the property above, had filled the canal tunnel with rubble. This, unfortunately, dammed the tunnel and blocked drainage, with the result that water so saturated the clay on which the railway tunnel stood that it collapsed. Until matters were corrected, a horse-drawn bus service linked the two Southampton stations.

The tunnel collapse caused confusion on the opening day, 1 June, as that morning the notice on the doors of Ringwood station proclaimed the postponement of the opening but then had to be hastily removed when the first train arrived at 10.00 a.m. and proved it a lie.

This tunnel caused further trouble in 1964 when its floor moved up towards the roof and for six months single line working had to be adopted while repairs were carried out. The trouble then re-occurred in 1984.

On 1 July 1847 the Newcastle & Berwick opened to Tweedmouth on the south bank of the Tweed so passengers for the North British were carried across the river bridge in an omnibus, on most days one bus sufficing. This service was withdrawn when the Royal Border Bridge opened on 29 August 1850.

The York & North Midland Railway opened the line between Church Fenton and Spofforth on 10 August 1847, York to Market Weighton on 4 October and Filey to Bridlington on 20 October. The York & North Midland proved to be part of an early railway scandal.

With George Hudson as chairman, the York & North Midland and other lines under his control seemed to be highly prosperous, but, like all booms, there was a bust. Until 1849 railway companies needed no independent audit, so initially it was not obvious that Hudson had been operating a pyramid scheme and the lines were not making the profits he claimed. By 1853 Hudson was bankrupt and in a debtors' prison. Unfortunately some small shareholders who had invested their life savings in his schemes also lost their money, people such as Charlotte Brontë. When he was discredited, Hudson Street in York became Railway Street. To give Hudson his due, he sold all his possessions to pay back some of his creditors before seeking refuge abroad to live in poverty.

The London & North Western opened 39¾ miles of line between Rugby and Stafford on 15 September 1847.

The East Anglian Railway opened the 5¼ miles from St Ives to Huntingdon on 17 August 1847 and the 14¼ miles from Downham to Ely North Junction and the 3 miles from Swaffham to Sporle on 26 October 1847.

The Midland Railway opened the line from Long Easton Junction to Codnor Park and the branch line to Ilkeston on 6 September 1847.

One of the important companies making the West Coast Main Line was the Caledonian Railway and this opened the 39¼ miles from Carlisle to Beattock on 9 September 1847. It was engineered by Joseph Locke, who had managed to build the line without a tunnel.

The Edinburgh & Northern Railway opened 24¼ miles from Burntisland on the north bank of the River Forth to Cupar, and 4½ miles from Ladybank to Lindores on 20 September 1847, and a 1½-mile extension from Lindores to Glenbirnie on 9 December 1847.

On 21 December 1847 the Great Western opened 25¼ miles of broad gauge line from Reading to Hungerford. Built by the Berks & Hants, it had been absorbed by the GWR in 1846. In due course, this line became invaluable when the GWR created a short cut to the West avoiding Bristol.

6

An Era of Innovative Railway Bridges

1848

The Newmarket Railway opened to goods from Great Chesterford to Newmarket on 3 January 1848 and 4 April for passengers.

On 1 February 1848 the Eastern Counties Railway opened 19 miles from March South Junction to St Ives.

In February 1848 W. H. Smith chartered a special train to deliver the budget editions of London newspapers to the provinces. It ran from Euston to Glasgow via Rugby, York, Newcastle and Edinburgh, 476 miles, in less than 10½ hours giving an average speed of about 50 mph. This timing included stops, engine changing and transfer from one train to another as there were no railway bridges over the Tyne and the Tweed rivers.

On 15 February 1848 the Caledonian Railway opened 61½ miles of line between Beattock and Edinburgh via Carstairs, thus completing the West Coast route to Scotland and, for the first time, offering a through route without the need to change carriage. Although the East Coast line to Edinburgh had been open for almost a year, it involved train changes at the Tweed and the Tyne. This new line involved a climb for 10 miles at 1 in 74/88 to Beattock Summit before a more gradual descent through the Clyde Valley. On 10 March 1848 the Post Office transferred the carriage of its London to Edinburgh mails from the East Coast to the West Coast.

Eight to ten fat cattle were carried to London for £8 7s 0d and sheep 'new out of the wool' at 2s 3d per head. Farmers were told that the journey was so short that the animals did not need to be watered or fed during transit, but initially farmers insisted on sending drovers, the railway company having to provide a third-class carriage for them. The trip to London took 25 hours. Although the railway had only intended sending one cattle train a week, by 21 October 1848 one ran every night. Sheep were carried in double-deck wagons.

The arrival of the railway at Gretna Green made it easier for the English who desired runaway marriage, because instead of a costly post-chaise they merely required a relatively inexpensive railway ticket. But the railway brought trouble to the Customs & Excise. The law stated that whisky could not be imported into England from Scotland in quantities of less than 20 gallons and that each consignment required a certificate stating that duty had been paid. The new railway offered ample opportunity for passengers and employees to transport whisky across the border in smaller quantities than the legal minimum and on which duty had not been paid. After several passengers and employees had appeared in court the Caledonian displayed in all its station a poster:

> The Caledonian Railway Company refuse to undertake the Conveyance of Spirits, except when conditions of the Excise Regulations have been complied with, and when they are supplied with the name and address of the party sending and the party to receive the Consignment. All Packages containing Liquids of any description are liable to detention on suspicion to avoid which it is desirable their contents should be stated at the time of booking.

The Carstairs to Edinburgh section gave the Caledonian a route between Glasgow and Edinburgh. Although steeply graded and 8 miles longer than the flatter and more direct line of the Edinburgh & Glasgow Railway, the Caledonian announced that it would operate expresses between the two cities starting on 1 April 1848. It proved a very apt date to start because of the expensive rivalry between the two companies. Initially it was about providing a quicker service and then ticket prices were reduced, but the reduced fare only applied between the termini, thus intermediate passengers paid one-third more than through passengers for half the distance. Realising that competition was ruining both companies, eventually a truce was declared.

On 9 July 1869 the Caledonian avoided the Carstairs detour by opening a more direct line between the two cities via Cleland and Mid Calder. Competition with the North British was so great that between them the two companies were running 54 trains daily between Edinburgh and Glasgow, many only sparsely filled. Again sense prevailed and the service was reduced to about 20 North British and 15 Caledonian trains each way. Between Glasgow and Edinburgh the Caledonian ran branches to many collieries and shale mines, but as the minerals were worked out these lines closed.

The East Lincolnshire opened 14 miles from Louth to Grimsby and New Holland on 1 March 1848, Firsby to Louth on 4 September and Boston to Firsby on 2 October 1848. Also on 1 March the Manchester, Sheffield & Lincolnshire opened from Great Grimsby to Ulceby and New Holland, from Ulceby to Market Rasen and from Barnetby to Brigg on 1 November, and from Market Rasen to Lincoln on 18 December.

The Midland Railway opened from Melton Mowbray to Stamford on 20 March for goods and 1 May for passengers, from Nottingham to Kirkby on 2 October, and from Coalville to Burton-on-Trent on the same date. The Lancashire & Yorkshire opened between Wakefield and Goole on 1 April, from Knottingley to Askern Junction on 6 June and from Walton Junction to Wigan on 20 November 1848.

The North Staffordshire Railway, familiarly known as the 'Knotty', was busy with openings in 1848: Stoke-on-Trent to Norton Bridge on 17 April, Stoke-on-Trent to Uttoxeter on 7 August, Uttoxeter to Burton Junction on 11 September, and Stoke-on-Trent to Crewe and Congleton on 14 October.

On 5 May 1848 the South Devon Railway opened to passengers from Totnes to Laira Green near Plymouth, goods traffic starting on 13 September 1848. Brunel had intended the line to be worked on the atmospheric system (*see* page 75), which was thought to have been able to cope better with steep gradients than a steam locomotive. Crossing Dartmoor, a Down train faced a gradient of 1 in 46 up to Rattery and 1 in 42 on the descent from Hemerdon. It was not until the advent of dieselisation that this section ceased to be an operating problem with the need for assisting engines to be held ready.

The locomotive-worked Scottish Central Railway opened from Stirling to Greenhill Upper Junction with the Edinburgh & Glasgow Railway on 1 March 1848 and the 33 miles from Stirling to Perth on 22 May. The sharpest curve was 40 chains and the ruling gradient for northbound trains was 1 in 91 and 1 in 74 for those southbound. The line had been built by probably the most successful contractor, Thomas Brassey, through whose accounts, it is said, more flowed in a year than through the treasuries of a dozen duchies and principalities. A tunnel near Perth was cut through 'bastard whinstone' with quartz veins. Trouble was experienced with a seepage of water coupled with the fumes from trains rotting the roof of the tunnel so severely that it required brick relining in 1901–1904. The Scottish Central, as did the Caledonian, ordered Crewe-type 2-2-2s, perhaps to show its allegiance to the West Coast line.

The Chester & Holyhead opened 57¾ miles from Saltney Junction, south of Chester, to Bangor on 1 May 1848 and the 21¾ miles on Anglesey from Llanfair to Holyhead on 1 August, the difficult crossings of Conway and Britannia Bridges delaying complete opening. Robert Stephenson was the engineer while the stations were designed by Francis Thompson. As Anglesey was still inaccessible by rail, two locomotives for working the line were shipped to Holyhead. Following the opening, passengers were carried by coach between Bangor and Llanfair using Telford's suspension bridge – in fact at one time it was thought that, to avoid the expense of a railway bridge, railway carriages could be drawn across Telford's bridge by horses.

It was also on 1 August 1848 that the Irish Mail train first ran, as did the Chester & Holyhead's ferry service from Holyhead, but the mail contract was given to the City of Dublin Steam Packet Company, which operated at a loss. To protect the harbour at Holyhead a great breakwater was built, 7,860 feet in length, a 7-foot gauge line carrying stone from Holyhead Mountain. The breakwater was not finished until the 1870s. During World War I Holyhead became a destroyer base.

The opening of the Chester & Holyhead had a serious effect on the coastal shipping from Liverpool along the coast of North Wales as passengers deserted the steamers almost immediately. Some of the coastal settlements on the route developed into resorts. In the early 1880s, a fast businessmen's train ran each way between Llandudno and Manchester, and from 1908 two club carriages were provided. Tea was served on board and each member was allocated an armchair and a locker. Later, a third-class club was established on this route.

The first club coaches had been inaugurated in 1895 on the Lancashire & Yorkshire's Blackpool–Manchester line. Users were required to pay a supplement in addition to the cost of the season ticket and new members were elected by a committee. One rule was that no windows should be opened while the train was in motion. Other club trains ran to and from Manchester, from Liverpool and Windermere, while the wool magnates from Bradford were carried home to Morecambe in two club cars. It is surprising that season ticket holders in the London area did not adopt the idea. The North Eastern Railway operated club cars between Bridlington and Hull. All the club cars were withdrawn during World War II and were never reinstated.

Stephenson had a problem crossing the Menai Strait. As there was only one rock available for intermediate support, he needed to provide spans of in excess of 450 feet. Normal suspension bridges were too flexible for use by trains and arches were no solution as they would have been an obstruction to sailing ships. A completely new design was needed.

In 1845, Stephenson, with William Fairbairn and Eaton Hodgkinson, spent two years experimenting with tube-shaped bridges. The result of this careful research was that chains were unnecessary and that a square, rather than round, tube was found to be best, with a cellular top and bottom to offer stiffness. Curiously, a mishap at Blackwell with the launch of the iron steamship *Prince of Wales* gave him the help he needed. Due to a failure of the launching tackle, the vessel stuck so that her hull was completely unsupported for 110 feet, yet was not strained. This was the proof Stephenson needed that a wrought-iron tubular bridge would offer sufficient strength to stand without the aid of suspension chains.

The single-span Conway Bridge, with a 400-foot-long tube for each road, became a dress rehearsal for the Britannia Bridge. The masonry of both bridges was started in the spring of 1846 and as sufficient lodgings were unavailable locally, the workmen lived in timber huts on the shores of Conway and Menai. Some of the plates were flattened by hand with 40 lb sledge hammers. The tubes were built near each bridge site.

The view of the yard at night from Anglesey was an amazing sight. Forty-eight rivet hearths each had flames and from them a golden rain of sparks shot skywards, reflected in the sea. This golden rain was produced by the rivet boys who hurled the white-hot rivets 40 feet into the air, to be dextrously caught by the riveting gangs at work on top of the tubes. Altogether 90 tons of rivet iron was used, every rivet having to be closed by hand.

In 1848 the first of the wrought-iron tubes, that carrying the Up line, was floated into position, raised by hydraulic jacks and then supported by masonry. Stephenson was assisted by his friend Isambard Kingdom Brunel, while Captain Christopher Claxton, RN, having just returned from refloating Brunel's SS *Great Britain* at Dundrum Bay, superintended the nautical and signalling arrangements for the floating. This was the first time an hydraulic press had been used for bridge building and Brunel adopted this method for his bridges at Chepstow and Saltash. A special train was able to pass through this tube on 18 April 1848.

When the second Conway tube had been raised to within 2 feet 6 inches of its correct height, a crack several inches in length appeared in the crosshead of one of the lifting presses. The tube was quickly supported with timber packing and lifting continued. The Down Conway tube was completed by January 1849.

The Britannia Bridge consisted of three towers, one on either shore, with a central tower built on a rock. This central tower, the Britannia, was 221 feet 3 inches tall, while the side towers were each 18 feet shorter. Up and Down tracks were carried in two parallel tubes, each of which consisted of four sections. The total weight of the tubes was 5,188 tons and the length of each tube 1,511 feet. They were rigidly mounted in the central pier, but to allow for expansion were free to move over bearings on the shore piers. By doing this, Stephenson had involved the cantilever principle and thus made a strong structure even stronger.

The first tube section was to have been floated out on 19 June 1849 and a spectacular event was expected. The three great tubes on the Caernarvon shore had been converted into a grandstand thronged with spectators and cannons were ready to fire a salute. Brunel stood beside Robert Stephenson as did Joseph Locke. The pontoons supporting the tube were lifted by the tide and at 6.00 p.m. Stephenson signalled 'Cut away!' The result was an anti-climax. The capstan on one of the pontoons gave way and the project had to be temporarily aborted.

On the morning of 20 June 1849 the tide was running so quickly through the strait that it was impossible to lay out the hauling lines. Buoy moorings were uprooted, heavy cables torn away – the crowds had plenty of excitement. At 7.30 p.m. order had been restored and Stephenson again gave the order to 'Cut away!' The huge tube glided smoothly out into the tideway and the wind and current began to speed its movement. Stephenson ordered the screw cable-stoppers to be applied to check the speed, but one stopper failed to grip and then an 8-inch-diameter checking cable snapped like a thread.

It was imperative that the Anglesey end of the tube butted against the Anglesey pier so that when it was safely lodged there the other end could be swung to the Britannia tower. At the critical moment the tube swung too far, and as the men tried to check it the capstan seized, was torn from its foundations and it and the men thrown into the sea.

Fortunately Foreman Rolfe kept his head; he seized the heavy cable and staggered up the beach, dragging the heavy cable and shouting for the crowds to help. Slowly they pulled it to the Anglesey pier, which it struck with a thunderous reverberation. The Caernarvon capstans spun into action and the other end of the tube was safely home under the Britannia tower. 'Now,' remarked Robert Stephenson to Brunel, 'I shall go to bed.'

On 22 June 1849 Robert Stephenson laid the final stone of the Britannia Tower. The tube section rested for two months above high water while the lifting apparatus was set up, and when this was completed the tube was gradually raised between August and 13 October 1849 to a height of over 100 feet above high water. On one occasion one of the hydraulic presses failed and the tube fell, fortunately not far, as Stephenson had the foresight to provide supporting masonry so that the tube fell just a few inches.

In due course the other three sections of the first tube were completed and on 5 March 1850 Robert Stephenson and the contractor C. J. Mare drove in the last rivet. Then, accompanied by Francis Trevithick and other engineers, they boarded a long train containing 700 passengers and 45 loaded coal wagons, which was slowly drawn through the tube by three locomotives, the whole train weighing more than 500 tons.

On 18 March 1850 the line between Bangor and Llanfair opened, the 2.30 p.m. Holyhead to Euston express having the honour of being the first public passenger train to travel the whole length of the Chester & Holyhead. The Down tube was opened on 19 October 1850; building the bridge had cost 19 lives. Its ironwork had cost in excess of £300,000 and the total was double this amount.

Unfortunately the Britannia Bridge cannot now be seen in its original state. On 23 May 1970 some lads entered the tubes in search of birds' eggs. To light the darkness they used torches made from lit newspaper. To protect the wrought-iron plates above the line, engineers had built a timber roof which even later was sealed with tarred hessian – and this ignited. Despite the efforts of the Caernarvonshire and Anglesey fire brigades, the bridge's height, construction and lack of an adequate water supply meant they were unable to control the fire. The heat split the bridge, which was totally lost. As there were no longer any square-rigged men-o'-war which the Admiralty deemed should be able to pass, Stephenson's spans were replaced by an arched steel bridge.

As Holyhead and Anglesey were now cut off from the rest of the railway system, stranded locomotives were transferred to the mainland on low-loader lorries, frightening one drinker who staggered out of a public house just as a main-line diesel passed.

It was debated whether it was worth the expense of rebuilding the bridge, but when it was considered that a successful container service between London and the Republic of Ireland had been set up in January 1968, this fact swayed the argument for making a replacement. Soon after its reopening on 30 January 1972, a road deck was added above the railway. This echoed Stephenson's High Level Bridge at Newcastle built 1845–1849 across the Tyne. Here he used a railway deck supported on wrought-iron arches from which the road deck hangs on hangers.

Another interesting construction on the route was Foryd Bridge, west of Rhyl. An iron girder bridge with a central opening span over the River Clwyd, it was not a good bridge to have on a main line as it took about 40 minutes to open the span, warp a vessel through and then close it. An unusual feature near Penmaenmawr was the timber avalanche shelters to protect trains from falling rock.

On 4 May 1848 the North British Railway opened from Gorebridge to Bowland Bridge, part of a line that was projected by the Edinburgh & Hawick and acquired by the North British in 1846 in an effort to reach Carlisle.

The lack of interlocked signals and points caused a disaster on the Great Western at Shrivenham on 10 May 1848. In order to clear a wagon turntable, two porters pushed a horsebox and cattle truck onto the main Up line, their actions unseen by the policeman who at that time was responsible for signalling and who was placed at the opposite end of the station. The result was that the wagons were struck by *Sultan*, a 4-2-2 heading the 12.00 noon Up express from Exeter, and hurled onto the platform. *Sultan* kept to the rails and was virtually undamaged, but the wreckage ripped out the side of the leading coach, killing six passengers and injuring 13.

On 17 May 1848 the Edinburgh & Northern opened 11½ miles from Cupar to Newport-on-Tay, and Glenbirnie to Abernethy Road on the same date, Abernethy Road to Perth on 25 July, and Cross Gates to Thornton Junction on 4 September 1848. The Edinburgh & Northern was unusual in the fact that it had an office in Edinburgh, yet all its track was across on the other side of the River Forth.

On 5 July 1848 the Edinburgh & Glasgow opened its 5½-mile-long Campsie branch. It proved most popular due to its attractive scenery and many Glaswegians enjoyed their first trip into the countryside and their first train journey when travelling to this line. It was actually advertised as the 'picnic branch'.

The Liverpool, Crosby & Southport Railway opened from Waterloo to Southport on 27 July 1848.

On 1 August 1848 the York & North Midland Railway opened from Selby to Market Weighton.

On 22 August 1848 the Scottish Midland Junction Railway opened throughout from Perth to Forfar via Cargill & Coupar Angus.

22 August also marked the opening of the Windsor, Staines & South Western Railway from Richmond through Staines to Datchet on the Thames opposite Windsor, the Commissioners of Woods &

Forests having opposed a railway approaching closer to Windsor. In truth, earlier that year, the London & South Western chairman had stated that 'Her Majesty having graciously consented to an extension of the Windsor, Staines & South Western line from Datchet across Home Park into Windsor'. Behind this statement was the fact that Prince Albert needed £80,000 to drain Home Park and, not wishing to beg this sum from Parliament, persuaded the South Western to fork out this sum. Its line to Windsor opened on 1 December 1849.

On 23 August 1848 the Glasgow, Dumfries & Carlisle Railway opened the 24½ miles from Dumfries to Gretna, two years later amalgamating with the Glasgow, Paisley, Kilmarnock & Ayr to form the Glasgow & South Western, which provided an alternative route between Glasgow and England. The Kilmarnock line had opened between Kilmarnock and Muir via Auchinleck on 9 August 1848.

On 1 September 1848 the Leeds & Thirsk opened Wormald Green to Weeton, extending it from Wormald Green to Ripon on 13 September. A 23-arch viaduct across the River Aire at Leeds preceded the 2-mile-241-yard Bramhope Tunnel, which was almost immediately followed by a curving 21-arch viaduct across the River Wharfe. The Leeds & Thirsk was intended to serve Harrogate by a direct route and break George Hudson's monopoly using an indirect route between Leeds and the north-east via York. In 1851 it was renamed the Leeds Northern Railway.

The first section of the Wilts, Somerset & Weymouth Railway opened from Thingley Junction, just west of Chippenham, to Westbury on 5 September 1848. The Wilts, Somerset & Weymouth proved to be a very important line as it gave the Great Western access to Weymouth and the valuable ferry service to and from the Channel Islands, profitably carrying passengers and market-garden produce. As the line ran south it also had the advantage of acting as somewhat of a barrier to the westwards growth of the London & South Western.

The East Anglian Railway opened the 9 miles between Spore and Dereham on 11 September 1848; on 2 October 1848 the Leeds & Bradford opened between Skipton and Colne; on 14 October 1848 the Shrewsbury & Chester opened from Ruabon to Shrewsbury; and on 23 December from Gobowen to Oswestry. The Shrewsbury & Chester's second-class coaches actually had glass windows and partitioned compartments, both a luxury at that time. The ceremonial opening on 12 October was the usual spectacular affair with three locomotives hauling 59 carriages leaving Chester for a banquet at Shrewsbury. Normally Board of Trade inspecting officers appear practical rather than romantic, but Captain Wynne wrote regarding the railway's 269-yard-long Chirk Viaduct marring Telford's canal viaduct:

> It is to be regretted that the two works are necessarily placed so closed (*sic*) together for the more recent one completely degrades the other which has so long given celebrity to the valley and been looked upon as one of its leading features, the two are so mixed up by their close juxtaposition that the proper effect of each is lost, and the scenery which is very beautiful not improved.

On 17 October 1848 the Great Northern opened 59 miles from Peterborough to Boston and Lincoln.

The Great Western Railway made another invasion of London & South Western territory when it opened a branch from Southcote Junction to Basingstoke on 1 November 1848.

Just as Chat Moss caused a problem to the Liverpool & Manchester, so the quaking bog over the fens near Whittlesea Mere caused problems to the Great Northern. A hundred acres of faggot wood were cut, stakes placed end to end to form a platform for a layer of peat sods and then another layer of stakes laid down, then more peat sods and so on. This was done gradually to give the water time to run out. Similarly, brick abutments for bridges were founded on timber rafts.

1849

This year was to prove an exceptionally busy one for railway openings. On 1 February 1849 the East Lancashire Railway opened the 6 miles from Burnley to Colne and 22¾ miles from Lostock Hall Junction near Preston to Walton Junction near Liverpool on 2 April. On 12 February the Manchester, Sheffield & Lincolnshire opened the line from Sheffield to Beighton and on 17 July extended it from Beighton to Gainsborough, while on 2 April it had opened Brigg to Gainsborough. On 1 March 1849 the North British opened its line from Bowland to Newtown St Boswells, extending it to Hawick on 29 October; Reston to Duns was opened on 10 August and Drem to Williamstown on the same day. On 20 March 1849 the Norfolk Railway opened the line from Dereham to Fakenham.

On 9 April 1849 the South Staffordshire Railway opened from Walsall to Alrewas, while also on 9 April the Great Northern Railway opened the 16 miles between Lincoln and Gainsborough, and between Retford and Doncaster on 4 September.

1 May 1849 was an important date for the Bristol & Exeter for that was when it took over its own working. Although initially it had been worked by the Great Western, it was decided that it was large enough to provide its own locomotives and rolling stock. In addition to 20 passenger and eight goods locomotives based on Great Western designs, it had a very interesting and unusual combined locomotive and carriage, designed and constructed by W. B. Adams at the Fairfield Works, Bow. It had a vertical boiler above the four-wheel power section, while the coach portion accommodated 16 first and 32 second-class passengers. Initially, the Bristol & Exeter's engineer, C. H. Gregory was in charge of the locomotive department.

James Pearson was appointed locomotive superintendent and designed his own engines. In 1853 he produced a 4-2-4 express tank locomotive with 9-foot-diameter driving wheels; one reached an authenticated speed of 81.8 mph down Wellington Bank where, rather later, *City of Truro* was to make its record run. Unlike those of the Great Western, none of its engines was named. The Bristol & Exeter works at Bristol turned out its first engine in 1859.

1849 was a busy year for the North Staffordshire Railway as it opened Stone to Colwich on 1 May, Congleton to Macclesfield on 13 June, North Rode to Uttoxeter on 13 July, and Marston Junction to Willington Junction on 13 July.

The Shrewsbury & Birmingham's line opened from Shrewsbury to Oakengates on 1 June and Oakengates to Wolverhampton on 12 November, unseasonable weather having delayed the construction of the 671-yard-long Oakengates Tunnel. Also on 1 June the Shropshire Union Railways & Canal Company opened its line from Shrewsbury to Stafford.

On 4 June 1849 the Manchester, Buxton, Matlock & Midland Junction Railway opened between Ambergate and Rowsley. On 2 July 1849 the Colchester, Stour Valley, Sudbury & Halstead Railway opened from Marks Tey to Sudbury. On the same date the Eastern Union opened between Finningham and Burston, extending to Norwich (Victoria) on 3 December.

On 4 July the Reading, Guildford & Reigate opened from Reigate to Dorking and also from Reading to Farnborough; from Dorking to Shalford and Farnborough to Ash Junction on 20 August; and from Shalford to Shalford Junction on 15 October. The company enjoyed running powers over the London & South Western's line from Ash Junction to Shalford Junction.

On 10 July 1849 the Leeds & Thirsk opened 11¼ between Weeton and Leeds; on 27 July 1849 the York, Newcastle & Berwick opened from Tweedmouth to Sprouston; Washington to Pelaw on 1 September; and Chevington Junction to Amble on 5 September.

On 30 July 1849 the South Eastern opened from Deptford to Gravesend, enabling the company to provide a through service from London to Strood. On 21 July 1849 the Whitehaven & Furness Junction Railway opened from Whitehaven to Ravenglass.

Standedge Tunnel on the Manchester Sheffield Lincolnshire line between Leeds and Stalybridge was opened on 1 August 1849. Single bore, 3 miles 62 yards in length, when opened it was the longest railway tunnel in England and today is only beaten in length by the Severn and Totley tunnels. It runs parallel with the earlier canal tunnel, and when it was being cut, connecting passages to the waterway allowed the canal to remove spoil and bring in material, thus speeding work. Additionally, the canal tunnel enabled more accurate estimates to be made of construction costs as the strata was known, while the old shafts were reused. The tunnel cost £201,608 compared with an estimate of £147,200, provided employment for almost 2,000 men and used more than 150,000 lbs of candles. As with the Woodhead Tunnel, to avoid a head-on collision a pilot engine was required to be attached to each train.

A second single-line parallel bore was started in 1868 and opened 12 February 1871. As the twin tunnels had the only suitable level stretch, by 1878 water troughs had been laid in the tunnels. In 1883 the London & North Western began quadrupling the Colne Valley line and a double-line tunnel opened 5 August 1894. The two single-line tunnels were closed on 31 October 1966, shortly after being used for tests in connection with the Channel Tunnel project, but are maintained to help maintain the operating twin-track tunnel and could be reopened should increased capacity be needed.

Also on 1 August 1849 the North Western Railway – referred to as the 'Little North Western' to distinguish it from the much larger London & North Western – opened from Skipton to Ingleton, and from Lancaster to Wennington on 17 November.

On 13 August 1849 a branch was opened from Drem, on the Edinburgh–Berwick main line, to Williamstown and extended to North Berwick on 17 June 1850. The North British hoped that North Berwick, situated 23 miles from Edinburgh, would develop as a high-class residential suburb. To encourage this development the company advertised Line of Residence tickets granted to a householder who lived within a mile of a North British station and worked in Edinburgh. Traffic failed to develop to expectations and by the winter of 1856 the steam-hauled service between Drem and North Berwick was replaced by a horse-drawn rail vehicle, however the branch came into its own in the summer when holidaymakers flocked to the resort. To make it more accessible to Glasgow residents, the Lothian Coast Express was introduced 3 June 1912 and it also had the distinction of being the first to run between Edinburgh and Glasgow in exactly an hour.

Two carriages left Dunbar at 7.55 a.m. and travelled along the main line to Drem where it picked up a three-coach set with restaurant car, which had run from North Berwick. At Longniddry Junction two coaches from Gullane were attached and, after a six-minute halt at Waverley, left at 8.49 a.m., arriving at Glasgow, Queen Street, at 9.49. It returned from Queen Street at 3.50 p.m., reached Waverley at 4.50, left at 4.56 and arrived at Gullane 5.34, North Berwick 5.40 and Dunblane 5.45. Suspended during the First World War, the Lothian Coast Express reappeared during the summer from 1921 and by 1929 even carried a Pullman restaurant car, but by 1939 no through coaches were being run from Glasgow and North Berwick or Gullane.

3 September 1849 was the date of the Methley Incident. The following day was to be the opening of the Great Northern's route to Leeds, which used running powers over the Midland from Methley Junction for the last section. The Midland wanted the Great Northern to give an undertaking that it would never construct a rival line to Leeds and threatened that if an assurance was not given all its trains would be stopped at Methley and maximum tolls extracted from every passenger.

What followed was described by the *Doncaster Chronicle*:

Atrocious Conduct in a Railway Company
The [Great Northern] Superintendent at Doncaster, having heard it whispered that something was going on at the junction of the Doncaster line with the Midland Railway at Methley, sent over a special engine before the trains and found the servants of the Midland Company had removed the points at the junction, so that had the train proceeded thither it would inevitably run off the road.

The Great Northern protested and it was 1 October 1849 before matters were settled and the Great Northern reached Methley and Leeds, the official opening of the line taking place on 1 December 1849.

On 14 September 1849 the 10 miles of the Chester & Holyhead between Mold Junction and Mold were opened; its first 7¼ miles were double track, the remainder being single. From October the line was worked by an engine specially built by the London & North Western. This was No. 247 *Mammoth*, a Crewe goods 2-4-0 converted into a tank engine. As a result of under-powered locomotives failing while trying to climb the 1 in 43 incline between Broughton and Hope, the London & North Western designed an experimental 0-6-0 goods locomotive, which proved to be the precursor to the DX class.

On 15 October 1849 the Glasgow, Dumfries & Carlisle Railway opened from Closeburn to Dumfries. The Aberdeen Railway opened between Dubton Junction and Limpet Mill on 1 November 1849, extending from Limpet Mill to Portlethen on 13 December; this line was to become part of the Caledonian Railway's route to Aberdeen. On 12 November 1849 the Edinburgh & Bathgate Railway opened 11¼ miles from Ratho to Bathgate. This line was intended to form part of the Edinburgh & Glasgow's secondary route from Edinburgh to Glasgow.

1850
The world's first train ferry opened on 1 March 1850 to link Granton, near Edinburgh, across the Forth to Burntisland. It was designed by the Edinburgh & Northern Railway's engineer

Thomas Bouch. The *Leviathan* was able to carry thirty-four wagons. When first tried on 7 February 1850, it only carried 20 loaded wagons and a passenger carriage containing the company directors and friends. The vessel was only partly loaded as no other rolling stock was available. Despite the heavy swell, the vessel proceeded 'smoothly and steadily as if the sea had been placid and calm'. Initially goods, minerals and livestock were conveyed without transshipment, while passengers could be conveyed in a through coach.

When first planned it was thought to overcome the rise and fall of 20 feet between high and low tide by using hydraulic or steam cranes to lift wagons on board, but this was thought to be slow, expensive and liable to damage the rolling stock. Then a floating bridge was suggested with one end hinged on shore and the other end attached to a float, to rise and fall with the tide. This would have answered remarkably well had the water always been smooth, but in stormy weather would have required protection by expensive jetties.

The system adopted was a masonry slip constructed alongside the piers at Burntisland and Granton on which were laid two railway tracks. Upon this incline was placed a movable platform, 61 feet in length and 21 feet wide resting on 16 wheels. At the front of this platform were attached, by universal joints, four malleable iron girders 35 feet long, constructed of boiler plate to span the distance from the platform to the vessel and affording a sufficient depth of water for the ship's keel to clear the slip. The girders were raised and lowered on the arrival or departure of a vessel by means of a winch. The whole platform was raised or lowered to suit the tide by a small stationary steam engine, which was also used to move wagons on or off the vessel. The ship could be fully loaded in 5 minutes and discharged in about the same time by stationary engines ashore.

The *Leviathan* was unconventional. In order to leave the centre of the deck clear to allow wagons to pass along the deck, the ship had two engines each driving an independent paddle wheel. The ship could be navigated into any position required without ropes or assistance from the shore by working one engine ahead and the other astern. The *Leviathan* and the stationary engines were constructed by Robert Napier of Glasgow. When it was advertised that goods would be carried across the Forth without transference 400 tons of turnips were offered.

Bouch's idea of a floating bridge boosted the company's dividends and won him an associateship of the Institute of Civil Engineers. He resigned from the railway and set up business as a consulting engineer. In 1851 a similar ferry opened across the Tay. Both ceased operation when replaced by the respective bridges.

The Buckinghamshire Railway was busy in 1850. 1 May saw Bletchley to Banbury opened for passenger traffic, goods starting a fortnight later. The line from Verney Junction, near Winslow, to Islip was inaugurated on 1 October and from Islip to Banbury Road, Oxford, on 2 December.

The South Wales Railway was a very significant broad gauge line stretching from Gloucester to Fishguard, totalling with its branches 175 miles, and was, of course, a rival to Stephenson's Holyhead route to Ireland. On 18 June the South Wales Railway opened the 74¾ miles from Chepstow to Swansea. The section from Grange Court Junction just west of Gloucester to Chepstow East opened on 19 June 1851, the gap between the two sections caused by the incompletion of the significant bridge over the River Wye being filled by horse buses, which conveyed passengers across the road bridge between the two Chepstow stations.

Although most of Brunel's bridges were symmetrical, the one at Chepstow was the exception due to a 120-foot-high cliff on one side and low-lying land on the other. The cliff provided an abutment for one end of the 300-foot span, but the other end, with the three approach spans, were carried on piers.

Cast-iron cylinders were sunk through the soft ground to a solid foundation and then filled with concrete. To sink large columns for the main span, Brunel used the pneumatic method whereby the upper ends of the cylinders were sealed and compressed air introduced to keep the water out, workmen and materials of necessity then entering through airlock doors.

The river span was something never seen before. It consisted of girders supported by suspension chains hung from a circular tube, 9 feet in diameter. These tubes, very slightly arched to improve their appearance, prevented the chains from dragging the piers inwards. On 8 April 1852 a tube was floated into position below the piers and then lifted by chain tackle attached to specially designed winches. Brunel was in charge, assisted by R. P. Brereton and Captain Claxton, the latter responsible for the shipping side of the operation.

The first tube was placed at right angles to the Wye and thrust forward on trolleys until it overhung the river; beneath was a pontoon of six iron barges. This pontoon took the weight of the span as the tides rose and was guided across the river by two chains anchored to the opposite cliff. By sunset the tube had been lifted to rail level and the next day was set on its piers. A single-line bridge opened on 19 July 1852, the second following on 18 April 1853. This bridge at Chepstow proved to be a dummy run for the Royal Albert Bridge at Saltash. Chepstow Bridge is no longer in its original condition as the main river spans were replaced with steel trusses in 1962.

Before the opening of the South Wales Railway, the journey from London to Swansea, partly by rail and partly by coach, took 15 hours, but with the opening of the railway the journey took only 5 hours and the trip was carried out in much greater comfort.

22 June 1850 marked the opening of the 12¾ miles from Blackburn to Chatburn and the Horrocksford branch of the Bolton, Blackburn, Clitheroe & West Yorkshire Railway, while on 1 July 1850 the Lancashire & Yorkshire opened from Huddersfield to Penistone. The Ambergate, Nottingham, Boston & Eastern Junction Railway opened from Colwick at its junction with the Midland Railway to Grantham on 15 July 1850. This line was the subject of intense rivalry between the Midland and the Great Northern, finally being leased to the Great Northern from 2 April 1855.

It was felt that Loch Lomond needed railway access and this was provided by the Dumbartonshire Railway, passengers from Glasgow using a steamer to Bowling, and then rail from Bowling via Dumbarton to Balloch at the southern end of the loch. Piers with a railway connection were provided at Bowling and Balloch. From the northern end of Loch Lomond, road connection could be made to Oban. The line opened on 15 July 1850.

1 August 1850 was the day of the Highland Agricultural Society's show at Glasgow. The Scottish Central Railway cashed in on the event and ran three lengthy trains from Perth and other stations

at 5-minute intervals – the time interval system still being used rather than the much safer block system, which offered a space between each train. Although the second of these trains consisted of thirty-five coaches it became so overcrowded that passengers swarmed on to the carriage roofs, and Harrison, the locomotive superintendent travelling on the footplate, had no success in trying to bring them down. The railway staff then refused to start the train until the passengers descended, but still they refused to budge. The matter was resolved by coupling on to the rear some open sheep wagons with hurdle sides into which the roof passengers scrambled. At the summit of Cowlairs Incline (*see* page 63) the train stopped at the ticket platform for the locomotive to be detached and run round using one of two crossovers to the rear of the train, which would then descend under the control of the brakesmen.

When the first train arrived at Cowlairs it was so long it blocked the first crossover, and before he could reach the second crossover the second train had arrived and blocked that one. While the crews were discussing how to solve the problem, the third train arrived and crashed into the flimsy sheep wagons, breaking them into matchwood. The more agile passengers had been able to leap out before the engine crashed into them, but five were killed and many seriously injured. The Board of Trade inspector found that the cause of the accident was due to the fact that the second train had not been promptly protected in the rear by one of the guards. The guard should have run back down the line laying detonators at the prescribed intervals, but it was found that if he did, often the driver would get his train moving and the guard would be left behind. To obviate this he would wait for instructions from the driver, and with the time-interval system, time was perilously short. Another drawback to the time interval system was that station clocks were not always accurate. A passenger train on the East Lancashire Railway ran into the rear of a goods trains that had stalled in a tunnel near Bootle in November 1849, it had been despatched only 3½ minutes after the goods train. A witness explained that the Bootle station clock 'went wildly'.

The Caledonian Railway opened to Aberdeen (Ferryhill) on 2 August 1850 and the line extended three-quarters of a mile to Aberdeen (Guild Street). With the development of steam-powered trawlers, Aberdeen developed into a major fishing port and from about 1885 a daily fish train left for London enabling fish to be sold at Billingsgate within 24 hours of their landing.

On 8 August 1850 the Great Northern Railway opened from a temporary station at Maiden Lane (now York Way), London, to Warrington Junction, north of Peterborough. The 528-yard-long Gas Works Tunnel dips below the Regent's Canal and then climbs at 1 in 105, closely followed by the longer or Copenhagen Tunnel. The line ended at Maiden Lane as King's Cross station was incomplete. A feature of the new line was Welwyn Viaduct of forty arches, which spanned the Mimram Valley.

On 28 August 1850 the Stirling & Dunfermline opened its line between Dunfermline and Alloa, extending to Tillicoultry on 3 June 1851, finally reaching Stirling on 1 July 1852.

On 29 August 1850, the Royal Border Bridge was opened across the Tweed, thus allowing through trains to run from Edinburgh to London. In 1849 when the Berwick–Newcastle gap was still filled by stagecoach, only 5,792 passengers were booked by the North British from Edinburgh to London, yet 11,584 travelled by sea over the same period. In 1851 thousands travelled by train from Scotland to London to see the Great Exhibition, paying £1 11s 6d for a third-class return.

On 2 September 1850 the Great Western, already having secured much of western England, now extended from Oxford to Banbury, thus thrusting itself northwards.

On 12 September 1850 the London & North Western opened between Coventry and Nuneaton but the section between Coventry and the first station, Coundon Road, was closed for nearly three years when in 1857 the 23-arch Spon End Viaduct collapsed and had to be partly replaced by an embankment.

Also on 12 September 1850 the Scottish Central opened a branch from Alloa Junction to the harbour of South Alloa from where passengers and goods could be ferried across the Forth to Alloa. The ferry became redundant on 1 October 1885 when the Alloa Railway opened an extension with a 1,600-foot-long 20-span bridge, including a swing section.

On 21 October 1850 the Royston & Hitchin opened between the two towns, and was extended on 1 August 1851 from Royston to Shepreth.

The Glasgow, Paisley, Kilmarnock & Ayr amalgamated with the Glasgow, Dumfries & Carlisle to form the Glasgow & South

Western Railway; the first line to be opened with this new name being from New Cumnock to Closeburn on 28 October, the date of the new company's formation. William Johnstone, resident engineer on the Glasgow, Paisley, Kilmarnock & Ayr, became first its manager and then manager of the Glasgow & South Western until 1874. This was an unusual example of an engineer changing to railway management.

In 1850 Clemente Masserano interested the London & South Western directors in a cheap form of locomotive named *Impulsoria*, basically a 2-2-0 locomotive frame with an endless belt on which two horses trotted. An excellent feature was that its axles had roller bearings and its advantage was that horses cost 2s 0d a day, whereas steam locomotives used 6d worth of coal per mile. As gearing allowed the power output to be adjusted to suit the load and gradient, *Impulsoria* could draw 30 wagons up the incline at Nine Elms goods depot, but in the event, none of these machines were ordered.

On 18 December 1850 the Birkenhead, Lancashire & Cheshire Junction Railway opened from Chester to Walton Junction.

Although only having a length of approximately 12 miles, the North London Railway was very successful until the advent of tube railways. Its trains had running powers over other lines to Alexandra Palace, High Barnet and Enfield, as well as to Willesden, Acton, Kew and Richmond, forming a valuable connection between railways north of the Thames and those to the south. It opened in sections between Bow Junction and Chalk Farm in 1851–2, while that to Richmond opened in 1860.

Goods trains were formed of loose-coupled, unbraked wagons, the only braking available being on the engine and tender, and it was not always available on an engine, some engineers believing that the heat from the brake blocks caused tyres to expand and come loose. With the increase in the length of goods and mineral trains, a brake van at the rear was necessary, both to assist in braking and also making the guard available to give warning should a train become divided. Brake vans came into general use about 1850. The vans were generally on four wheels, and were spartan with just a coal-fired stove and handbrake. A verandah was at either one or both ends and the van was ballasted to increase its braking power.

It is interesting to notice the effect of the 1845 Act, which insisted on providing a closed third-class carriage. This can be seen in the passenger ratios for every hundred passengers:

Year	First Class	Second Class	Third Class
1845	17	43	40
1850	12	36	52

Freight traffic increased relatively to passenger traffic:

Year	Passenger Traffic per £100	Freight Traffic per £100
1845	£63	£37
1850	£52	£48

The average charge for conveying 1 ton of freight 1 mile was almost exactly the same as that paid by an average passenger for the same distance.

7

The Great Exhibition, Its Aftermath and the First Underground Railway

The opening of railways had a great effect on life in Britain. In 1820 about 75 per cent of the population lived in the countryside, yet by 1850 more than half the population was working in cities. Until the coming of railways many folk only moved a handful of miles from their village, but railways enabled both goods and people to be moved quickly and relatively cheaply about the country. The fact that railways offered easy travel, allowing people to go outside their parish and meet members of the other sex further away, widened the gene pool and eased the problem of the village idiot due to intermarriage. Railways brought cheap coal, slate and building materials. They allowed food firms to produce for a countrywide or even international market, not just a local one. Firms such as Crosse & Blackwell, Huntley & Palmer, James Keiller and the Maconochie Brothers, which had originally supplied just their locality, were able to use rail transport to develop into national firms. Railways enabled W. H. Smith's to become the first chain store in the world.

It is not generally realised how much the coming of railways affected book production. In 1840 almost all publishers and printers were in Cambridge, Edinburgh, London or Oxford, but the growth of railways and the penny post allowed publishers to send work to printers at a distance and who could print at a cheaper rate. Book production was speeded to times unthinkable

30 years before. George Eliot finished *Felix Holt* in London on 31 May 1866, and as it was published and printed in Edinburgh the proofs had to travel 800 miles, yet it was in the book shops by 12 June. This would have been impossible 40 years earlier.

Railways carried raw materials inland so places away from the sea were able to develop industries, and towns and cities expanded, while later in the nineteenth century commuting by rail developed. As railways conveyed goods faster there was far less time for theft, often a problem with canal transport.

Henry Booth, treasurer of the Liverpool & Manchester Railway, wrote: 'Speed, dispatch and distance are all relative terms, but their meaning has been totally changed. What was quick is now slow; what was distant is now near and this change in our ideas will pervade society at large.'

1851

This was the year of the Great Exhibition in Hyde Park, where it opened on 1 May. There were 19,000 exhibits in the Crystal Palace, which was twice the width and four times the length of St Paul's Cathedral. It attracted visitors from all over the country: numbers attending equalled a third of the population of England and Wales. Without railways it would have been impossible to bring together the exhibits or carry such numbers of visitors. By 1851 almost every important town in England had a rail link to the capital. Special excursion fares to visit the exhibition were within the means of all but the poorest, and some businesses offered employees, and their families, free trips. The Caledonian Railway took the opportunity of the Great Exhibition to popularise Anglo-Scottish travel. In 1851 the Caledonian offered return tickets to London for £2 0s 0d, while the proprietors of Murray's Time Tables arranged for an excursion at £1 10s 0d return, but those who bought the first 200 tickets could get them for £1 7s 0d. For some people it was the first time they had visited London, or perhaps even left their own town or village.

Thousands came from the Continent to see the Great Exhibition, some using the 'eleven hours' route from Paris.

One female passenger from Bath had good reason to remember her trip. The *Bath & Cheltenham Gazette* of 6 August 1851 recorded:

On Monday fortnight [23 July] a servant girl from Bath decided to see the wonders of the Great Exhibition. For reasons of economy, she selected a Parliamentary train, but she missed it. Nothing daunted, with a quarter's wages in her pocket, and something more, she preferred the next train to the next day and soon she found herself passing the engine which was to have conveyed her to London, and this in some degree satisfied her for the extra outlay, forgetting that her altered plans in Bath would also operate at the London terminus. Here she failed to meet the friends who were to conduct her safely to her destination and in her dilemma sought refuge in a cab, with the request to the driver to take her to a certain street in Kensington; but, after numerous fruitless inquiries, Kennington was found to be the desired haven, which after much perplexity, was reached at the cost of a six shilling cab fare.

Happy in meeting her friends, the young woman found no further annoyance till she went to the Crystal Palace, where her gratification was alloyed by a tremendous shower on leaving the building, which rendered her Exhibition bonnet and dress useless for the future.

The mishap which attended her at starting, appeared to follow her, for on her return, wishing to call on a relative in Gloucestershire, she inquired for the Railway which would take her to Stroud, perhaps without designating the county. She was referred to the London Bridge terminus and having purchased her ticket, a pleasant ride followed; but the sight of the sea gave her misgivings that she was wrong, and finding her journey at an end, asked the guard if that was Stroud, in Gloucestershire, when to her great dismay, she found herself at Strood in Kent.

Here, to the credit of the Railway authorities, no advantage was taken of the error, and being satisfied of the truth of the servant's statement, they returned her fare and sent her back to London, and the girl sustained no other inconvenience other than a return to Kennington. She was more careful in her next exploit, and on Monday evening reached home a little the worse for her numerous calamities, but with the full conviction that she never wished to see London again.

The distribution of each £100 of working costs in 1851 were:

	£
Direction and Management	10.52
Permanent Way and Works	15.76
Locomotive Power	35.15
Rolling Stock	38.57

The South Eastern Railway opened from Ashford via Hastings to St Leonard's on 13 February 1851, and Tunbridge Wells to Robertsbridge on 1 September 1851. The London & North Western Railway opened from Rugby to Leamington on 1 March 1851.

The 887-yard-long Mickleton Tunnel, later known as Campden Tunnel, was the scene of a battle in June 1851. When the contractors Messrs Williams and Marchant ceased work, the Oxford, Worcester & Wolverhampton Railway took possession and handed the contract to Messrs Peto & Betts, but the original contractor, Robert Marchant, objected and kept his men on guard. Brunel then arrived with an army of navvies to take possession. As Marchant had heard of this intention and was anticipating a fight he asked to magistrates to attend:

The magistrates were early on the ground, attended by a large body of police armed with cutlasses. Mr Brunel was there with his men and Mr Marchant the Contractor, also appeared at the head of a formidable body of navigators. A conflict was expected, but happily through the prompt action of the magistrates who twice read the Riot Act to the men, they were dispersed.

The following day, a 2,000-strong army of Peto & Betts's men were assembled from various parts of the line and marched that night to the tunnel, arriving in the early hours of the following morning. Marchant and his 100 navvies, overawed by the 2,000-strong Brunel army, decided to come to an agreement. The Battle of Mickleton Tunnel was over and troops from Coventry, who had been summoned to support the police, arrived to find that all was at peace.

On 24 September 1851 the broad gauge Vale of Neath Railway opened for passenger traffic, goods starting in December. Due to the state of the money market, the company had experienced difficulty in raising funds and the line required heavy earthworks, including the 526-yard-long Pencaedrain Tunnel, the construction of deep cuttings and several timber viaducts, the longest of which was 270 yards. The line was double from Neath to Hirwain, then single to Aberdare. Gradients were severe with a 5½-mile bank at 1 in 47–50 followed by a fall at 1 in 50 for almost 2 miles. Initially traffic was hampered by the fact that the company had no facilities for shipment of coal, but this problem was solved in April 1852 when the Briton Ferry Dock Company opened a branch to a wharf on the Neath River. Coal traffic then started from Aberdare, with iron ore travelling in the opposite direction.

Just as it was the custom of the driver of a British horse-drawn vehicle to sit towards the right-hand side of the box to enable him to see the clearance available between his own and an opposing vehicle, with the coming of the railway the right-hand side of the footplate was allocated to the driver, even though running on fixed track eliminated the condition applying to his coach predecessor. With the driver on the right, the fireman could shovel more comfortably; the reversing lever was more readily operated by the driver's right hand, and the driver could see better if anything was amiss with the adjacent track and observe any signs that might be made to him from a train coming in the opposite direction. Some lines such as the London & North Western, the Lancashire & Yorkshire and some Scottish railways transferred the driver to the left with the argument that at most stations the driver could take the signals directly from the guard and see signals that were mostly situated on the left of the road. He was also better placed for seeing a fog-man's hand signals. Some locomotive engineers, such as the Drummonds, took their own practice with them when moving to another company and there was at least one instance of the driver's position being changed over by one engineer and reversed again by his successor. At grouping in 1923, the enlarged companies found themselves with both kinds of drive. The LMS, LNER and the SR made the left-hand drive standard, although engines of the opposite type inherited from the constituent companies lasted almost to the end of steam. The GWR continued to use the right-hand position for the driver and converted any engines with left-hand drive which came into its possession, such as those of the former Midland & South Western Junction Railway, to right-hand drive. Left-hand drive was selected for BR Standard locomotives. Closely connected with this question is that of the placing of signals. Curves and obstructions partly determine the location, but all things being equal, right-hand-drive railways placed signals on the right, and those of left-hand drive on the left.

1852

On 31 May 1852 the Leeds Northern Railway opened 29 miles from Melmerby to Stockton, the line's major feature being a viaduct over the River Tees and the town of Yarm, 760 yards long and consisting of 42 arches. On 1 July 1852 the Monmouthshire Railway & Canal Company opened its line from Newport to Pontypool. In order to facilitate traffic, the company had been forced to convert some of its plateway tramroads into locomotive-worked standard gauge lines using flanged wheels.

An accident at Burnley on 12 July 1852 showed the unbusinesslike way in which some railways operated. At the Lancashire & Yorkshire station there was a single passenger platform at the end of the branch line but there were also two through roads to the East Lancashire Railway's sidings. Points, known as 'East Lancs' points, were weighted to give access to the passenger platform and had to be held over by hand to admit a train to the East Lancashire's sidings. The platform was only long enough to hold a six-coach train, but on this day two double headed school excursion trains were being run respectively to York and Goole, one of 45 coaches and the other of 35. The platform being far too short, the trains were despatched from the East Lancashire sidings. When they returned that evening, in order not to trap the locomotives at the buffer stops, it was decided that the engines would be uncoupled at the station throat, run to the shed and then the train run by gravity into the East Lancashire sidings. Only two employees were on duty: porter Parker and night watchman Grant. Realising that they could not cope alone, they enlisted the help of two non-railway friends: James Crabtree, a calico printer, and Tom Bridge, a blacksmith. They dealt with the train from York quite successfully, Tom collecting the tickets in his hat.

When the Goole train arrived, Parker told Crabtree to hold over the weighted points, but Crabtree decided he ought to help Parker and Grant so called to the blacksmith: 'Tom, hold these points while I go up the line.' Tom was holding the points over when one of the engines which had been uncoupled from the train passed and its driver called: 'Turn me into the shed.' Anxious to help, Tom let go of the weighted points lever to move the shed points. Not being held, the weighted points clicked over and the descending passenger train ran into the platform and crashed into the buffers. Three children and a teacher were killed and many injured.

The Board of Trade inspector observed that the damage and casualties would have been less had the buffer heights been standardised and prevented the buffers from overriding; he was also unimpressed by the company's staffing arrangements. This accident led to the requirement that signals should be connected with points in order to work in conjunction with them – this was the first step in introducing interlocking frames whereby a signalman was mechanically prevented from setting up conflicting routes.

On 29 July 1852 a London & North Western Railway engine, No. 234 *Mazeppa*, ran away. It was very aptly named, for Lord Byron, in his narrative poem *Mazeppa* published in 1819, tells how Ivan Mazeppa was punished for an indiscreet love affair by being bound naked to the back of a wild horse. The horse galloped off across the steppe, never stopping until it fell dead.

When *Mazeppa* arrived at Shrewsbury with the 9.05 a.m. from Stafford, her driver reported to the shed foreman that the regulator gland was blowing and needed repacking. The engine was entrusted to Joseph Thompson, the night cleaner, at 11.00 p.m. He drew the fire, blew down steam and, using another locomotive, propelled *Mazeppa* into the shed. He and his assistant packed the gland, cleaned and oiled the engine and lit the fire at 4.00 a.m. His assistant left at 5.00 a.m. to knock up some workmen, leaving the foreman alone in the shed. Thompson made up *Mazeppa*'s fire at 5.45 a.m. and went home at 5.50, five minutes before he should have done. The day cleaner should have arrived at 6.00 a.m., but was 10 minutes late, so for 20 minutes the shed had been unmanned. A fireman who asked for the whereabouts of *Mazeppa* was told she must have gone out early, and she most certainly had.

At this very moment an excited platelayer arrived to say that he had seen an unmanned engine on the line to Stafford. Thompson had unfortunately left *Mazeppa* in forward gear with the regulator open and she had made her escape.

At Shrewsbury an engine in steam was commandeered and sent off in hot pursuit. 3 miles from Shrewsbury the driver spotted her in the distance but then lost sight of her. Meanwhile, at Donnington, 14 miles from Shrewsbury, the 6.00 a.m. from Shrewsbury was standing at the platform when its driver glanced back and saw a light engine approaching at speed. With her only 60 yards away and obviously not going to stop, he opened his regulator in an effort to escape, but had left it far too late. The brake van of the three-coach train was smashed, as was the second-class coach and the first-class coach, but the few passengers were fortunately all in the third-class coach at the front of the train and only one was killed. Joseph Thompson awoke from his sleep to be charged with manslaughter and the Board of Trade inspector made some apt remarks on the importance of strict timekeeping and observing shed regulations regarding stationary locomotives.

On 1 August 1852 the Great Northern Railway opened the 59 miles from Peterborough to Retford and on 14 October extended the line three-quarters of a mile from the temporary Maiden Lane station to a simple yet splendid terminus at King's Cross. It had an arrival platform and a departure platform with 14 intermediate tracks, the whole covered by a great twin-arched roof, each with a 71-foot span. All the offices were set along the departure platform. The station, now Grade I listed, was designed by Lewis Cubitt, nephew of Sir William Cubitt, the Great Northern's consulting engineer and whose son Joseph Cubitt was the railway's chief engineer. King's Cross has been called an engineer's station, all its elements being visible, its front merely a brick screen, but cleverly relieved with an Italianate clock tower.

1 August 1852 was also the date of a scuffle between the Great Northern and the Midland. It happened because the Ambergate, Nottingham, Boston & Eastern Junction Railway had opened on 15 July 1850. It was really an extension of the Great Northern to Nottingham, but the line from Nottingham to Ambergate was in what was considered Midland territory. On 1 August 1852 passengers from King's Cross were hauled into the Midland station

at Nottingham (the Ambergate line had running powers for this) by a Great Northern locomotive. Midland officials arranged for the Great Northern train to be hemmed in front and rear by several Midland engines. The Great Northern driver made a bold attempt to break out, but his engine was captured and pushed into a shed. The rails were lifted to prevent its removal and there it remained for seven months.

On 1 October 1852 the Great Western opened the 66 miles from Banbury to Birmingham.

1853

In the 1850s the streets of London were becoming crowded and a speedier method of transport was required. The Great Western provided what was an almost ideal answer, a 3½-mile-long line from Paddington to Farringdon Street forming the Metropolitan Railway, the world's first underground passenger-carrying line. As the area was built up and the purchase price of property would have been prohibitive, the cut-and-cover principle was adopted, whereby for most of the route the railway would follow roads.

To keep expense within reasonable limits it was built relatively cheaply by excavating a huge trench in a street, covering it with a brick arch and then relaying the road on top. As steam traction was to be used, ventilation holes were placed on islands in the road through which the steam and smoke could disperse. These grilles were loved by young clerks – if a young lady was unwise enough to stand over one while a steam engine was passing below, the blast would raise her skirt in a satisfying manner! Most of the stations were open to fresh air. The Act for the North Metropolitan Railway (later the 'North' was dropped) was dated 15 August 1853.

A mixed gauge line, its Act empowered the Great Western to subscribe £175,000, and an unusual feature was that the City of London subscribed £200,000 towards the £1 million required, though normally public bodies did not invest in railway companies. Around this time a new meat market was being established at Smithfield and the Great Western and Metropolitan leased its basement for a goods station; in fact Great Western condensing-steam locomotives continued to work through to Smithfield until 30 July 1962. It was to be the world's first underground passenger-carrying line, but *The Times* of 30 November 1861 was not encouraging. It described the scheme as 'a subterranean railway suggestive of dark, noisome tunnels, buried many fathoms deep beyond the reach of light or life'. However, when it opened on 10 January 1863, *The Times* was less critical (*see* page 127). The Metropolitan was one of the first railway companies to provide cheap fares for workmen.

1854

Very surprisingly, the earthworks for the Leeds, Halifax & Bradford Junction Railway, opened on 1 August 1854 to passengers and to freight on 7 August, were carried out in the Ice Age! The heavy tunnelling that would usually have been essential for the line to enter the Bradford basin was not required due to the utilisation of the overflow channel of a glacial lake, which had formed a deep cutting sufficiently wide for double track.

As the approach to its Adolphus Street terminus involved a steep climb, and despite the route from Leeds being 4 miles shorter than the rival Midland line, the directors realised that it had not captured sufficient traffic. The answer was to make a ¾-mile-long line down 1 in 49 to the Lancashire & Yorkshire station. Although a short length, it took no less than two and a half years to build as it ran through a cutting up to 60 feet deep. Most of the excavated spoil was fireclay and kept 60 men in employment for 15 years making bricks, drain pipes and chimney pots. The line opened in 1867, the company having been taken over by the Great Northern two years previously.

The chief architectural feature of the permanent Paddington station was the awe-inspiring train shed, influenced by the Crystal Palace of 1851. It was the first large British station to have a metal roof. Brunel's son in *The Life of Isambard Kingdom Brunel* describes it:

> The interior of the principal part of the station is 700 feet long and 238 feet wide, divided in its width by two rows of columns into three spans of 69 feet 6 inches, 102 feet 6 inches and 68 feet, and crossed at two points by transepts 50 feet wide, which give space for large traversing frames. The roof is very light, consisting of wrought iron arched ribs, covered partly with the Paxton glass roofing, which Mr Brunel here adopted to a

considerable extent. The columns which carry the roof are very strongly bolted down to large masses of concrete, to enable them to resist sideways pressure.

As Queen Victoria used the station frequently en route to Windsor, a suite of royal waiting rooms was provided for her with the convenience of direct access from the carriage approach to the station platform. The new station cost £650,000 and covered 8 acres. Unlike other major London termini, because it is set in a cutting, Paddington lacks an imposing exterior facade. The departure side was brought into use on 16 January 1854 and the arrival side on 29 May 1854, the temporary Bishop's Road station then being demolished.

In 1854 the Eastern Counties Railway opened a shipping service between Harwich and the Continent. In 1863 the Great Eastern received Parliamentary approval for providing its own steamers, hitherto having to charter vessels. Because land at Harwich was not available for expansion, in 1874 the decision was made to build a new deepwater port 2 miles upriver from Harwich at Parkeston Quay, named after Charles Parkes, chairman of the Great Eastern. The new port opened in 1883, and traffic increased even further when a new port at the Hook of Holland opened in 1893. Harwich was the most important base on the east coast south of Harwich for the Royal Navy, and during WWI most of the port was given to the navy. In the early months of the war thousands of Belgian refugees arrived at Harwich and Parkeston Quay and were taken to London by the Great Eastern. When the north curve was laid at Manningtree, this allowed access to Harwich from the north and thus tapped this traffic, as well as that from London. Although the Harwich Boat Express took only 1½ hours for its journey, it was able to serve 111 meals from a kitchen measuring just 6 feet by 17 feet, though some food such as soup, bread and pastries were prepared beforehand in the kitchens of Great Eastern Railway hotels. In 1924 Harwich also had the honour of being the terminus of the first public Continental train ferry when a link was made with Zeebrugge, but only for freight wagons (*see* page 277).

The coming of railways affected city people's diets because until the development of the railway network, lack of refrigeration meant that they could only eat food that had a long shelf life. Now they had considerably more choice.

Although some cows were kept in cities, the milk was likely to be watered. Railways altered the situation and as early as 1832 the Liverpool & Manchester carried fresh milk to Liverpool. Charles Barham founded the Express Country Milk Supply Company in London in 1864, and when cattle plague struck cow keepers in the metropolis in 1865 he seized the opportunity to bring milk in from the country. In a way this proved disadvantageous, as it meant that bovine tuberculosis, instead of being confined locally, was dissipated; it is reckoned that 800,000 people died of this disease between 1850 and 1960. His enterprise was renamed the Express Dairy Company in 1882. To prevent milk from deteriorating during transit, it was cooled at the farm or railhead depot. Many of these depots were creameries, which balanced the cities' demands and the milk supplies by turning any surplus into butter or cheese. The dairy companies supplied farmers with conical churns holding 17 gallons and weighing 2¼ cwt when full. Although two men were needed to lift one churn into a ventilated van, two churns could be rolled along a platform by a dextrous porter. About 1930, more manoeuvrable cylindrical 8–12-gallon cans were introduced.

Fish fresh from the sea could be moved around the country, allowing fish and chips to become a popular and cheap food. Grimsby grew from a small harbour to become the largest fishing port in the world. In six years, its fishing fleet grew from twenty-two vessels to more than a hundred. In 1909 some 173,735 tons of fish were landed there, most of which were moved by rail, thus it can be said that the railways were responsible for fish and chips becoming a national dish.

Before the railways, fresh meat for London arrived on the hoof, animals growing thin on the journey, whereas when carried by rail they remained fat. Meat was fresher, animals either being sent by rail to cities for slaughter – many stations had cattle docks – or their carcases were despatched in wagons. Irish cattle were also sent onwards by rail. As we have seen, Smithfield Market was directly connected by rail. Turkeys were sent by rail from Norfolk.

Railways enabled fresh fruit to be quickly taken to market, and this was especially useful for soft fruit with a short shelf life such as strawberries, grown in areas like the Cheddar Valley and Hampshire, which also produced watercress. Fruit from the Vale of Evesham, early potatoes and tomatoes from the Channel Islands were landed at Weymouth and distributed by rail. Cornwall produced flowers and early vegetables. Rhubarb was sent from the Wakefield area, with the rhubarb express running from Ardsley to London, some rhubarb even being sent on to Paris. Railways enabled bananas to be quickly distributed and become a common sight.

Rail travel turned some seaside towns into tourist destinations – Scarborough, Southend and Blackpool being good examples – while industrialisation allowed more people to have disposable income and time to spend it by travelling to such destinations.

The railways also had a considerable influence on manufacturing. Michael Nairn owned a sailcloth business at Kirkcaldy, but with the increase of steam-powered ships, the demand for sailcloth fell and he decided to diversify into the manufacture of floor cloth for which there was an increasing demand due to the housing boom and raised standards of living. In 1847 Nairn set up his new factory at Sinclairtown adjoining the railway station. Railways caused brands to develop – when a manufacturer and a customer were separate, and not local, trust in the product was essential, and brands provided this.

1855

On 15 May 1855 three crates containing bullion worth £14,000 were sent from London to Paris, but when unlocked on arrival it was found that lead shot had been substituted. No culprit was discovered, but over a year later Edward Agar was arrested for cheque fraud and sent to a prison hulk on the Thames. When he discovered that a portion of the takings from the gold robbery had not been passed to his girlfriend by his co-conspirator William Pierce, a furious Agar revealed that Pierce, an ex-railwayman, had made duplicate keys for the bullion van and, with the assistance of the guard James Burgess, swapped the gold for lead en route to Folkestone. Pierce was sentenced to only two years' imprisonment, while William Tester, the roster clerk who arranged for Burgess to be guard on that train, and Burgess himself, both received fourteen years' transportation to Australia for being in breach of trust.

1856

In January 1856 the South Yorkshire, Doncaster & Goole Railway opened its branch to Thorne Waterside to a warehouse and coal staithes along the River Don. Then, alas, with the Board of Trade inspector almost due, leaving no time to correct the mistake, it was realised that no run-round loop had been provided at the terminus. Imaginative thinking suggested that well-dressed navvies be placed in wagons attached to the inspector's train, giving the appearance of shareholders celebrating the occasion. On arrival at Thorne the inspector was taken to an inn for a drink, and while he was out of sight the navvies lifted the locomotive off the track, propelled the coach and wagons past it before re-railing the engine so everything was ready for the return trip when the inspector emerged from the hostelry. The ruse worked and the inspector failed to spot the omission of a run-round loop. This was quickly installed a few days later.

The Eastern Counties Railway became a scapegoat due to its chronic record of unpunctuality. So dreadful was it that in 1856 George Hoy of Bethnal Green issued a challenge to the directors to pit some of the business trains against his donkey. The line provided wonderful material for cartoonists, and in one a voice from the storekeeper's department asked: 'What shall we do with the crest?' To which the passengers replied: 'Make a fool's cap of it!'

1857

It was the custom for the locomotive of a St Helens Railway train arriving from Runcorn Gap to be detached approaching Arpley station and accelerate into a siding, the points being turned to allow the carriages to run into a platform. On 24 December 1857 at Runcorn Gap the guard allowed a porter to take his place and at Sankey Bridges the porter left the train in the charge of a ticket collector. Lacking sufficient skill, the latter turned the brake handle the wrong way and the carriages crashed into a train waiting to start from Arpley.

Robert Forester Mushet made the first steel rail and this was laid experimentally at the Midland Railway's Derby station, on a line carrying heavy traffic. It remained in service until June 1873. The first steel rails on the London & North Western Railway were laid at Chalk Farm in 1863 and they came into general use on British railways in the 1870s.

1858

On 28 May 1858 the Glasgow, Dumbarton & Helensburgh Railway opened, and at Dumbarton most trains were divided – one portion going to Helensburgh and the remainder to Balloch. This meant that the Glasgow to Bowling steamer service for Balloch passengers was severely hit, so paddle-boat operators changed from Bowling to Dumbarton and encouraged passengers to use road service to Balloch. On 14 August 1862 the Edinburgh & Glasgow absorbed the Glasgow & Dumbarton & Helensburgh and the Caledonian & Dumbarton, these being taken over by the North British on 31 July 1865. Helensburgh was useless as a river/rail connection, the two being distant, so the North British established a station and pier at Craigendoran just to the east, thus enabling the North British to challenge Caledonian Clyde traffic.

A dramatic accident occurred at Sankey Bridges, near Warrington, in November 1858. The locomotive of the Euston–Garston train failed at Guide Bridge and was replaced by *Actaeon*. Unfortunately no one had informed the Sankey Bridges station master that she was required to return to Guide Bridge that evening. Consequently, as usual after the last train had passed, he swung the bridge open for canal traffic to pass during the night. Returning from Garston, fog caused *Actaeon*'s driver to miss the signal and she plunged into the canal. She was hauled out, little worse for her ducking.

8

Problems of
Inappropriate Behaviour

1859

Travelling by train in 1859 was not always a delight and tells of conduct not so likely today. That year a correspondent wrote to *The Times*:

Sir,

Many respectable, including many well-bred and refined people are obliged, through lack of means, to travel second or third class. Why should they, simply for want of money, be subjected to rude, coarse, disgusting, ay, and almost blasphemous conduct from their fellow-travellers, which might easily be prevented if some railway officials would be on the alert and exert their temporary authority.

Some weeks ago I, with two young friends and my little daughter, had been seeing all the wonders of the quaint old city of Chester, and were leaving by the 6.45 train on the Chester and Warrington line.

For private reasons we took second class tickets. It was on a Monday – the crowd was great. At last a porter showed us a second-class carriage; it was in two compartments, and in one part were four girls of the working class, the eldest about 17 years old. In the other division were some decent people and a man, who, directly the train was in motion, pulled out a pipe and some matches. After several attempts he lit the pipe and puffed away. His neighbours requested him to cease. He was stubborn. Then I turned and, speaking slowly, and civilly,

asked him not to smoke. He was impertinent in manner, and said 'I shall do as I like'. Of course I did not say another word, but determined to speak to an official, but none came near, and I was on the off side. Also one of the girls was very free in her conduct, and at three stations some men tried to get in, though the carriage was full, and their language and jests were extremely painful. At last, the occupants of the next division got out, and a man entered, evidently drunk. Then began a scene of noise and shouting and roaring out of hymns, which made one shudder and long for release, especially as it was fast becoming dark, and there was no lamp. It ended in the man trying to climb over into our part, but, not succeeding, he fell into a corner, and subsided into a kind of noisy stupor. In the meantime fearing lest the girls should irritate him, I managed by gravely conversing with them, and bestowing some small silver on them, to quiet them, and in that state we left the carriage. Now, sir if I travelling second class for once was exposed to such scenes, certainly I may conclude that others as well born and well bred as myself, and who are constantly from necessity second-class passengers, do not escape similar ones.
I am, Sir, your constant subscriber,
J. J. M.

Certainly standards of behaviour in public were not what we expect today; there were greater differences in the various classes and the personal hygiene of some was not so scrupulous and exceedingly filthy habits could be observed, so it was not surprising that railway management did not provide upholstered seats, which would have been cut to ribbons by hooligans, while the leather straps used for lowering and raising windows would have been cut off and used for stropping razors or other purposes.

Another correspondent wrote to *The Times* in November 1859 and gave details of a frightening train journey he had experienced:

Sir,
On the evening of Thursday one of our citizens, accompanied by a male and female friend, entered a second-class carriage at the Canterbury Station, for the purpose of proceeding to London. In the same carriage, at one corner, sat a man evidently under the influence of drink. The train started, and the strangers began to

'chaff' each other, and then to quarrel. At length the tipsy man took off his coat, turned up his sleeves, and prepared to do battle with his antagonist, who appeared to be in the same mood. This scene so alarmed the woman that she went off in hysterics, and on reaching Wye our citizen and his two companions went into the next carriage. Here sat two dragoons – a sergeant and a private; the former was enjoying a nap in the corner, but the other was looking wildly about him. The movements of this man were most extraordinary and alarming. A few moments after the newcomers had taken their places he plunged his arm under the seat occupied by the sergeant, and brought forth a forage bag. This he carefully examined, and at length drew out razor, which he opened and proceeded to strop, to the terror of the other passengers who could not possibly imagine what the fellow was going to do, his countenance being anything by prepossessing, and his actions those of a maniac. Having well stropped the razor, he helped himself to a lump of meat and bread, which he cut with the razor and masticated with great rapidity. His hunger appeased, the remainder of the bread and meat was deposited in the bag, and the man again deliberately set about sharpening the dangerous instrument. At this juncture the terror of the woman was extremely painful to witness, while that of her companion was hardly less intense: but there was no escape. Fortunately the light at the top of the carriage enabled them to watch – with breathless silence – the extraordinary manoeuvres of their singular travelling companion, but did not tend in the slightest degree to calm the intense excitement and fear which they had produced. At length the sergeant woke from his slumbers, and no sooner did he open his eyes than he immediately grasped the dragoon by the throat, and forcibly took the razor from his grasp, which he immediately placed in a place of safety. The fact was then elicited that the man who had been playing such antics with the razor was a maniac, and that he had been sent from one of the transports in charge of the sergeant, who was taking him to headquarters prior to his dismissal from the service.

Shunting involves sorting wagons into various sidings. Initially this entailed an engine going backwards and forwards, but in 1859 the North Eastern Railway at Tyne Dock introduced gravity shunting where a locomotive slowly propelled a raft of wagons over a hump and they were then cut off and allowed to gravitate into the respective sidings.

1860

A locomotive consumes a vast quantity of water, and the greater part of a locomotive tender contains not coal but water. In the mid-1800s, when long-distance trains were being speeded in order to avoid stopping to replenish water supplies or having to pull a vast tender, John Bland, a draughtsman in the London & North Western's Crewe works, sketched a device for picking up water without stopping. Basically it was a scoop on the tender which would pick up water from a trough between the running rails.

The first troughs were laid near Aber between Chester and Holyhead in 1860 and the idea was soon adopted by all the other large English railway companies except the London & South Western. Following dieselisation some troughs remained in use to allow the heating-boiler tanks to be topped up, permitting the diesel-electric Deltic locomotives to run non-stop between King's Cross and Edinburgh.

The Lancashire & Yorkshire Railway was one of the first users of water troughs, after the London & North Western. Later their 2-4-2Ts collected water either running forwards or in reverse by means of a vacuum-worked pick-up apparatus operated from the brake supply.

Even in the early days of railways, pollution was frowned on. Parliament required engines 'to consume their own smoke'. To comply with this ruling not to emit smoke, most railways used coke as a fuel, building coke ovens, which, being static, did not have to consume their own smoke. Coke was used extensively and some locomotive engineers tried to find a method of burning coal without making smoke. These attempts were complicated, and coal could not be used until the Midland's Matthew Kirtley and his assistant Charles Markham discovered the simple and cheap method of using a deflector plate and brick arch to admit air above the fire and thus burn off any smoke. After 1860 most locomotives had this modification and burnt coal.

1861

The railway reached Stranraer on 12 March 1861 and the extension to the harbour was brought into use on 1 October 1862. In 1874 it supplanted Portpatrick as the short sea route to Ireland, Larne being the corresponding railway port on the far shore.

Railway passengers have always been at least slightly scared of tunnels, and their fears were realised on 25 August 1861 when primitive signalling and human frailty caused the worst British railway disaster to that date, in Clayton Tunnel, north of Brighton,.

Three trains left Brighton for Victoria at 8.28, 8.31 and 8.35 a.m. with 16, 17 and 12 coaches respectively. The line was worked on the time-interval system, a minimum of 5 minutes separating each train. Since 1841 Clayton Tunnel had been equipped with a telegraph system between signal boxes at both portals. This meant that a signalman would be aware of a train entering the tunnel, and if it broke down before emerging he would be aware of the fact.

The distant signals were Whitworth's patent, and when a train passed over a treadle, that signal was automatically placed at danger. If this did not occur, an alarm bell rang in the signal box.

Henry Killick was on duty at the South box, and as a Sunday marked the change of shift from day to night duty, and in order to have one free day a week, he worked a continuous turn of 24 hours instead of the regulation 18.

The 8.28 sounded the alarm bell when it passed the distant signal as it had failed to return to danger. Unfortunately the sleepy Killick did not immediately respond and, as the 8.31 approached his box having passed the distant signal showing 'clear' when it should have displayed 'danger', he waved a red flag to stop it, but it went on into the tunnel.

Killick then telegraphed to Signalman Brown at the North box to inquire if the tunnel was clear. Brown, overlooking that Killick had sent two 'Train in tunnel' messages, saw the 8.28 emerging and signalled 'Tunnel clear'.

The driver of the third train, the 8.38, seeing the distant signal now correctly set at danger, braked, but Killick, believing the tunnel clear, waved his white flag so Driver Gregory opened his regulator and entered the tunnel.

Unfortunately Driver Scott, of the second train, had glimpsed the red flag, stopped in the tunnel and started to set back to find out what was wrong. Driver Gregory's engine, heading the third train, smashed into the rear of the second with such violence that it was thrust forward 50 yards. Twenty-three passengers were killed and 176 seriously injured.

At the subsequent inquiry Captain Tyler recommended that an interval of space, rather than time, should be observed, but the block system was not universally applied throughout the London, Brighton & South Coast Railway until 31 December 1874.

1862

On 1 July 1862 the Border Union Railway was opened throughout by the North British from Edinburgh to Carlisle and advertised as the 'Waverley route', the title inspired by Sir Walter Scott's Waverley novels. The West Coast companies, the London & North Western and the Caledonian were peeved at their monopoly being threatened and tried to stop traffic from using the Waverley route. One ploy was that Edinburgh traffic from the south arriving at Carlisle should be sent by the Caledonian unless specifically consigned by the North British route. Even stores from the Midlands to the North British St Margaret's works in Edinburgh were labelled 'via Caledonian Railway', so what had been intended to be an important main line was receiving very little traffic. It was only when the Midland Railway arrived at Carlisle on 1 May 1876, when the Settle and Carlisle was opened, that the Waverley route became important and the Midland and North British used it to inaugurate an express from St Pancras to Edinburgh. Traffic over the line declined in the middle of the twentieth century and the line closed on 5 January 1969, the last train being the Up sleeper.

In December 1862 the Vale of Clwyd Railway, at the request of local inhabitants, started to attach passenger coaches to its goods trains, thus offering a more frequent service, the operator wisely observing: 'The company do not of course guarantee the exact time with the goods trains'.

1863

Regarding the opening of the Metropolitan Railway on 10 January 1863, the *Illustrated London News* reported:

It was calculated that more than 30,000 persons were carried over the line in the course of the day. Indeed, the desire to travel by this line on the opening day was more than the directors had provided for; and from nine o'clock in the morning till past midnight it was impossible to obtain a place in the up or Cityward line at any of the mid-stations. In the evening the tide turned, and the crush at the Farringdon-street station was as great as at the doors of a theatre on the first night of some popular performer. Passengers were unanimous in favour of the smoothness and comfort of the line.

The 11.8 million journeys made on the Metropolitan in 1863 have risen today to 70 million.

As it was anticipated that tunnels full of smoke would not endear the system to passengers, a smokeless locomotive was designed by the line's chief engineer, Sir John Fowler. Its fire heated firebricks and these in turn heated the boiler and retained the steam. This 2-4-0T, known as 'Fowler's Ghost', when tested on the Great Western Railway's main line ran out of steam after only 7½ miles: like King Alfred's hot cakes, Sir John's hot bricks were a failure. Something more efficient was required and this was provided by Daniel Gooch, the Great Western's locomotive engineer. It was a 2-4-0 well tank engine fitted with condensing apparatus. Flaps, worked by rods from the footplate, sent exhaust steam up the chimney in a normal fashion when working in the open, or directed it into the water tanks when in tunnel. Although to some extent successful, the water in the tanks became overheated and often it was necessary to exhaust the steam into the tunnel with the result that the air was far from fresh. This was the very first condensing locomotive in Britain and the only broad gauge engine Gooch built for the Great Western with outside cylinders.

It was often necessary to exhaust the steam into air in the tunnel, and on 7 October 1884 *The Times*, reporting a journey from King's Cross to Baker Street, likened it to 'a mild form of torture which no sane person would undergo if he could help it'. Despite all these unpleasant fumes issuing from its locomotives, curiously the Metropolitan banned smoking in its coaches, though this ruling was overturned in 1874 as a belated result of an amendment to the Railway Regulation Act of 1868, which required all railways to provide a smoking carriage on every train.

For Metropolitan passengers the Great Western provided 45 eight-wheel broad gauge coaches. Six of these were ten-year-old composites, but the remainder were a new design. A fresh departure for the Great Western was that all were illuminated by gas carried in rubber bags on the roof. *The Times* commented that 'the novel introduction of gas into the carriages is calculated to dispel any unpleasant feelings which passengers, especially ladies, might entertain against riding so long a distance through a tunnel'. The fact that the gas which provided that light was stored in rubber bags on the roof is surprising in our safety-conscious days.

The Metropolitan Railway was safety conscious and worked the line by block telegraph, so distance, rather than a time interval, separated trains of which four were run each hour.

As the line had been sponsored and worked by the Great Western, it was not surprising that it was laid to the mixed gauge. The two companies did not always see eye to eye, and on 18 July 1863, hoping to force its own way, the GWR gave notice that it would stop working the line on 30 September. The Metropolitan calmly replied, saying it would take over working on 1 October. The GWR retaliated and said it would withdraw on 10 August. The Metropolitan took over services using standard gauge stock borrowed from the Great Northern Railway and the London & North Western, but they did not have the necessary condensing locomotives. Archibald Sturrock, the GNR's locomotive superintendent who had been the first manager of the GWR's Swindon works, quickly adapted some GNR locomotives to exhaust their steam into the water tank in the tender. Unfortunately the flexible pipe between engine and tender frequently burst. Sturrock's conversions were used until the Metropolitan was able to purchase its own condensing tank engines from Beyer, Peacock & Company.

Relations with the GWR improved in the autumn, and on 1 October 1863 the GWR inaugurated a service of through broad gauge trains between Windsor and Farringdon Street, but from 1 March 1869 it agreed to work over the Metropolitan Railway exclusively on standard gauge, which allowed the broad gauge rails to be lifted. In fact, BR Western Region condensing steam locomotives continued to work over the Metropolitan lines to Smithfield meat market until 30 July 1962. On 1 October 1863 the Great Northern also ran through trains to and from the City and the commuters on the first train were so pleased that they drank the station buffet dry.

The line was extended to Moorgate Street station on 23 December 1865 and that year 15 million ordinary tickets and 5,498 seasons were sold, ten years later sales had increased to 43.6 million and 32,941 respectively.

As the Metropolitan was used to link the Great Northern with the London, Chatham & Dover Railway, and because the double track was insufficient to handle all the traffic, a second pair of tracks known as the Widened Lines was provided between King's Cross and Moorgate.

In due course other cut-and-cover lines were opened in London and on 6 October 1884 the Circle Line was completed, thus linking many of the main line termini with the City and with each other.

Paradoxically the Metropolitan now has only about 15 per cent of its lines in tunnels due to the policy of its manager, Edward Watkin, who extended the line out into the country in an effort to seek new commuters. He secured parliamentary powers to purchase land for non-railway purposes and initiated housing estates at Willesden Green in 1880, Pinner in 1900 and Wembley Park in 1906. In 1915 the Metro-land slogan was first used, while in 1919 a subsidiary company, the Metropolitan Railway Country Estates was set up. In fact, by the mid-1920s, the Metropolitan earned more than twice per third-class seat than the three largest main-line companies.

An initiative of Edward Watkin in 1890 was to purchase 280 acres of countryside at Wembley and to attract people there by constructing pleasure gardens and a tower taller than the Eiffel Tower, but then, with only one stage of the tower complete, it started sinking into marshy ground. Money ran out, the gardens failed to attract crowds and early in the twentieth century the stump was demolished. In 1924 the decaying gardens were transformed into the Empire Exhibition and Wembley Stadium was built on the site of Watkin's tower.

Edgware Road station has been particularly unfortunate; on 30 October 1883 Irish republicans detonated a bomb there, and then on 7 July 2005 it was subject to a terrorist attack. The Underground did not always just convey commuters: in May 1898 the corpse of William Gladstone was brought from his country estate at Hawarden, Flintshire, to the Underground station at Westminster.

The Metropolitan wisely changed to electric working in 1905, obviating the very unpleasant atmosphere, though according to E. L. Ahrons in *Locomotive & Train Working in the Nineteenth Century* some found it beneficial.

> The former steam railways – at least the Inner Circle portion – had one advantage which disappeared with the steam locomotive. In the old days they provided a sort of health resort for people who suffered from asthma, for which the sulphurous and other fumes were supposed to be beneficial, and there were several regular asthmatical customers who daily took one or two turns round the circle to enjoy the – to them – invigorating atmosphere. But today the sulphur has all gone, except in the speech of a few irritable travellers, and has been replaced by an indescribable atmosphere of squashed microbes, and the sounds emitted by a hustler with a trumpet.

When the Metropolitan was electrified, its 66 steam locomotives were redundant and sold: six to the Cambrian Railways, two to the Nidd Valley light railway in Yorkshire running between Pateley Bridge and Wath-in-Nidderdale, one to the Somerset Mineral Railway and two to collieries. Its four-wheeled coaches were also sold to such companies as the Nidd Valley and the Weston, Clevedon & Portishead Light Railway. The doors of the Metropolitan coaches were round topped so that if opened in the tunnel they would not foul the walls.

The Metropolitan considered itself a main-line railway, which happened to have its London end in a tunnel, but provided for three classes of passenger, two from 1905 and one from 1941, and also had refreshment rooms and handled freight and parcel traffic. In 1933, with the other underground lines, buses and trams, it became part of the London Passenger Transport Board. Actually 55 per cent of London's 'underground' lines are actually on the surface. Today more people use the Underground than the national network.

Archibald Sturrock was imaginative. Apart from quickly adapting an ordinary engine to one of the condensing variety to aid the

Metropolitan in its difficulty, he also tried a steam tender. This was a tender with coupled wheels, a crank axle and cylinders supplied by steam from the boiler. It was used on heavy coal and goods trains, but repairs proved expensive and the idea was dropped.

Sturrock's engines were strong. No. 210 *Oliver Hindley* was speeding down Retford Bank with the Scotsman when the driver spotted a goods train ahead on a crossing. Realising he could not stop in time, he tried the alternative, opened the regulator and smashed through the goods train, causing no damage to No. 210 apart from dents and scars!

The Severn Estuary was a severe hindrance to trade between Bristol and South Wales. The bee-line distance of 18 miles between Bristol and Newport required no less than 81 miles travel by rail. The Bristol & South Wales Union Railway was proposed to ease the connection. It obtained its Act for building broad gauge line from Bristol to New Passage Pier on the south bank of the Severn, from where a ferry would link with Portskewett Pier across 2 miles of water. From that pier, a short branch connected with the South Wales Railway.

Brunel was appointed engineer and he invited Charles Richardson to be resident engineer. Richardson had worked with Brunel on the Great Western Railway and had the necessary tunnelling experience to deal with the 1,246-yard Patchway Long Tunnel and the 62-yard Patchway Short Tunnel.

The building contract was carried out by Rowland Brotherhood of Chippenham. As he required locomotives for use in his various contracts, and moving these from one location to another was difficult, Brotherhood's son Peter designed an engine capable of travelling on either road or railway. One of these 11-ton machines travelled from Chippenham to the Bristol & South Wales Union contract at Patchway over ordinary roads at an average speed of 6 mph.

Richardson designed the two piers of timber on a stone base and allowed trains to run to the end. Stairs led passengers to pontoons of hulks moored alongside, enabling ferry steamers to land passengers at any state of the tide, despite rises of as much as 46 feet. Steam-operated lifts took merchandise and luggage to the correct level. New Passage Pier was 1,635 feet in length and Portskewett Pier 708 feet. While engaged in building the piers, Richardson was led to consider the project of cutting a tunnel beneath the Severn.

The Bristol & South Wales Union was ceremonially opened on 25 August 1863 and to the public on 8 September 1863.

On 23 May 1881 the night watchman discovered Portskewett Pier was ablaze. Telegrams were sent to summon the Chepstow fire brigade, which failed to respond. The Cardiff fire engine arrived at 6.00 a.m. and its pump handles were operated by navvies from the Severn Tunnel works; the Newport fire engine arrived shortly after. The glow alerted the watchman at New Passage Pier on the far bank of the Severn. He roused other employees and the paddle steamer *Christopher Thomas* left. A fire engine and hose from Bristol was placed on the 7.15 a.m. train to New Passage and this engine, afloat on the *Christopher Thomas*, and the others ashore, eventually doused the flames.

As the ferry was inoperable without the use of Portskewett Pier, passenger trains were run from Bristol over the Midland Railway to Berkeley Road, then crossed the Severn Bridge and joined the South Wales line at Lydney. This alternative route was actually 25 minutes faster, but after temporary repairs to the pier had been carried out, the ferry reopened on 16 June 1881 to avoid the Great Western having to pay for running over the Midland line.

Railways were affecting the lives of the British in many ways – a skilled artisan was no longer tied to employment within walking distance of his home, he could seek work at a distance either travelling by train daily, or returning home at weekends. For example, the South Eastern Railway offered special Saturday evening cheap tickets available for return either on Sunday evening or Monday morning.

There was a phenomenal expansion in the number of cheap excursion trains available, such as to Epping Forest by the Great Eastern for 1s 0d or to Windsor by the Great Western, or South Western, for 2s 6d. In September 1863, four trains ran daily on the London, Chatham & Dover to Herne Bay and back for 1s 6d, including admission to a series of amusements, while you could see something of the Continent on a day trip from London to Calais, or Boulogne, for 7s 6d.

1864

The growth of London, coupled with the cholera epidemic of 1848–9, meant burial space was proving a problem so, from

October 1849, each night the London & South Western carried coffins to Woking in goods trains. The London Necropolis and National Mausoleum Company obtained a Private Act on 30 June 1852. Two years later, it bought almost 2,200 acres of land at Woking and arranged with the London & South Western to have a dedicated platform at Waterloo. There was a grand hall and staircase for those attending the better classes of funerals, and another hall and staircase for the lowest classes. Steam-powered coffin-lifts linked all floors. Brookwood was the largest cemetery in Western Europe; it was served by its own ¾-mile-long branch line, which opened on 13 November 1864. Not far inside the cemetery gate was the North station, serving the Nonconformist chapel, while at the far end was the South station and the Church of England section. Just as the mourners' coaches were divided into three classes, so the hearse vans also were divided into three sections, the main distinctions being the quantity of ornamentation on the doors. A train had Anglican and Nonconformist portions, the hearse vans placed in the rear of the relevant portion of the train. Initially black horses drew the train along the cemetery branch, but locomotive working began in 1864, the train being propelled through the cemetery under the guard's supervision. The funeral train, known colloquially as 'The Dead Meat Train' or 'The Stiffs' Express', generally consisted of two brake-firsts, a saloon and some hearse vans. As the fares were fixed under the Necropolis Company's Act, they could not rise. By 1902 the normal fares for Waterloo–Brookwood had increased, so some economically minded golfers dressed as mourners and used the Necropolis train to reach the links at Brookwood. Funeral trains ceased when a parachute mine fell on the Waterloo terminus on 16 April 1941 and as the motor hearse had taken over, the Necropolis station was not rebuilt after the war.

In 1864 Robert Fairlie patented a double-ended locomotive, basically two tank engines back-to-back, sharing one cab. The driving wheels were set on bogies giving the advantage of flexibility on curves and also easing the engine round, rather than thrusting it into the curve as a fixed-wheelbase machine did. The narrow gauge Festiniog Railway built a Fairlie locomotive in 1869, found it ideal, and they still work the line today. His idea was not generally adopted elsewhere, either the Beyer-Garratt or Mallet design of a flexible wheelbase being proved to be better.

Although W. R. Sykes had experimented with track circuits in the 1860s, he was a little before his time as many passenger coaches had Mansell wheels with wooden centres (*see* page 145). These would not conduct current, and wet ballast could also prevent a train being detected. The track circuit was a means of detecting whether a train or vehicle was on a stretch of line. This was done by passing an electric current through the rails and if present, wheels and axles would complete the circuit. It was not until about 1910 that the larger British companies installed track circuits on a large scale.

The mixed gauge Hammersmith & City opened a line from a junction with the GWR at what is now Westbourne Park to Hammersmith on 13 June 1864. Built by the GWR and the Metropolitan, it was set up as a separate company. It used land that had craftily been purchased by two of the Hammersmith & City directors and then resold to the railway at a handsome profit. Laid to the mixed gauge, it was worked by the GWR on the broad gauge until April 1865 when the Metropolitan took over working, the GWR broad gauge trains simply operating to and from Kensington, Addison Road, until 1869 when the broad gauge rails were lifted. It became the joint property of the Great Western and the Metropolitan on 1 July 1867, both owners operating services with their own stock. The line was converted to electric operation in 1906, the GWR erecting a power station at Royal Oak for both working trains and lighting purposes in the Paddington area. Some trains were electrically powered on 5 November and the entire service between Hammersmith and Addison Road and the City electrified on 1 January 1907 using joint stock. The multiple-unit cars were of Metropolitan design, numbered in that company's series and maintained by the Metropolitan. These were the only electric trains owned by the GWR, whereas after 1923 the LMS, LNER and SR operated quite extensive electric systems.

On 9 July 1864, in a first-class compartment on the North London Railway, Thomas Briggs was bludgeoned to death by Franz Muller, near Old Ford. To prevent a repetition, windows were inserted in compartment walls to render them less private.

These openings were called 'Muller's lights'; they were not appreciated by couples who enjoyed canoodling.

1865

Although the railway to Greenock speeded passengers to the lower Clyde resorts, steamers for Rothsay and beyond had to spend time passing the headland at Gourock, but a pier at Wemyss Bay would only be half an hour's sailing from Rothsay. The line to Wemyss Bay was opened on 13 May 1865, worked by the Caledonian Railway. Initially results were poor due to operating failures, but in 1869 the service became reliable and cheap, the fare Glasgow to Rothsay being only 2s 6d.

Much coal was mined in Fife, some of it coming from beneath a railway, Thornton station was particularly affected and from the 1860s, the platforms and buildings began to subside, eventually crumbling. The area was flattened, ash laid and a new station built over the old. As the sinking continued, the station buildings were raised and the permanent way packed with ash to maintain the rail level, but eventually it became necessary to build a third station.

The Perth & Inverness was a difficult railway to construct. It reached the highest point of a British main line at Druimuachdar Summit at 1,484 feet in the Pass of Drumochter. Snow and floods are a hazard, while in the Pass of Killiecrankie the line has to be supported on a retaining wall 690 yards in length and with an average height of 55 feet. Deep drains had to be cut to drain the surface water and, where peat was more than 20 feet deep, the track undulated about 4 inches when a train passed. Extra sleepers were added to offer greater stability. As the ground dried and the earth consolidated, the rails were lifted fortnightly and extra ballast inserted. In some places, due to the shrinkage of peat, the ballast is 30 feet deep. The line opened on 1 August 1866. To handle the heavy freight trains over the line, in 1894 David Jones designed the first British 4-6-0.

The main road paralleled the railway up through the Drumochter Pass and its original surface was atrocious. The Highland Railway was able to make capital out of this by advertising the fact that a disagreeable car journey could be avoided by placing the vehicle on a train at Dalwhinnie or Blair Atholl. The railway company insisted that a car's petrol tank should be empty. A Blair Atholl porter once checked this by thrusting a naked light inside; unsurprisingly, that particular car was unable to make the journey by train.

William Stroudley was the first locomotive superintendent of the Highland Railway and when appointed in 1865 he designed snow ploughs. At the start of the snow season, every engine was fitted with a small plough; at ordinary running speeds it could clear 2 feet of light snow. In severe weather a larger plough was fitted, which could deal with up to 9 feet, while the largest plough was a sharp-nosed battering ram which, with five locomotives behind it, could be forced through 11-foot-deep drifts.

On 17 December 1880 a train near Dava, south-east of Inverness, was buried to a depth of 69 feet, but fortunately its passengers were able to escape before the snow grew to this depth. A train travelling in the opposite direction was trapped as well. Its passengers were also able to escape, but the cattle were too frightened to be coaxed from the wagons.

In places prone to drifting, snow fences were erected to prevent snow from being blown into cuttings. On the Caithness–Sutherland border a blower was built consisting of boarded fences both sides of the track, the inner edges of the blowers nearly touching the ground but their outer edges 8–10 feet above. This deflected the wind away from the railway so that the snow was deposited away from the track.

A hazard in summer was fire, the Highland engines toiling up the gradients spraying red-hot cinders over pine trees and bracken. To avoid paying damages to landowners, the answer was to cut fire breaks between the railway and the pines, or alternatively plant rows of deciduous trees between the line and the conifers.

In the early days of rail travel, the wise placed a pot in their luggage, the contents of which were tipped out of the window – or sometimes there was a rash and highly dangerous opening of a door. Gentlemen had an alternative: instead of using a pot, they could fix a rubber tube down the trouser leg to end in a suitable container. There was no such comparable invention for ladies. In the 1860s lavatories were provided in family saloons; they made their appearance in sleeping cars in the 1870s and, when corridor coaches were introduced in the 1880s, lavatories became more common. It meant that the railway companies had to haul around more unproductive space as both corridors and lavatories reduced seating accommodation on a coach. For many years the water closets were flushed directly on to the track, the train's speed generally breaking the solid waste – hence why passengers were requested not to use them when in a station. In due course this simple and economic system was believed to be unhygienic and in 1984 the Department of Transport stated that toilets be fitted with retention tanks, so no longer could you lift the seat and see the ballast whizzing by.

1866

The Wrexham, Mold & Connah's Quay Railway opened to goods and minerals on 1 January 1866 and to passengers on 1 May the same year. In the early days it combined passenger and goods into mixed trains worked by an old 0-6-0 with a four-wheeled tender. The company was so poverty-stricken that its staff were without uniforms and passenger accommodation could be so short on market days that passengers sat on the coal in the tender and crowded onto the footplate.

The Potteries, Shrewsbury & North Wales Railway was a curious line. Opened on 13 August 1866, it ran nowhere near the Potteries, but from a junction with the Cambrian Railways at Llanymynech to Shrewsbury. Built with a double track, it hoped to be part of a line to an Irish ferry. These hopes never came to fruition as bailiffs took possession and the line closed on 21 December 1866. Some locomotives were sold, the line singled and it reopened in December 1868. An inspection by the Board of Trade in 1880 found timber bridges rotting, while sleepers and fences were seriously decayed, so it closed completely on 22 June 1880. It lay derelict until 1909 when a Light Railway Order was applied for. This was granted and the line reopened as the Shropshire & Montgomeryshire Light Railway on 13 April 1911 under the managership of that light railway enthusiast Holman F. Stephens. Locomotives and rolling stock were acquired from a variety of sources and included a Wolseley-Siddeley two-coach railcar, a Ford three-car set and an ex-London County Council horse tramcar for use behind the diminutive locomotive *Gazelle* on the rather insubstantial Criggion branch. Regular passenger services were withdrawn on 6 November 1933. With the coming of World War II, the War Department saw that the sparsely populated countryside the railway traversed was ideal for establishing an ordnance depot, so in 1941 the line was taken over by the military, repaired and worked by War Department locomotives. In 1948 it was transferred to British Railways but remained on lease to the War Department. The Criggion branch closed 4 January 1960 and the remainder 29 February 1960.

In 1866 the service inaugurated between Charing Cross and Cannon Street took 7 minutes and this brief time of seclusion in a compartment was valuable to certain ladies and gentlemen who were not unknown to practise vice, having discovered that buying a first-class ticket was cheaper than paying for a hotel room.

The 2-foot-3-inch gauge Talyllyn Railway opened on 1 October 1866 to carry slate to Towyn and it also operated passenger services. In 1911 the quarries were sold to Sir Henry Haydn Jones, MP for Merioneth, who promised to keep the railway open in his lifetime. The quarries closed in the late 1940s, but services ceased on 6 October 1950 following Sir Haydn's death. A group of enthusiasts felt that closure of the line was a great loss and that it should be possible to run it with volunteers. His widow, Lady Jones, was very co-operative and the Talyllyn Railway Preservation Society was established, the very first example of this movement in Britain. The line reopened on 14 May 1951 and has flourished, attracting tourists to the delightful scenery.

The Victorian builders could certainly work quickly. On 16 November 1866 the viaduct over the River Aire at Apperley, north-west of Leeds, was washed away by floodwater, a goods train plunging into the gap. John Crossley, the Midland's civil engineer, worked so rapidly that he had the structure rebuilt and opened by 1 January 1867, his directors being so pleased that they gave him 300 guineas.

1867

On the morning of 20 August 1867 a goods train consisting of 43 wagons called at Llandulas on the London & North Western Railway in North Wales. Time was approaching for the arrival of the Irish Mail and it was decided that this train should be placed into a siding to allow the Mail to overtake. Unfortunately some wagons were already occupying the sidings and this meant that the train could not be backed in as a whole but divided using two sidings. The rear half was left on the main line while the front portion was shunted into a siding but then, although time was getting short before the approach of the Mail, the stationmaster decided to shunt three wagons to the front of those standing on the main line.

Unfortunately these three wagons were shunted onto those others at far too great a speed, the shunter failed to apply the wagon brakes with the result that they struck the standing wagons so hard that the brake van's brakes were broken and the rear of the goods train ran down the gradient of 1 in 147 towards the previous station and the 13-coach Irish Mail hauled by 2-2-2 No. 291 *Lady of the Lake*.

The Mail was travelling fairly slowly up the gradient and its driver had about 150 yards warning to apply the brakes and reverse, so the collision at Abergele was relatively gentle, but unfortunately the leading wagons of the runaways contained casks of paraffin oil and some burst spraying the engine, tender, a van and three coaches. The paraffin immediately ignited, giving no chance to release the trapped passengers of whom there were thirty-two. None survived.

Thinking quickly, the remaining nine undamaged vehicles still on the rails were uncoupled and on the falling gradient it was easy to push them away from the fire.

9

Light Railways – the Solution to Serving Sparsely Populated Areas

1868

Unless a railway company owned the land on which it wished to build a railway, an Act of Parliament was required in order to gain powers of compulsory purchase. Such an Act was expensive to obtain, and in some areas of Great Britain a railway was desirable but would be barely economic, and so it was believed that it should be possible to build a line which needed less expenses to set up and then, when running, could be cheaper to operate. It was hoped that building a light railway would bring economic recovery to an area.

The first attempt at this was the Railway Construction Facilities Act of 1864. Instead of an Act, a Board of Trade certificate could authorise a line, but would still require Parliamentary and landowners' approval. This method proved ineffective.

A better attempt was the Regulation Act of 1868 which mentioned the term 'light railway'. This was a line authorised by the Board of Trade with axle loads restricted to 8 tons and a maximum speed of 25 mph. A few lines were built under this ruling, such as the Easingwold and Southwold railways, but the best solution came with the Light Railways Act of 1896. Its main provisions were:

1. A Light Railway Commission of three members to receive applications and determine their worth.
2. Instead of an authorising Act, the Commissioners could grant a Light Railway Order subject to the Board of Trade's approval of the technical aspects.

3. Local authorities could make loans, or subscribe. Where money was advanced, a treasury loan of 25 per cent was also available.

4. The Treasury could make grants or loans up to 50 per cent of capital cost if the Board of Agriculture certified that a light railway was necessary to develop the district.

5. The Commissioners and the Board of Trade could relax provisions of general railway regulation (this would enable a railway to be run more cheaply).

6. Compulsory purchase of land was authorised and landowners' compensation would take into account the benefits the railway would bring.

7. Existing railways could be converted to light railways by applying for an Order.

Between 1898 and 1918, 687 applications were received for light railways, covering 5,015 miles. Of the 2,100 miles authorised, only 900 miles were built and 350 miles of these were street tramways. In the event, the Board of Trade was reluctant to alter its thinking: despite low speeds, many light railways were forced to provide signals, full-height platforms and level crossing gates rather than cattle grids, though the Great North of Scotland Railway's branch from Fraserburgh to St Combs was allowed to be unfenced provided that the locomotives were fitted with cow catchers. Flat-bottomed rail, spiked directly to the sleepers, was used on light railways rather than the bull-head rail and chairs then generally used by the main line companies. Most of the independent light railways were poor, suffering high interest charges and using unreliable second-hand equipment. Following World War I they suffered from road competition. By the time of World War II, only sixteen independent light railways were still operating and three were nationalised in 1947: the East Kent, the Kent & East Sussex and the Shropshire & Montgomeryshire. Arguably the most successful, the Derwent Valley Light Railway in Yorkshire, lasted until 1988. A preservation society has reopened the Kent & East Sussex Railway.

The Mid-Suffolk Railway was a good example of a light railway being laid cheaply, for in places it was just laid directly on the ground after ballast had been thrown down. To save on the cost of bridges, it had 114 level crossings in 18 miles while its terminus at Laxfield was clad in zinc sheeting printed with a brick pattern. Two trains ran each way daily, but passenger numbers were disappointingly low as the stations were far from the communities they were intended to serve. From 1906 it was in receivership, so when in 1908 a locomotive was delivered by Hudswell Clarke, it was chained to the rails as the cheque to pay for it had yet to arrive. The line had opened to goods traffic on 20 September 1904 and to passengers on 29 September 1908 using four-wheeled ex-Metropolitan District coaches. It was taken over by the London & North Eastern Railway in 1924. The last train ran on 26 July 1952. Preservationists have reopened a station and length of rail at Brockford.

The Leadhills & Wanlockhead Light Railway opened to Leadhills on 2 July 1901 and was extended to Wanlockhead on 1 October 1902. Worked by the Caledonian, it was a happy-go-lucky line, which stopped anywhere to pick up passengers or parcels. Usually one carriage and a van were sufficient to handle the traffic. The expected development in lead mining failed to occur and the line closed on 2 January 1939.

Colonel Holman Fred Stephens was the King of Light Railways, ruling 13 companies under the title of Associated Railways from an office in Tonbridge. Although much of the equipment was second-hand he was up-to-date, using internal-combustion propulsion for some railcars and shunters and concrete pot-type sleepers.

Today Light Railway Orders enable preservation societies to gain authorisation to operate their lines, while since 1972 the Heart of Wales Line between Llanelli and Craven Arms has been operated under a Light Railway Order.

The second underground passenger railway in the world was the Metropolitan District Railway, usually known as the 'District'. It opened from South Kensington to Westminster Bridge on 24 December 1868 as part of the Inner Circle proposed by the House of Lords Committee. It was envisaged that the Metropolitan and the Metropolitan District companies would be merged on completion of the Circle in 1884, but this did not happen, the Metropolitan sending its trains round the Circle clockwise and the District anticlockwise. Each company had its own booking office at the stations and one had to be careful when buying a ticket for a short journey that you used the right office or you would find yourself having to go almost all the way round to reach your destination.

The Aylesbury & Buckingham Railway between Aylesbury and Verney Junction opened on 23 September 1863. Florence Nightingale frequently used the latter station when making visits to Sir Harry Verney at Claydon House. In 1890 this very minor branch line became important when it was taken over by the Metropolitan Railway to become part of a line from the Manchester, Sheffield & Lincolnshire Railway via the Metropolitan Railway to the South Eastern Railway, the plan being to link them with a Channel tunnel. The line was isolated from the rest of the Metropolitan system until 1 September 1892. Although in theory the Metropolitan could from that date work its trains to Verney Junction, in practice this was impossible as the light track and weak underline bridges precluded the use of existing Metropolitan locomotives, so the Great Western continued to work trains. The Metropolitan improved the line by rebuilding stations and relaying the track to main line standard with heavier rail, purchasing additional land and adding a second track, this doubling being completed by 1 January 1897. The Metropolitan sidings at Verney Junction had such a severe curve that a visiting London & North Western engine was highly likely to be derailed. Some trains ran through from Verney Junction to Baker Street and in 1922 six such trains were run daily, including a Pullman service using either *Mayflower* or *Galatea*.

1869
The Caledonian took over the Glasgow, Paisley & Greenock Railway in 1851 with its irritating walk between the railway and steamer. Greenock merchants conceived the idea of a line from a waterside pier at Greenock to an end-on junction with the Glasgow & South Western's branch at Bridge of Weir. It was also hoped that the line would attract coal and mineral traffic from Ayrshire and help develop Greenock as a port. The line, the Greenock & Ayrshire, worked by the Glasgow & South Western, opened for mineral traffic on 1 September 1869, for goods on 1 October and passengers on 23 December 1869. Each route reduced Glasgow to Greenock fares to just 6*d*, the Glasgow & South Western passengers having the advantage of much easier access to the steamers.

As the steamers called at the Custom House Quay pier first and then the Glasgow & South Western's Princes Pier, the Caledonian deliberately slowed its trains so that the connecting steamers were delayed and thus passengers waiting to board at Princes Pier delayed. The ploy backfired as the Caledonian lost the mail contract to the Glasgow & South Western and also most passengers preferred the latter's route, which entailed less walking.

In the early 1860s, the West Cumberland iron ore mines increased their production and much of the ore was destined for the Lanarkshire steelworks. It was seen that if, instead of going via Carlisle, a new line was built across the Solway to the south-east area of Dumfriesshire to join the Caledonian main line at Kirtlebridge, this would save about 20 miles. Work on the Solway Junction Railway started in 1865 and opened for goods and minerals on 13 September 1869 and to passengers on 8 August 1870. The 1,940-yard-long Solway viaduct was carried on 193 cast-iron piers, 181 single piers and 12 double piers, each carrying 30-foot spans. The rails were 35 feet above low water. Only a single track was laid but enough land was purchased to allow doubling and all bridges, were built to support two tracks. The line was worked by Solway Junction engines and staff. In 1873 the Caledonian leased the Scottish section of the line and took over the remaining section in 1895, but the Solway Junction Company remained nominally independent until 1923.

The viaduct proved costly to maintain. In the winter of 1875–6 ice formed inside the 1-foot-diameter cast-iron columns and created cracks, while in January 1881 ice floes demolished 45 piers and 37 girders collapsed. One floe was 27 yards square and 6 feet thick. As the damage would cost £30,000 to repair and the company lacked sufficient funds, an Act of Parliament was sought to raise this amount. The line was not reopened until 1 May 1884. By the end of the nineteenth century the best ore had been worked and the Lanarkshire steel mills changed to Spanish ore. During WWI, from 1 January 1917, the line from Annan to Brayton, including the Solway Viaduct, was completely closed. It reopened on 2 March 1919 but it soon became evident that the viaduct was again in need of expensive repairs. These were not justified by receipts so from 1 September 1921 goods and passenger services were withdrawn. Left in situ, the viaduct was used as an illegal footpath to licensed hospitality denied to Scotsmen on a Sunday. A barbed wire fence was erected, but this was no barrier to the enterprising Celt; eventually a Sunday bus service between Annan and Carlisle rendered the walk unnecessary. The viaduct was demolished between 1933 and 1935.

It is interesting that English railways did not enter Scotland, yet Scottish railways not only came to the border towns of Berwick and Carlisle but the North British managed to reach Hexham in Northumberland and the Caledonian Silloth and Brayton in Cumberland. Wales was invaded by the Great Western Railway and the London & North Western Railway, the Cambrian Railways only crossing the border to Whitchurch.

The East London Railway was a short but important line opened on 6 December 1869 uniting existing railways north and south of the Thames using the Thames Tunnel built by Marc Brunel, which had been opened as a footway in March 1843. The tunnel failed as a commercial enterprise and closed in the early 1860s, the East London purchasing it. With rail links at each end, the only modification to Brunel's work was the removal of some of the central row of tunnel piers to allow clearance on curves.

When an engine is running downhill, the blast is very soft and steam can drift down from the chimney and obscure a driver's view. To obviate this problem, David Jones, appointed locomotive superintendent to the Highland Railway in 1870, designed a chimney with an outer casing into which slots had been cut at the front. When running, air entered at the front, passed around the casing to the rear and emerged to thrust the exhaust steam upwards. Use of these louvres had another advantage: pounding through the forests, red-hot sparks and cinders caused lineside fires for which the company had to pay compensation; the louvres threw these sparks higher and they were thus cooler when they descended.

1870

Although thankfully there have been few instances of wagons running away during shunting operations and striking passenger trains, one such accident occurred at Barnsley on 12 December 1870 when 15 people were killed and more than 50 injured in an accident which was almost a repetition of that at Abergele three years earlier.

During shunting operations, 10 wagons were left on a gradient of 1 in 119 and were only held by a single sprag thrust through the spokes of a wagon wheel. When two wagons were shunted against the raft of 10 wagons, the sprag broke and the guard failed to couple up. A pointsman at the yard's outlet heard the guard's shout, managed to pin down the brake on one wagon, but slipped and fell in an attempt to secure another. Another pointsman tried to make an heroic attempt to stop the runaways as they passed at about 7 mph, took a running jump, but was knocked off by the girder of an underbridge. Signalmen at three junctions looked on helplessly as the wagons sped by; there were no facing points they could operate to deflect the runaways. One and a half miles away, a passenger train was standing at Stairfoot station and people on the platform heard a roar as the runaways crossed an iron bridge about 200 yards distant. They struck the back of the passenger train at about 40 mph and its driver was knocked down on the footplate. The guard and stationmaster, both standing on the platform, were hurled several feet and struck unconscious. The rear coaches were completely shattered, 15 passengers lost their lives and 59 were injured. Colonel Rich criticised the fact that no trap points had been provided to protect the running lines in the event of a mishap.

Another unusual accident occurred on Boxing Day 1870. As the 4.25 p.m. King's Cross–Peterborough passed Marshmoor level crossing 2 miles south of Hatfield, the driver looked back to check that all was well with the train but to his amazement found it was not there! He stopped and slowly reversed, wisely sending his fireman ahead with a red hand lamp.

After proceeding for about half a mile they met the guard, who informed them that there had been a disaster. The driver reversed and continued to Hatfield to warn any oncoming train and to seek help.

Apparently as the train approached the crossing, the tyre of a van at the head of the train had broken and the wheel disintegrated. The coupling between the van and engine snapped and the van and the first two coaches ran off the rails and into the road, demolishing a wall and in the roadway fatally crushing the mother and sister of the signalman; six passengers also lost their lives. The Board of Trade inspector criticised the method of tyre fixing and recommended the use of Mansell wheels on passenger stock.

Richard Mansell, carriage superintendent of the South Eastern Railway, took out a patent in 1848 for an improved carriage wheel. An iron, later steel, centre boss was surrounded with a disc built from 16 teak segments, the disc then forced onto the tyre by hydraulic pressure. A securing ring was fixed on each side and the whole lot joined together by nuts and bolts. By 1874, 20,000 sets of Mansell wheels were in use and no failure had ever been experienced.

The first tube railway was the Tower Subway, built by Peter Barlow who was assisted by his pupil James Henry Greathead. When Barlow proposed constructing the tunnel, as Marc Brunel had encountered such difficulties tunnelling below the Thames, no contractor was willing to undertake construction of this subway until Greathead, then aged 24, tendered for the tunnel and shafts at £9,400. He devised a tunnelling machine consisting of a cylindrical wrought-iron shield thrust forward by six powerful screws. The Tower Subway Tunnel opened in 1870, passengers travelling the 450 yards in a cable car on a 2-foot-6-inch gauge track. The tunnel soon became just a footway and closed in 1894 when Tower Bridge opened.

1871

The railway between Quainton Road, on the Aylesbury & Buckingham Railway, and Wotton opened on 1 April 1871. It was an unusual line in several respects. Built to serve the Duke of Buckingham's estate, he paid its cost and gave his own land for the greater part of the line's length and leased the remainder from Winwood's Charity. As no land needed to be purchased, no Parliamentary powers were required. As work was carried out by the estate, unusually no contractor was employed except for a short period when bridge rails were laid on longitudinal sleepers similar to those used by the GWR in its early history. Longitudinal sleepers were sensible because horse traction was used and this design of track meant that there were no cross-sleepers for horses to trip over. It was not intended to carry passengers other than estate workers and stockmen, but so many requests were made that a coach was borrowed and began a service in January 1872. Two months later, the line was extended the final ¼ mile to Brill. From 1872 the line was worked by the firm of Chaplin & Horne, who introduced steam power in the form of two highly unusual 6 hp four-wheeled traction engine-like locomotives from Aveling & Porter at £400 apiece. Each weighed 10 tons in working order and had a single cylinder above the boiler. This imparted motion to a flywheel from where a chain drove the wheels. A spark-arrester was fitted to the tall chimney. As the locomotive travelled at little more than 4–8 mph, the journey of 6½ miles took about 90 minutes. The topography made the engines work hard as between Wotton and Brill there was an almost continuous incline for 2¾ miles, varying from 1 in 100 to 1 in 51. Another curiosity was that it was probably the only line to use a farthing in its fare table: a ticket from Quainton Road to Wood Siding cost 5¾*d*.

With a view to extending the line for 11 miles to Oxford, the line was taken over in 1888 by the Oxford & Aylesbury Railway and the line relaid. Although still owned by the Oxford & Aylesbury, from 1 December 1899 the line was worked by the Metropolitan Railway. With the formation of the London Passenger Transport Board in 1933 the LPTB took over the line's working, leading to the curiosity of London Transport engines working an extremely rural single line in the depths of Buckinghamshire.

The LPTB then made the decision not to run trains north of Aylesbury, so the branch closed from 1 December 1935. The last train, comprising an old coach and a newer one, carried so many passengers that more than half were required to stand. This was quite a contrast to an ordinary day, as in its last years daily traffic averaged 58 passengers and 34 tons of goods, the branch creating an annual loss of £4,000.

19 June 1871 marked the opening of the 17¼-mile-long line between Golspie to Helmsdale built at the Duke of Sutherland's expense when the Sutherland Railway failed to reach its intended terminus at Brora. A private station served Dunrobin Castle, the seat of the duke. The line was worked by the Highland Railway, which bought it on 28 July 1884. The duke owned a 2-4-0T, which was used to draw his small four-wheel saloon to Inverness where the saloon was attached to main-line trains. In 1895 the next duke purchased a 0-4-4T, a full-width leather seat being provided in the cab for passengers who wished to travel on the footplate. As he was a director of the London & North Western Railway, in 1899 he had a large bogie saloon built at Woolverton, designed by carriage and wagon superintendent C. A. Park, and it was the prototype

for the royal train built in 1903 for King Edward VII and Queen Alexandra. When the duke was travelling by special train north of Aberdeen, his large saloon was steadied by having the smaller vehicle coupled behind.

1872

The first successful railway trade union was the Amalgamated Society of Railway Servants (ASRS) founded in 1872 at Derby; until then, any criticism of a railway company was regarded as insubordination. It was an all-grade union and within a year had enrolled more than 17,000 members. The local Liberal MP, Michael Thomas Bass, was the union's financial backer – helping it produce *The Railway Service Gazette*. As his firm sent half a million barrels of beer by rail annually, his was a voice or importance. Until the late 1880s, the ASRS was a friendly-society union and strikes were deplored as 'an evil to masters and men'. One of its initial acts was to collect accurate statistics on deaths and injuries; the Board of Trade had required companies to report accidents, but such recording was lax – for example the Lancashire & Yorkshire reported 73 injuries in 1872 whereas the ASRS listed 1,387. In 1875 no less than 767 railway employees were killed in Britain. Wagon shunting claimed a high proportion of fatal accidents until shunting poles came into use.

ASRS members tended to be drivers, guards and signalmen, rather than the more poorly paid porters and platelayers. Between 1887 and 1897 the union changed from a friendly society with a few mutual protection benefits into a trade union with benefit funds, this change being brought about mainly by members in the north-east, Scotland and South Wales. The Darlington programme of 1887 sought a 10-hour day with overtime at 25 per cent above normal rates and a guaranteed weekly wage. Union membership increased from 9,000 in 1885 to 26,000 in 1890.

One common risk of accident occurred when coupling wagons. Twice in the 1880s the union demonstrated automatic couplings that would have obviated the need of a shunter to pass between the wagons, but the companies rejected the plan on account of the financial cost. With the Railway Employment (Prevention of Accidents) Act of 1900, companies having yards where shunting was carried out after dark were required to provide fixed lamps and not merely illumination by hand lamps. To avoid men tripping over point rodding or signals wires and falling on the track, these were required to be enclosed. It was not until 1911 that railways were obliged to fit brakes on both sides of a wagon in order to avoid men making a dangerous crossing of the line to apply or release them, and even then the railways were allowed 20 years to carry out this modification. The peak of deaths came in the 1870s at more than 700 annually, but well into the twentieth century the number killed was in excess of 100.

Although the Factory Act of 1833 limited the hours worked in some industries, it did not apply to railway employment and Bass informed the House of Commons that on the Midland Railway, although a driver's standard working day consisted of 10 hours, he knew of thirty to forty men who worked almost double that. James Greenwood of the *Daily Telegraph* reported that one passenger guard who started work at 6.35 p.m. on 23 December did not finish until 2.00 p.m. on Christmas Day having worked for 43 hours and 25 minutes. When he was found asleep on Christmas Eve, instead of being replaced, a porter was assigned to travel with him and keep him awake. The Liability Law of 1880 offered employees the right to compensation in cases of negligence, but the companies were able to contract out of compensation to the provident societies, which paid lower rates. Staff were controlled by using reprimands, cautions, fines, suspensions and dismissals, all noted in a staff register.

1872 was memorable for the fact that it was the year when James Allport, general manager of the Midland Railway, first admitted third-class passengers to all trains, while from 1 January 1875 the second class was abolished and third-class passengers travelled in what had been second-class compartments and the old third-class coaches were broken up.

From the 1870s bogie coaches became more and more usual, though it was many years before all companies ceased building four- or six-wheeled coaches. Wheels were generally suspended, having laminated springs above the axle boxes with auxiliary springs at the ends of the spring hangers. These auxiliary springs were of the helical, volute or coil type, with rubber sometimes being used.

1873

The first British sleeping cars were built by Messrs Ashbury, of Manchester, in 1873 for the Great Northern and the North Eastern railways. They brought to an end the illegitimate custom of guards hiring two sticks and a spare cushion for passengers to place between opposite seats to form a bed. The West Coast route, not wishing to offer an inferior service, in February 1874 placed sleepers on the London and North Western.

High-speed derailments have fortunately been very rare, but one did occur on 1 August 1873. The 8.00 p.m. Euston to Scotland was a heavy train of 25 vehicles drawn by two engines. As it was speeding through Wigan in the early hours of the morning, driver Will Strawpert glanced back and saw sparks flying from the rear of his train. He whistled for the guards' brakes and cautiously applied his own, not wishing the weight behind to push off any lighter vehicles towards the front.

He walked back and was horrified at the sight. Fifteen carriages had successfully negotiated the points, but the sixteenth coach had derailed with the luggage van behind it. The latter demolished a shunters' cabin but the couplings held and both vehicles rerailed themselves at the far end of the platform. The coaches behind the van were all derailed and piled up, some landing on the roof of a factory; only the last coach and rear brake van remained on the track. 13 passengers were killed and 30 injured.

Captain Tyler's investigation lasted five weeks and 104 witnesses were examined. He concluded that the train had been travelling too fast and referred to the competition between East and West Coast companies, which tempted drivers to take risks. The actual cause of the derailment of the 16th carriage was inexplicable. An important result of the accident was that the Board of Trade required facing point locks to be installed on all passenger lines.

1874

The line to Thurso, the most northerly British station, opened on 28 July 1874 and it was at last possible to travel by rail all the way from the south-west tip of England to the north of Scotland.

The year 1874 marked the inauguration of the first cross-country service, from Birmingham to Bath by the Midland Railway and then over the Somerset & Dorset and the London & South Western to Bournemouth. Six years later, with the co-operation of the North Eastern, the service was extended to Newcastle.

The disaster caused by a broken tyre at Hatfield on Boxing Day 1870 was repeated on the GWR at Shipton on Christmas Eve 1874. The 10.00 a.m. Paddington–Birkenhead consisted of 14 heavily laden coaches drawn by 2-2-2 No. 478 assisted by a pilot engine. The latter was removed at Oxford and replaced by 2-2-2 No. 386 and to accommodate Oxford passengers on the already crowded train, an extra coach was added behind No. 478. This coach was an elderly little four-wheeled affair built in 1855 for the Newport, Abergavenny & Hereford Railway. When travelling at about 40 mph the tyre of the right-hand leading wheel of the first coach broke. The wheel disintegrated, and the coach derailed.

Driver Richard on No. 478, looking back to check that all was well with the train, noticed snow and ballast flying up, while on the other side his fireman observed the clapper of the alarm gong on the tender flapping, but not with sufficient movement to sound the gong. A man was leaning out of a window waving his arms and yelling, 'Whoa! Whoa!'

Unfortunately Driver Richard did what at the time seemed the best thing to do but which proved to be a fatal mistake. Continuous brakes not being fitted, he blew his deep-toned alarm whistle to warn the brakesmen on the train to apply their brakes, but before they could do this, both drivers had closed their regulators and reversed their engines while the respective firemen were busy screwing down the tender brakes.

This action meant that the derailed lightly built coach, which had been held upright by taut couplings front and back, was squashed to matchwood by the momentum of the heavy train behind. To make matters worse, this happened where the line crossed the Oxford Canal between Shipton-on-Cherwell and Hampton Gay. The nine coaches behind the little four-wheeler fell into the canal, killing 34 passengers and seriously injuring 65.

As the line was worked on the time-interval system and there was the severe risk that a following train could strike the wreckage, the rear guard, accompanied by two passengers, ran back along the line and reached Woodstock Road in time to warn the stopping passenger train. Meanwhile the leading engine of the Birkenhead express had been uncoupled and run on to Kidlington station to stop Up trains and summon help.

Colonel Yolland of the Board of Trade made comments. He was highly critical of the fact that the tyres of the little four-wheeler were secured by four countersunk rivets through the rims, a primitive form of construction that the GWR had agreed to discard as dangerous back in 1855, yet the carriage had been re-tyred by this means in 1868! Colonel Yolland recommended the use of Mansell wheels. He also criticised the fact that a vehicle was marshalled in front of the leading brake van and the fact that the GWR did not advise its drivers how they should act in such an emergency. This resulted in the company adding a new paragraph to its rule book:

If any of the vehicles be off the rails, the brakes in the rear must be instantly applied, in order that by keeping the couplings tight the disabled vehicles may be kept up and out of the way of the vehicles behind until the force of the latter is exhausted, it being desirable that the front portion of the train should be brought slowly to a stand. The application of the front brakes might result in further damage, and great care must be exercised in their application, In all cases the application of brakes behind a disabled vehicle, or the application by the Guard of the continuous brake at the rear of the train, will be attended with advantage, and rear Guards of trains fitted with continuous brake must apply the continuous brake as well as the hand brake.

10

Improvements to Railway Safety

1875

On 1 January 1875 the Midland Railway abolished second class, having found that the numbers of second-class tickets sold had decreased and those of third-class passengers increased, making it less profitable to provide carriages for this class of traveller, so former second-class carriages became third-class coaches and helped the Midland poach passengers from other railway companies. In due course, the other companies had to follow suit and abandon second class. In 1956 the curiosity of having just first and third class was abolished when third class was renamed standard class.

In the early days of newspaper production, papers had to be folded by hand and this delayed despatch. In 1875 W. H. Smith and *The Times* devised an improvement whereby the London & North Western introduced vans with tables and lights so that the papers could be folded en route, even though this was a task that needed skill in those fast, rough-riding vans. Not to be outdone, other railways copied this scheme.

The Great Western's newspaper service to Swansea was very slow, taking more than 10 hours. This suggested to the London & North Western that it should run a newspaper train from London to Swansea even though its route was 62 miles longer. This stirred the Great Western, which speeded up its own train to arrive at 1.30 p.m. instead of 4.30 p.m.

Initially trains were regulated by a time interval. No train was allowed to pass a railway policeman unless the previous train had passed at least 10 minutes earlier. This, of course, was not entirely safe as the previous train may have broken down and come to a halt just out of sight of the policeman. The only safeguard was that the guard of a train stopped between stations was required to go back and protect the rear of his train by placing detonators on the line.

With the increasing speed of trains, drivers experienced difficulty in seeing a policeman and obeying his red flag to stop, because train brakes left something to be desired. The only brakes available were those on the engine, or tender, and on manned brake vans distributed throughout a passenger train. This sighting problem was solved by having a moving arm mounted on a tall mast. To prevent the rear-end crash problem, with the introduction of the electric telegraph the line was divided into sections and no train allowed into a section until notification had been received that the previous train had been cleared.

Initially passenger train braking was by hand brakes on a tender, or in vans marshalled at intervals along the train. The North London and the London & North Western used an early type of continuous brake, the Clark, or Clark & Webb's chain brakes, applied when a friction clutch on the axle of a brake van operated a windlass that tightened a chain, which applied brakes to adjoining vehicles. The Lancashire & Yorkshire used Fay's brake, while the Highland used Newall's, both designs worked by handwheels through longitudinal rotating shafts below the carriages, with jointed couplings between each vehicle.

There were three pneumatic systems, the cheapest being the 'simple' vacuum developed by the American James Young Smith. An ejector (similar to an injector but pumping air rather than water) on a locomotive was turned on to exhaust a pipe running through the train and this applied the brakes. It was slow to act and would not work if a hose parted. An improved version was that invented by James Gresham whereby the ejector was on all the time the train was in motion, maintaining a vacuum in the train pipe and on both sides of each cylinder. To apply the brake, the vacuum was destroyed, air flowed into one side of the cylinder but could not pass a non-return valve and pressure applied the brake. The division of a train automatically caused the brakes to be applied. The best system tried at Newark was the Westinghouse air brake, which was automatic and rapid in action, stopping a train weighing

203.2 tons with engine from 52 mph to a halt in 19 seconds and covering 913 feet. The only disadvantage with the Westinghouse brake was that once applied it was not possible to ease the brake off without fully releasing and then reapplying it. Most railways chose the vacuum brake, but those who chose the non-automatic Smith variety realised that the automatic type was essential and then adopted it. Due to the differences between the Westinghouse and the automatic vacuum, dual-fitted carriages had to be supplied for through running between railways.

1876

A severe snowstorm occurred on the evening of 21 January 1876. Driver Joseph Bray was in charge of a 37-wagon coal train trying to spot signals in the blizzard. Twenty minutes behind was the Up Flying Scotsman. As the mineral train was 18 minutes late, the signalman at Holme was instructed to shunt the goods to let the Scotsman overtake, so set his signals to danger. The coal train, instead of stopping, ran through, because instead of showing 'Danger' as the signalman had intended, they had become frozen at 'Clear'.

The first two signal boxes to the south were not in telegraphic communication with Holme, Abbots Ripton being the next one so equipped, and here the coal train stopped and the signalman asked Bray to back into a siding. At this moment the signalman at Wood Walton, the previous box, saw the Scotsman fly by, even though his levers should have set the signals at 'Danger'. Six wagons were still on the main line and still had to be propelled into the siding when the Scotsman, headed by 2-2-2 No. 269, ploughed into the wagons, derailing its engine to lay across the Down line.

The Abbots Ripton foreman platelayer ran south along the Down line, laying detonators. Driver Bray, whose engine lay undamaged and safe in the siding, uncoupled his locomotive and, unaware that the foreman was doing the same, sent his fireman forward to protect the Down line. Having received permission to do so, Bray, with his guard, Hunt, on the footplate waving a red lamp, set off southwards.

Meanwhile driver Wilson was driving 2-2-2 No. 48 heading the 5.30 p.m. King's Cross to Leeds express and attempting to keep time despite the blizzard. He sped through Huntingdon and

Stukeley before he received the warning. The foreman platelayer had managed to place detonators by the Abbots Ripton Down distant signal, 1,100 yards from the accident, and had run on further and was about to place another detonator when the express passed him at more than 50 mph. When Wilson heard the detonators at the distant signal it was frozen at 'Clear', though had it been correctly indicating 'Danger' it would have given Wilson another 200 yards to stop. He closed the regulator, reversed and whistled for the brakes, the engine itself not being fitted and the train not having continuous brakes. He immediately saw a red light and heard an engine whistling, which was Hunt and Bray on the goods locomotive. Unfortunately on the falling gradient and with the rails slippery with ice and snow, Wilson was unable to stop and struck the tender of the Scotch express at 15–20 mph. His engine tipped over on its near side, the following coaches adding to the wreckage already there. 13 passengers died and 24 were injured, most casualties being in this second collision.

This accident had a great influence on railway operation. Captain Tyler, the Board of Trade inspecting officer, said that both accidents could have been avoided if fogmen had been placed at distant signals. He criticised the Great Northern's working of the block system that allowed the Abbots Ripton signalman to accept the Flying Scotsman to his home signal while a goods train was shunting only 68 yards ahead. He observed that 'the space interval had been reduced to the thickness of the signal post' and concluded that 'the block system so worked becomes a snare and a delusion'.

The Great Northern used slotted signal posts, and when the arm showed 'Clear' it was tucked inside the post. Ice and snow had frozen the arm in the slot and when the signalman pulled the arm up to Danger, it had failed to move and remained in the slot. Captain Tyler recommended that signals should normally show 'Danger' and only be cleared to allow a train to pass. The Great Northern replaced its slotted signals with those centrally balanced that automatically swung to 'Danger' if connecting wire snapped. It was not until 1892 that balanced signal arms were made a Board of Trade requirement. Another 1892 requirement was that the 'All Clear' light should be green and not white, which could so easily be confused with other lights.

1 May 1876 marked the opening of St Enoch station, Glasgow, with a through service to St Pancras. St Enoch was opened officially on 17 October 1876 by the Prince and Princess of Wales, who later became Edward VII and Queen Alexandra. Its glazed arch roof, 504 feet in length and 80 feet high, had a span of 198 feet. Initially a joint station, in 1883 it was taken over by the Glasgow & South Western.

Scottish railway companies adopted the shop parcel system, not taken up in England. At stations a passenger on a shopping trip could buy a packet of labels, priced at a penny each. A perforation ran through the centre of each label and when something was purchased at a shop you stuck on half of the label, then, when you finished your shopping, you went to the station cloakroom and on production of your half-labels were given your parcels, which the shop had delivered to the station.

Although goods trains had worked over the Settle & Carlisle line from 2 August 1875, it was not until 1 May 1876 that the line opened to passengers. As its route was longer than that of its rivals, to attract passengers wishing to travel from England to Scotland it offered superior luxury – Pullman cars as well as sleeping and drawing-room cars. A joint stock of vehicles was formed by the Midland and the two Scottish companies, the Glasgow & South Western and the North British, most of it of Midland design.

The line began when the Midland covetously eyed passengers going to Scotland by the West and East Coast routes and wished to cream off some of the profits. Already being able to get as far north as Settle, it realised that by building a 72-mile line from Settle to Carlisle, it could link there with the Glasgow & South Western and reach Glasgow over its lines and to Edinburgh over those of the North British. The idea was almost scuppered in 1866 when the Glasgow & South Western nearly amalgamated with the Caledonian Railway.

Construction of the line was far from easy as it climbed to a summit of 1,151 feet at Ais Gill with a ruling gradient of 1 in 100. The line was surveyed by Sharland, a young Tasmanian engineer. At one stage, his theodolite group were snowed in for three weeks at Gearstones Inn. Snow lay 18 inches above the lintel of the front door, which was 6 feet high. The stress of this work affected his health and he died a few years later at Torquay.

The first sod was cut in November 1869. The line was not simple to build as it required 19 viaducts, 3¼ miles of tunnelling, miles of cuttings blasted through rock or torn through clay of the most extraordinary tenacity, and embankments piled on peaty moors, on some parts of which a horse could not walk without sinking. To carry provisions to some of the navvies, a special cart was designed with a large barrel, instead of wheels, beneath the cart body. One visitor stated: 'I've often seen three horses in a row pulling at that concern over the moss till they sank up to their middle, and had to be drawn out one at a time by their necks to save their lives.'

John Sydney Crossley, the Midland's chief engineer, said: 'I have known the men blast the boulder clay-like rock, and within a few hours have to ladle out the same stuff from the same spot like soup in buckets. Or a man strikes a blow with his pick at what he thinks is clay, but there is a great boulder underneath, almost as hard as iron, and the man's wrists, arms and body are so shaken by the shock, that, disgusted, he flings down his tools, asks for his money, and is off.'

The wind in the Ingleton Valley could be so strong in the winter that for days bricklayers on the viaduct were unable to work for fear of being blown off the structure. There being little accommodation available for the hundreds of navvies engaged on the work, temporary accommodation had to be provided. In the stinking hovels, smallpox broke out in May 1871 and the toughest men in Europe died.

Normanton station was the refreshment stop and in 1871 it had been rebuilt with a long island platform, almost ¼ mile in length and the fourth longest in the country. Food could be ordered in advance and the Midland's summer timetable of 1887 stated that: 'A dinner of five courses, with dessert, and no fees to waiters, is prepared at Normanton and half an hour is allowed for the discussion and dispersal of the good things so liberally provided.'

The long gradients of the Settle and Carlisle made the line costly to work and in winter it could be blocked by snow, so in the 1960s British Railways began to run it down and in 1970 closed all the stations except Settle and Appleby. The last through trains were withdrawn in 1982, leaving only two local trains and almost no freight. Local authorities subsidised excursions for walkers, some stations being reopened on such occasions. Friends of the Settle &

Carlisle Line was formed as a support group and in 1989 the government stated that the line would be retained and developed so services were improved and eight stations reopened. The English Tourist Board set up the Settle & Carlisle Development Company to encourage small businesses to expand in the area.

From the summer of 1876, services provided by the three routes to Edinburgh were:

Departure time	10.00 a.m.	10.10 a.m.	10.35 a.m.	10.00 a.m.
Station	King's Cross	King's Cross	St Pancras	Euston
Class of passenger	1st & 2nd	1st, 2nd & 3rd	1st & 3rd	1st, 2nd & 3rd
Mileage	393	393	413	400
Arrival	7.00 p.m.	8.10 p.m.	8.42 p.m.	8.00 p.m.
Average speed (mph)	43.7	39.3	40.6	40.0

Bank Holiday Monday 7 August 1876 was very busy on the Somerset & Dorset (S&D) and 17 extra trains were being run. As the S&D had only a single line, in addition to the Absolute Block system, trains had booked crossing points in order to pass trains running in the opposite direction. Caleb Percy, in his office at Glastonbury, was responsible for crossing trains running out of course and was in contact with stations by means of the single-needle telegraph.

Because the 7.10 p.m. Special from Wimborne to Bath was hauled by 0-6-0ST No. 5, a powerful engine only a couple of months old and good at climbing banks, it reached Radstock 15 minutes before Percy's calculations.

Stationmaster John Jarrett at Radstock tried to contact Percy for instructions whether to hold it or send it on, but was unable to get through. Instead of holding it until an answer was received, he foolishly despatched it at 11.02 p.m.

Now between the crossing loops at Radstock and Wellow stations, Foxcote signal box had been opened the previous year when a colliery siding was laid. There was no crossing loop there, the box merely working the siding and passing on trains. Things were slack at Foxcote: regulations required that the train books were to be examined by the Radstock stationmaster, but he had omitted to do so. Furthermore, only the home signals were lit, both distant signals were unlit because they had run out of oil and it was the frugal practice of the S&D not to light them on moonlit nights.

In charge of Foxcote that night was Alfred Dando, aged 20. Formerly a miner, he had been appointed porter at Radstock on 22 May that year and, showing promise, was appointed to the Foxcote box. After a week's training there, he took charge.

When the 7.10 p.m. Wimborne–Bath arrived, as the block was still occupied by the previous Up train Alfred held his signals at danger. In due course the block was cleared and the train sent forward.

Unfortunately things were every bit as slack at Wellow as they were at Foxcote and Radstock. Stationmaster James Sleep had been on duty from 5.00 a.m. until 6.30 p.m. for £1 3s 0d a week. On such a busy day he should have remained at his post and not gone off to quench his thirst at the Hope & Anchor, Midford. Assisting him, and in charge during his absence, was 15-year-old James Hillard, also in charge of the telegraph despite a rule which stipulated that the telegraph clerk was not allowed to signal 'Line clear' unless authorised by the stationmaster.

A special train carrying spectators from the Bath Regatta should have left Bath at 9.15 p.m., but due to a shortage of coaches did not actually leave Bath until 10.43. In due course it arrived at Wellow with Sleep travelling on it from Midford and at 11.03 was sent on by Hillard, who claimed that he had received 'Line clear' from Foxcote. Now two trains were approaching each other head-on between Wellow and Foxcote.

Driver John Hamlin on 0-6-0ST No. 7 heading the 9.15 saw the red signal at Foxcote, applied the brake, blew his whistle and saw the Up train approaching him about 25 yards away, but was able to place his engine into backward gear before the crash. Henry Pullin, assistant guard in the rear van, when he heard the whistle, acted and had his brake fully applied when the collision occurred.

Only No. 7 was derailed, but the first three coaches of its train were smashed, killing 10 adults and two children – plus the front guard. None of the passengers of the other train were killed and its coaches only slightly damaged. Rescue work was helped by

The opening of the Glasgow & Garnkirk Railway on 27 September 1831, seen from Proven Mill Bridge, Glasgow. (David Hill)

A Liverpool & Manchester Railway train at Rainhill, 1831. Passengers on a stage coach look down at the new form of transport. (T. T. Bury)

The London & Birmingham Railway's Euston station, 1837. Most of the carriages on the far left are open. The closed coach has a luggage rack on its roof. (T. T. Bury)

A London & North Western Railway 4-4-2T Precursor Tank passes over Bushey water troughs. (Author's collection)

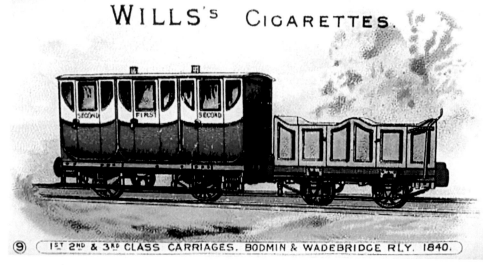

WILLS'S CIGARETTES.

⑨ 1ST 2ND & 3RD CLASS CARRIAGES. BODMIN & WADEBRIDGE RLY. 1840.

Bodmin & Wadebridge first-, second- and third-class carriages in 1840 depicted on a cigarette card. First-class passengers have a smoother ride in the centre of the coach, while the second class are bumped up and down above the axle. The third-class passengers enjoy the brakeman's company and plenty of fresh air. (Author's collection)

An early aircraft tries to race a London & North Western Scottish express over Shap Summit. (Author's collection)

A North British Railway 4-4-2 leaves Edinburgh Waverley station. (Author's collection)

Lancashire & Yorkshire Railway 4-4-2 No. 1421 with 7-foot-5-inch-diameter driving wheels. (Author's collection)

South Eastern & Chatham Railway 4-4-0 No. 504. (Author's collection)

Caledonian Railway goods 4-6-0 No. 918. (Author's collection)

Woodhead Tunnel
on the Great Central
Railway: No. 264
is leaving while
two 4-4-0s enter.
(Author's collection)

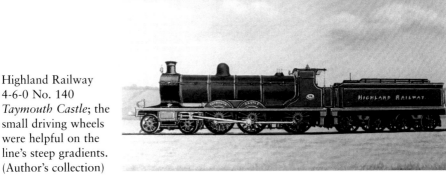

Highland Railway
4-6-0 No. 140
Taymouth Castle; the
small driving wheels
were helpful on the
line's steep gradients.
(Author's collection)

London & South Western Railway T14 class 4-6-0 No. 443, probably on a
working to or from Bournemouth *circa* 1912. The class had two nicknames:
'Double-breasters' due to the massive front end and 'Paddle-boxes' due to the
enormous splashers. (Author's collection)

Great Northern Railway 4-4-2 No. 251. Having a pony truck rather than a set of driving wheels as the last axle enables it to have a wide firebox. (Author's collection)

Great Western Railway 4-6-0 No. 4001 *Dog Star*. (Author's collection)

Midland & Great Northern Railway 4-4-2T No. 41. (Author's collection)

North Staffordshire Railway 0-6-2T No. 167. (Author's collection)

A train of what looks like Midland Railway stock hauled by Glasgow & South Western Railway 4-4-0 No. 86 and a 4-6-0. (Author's collection)

Glasgow & South Western Railway railmotor No. 1. (Author's collection)

North Eastern
Railway 4-6-0T
No. 695. (Author's
collection)

Victoria station
circa 1910 with a
Brighton express
hauled by H1 class
4-4-2 No. 40.
(Author's collection)

A train on the London, Tilbury & Southend Railway hauled by 4-4-2T No. 54
Mile End. (Author's collection)

Midland Railway Compound 4-4-0 No. 1013 heading a Liverpool and Manchester express. This class was the only really successful British compound. (Author's collection)

Metropolitan Railway 0-6-4T No. 94 *Lord Aberconway*. (Author's collection)

A Great Eastern Railway 4-4-0, later LNER class D15, crosses Trowse swing bridge. (Author's collection)

Left: This oil-fired Great Eastern Railway 2-4-0, decorated to haul the royal train, has No. 751 on the cabside plate, though the colour artist has painted the wrong number on the buffer beam. The locomotive was built in 1886 and this picture was made before 1908 when it was rebuilt as a 4-4-0. (Author's collection)

Left: A Great Northern, Piccadilly & Brompton Railway train at Piccadilly *circa* 1907. (Author's collection).

A 1954 advertisement for the Snowdon Mountain Railway.

GOLDEN ARROW
JIG-SAW PUZZLE

40 Pieces Interlocking.

The GOLDEN ARROW LIMITED
(London — Paris de Luxe service)

A Southern Railway Golden Arrow jigsaw depicting Lord Nelson class 4-6-0 No. 853 *Sir Richard Grenville*. This engine once became partly derailed and then rerailed itself. (Author's collection)

A London & North Eastern Railway Pullman express to Edinburgh approaches Hadley Tunnel headed by 4-6-2 No. 2549 *Persimmon*. (Author's collection)

A London Midland & Scottish Railway poster depicting the construction of a Coronation class 4-6-2 in 1937. (Author's collection)

A postcard depicting the Forth Bridge. (Author's collection)

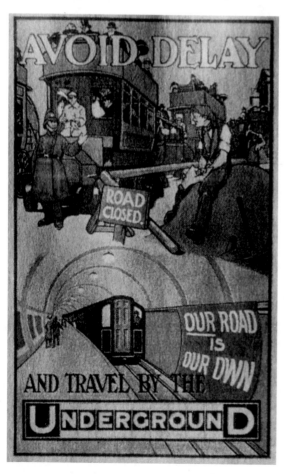

An early poster advocating a tube railway. (Author's collection)

A 1908 poster showing how easy it is to use the underground. (John Hassall)

Who could resist renting a London & North Eastern Railway camping coach in 1939? (Author's collection)

Above left: In 1935 the London & North Eastern Railway advertised its new express service by depicting streamlined A4 class 4-6-2 No. 2059 *Silver Link*. (Author's collection)

Above right: The Southern Railway advertises its road-rail container service in the 1930s. (Author's collection)

Below: The Britannia Bridge over the Menai Strait around 1934. Damaged by fire in 1970, a road deck was added in 1980. (Author's collection)

Above: A London, Midland & Scottish Railway poster of 1930 publicises the Liverpool & Manchester Railway centenary celebrations. (Author's collection)

Below left: A WWII poster issued by the Big Four and London Transport. (Author's collection)

Below right: A WWII poster issued by the Railway Executive Committee. (Author's collection)

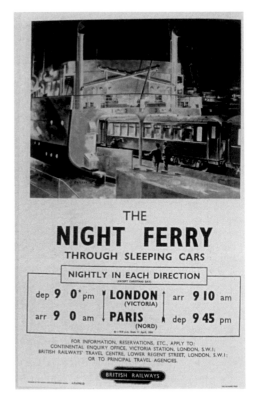

Above left: The Western Region advertises a car-carrying service. (Author's collection)

Above right: The Southern Region advertises through sleeping cars between Victoria and Paris, 1953. (Author's collection)

Left: The all-Pullman Brighton Belle in 1958. (Author's collection)

the light of bonfires made from the wreckage. Those who walked from the accident scene to Bath did not arrive until 6.00 a.m., 'exceedingly tired and footsore, as well as being out of sorts'.

The corpses were taken to the barn of the adjacent Paglinch Farm and laid out to be identified. Unfortunately they proved to be a magnet for the ghoulish and both the coroner and the local vicar addressed the crowd, saying that they hoped only immediate relatives would view the bodies. The local paper reported: 'Notwithstanding the distance from Bath [about 7 miles] hundreds of the inhabitants of the city visited the spot during the day.'

Clearance was much quicker than today. By noon the line was open again for traffic, but numerous articles belonging to the killed and injured were stolen from the wreckage including a bag belonging to Miss Noke, which contained her ticket confirming that she was insured with the Railway Passengers Association Co., entitling her to £1 10s 0d per week in case of accident. The police eventually recovered this ticket. Messrs Powell & Powell, upholsterers and auctioneers of Bath, provided coffins for the 11 adults and two children for £46, and the day following the accident they were conveyed to Paglinch Farm by special train.

Events held to raise money for the widow and children of guard Wills, who lost his life, raised £600. Four children orphaned by the accident were offered employment on the railway, three eventually rising to become stationmasters and one a head office inspector.

At the inquest the jury's verdict was the accident had been caused by the criminal carelessness of the Wellow stationmaster, James Sleep. It said that John Jarrett, the Radstock stationmaster, although not guilty of manslaughter, deserved severe censure for sending on a train without a crossing order, as did Caleb Percy for not providing a crossing order. Young Hillard, due to his age and long hours of duty, was considered free of consequences. At the Somerset Spring Assizes, James Sleep was charged with manslaughter and found guilty, but the jury recommended him for mercy considering his 'high character'. The judge sentenced him to 12 months' imprisonment without hard labour. Percy was dismissed with a month's salary in lieu of notice and Sleep and Jarrett sacked.

An interesting aside to the accident is that George Alfred Quick, later chief clerk at Bath S&D locomotive depot, was unofficially taking a ride to Radstock on the footplate of the

9.15 and jumped off before the collision, so injuring an already defective leg that it had to be amputated.

Known as 'Crutchy Quick', he certainly lived up to his name. Once a driver had arrived at Bath, gone to Quick and said that he had been given green signals all the way to Bath – although in truth he had run through many reds. He also mentioned that he had a revolver. Quick said: 'Let's see.' The driver took it out of his pocket to show him. Quick as a flash, Quick whipped it into an open drawer, locked it and threw the key to someone on the other side of the office. The driver was in fact mad, and had to be taken to Wells Asylum.

The 1870 Education Act meant that most people in the country became literate, and this benefitted station bookstalls. By this time W. H. Smith had 290 in England and Wales and was probably the world's first multiple retailer. The price of books had been reduced. At the beginning of the 1860s, the first editions of new novels were issued in three volumes at £1 11s 6d, and as this was more than a working man's weekly wage most were purchased by circulating libraries. By the 1890s, a novel had become a single volume selling for 6s 0d. Some novels were printed in cheap editions for 1s 6d or even 1s 0d. Fast trains could cause problems to bookstall staff: expresses speeding through Tiverton Junction blew the papers about. The manager's solution? Large green curtains to shield the stock. In 1891 the Railway & General Automatic Company had a lending scheme whereby you could pay to take a book from a slot machine and then replace it at the end of a journey. Unfortunately the faith that passengers would, in fact, do this was more praiseworthy than practised.

1877

The first British express to be named (or one of the first) was the Granville Express, which started running in March 1877 between Charing Cross and Ramsgate. It was initiated by the proprietor of the Granville Hotel in Ramsgate who arranged with the South Eastern Railway to run special trains for his weekend visitors, Down on Friday afternoons and returning on Mondays mornings. Initially first class only, from June second-class passengers were admitted. Not to be outdone, in April 1878 the rival London, Chatham & Dover Railway inaugurated the Granville & Westgate-on-Sea Special, running each weekday and catering for all three classes.

On 14 April 1877 a line was opened that offered passengers free travel. It was the Stocksbridge Railway, nearly 2 miles in length, built by Samuel Fox to serve his ironworks near Sheffield. Most of the passengers were either Fox employees or Penistone Grammar School pupils and travelled at their own risk until services were withdrawn in 1931.

The North British Railway, which had absorbed the Edinburgh, Perth & Dundee in 1862, could only reach Dundee by the ferry crossing from Tayport, the whole journey from Edinburgh to Dundee taking a minimum of 3 hours and 20 minutes for a journey of 46 miles when the weather was favourable.

E. L. Ahrons in *Locomotive & Train Working in the Latter Part of the Nineteenth Century* has a good account of this trip.

The most awkward portion of the North British system was that which professed to form some sort of connection between Edinburgh and the northern cities of Dundee and Aberdeen. A journey northwards from Edinburgh through Fifeshire was not one to be undertaken lightly. From Edinburgh a local train conveyed the passengers to Granton, where they were transshipped to the ferry boat which crossed the Forth to Burntisland. The waters of the Firth of Forth can be very unpleasant at certain seasons of the year, and a bitterly cold east wind can blow there in a manner which seems to beat its method of blowing anywhere else.

The passengers' luggage was placed on barrows at [Edinburgh] Waverley station and these were wheeled on to a couple of fish trucks attached to the Granton train. At Granton these barrows were trundled off the fish trucks on to the ferry boat and it was only on their arrival at Burntisland that the luggage was removed from them and placed in the vans of the train waiting to take the passengers to Tayport. Then there ensued a journey of exceeding slowness from Burntisland to Ladybank Junction, where a few coaches for Perth were detached, and the slowness increased with painful impressiveness from Ladybank to Tayport, where the unfortunate through passengers were again transferred to another ferry in order to cross the Tay. Eventually they were landed at Broughty Ferry Pier. Here another train had to be requisitioned, which ran over the branch to Broughty Junction, where the engine had to reverse, and eventually the saddened cavalcade reached Dundee.

Thomas Bouch proposed a bridge be built across the Tay, and the railway shareholders were excited that Scotland would possess the longest bridge in the world. Unfortunately they did not realise that Bouch was really a very inefficient engineer. He had been appointed consulting engineer to many small railway companies, but they had overlooked his deficiencies: one had timber bridges of inadequate dimensions made with untreated wood, while the rails had been insecurely fixed and the sleepers laid at 4-foot instead of 3-foot spacing. Another railway engineered by Bouch found its track was substandard; level crossing gates failed to close properly and an engine pit lacked drainage and was too small for a man to enter.

The Act for building the Tay Bridge was passed in 1870, the building contract placed in 1871 and the first train crossed on 26 September 1877, Bouch receiving a knighthood for his work. The opening of the bridge led to the North British carrying 85 per cent of Edinburgh–Dundee traffic. Then on 28 December 1879 tragedy struck – the bridge collapsed under the last train of the day. All 75 passengers and the train crew on board died, making this the only British railway accident where no passenger survived.

Subsequent investigation showed that imperfect castings for the bridge had been delivered, with holes and cracks filled with Beaumont egg, a concoction of carbon and wax; that no one was aware that the concrete had burst the iron columns it filled; that trains had crossed the bridge at speeds in excess of 40 mph when the restriction was 25 mph; that bridge maintenance was in the charge of a man whose experience was in bricklaying; and that Bouch had made no allowance for wind speed, which at times reached 90 mph. Sir Thomas Bouch died 10 months after the collapse of the Tay Bridge.

After his death another Bouch bridge was found to be seriously faulty. This was the bridge over the South Esk on the North British Arbroath & Montrose Railway. Colonel Yolland, who had sat on the Court of Inquiry into the Tay Bridge disaster, as inspecting officer for this new line, observed that the South Esk Bridge was curved, whereas that on the plans was straight, and that some of the piers were not perpendicular. He tested the bridge with dead and rolling loads and it became distorted. It was demolished and rebuilt.

A new Tay Bridge was built 60 yards west of the old structure and some of the old girders were recycled, though the new bridge had double track rather than single. Opened on 11 July 1887, it is more than 2 miles in length and consists of 85 spans, the widest with a span of 245 feet.

In 1880 only 51 per cent of passengers used the North British between Edinburgh and Dundee, the remaining 49 per cent travelling all the way by the Caledonian Railway. 28 old timber bridges on the Caledonian were being reconstructed, these causing delays on that line and passengers used the North British route, which despite having to use two ferries, beat the Caledonian time between Edinburgh and Aberdeen.

On 1 June 1877 the St Ives branch was opened, the last broad gauge line to be constructed. Although it had to be converted to standard gauge 15 years later, it would not have been practical to construct it to standard gauge as the lines serving it were broad gauge.

In 1877 a Royal Commission on Railway Accidents was instigated. The appalling facts were disclosed that in the years 1874–76 as many as 3,982 persons were killed and 16,762 injured on railways in the United Kingdom; 2,249 of those killed and 10,305 of the injured were railway servants.

Some of the statistics that emerged at the Royal Commission make startling reading in these days of health and safety. 'Mr Hargreaves, a station master on the Manchester and Liverpool line said "Drivers sometimes make ten hours overtime at a stretch and four to five hours' overtime is quite a regular thing. This overtime is usually unpaid."'

Driver Weston on the North British Railway complained that he had great difficulty in keeping his eyes open. He told the Commission:

I have been on duty sixteen hours a day in succession and on the third day I went on the engine at 7.30 in the morning and left it at 11 or 12 at night. I took my meals and everything on the engine. I never left the engine. I complained to the foreman and told him I had difficulty in keeping my eyes open. Upon the third day I told him that I could not hold myself responsible if anything occurred to the engine or the passengers and that it was unfair to force us to do it.

He reported this to the Superintendent, Mr Wheatley. He called me up and said "Weston, unless you retract those words,

I will dismiss you." I said "Mr Wheatley, you have the power to dismiss me, but I cannot retract what I said."

This story reveals three facts: the incredibly long hours drivers spent on a noisy, vibrating footplate; the arbitrary power of a superintendent to sack anyone who complained; and the devotion to duty of Weston, who placed the safety of his passengers and his train above everything else.

1879

On 1 August 1879 Glasgow Central station was opened by the Caledonian Railway. To the north of the station was a four-track bridge across the Clyde, 700 feet in length and 55 feet wide, designed by William Arrol, who later designed the Tay, Tower and Forth bridges. The Central station suffered from poor planning: its eight platforms were short and narrow, long trains bottling shorter trains in adjacent platforms; the concourse was too cramped to allow free movement and there was no proper provision for carriage sidings. The result was that between 1901 and 1905, Central was widened to offer 13 platforms and the Clyde Bridge widened to carry eight tracks.

The first regular dining car to operate was inaugurated on 26 September 1879 by the Great Northern. Initially such cars were first class only and passengers sat in them for the whole of the journey. Cooking was by solid fuel or from gas cylinders carried below the floor, but later electricity was used, the current generated on board. Railway companies had mixed feelings about introducing restaurant cars as they were heavy vehicles and added to the weight of the train.

When Queensbury station, near Bradford, opened on 1 December 1879, it consisted of exchange platforms, 400 feet below the level of the town, which was situated 1,150 feet above sea level. In 1890 the Great Northern laid an approach road and opened a new station, which was almost unique as apart from Ambergate, it was the only British station with continuous platforms on all three sides of a triangular junction.

The year 1879 was a bad one for accidents, no fewer than 75 passengers being killed and 602 injured, while that year 1,541 defective rails had been found, 1,270 broken tyres and 496 broken axles. The most serious accident in 1879 was the Tay Bridge disaster on 28 December 1879 (*see* page 164).

In 1879 a dispute occurred between a group of Great Western enginemen and Sir Daniel Gooch, the company's locomotive superintendent. The footplatemen had framed a polite petition against new and inferior promotion prospects, and presented it to Sir Daniel. He glanced at it and said: 'Damn the signatures! Have you got the men to back them up?' The answer was 'No' because the Amalgamated Society of Railway Servants (*see* page 148) was weak.

One of the enginemen who had approached Sir Daniel was Charles Perry, who realised that their needs were different from those of other railway servants and so they should set up their own organisation. Colleagues at Birmingham, Bristol, Newport, Pontypool and Sheffield were contacted. On 9 February 1880 Perry wrote to the first member of the Sheffield branch of the Associated Society of Locomotive Engineers and Firemen:

> The matter lies in a nutshell – we want a large sum of money to protect us enginemen and firemen from the rapacity of our employers, and at once, we cannot afford to wait three or four years: we must wait one year: the larger sum we pay into it, the sooner our position will be impregnable, and once the directors know that we are preparing in reality to defend ourselves, superintendents will think twice before they turn the screw.

The London & North Western cast envious eyes at the Festiniog Railway's Blaenau slate traffic and on 18 July 1872 secured an Act for building a line from Conway, either on the Festiniog gauge or wider, but not exceeding standard gauge. The tunnel at Blaenau caused delay and expense: 3,861 yards in length and with the summit of the line 790 feet above sea level, it opened 22 July 1879.

The Great Western also desired to gain some of these slate profits and so attacked Festiniog from the south with a line from Bala opening on 1 November 1882. It met the short 1-foot-11½-inch gauge Festiniog & Blaenau Railway, which on 10 September 1883 was converted to standard gauge, while the narrow gauge rails lifted were economically recycled as check rails on tight curves. The London & North Western and Great Western remained unconnected at Blaenau until 20 April 1964, when a link was laid between Blaenau North (the ex- London & North Western station) and Blaenau Central (the ex-Great Western). This was so that Trawsfynydd nuclear power station could have access from the Conwy Valley line, as the Liverpool Waterworks reservoir in the Trewerwyn Valley had flooded part of the ex-Great Western route and rather than facing the expense of building a deviation, the Great Western line closed.

1880

An example of competition between rival railway companies could be seen between Leeds and London in 1880 when the Midland, Great Central and Great Northern all provided services. On 1 June 1880 the Midland replied to the Great Northern's introduction of a dining car by providing faster trains, the Great Northern responded by speeding up its own services, but by October 1880 economics forced it to withdraw three of its trains.

In 1880 F. W. Webb, chief mechanical engineer of the London & North Western, invented the foot warmer in which heat was generated by the chemical reaction of acetate of soda. Tins containing this compound were heated in a vat of boiling water prior to use and the recrystallisation of the salt as it cooled down gave off latent heat. One could give new life to an expiring foot warmer by giving it a violent shaking and it would provide heat for several hours.

The line to Oban opened on 30 June 1880. The contractor responsible for constructing the line in Glen Dochart built for his navvies wind- and water-tight huts 'on a dry stance alongside a running stream'. The timber huts were almost palatial, having double-skinned walls, the interspaces filled with sawdust for insulation, while the roofs were of tarred felt – much quieter in the frequent wet weather than corrugated iron. In the centre of each hut was a room for the keeper and his wife, who cooked for the men, with bunk beds for a dozen navvies being provided at each end.

The line has severe gradients: eastbound trains having to contend with 1 in 47 and those westbound, 1 in 49. Glaciation assisted construction by offering smooth straight valley slopes, which allow railways to gain height gradually by cutting a shelf on the mountain.

In the Pass of Brander, the Callander-Oban line passes along the steep slopes of Ben Cruachan – which is subject to landslides. Initially watchmen patrolled the line to warn trains of any fallen boulders, but in August 1881 the company's secretary, John Anderson suggested an automatic warning system. This was a wire fence beside the track; a falling stone would break a wire thus throwing a weighted signal to 'Danger'. The sound the wind made vibrating the wires gave rise to the nickname 'Anderson's piano'. It was extremely unfortunate that on one occasion a boulder fell when a train was approaching: the warning signals fell to 'Danger' but too late, the engine ran into the obstruction and most of the train was derailed. In recent years experiments have taken place with an electric sensor system to detect rock movements.

The Fenians tried to wreck a London & North Western train on the night of 12/13 September 1880 but were foiled when John Heath, a platelayer, discovered the dynamite beneath the rails near Bushey. Fishplates connecting the rails had been removed from the Down fast line and a brown paper parcel, 14 inches by 8 inches, placed in a hole beneath the outside rail. John Heath opened the parcel and found what he supposed to be red lead. He replaced the fishplates and carried the signal lamps back to Bushey station, for that was the purpose for which he had come to the spot. On the way back he told Ganger Joseph Holwood what he had discovered. Holwood immediately went to the spot, collected the parcel and took it to the station masters at Bushey and Watford. They telegraphed the information to Euston and soon afterwards Superintendent Copping, head of the detective department, accompanied by two subordinates, arrived at Bushey. There they were joined by an inspector from the Hertfordshire Constabulary and a detective from the Metropolitan Police. It was considered that the material in the parcel was dynamite. Four pieces of rubber tubing had been filled with gunpowder and at the end of each tube was a large percussion cap. It was designed so that a train would explode the caps, which would then set fire to the gunpowder and thus cause the dynamite to explode.

On 5 December 1880 a single line tunnel was opened at Farnworth for use by Down trains. This was because the original double-track 295-yard long tunnel gave insufficient clearance for the Pullman cars that the Midland was intending to run between Manchester and Scotland via Settle. From that date, the original tunnel only carried Up trains.

It is not always realised that it was not until the coming of the railway network that it was possible to have football and rugby leagues, as until the railway era it was impossible to move teams and supporters readily around the countryside as travel was difficult, slow and expensive, whereas railways enabled teams to play nationwide. Such teams as Arsenal, Manchester United and Chelsea deliberately built their grounds near railways stations to provide easy access for spectators. For about a century from 1880, football specials were a Saturday feature and enabled railway companies to use rolling stock and locomotives that might otherwise have been lying idle. Similarly, horses and racegoers could come from a wider area.

11

The Severn Bridge

1881

A highly scenic line was the North Wales Narrow Gauge Railway, which opened from Dinas to South Snowdon on 14 May 1881. It remained just a branch line until 30 March 1922 when the Portmadoc, Beddgelert & South Snowdon Railway made an end-on junction, the two lines becoming the Welsh Highland Railway. At Portmadoc a link was made with the Festiniog Railway and through working begun. This proved a mistake as the economically weak Welsh Highland soaked up the profits of the Festiniog. From 1925 trains, were summer-only on the Welsh Highland and ceased altogether on 29 September 1936, The line was dismantled in 1942, the scrap proving useful for the war effort. Fortunately, this was not the end of the story because with the development of tourism and the need to offer more activities to bring people into the area, yet not increase road traffic, the line was relaid, bringing economic benefits to the area.

Initially carriage lighting was by oil, then experiments with gas started in 1857, but the first use of electricity was in *Beatrice*, a Pullman car running between Victoria and Brighton and demonstrated to the press on 14 October 1881. It was a world first.

One of the first journals published by a railway company was the *South Western Gazette*, which appeared in 1881. This was followed in 1888 by the *Great Western Railway Magazine,* initially published by that company's temperance society, but taken over by the GWR in 1904. Under Felix Pole, its circulation rose from

3,000 copies of each issue to an amazing 65,000. By 1914 most of the English railways had similar journals, but there were none for Scottish lines.

The Severn Bridge between Sharpness and Lydney opened on 17 October 1879, exactly a century after the first iron bridge in the world was constructed, which was also built across the Severn. The Severn Bridge was the longest English railway bridge and third longest in Britain, (if the Solway viaduct is discounted), following those spanning the Tay and the Forth.

The 4,162-foot long bridge consisted of a series of iron bowstring girders resting on cast-iron piers filled with concrete and rock. It was jointly owned by the Midland and Great Western railways, giving the former company valuable access to coal in the Forest of Dean. An interesting feature of the bridge was that it had a swing span over the Gloucester & Berkeley Canal. An engine driver was required to be on duty on one of the day shifts in order to maintain the engine and ensure the machinery operating the span was in good working order, the signalman on the other shift assisting in cleaning and coaling. Two boilers were used alternately for a fortnight, one being in use while the other was washed out. The swing span was left open at night when the signal box was closed.

The opening of the Severn Tunnel in 1886 somewhat eclipsed the bridge but on winter Sundays, when the civil engineer was in complete possession of the tunnel, trains were diverted across the bridge.

The end of the bridge came on 25 October 1960 when it was struck by an oil tanker, destroying two spans. Unfortunately for British Railways, under the Merchant Shipping Act, the limited liability for damage through collision did not exceed the sum equal to about 24 times the net registered tonnage of the vessel, so British Railways only received £5,000, a quite inadequate amount to repair the damage amounting to £294,000. The bridge was dismantled in 1967.

On 1 November 1881 the North British signed an agreement with the Carron Company to provide merry-go-round trains between the company's iron field at Cadder and the Falkirk furnaces. Three trains of 30 wagons were used: one en route, one being loaded and one being unloaded. The merry-go-round concept was not generally adopted until 80 years later.

1882

In 1882 the Great Northern built the first British side-corridor coach, a six-wheel first class for the East Coast Joint Stock. It had four compartments, seating four persons, and separate toilets for ladies and gentlemen. The total seating accommodation was 16, whereas for an ordinary coach without a corridor and lavatories a further 14 could have been accommodated – so the provision of this facility came at considerable cost to the company.

Sometimes a railway company was short of rolling stock and needed to borrow some. Between about 1880 and 1890 the Midland Railway regularly borrowed three 20-coach trains from the Glasgow & South Western for the Bradford-Morecambe Easter excursion traffic, returning them about a week later.

With the aim of reducing costs by getting the steam to be used twice, Webb built his first compound locomotives for the London & North Western in 1882. The 2-2-2-0 had two outside high-pressure cylinders and one inside low pressure cylinder, steam first entering the outside cylinders before moving to the inside cylinder. To reduce friction and obviate the need for long coupling rods, the driving wheels were uncoupled, this occasionally leading to problems with the valve gear sending the driving wheels in opposite directions! This was because they had loose-eccentric gear fitted to the low pressure cylinder, which contributed to free-running but was not under a driver's control. When an engine backed onto its train, the gear would be in reverse and needed a few inches of movement forward to reset the gear, but sometimes, when starting, the wheels driven by the high pressure cylinders would slip and the exhaust steam enter the low pressure cylinder and cause the wheels to turn in the opposite direction. Once the high pressure cylinders got the train moving, all was well.

In 1886 Worsdell of the North Eastern built inside cylinder compounds, with both cylinders within the frame. Worsdell's chief draughtsman was Walter Mackersie Smith who devised a compound opposite to Webb's system. It had a high pressure inside cylinder feeding two low pressure outside cylinders. It was much neater than Webb's system as all cylinders were about the same size and avoided a huge inside cylinder with heavy working parts.

Its success inspired Johnson of the Midland to build a three-cylinder compound, which was continued by his successor Deeley. The Smith-Deeley compound, a powerful and economic machine, grew to a class of 240 engines, the mainstay of the LMS, the last of the class was built in 1932. With the Smith and Smith-Deeley compound, the engine could be worked as simple, semi-compound or full compound, this flexibility meaning that it could use simple expansion on all three cylinders when starting when the greatest power was needed; semi-compound working with a limited amount of high pressure steam being admitted to the low pressure steam chest when the engine was heavily loaded or climbing, and full compound working used when proceeding at speed. Tests in 1924–5 revealed that the Midland compounds offered greater fuel economy than the larger simple expansion 4-6-0s.

The original British Pullman Car Company was set up in 1882 and all cars running in Great Britain were built in the USA until 1908, all subsequent cars were built in Britain. On 1 January 1963 the Pullman Car Company became a wholly owned subsidiary of British Railways.

1883

An unusual private branch, which opened in 1883, was a ½-mile long branch off the Midland's Leeds to Ilkley line. It opened to carry materials for the construction of the West Riding County Asylum and later the building's completion brought supplies and fuel. A variety of motive power was used including steam, battery and overhead electric. The line closed in 1951.

On 3 August 1883, at Brighton, Magnus Volk opened the very first electric railway in England; it ran on a 2-foot-8½-inch gauge – the oldest electric railway in the world still in operation. This innovation was largely ignored by the main line railways and most of the subsequent early British electric lines were underground. Although electric trains were cheaper in the long run, they needed a huge initial investment with a third rail, or overhead wire, both costly, so large-scale electrification did not arrive in Britain until the 1960s when a demand grew for cleaner motive power.

On 15 September 1883 the Great Western Railway issued a revised rule book, other railway companies producing something similar. Some of the paragraphs give an interesting insight into the running of the line at that time.

24. Greenwich time, which is adopted throughout all the railways in Great Britain, will be sent to the principal stations daily by telegraph and clocks must be regulated accordingly.

25. In order to insure uniform time being kept at all the Stations on the Line, to which the time is not telegraphed the following regulations must be strictly observed:-
   (a) Each Head Guard must, before starting on his journey, satisfy himself that his Watch is correct with the Clock at the Station where his journey starts, and must again compare it, by the Clock at the Station where his journey ends, before commencing his return journey.
   (b) The Guard in charge of the first Passenger Train (starting after 10.15 a.m.) stopping at all Stations on the portion of the Main Line or Branch over which it runs, must, on his arrival at each Station, give the Station Master or other person in charge the precise time and, in the event of the time given by the Guard differing from that of the Station Clock, the latter must be altered to agree.

52. Every Guard, Signalman, Engine Driver, Gateman and Ganger or Platelayer, will be provided with Detonators, which he is always to have ready for use whilst on duty; and every person in charge of a station must keep a supply of these Signals in a suitable place known by, and easy of access at all times to every person connected with the Station.
   All the persons named will be held responsible for keeping up the proper supply of Detonators.

53. These signals must be placed on the rail (label upwards) by bending the clasp round the upper flange of the rail to prevent their falling off. When an engine explodes a Detonator, the Engine Driver must instantly shut off steam, and bring his engine to a stand, and then proceed cautiously to the place of obstruction, or until he receives an "All Right" signal.

54. Detonators must be carefully handled, as they are liable to explode if roughly treated. It is necessary to keep them well

protected from damp. At intervals of not more than two months, one from each person's stock must be tested, to ensure that they are in good condition.

61. During foggy weather or snow storms it is the duty of the Station Master to take care that Fog-signalmen are employed, when necessary, at all the places where their services are required.

149. The signalman must frequently examine and try his fixed Signals to see that they work well, are kept clean, and show properly. Great care must be used in putting on a Distant Signal; it is not sufficient merely to move the lever, but the Signalman must at the same time watch the Signal or its Repeater, so as to ascertain that it obeys the lever, and goes fully on to "Danger." He must take care that the Signal wires are kept at the proper length by means of the regulating screws or links, so as to compensate for the expansion and contraction caused by variations of temperature.

209. Should a Guard wish to attract the attention of the Engine Driver, he must, in addition to using the Communication [cord] where such exists, apply his hand-break (*sic*) sharply, and release it suddenly. This operation repeated several times is almost certain, from the check it occasions, to attract the attention of the Engine Driver, to whom the necessary "Caution" or "Danger" Signal, as the case may require, must be exhibited. Should the train be fitted with a continuous break, (sic), with which the Guard has a connection, or which he has the means of applying, he must apply it and thus attract the attention of the engine driver.

210. When the Engine Driver gives three or more short, sharp whistles, or sound the break (sic) whistle (when a special whistle is supplied for the purpose), or applies the Communication, where such exists, the Guard, or guards, must immediately apply the breaks.

212. When from any cause a train is unable to proceed at a greater speed than four miles an hour, the Guard, if there

be only one, or the Rear Guard, if there be more than one, must immediately go back, or send some other competent person, 1,000 yards, or to the nearest Signal-box if there be one within that distance, in which case the Signalman must be advised of the circumstances. The person who goes back must follow the train at that distance, and use proper Danger Signals, so as to stop any following train, until assistance arrives, or the train which causes the obstruction is shunted.

213. When a train is stopped by an accident or from any cause (except where it is efficiently protected by Fixed Signals), the Guard, if there be only one, or the Rear Guard if there be more than one, must immediately go back 1,200 yards to stop any following train, and in addition to Hand Signals, he must take no less than six Detonators (to be used by day as well as night), which must be placed upon the line of rails on which the stoppage has happened, as follows, viz:-

    1 detonator at a distance of 400 yards from his train,

    1 detonator at a distance of 800 yards from his train and

    3 detonators, ten yards apart, at a distance of 1,200 yards from his train.

He must also conspicuously exhibit his Hand Danger Signal to stop any coming train. The Guard must not return to his train until recalled by the Engine Driver sounding the whistle of his engine, and when recalled, he must leave the two most distant Detonators, and return to his train, taking up the other Detonators on his way.

244. When a deficiency of room occurs in a train while on the journey, the Guard must request the Station Master to telegraph to the next Station where carriages are kept, to have one or more in readiness to attach on the arrival of the train, reporting the fact in his journal, He must also report in his journal if he has habitually either an excess or deficiency of room in his train.

247. Prisoners under the charge of police, and persons afflicted with insanity, must not be placed with other Passengers, but in a separate compartment.

248. In the event of any Passenger being drunk or disorderly, to the annoyance of others, the Guard is to use all gentle means to

stop the nuisance; failing which, he must, for the safety and convenience of all, remove the offender from the train at the first Station. The Guard must obtain the name and address of the offender, and also of one, at least, of the Passengers present at the time; he must also take care that the offender's luggage is put out of the train before it proceeds on its journey.

252. Every Head Goods Guard must have with him his Watch, a Red, a Green, and a White Flag, a box of Detonators (not less than twelve), a Hand Signal Lamp, a full set of Tail and Side lamps, two or more spare Coupling Chains, a Break-stick, two Sprags, and two Hand-scotches.

258a. REGULATIONS FOR THE CONVEYANCE BY GOODS TRAINS OF EXPLOSIVES AND DANGEROUS GOODS.
The vehicles must be placed as far as practicable from the engine attached to the train, and no fire must be allowed in the Guards' break-vans when any Vehicles containing Explosives are attached to the train.

In loading or unloading any Explosive the casks and packages containing the same must, as far as practicable, be passed from hand to hand, and must not be rolled upon the platform or ground, unless hides, cloths, or sheets have been previously laid down on the platform or ground over which the same are to be rolled.

At every Station at which a train stops, the Guard in charge must make a special examination of the waggons containing Gunpowder or other Dangerous or Inflammable Goods, and must more especially examine the axle boxes, and if the axles show the least sign of heating, the waggons must be detached, and the attention of the Agent or Foreman specially directed to it.

260. The Engine Driver must have with him at all times on his Engine or Tender two short Chains with hooks, a complete set of Lamps, Crowbar, two large Links, a Screw Jack, a Fire-bucket, a box of Detonators (not less than twelve), two Red Flags, a complete set of Fire Irons, and such other tools as may be ordered by the Locomotive Superintendent from time to time.

265. When a Passenger Train is about to start from a Station or Ticket Platform, the signal to start given by the Guard merely indicates that the Station duty or the collection of tickets is completed; and previous to starting the train, the Engine Driver must satisfy himself that the Line before him is clear, either by observation, or by obtaining by means of his whistle the exhibition of the necessary signal as the circumstances of the case may require; and when starting the fireman must look back on the platform side until the last vehicle has drawn clear of the platform, to see that the whole of the train is following in a safe and proper manner, and to receive any signal from the Station Master of guard that may be necessary.

310a. Every person, upon entering the service of the Company, must be in good health, and become a member of the "Enginemen and Firemen's Mutual Assurance Sick and Superannuation Society," and be subject to the Rules of that Society.

Each Engineman shall provide himself with a good Watch.

310b. In addition to the Daily Pay of Enginemen on the Main Lines, Annual Premiums will be given for general good conduct, and the careful and efficient working of their engines, and the economical use of fuel and stores. The advances of wages of both Enginemen and Firemen will also depend on their general good conduct, and in the case of Firemen, upon each man keeping his footplate and front of firebox clean and neat.

310g. Each of the Engines is provided with TWO WHISTLES. The Small Whistle is to be used for the purpose of warning any persons who may be on the Line of the Engine and Train approaching, and generally a whistle to call the attention of the people within hearing to the Engine; and it is the duty of the Guards to look out to the Engineman on hearing such a whistle, in order to ascertain immediately the cause of its being used, and give any requisite assistance.

The Large, or Break Whistle, is to enable the Engineman to Signal to the Guards in the train, or the Engineman of any assisting Engine, whether working before or behind his train, when he wishes the Breaks applied to stop the train.

190. Before a rail is taken out, during relaying operations, or when the line is unsafe from any cause, a flagman appointed for the purpose must exhibit a "Danger" Signal and place two detonators on the line, 10 yards apart, at a point at least 1 mile from the place of obstruction, and, in the case of a Single Line, this must be done in both directions.

348. Each Platelayer working in a Tunnel, when trains are approaching in both directions, must, if he is unable to reach any recess in the walls, lie down either in the space between the two lines of rails, or between the Line and the side of the Tunnel, until the trains have passed. The width of the space depends on the construction of the Tunnel, with which every man must make himself acquainted, in order that he may select the place which affords the greatest safety.

CORD COMMUNICATION BETWEEN PASSENGERS, GUARD, AND ENGINE DRIVER

1. The Cord Communication *must be* applied to all passenger Trains (including a Slip Vehicle) which travel more than twenty miles without stopping.

2. Guards will be responsible for seeing, before their trains are due to start from the Terminal Stations, that the trains are provided with the means of communication, and that all the Bells and Cords are in proper working order before the train is ready to start. This Regulation will also apply to all Stations at which vehicles are attached to, or detached from, their trains, and at Stations where a change of Engine or Head Guards take place. A Testing Signal, (one pull) must be given by the Guard to the Engine Driver, and one pull by the Engine Driver as an acknowledgement.

3. The Communication to the Guard and Engine Driver will only be joined together so as to be available for signalling on the off or six-feet side of the train, while travelling.

4. As soon as the train is started, the Guard must see that the Cam of the Communication wheel fixed in his van is carefully adjusted to a distance of about ten inches from the tongue of the Bell, which will be struck by the Cam when the Cord is pulled, so as to enable Passengers to ring the Bell with ease, and also avoid any ringing which might otherwise be caused by the lengthening or contraction of the buffers, either when

the train is leaving a Station, after being brought to a stand, or is passing round a curve.

When the Guard hears the Bell ring, he must AT ONCE look along the train, and if he sees no reason to anticipate danger from its being stopped, he must at once ring the Bell on the Engine and signal to the Driver to bring the train to a stand as soon as possible, and if the train is not fitted with the Vacuum Break he must apply the Hand Break as hard as possible to assist in pulling up the train.

11.   When the train is stopped, the Passenger who gave the Signal may be expected to communicate with the Guard; but should he fail to do so the Guard must endeavour to ascertain from which compartment the Signal was given, and obtain information as to the cause, and the name and address of the Passenger who pulled the Cord. Should the alarm have been mischievously given, or for an insufficient cause, the names and addresses of all the Passengers in that compartment must be taken, in order that the offending Passenger may be properly dealt with.

BYE-LAWS OF THE GREAT WESTERN RAILWAY COMPANY

6.   At the intermediate Stations the Fares will only be accepted, and the Tickets issued conditionally; that is to say, in case there shall be room in the train for which the Tickets are issued. In case there shall not be room for all the Passengers to whom tickets have been issued, those to whom Tickets have been issued for the longest distances shall (if reasonably practicable) have the preference, and those to whom Tickets have been issued for the same distance shall (if reasonably practicable) have priority according to the order in which the Tickets have been issued, as denoted by the consecutive numbers stamped upon them. The Company, will not, however, hold itself responsible for such Order of Preference or Priority being adhered to; but the Fare or difference of Fare, if the Passenger travels by an ordinary train in a class of Carriage inferior to that for which he has a Ticket, shall be immediately returned, on application, to any Passenger for whom there is not room as aforesaid, if the application is made before the departure of the train.

On 30 October 1883 the Fenians made another attempt at wrecking an English train – this time one on the Metropolitan Railway. As a train approached Edgware Road from Praed Street, a bomb dropped from a first class carriage exploded beneath a third class injuring 40, but fortunately killing nobody. On the same day another bomb was dropped from a train between Westminster and Charing Cross; luckily there were no injuries.

1883 saw the passing of the Cheap Trains Act, which provided that penny-a-mile fares should be exempt from passenger duty. This duty was payable at 2 per cent on fares between urban stations in a district which contained not less than 100,000 inhabitants. Compulsory provision of workmen's cheap tickets was also included in this Act.

By the end of 1883, railways in Great Britain were operating 14,128 locomotives, 43,000 passenger carriages, 419,000 goods wagons while employing 25,000 drivers and firemen, 19,000 signalmen and 59,000 platelayers.

12

Tunnelling: The First Tube Railway and The Severn Tunnel

1884

Although the cut-and-cover underground lines had temporarily eased London's traffic problem, another method of urban transport was needed. The cut-and-cover method was costly, the answer was a deep tube that did not disturb the surface. A South African engineer, James Henry Greathead, had invented a shield that made the boring of a tube through the clay possible. Vertical shafts were sunk at various points along the route and then tunnels driven from the foot of the shaft in both directions. A shield supported the soil and as further protection, the space between the outside of the shield and the earth was filled with liquid cement, applied under pressure. The tunnel followed streets to avoid having to purchase the freeholds of property above. The City of London & Southwark Subway Company in 1884 obtained powers for a cable-worked line from King William Street, the City side of London Bridge, to the Elephant & Castle.

Work began in 1886 and it was decided that an extension to Stockwell was necessary. In 1888 it was decided that electric traction would be preferable and in 1890 an Act authorised an extension to Clapham Common, this latter Act also changed the name to the City & South London Railway.

The City & South London Railway, the first important tube line, opened between King William Street and Stockwell on 18 December 1890. It was not London's first, this being the Tower Subway (*see* page 183). Although the standard gauge was used, as the tunnels were narrow, with a diameter of 10 foot 2 inches north of the Elephant and 10 feet 6 inches to the south, the cars – the Underground uses American terminology – were smaller than main line stock. As there were no beautiful views to be seen, the only windows were set high and the cars received the nickname 'padded cells'. Access was through trellis gates to an end balcony. Signalling was by mechanical lock-and-block. Unlike most surface railways, there were no class divisions, the rich mixing with the poor and all initially paying a flat fare of 2*d*.

The opening day saw the line having 10,000 passengers using King William Street and by early 1891, 15,000 passengers used the line daily. It was extended to Moorgate on 20 February 1900, to Clapham Common on 3 June 1900, to The Angel on 17 November 1901, finally reaching Euston on 12 May 1907. The small locomotives hauled trains until the line between Moorgate and Euston was closed on 8 August 1922 to allow the tube to be enlarged from 10 feet 6 inches diameter to 11 feet 8½ inches and from 1 December 1924 the larger standard tube stock was able to run through via connections at Camden Town and Kennington.

Road competition kept fares low and shareholders felt that dividends were disappointing. A disadvantage of being the first in the field was that almost everything was too small. The locomotives were underpowered, the two-car trains too short, the tunnel diameter too restrictive and capacity at the City terminus inadequate.

Sir Ernest Cassel, financial adviser to the Prince of Wales, was convinced that people demanded a fast ride from their homes in West London to the financial centre in the City. To save costs, like the City & South London line, it was to follow roads thus avoiding having to pay large sums to run below some of the most expensive buildings in London. Time proved this a false economy as curves are so tight that rails have to be replaced more frequently, sometimes as often as every 18 months to two years. An ingenious feature is that to save electricity, when leaving a station a downhill gradient assists acceleration, and an uphill gradient to help braking when arriving.

The Central London Railway was incorporated on 5 August 1891 to build a line from Wood Lane to the Bank. Shepherd's Bush to the Bank opened on 30 July 1900 and initially electric locomotives were used, but their vibration was so severe that they started to cause cracks in the walls of the buildings they had been so careful to avoid. The answer was to replace the electric locomotive which had one large motor, with multiple units. With this system the smaller electric motors for propelling the train were placed on the axles of certain cars and controlled from either end of the train; this reduced vibration by 80 per cent. The system also allowed greater acceleration at starting as the motive power is more evenly distributed throughout the train. An additional advantage was the saving of time by eliminating the necessity of uncoupling the locomotive at the end of a journey and running it round to the other end, a motorman merely having to walk from what was the front of the train to what was the rear. The railway was classless and as a uniform fare of 2*d* was charged it became known as the 'Tuppenny Tube'. At the time it was unusual for a railway to let the upper and lower classes mix, though this happened on trams and buses.

The Central London line was also built under American influence and used terms such as 'cars' rather than 'carriages', and 'eastbound and westbound' rather than 'Up and Down'.

Bank station became the largest subterranean station in the world and now has 10 platforms and 10½ miles of foot tunnels. Its platforms are curved because Bank of England vaults are beside and below the line.

By 1893 there was a need for a north to south line from the West End to Waterloo and it was even said that Westminster business men wanted a speedy means to reach Lord's to enjoy the last hour's cricket. To meet this need, the Baker Street & Waterloo line was incorporated on 28 March 1893. Money was short and construction did not start until 1898. It opened between Baker Street and Kennington Road (now Lambeth North) on 10 March 1906, the extension to the Elephant opening on 5 August 1906. The line's portmanteau title 'Bakerloo', was coined by G. H. F. Nichols of the *Evening News*. G. A. Sekon, then editor of the *Railway Magazine,* disliked the nickname commenting: 'Some latitude is allowable perhaps to halfpenny papers... [but] to adopt its gutter title is not what we expect from a railway company.'

In July 1907 Sir George Gibb, general manager of the North Eastern Railway and chairman of the District Railway, in order to co-ordinate fares and services of the underground railway companies, set up the London Passenger Traffic Conference and when Albert Stanley took over in 1910, he brought in the UndergrounD sign and the surrounding lozenge.

On 1 July 1910 the Piccadilly became the London Electric Railway and absorbed the Hampstead and Bakerloo companies. The Common Fund Act of 1915 empowered the UndergrounD to control London Electric Railways, the District, the Central London, the City & South London, most of the tramway companies and the London General Omnibus Company, all retaining their legal identity. Only three large concerns remained independent: the Metropolitan, the Tilling bus group and London County Council tramways.

The Great Northern & City Railway was incorporated 28 June 1892 to build a line from Finsbury Park to Moorgate. Shares were taken up slowly and work did not start until August 1898. Tunnels were 16 feet in diameter so that the line could handle full-sized stock. It opened 14 February 1904. The Underground Electric Railway took the line over on 1 July 1913 and on 13 May 1939 the large-size stock was replaced by standard tube trains.

Another line which has always been unconnected with other London underground lines, is the Waterloo & City. A fair proportion of passengers arriving at Waterloo were destined for the City. An overground railway would have been prohibitively expensive and even a line with standard-sized tunnel, such as the Metropolitan, would have cost £5m. A tube railway would prove relatively inexpensive, only needing a capital of £540,000 and £180,000 loans, so the London & South Western, which owned Waterloo, backed the Waterloo & City Electric Railway. It obtained the necessary Act on 27 July 1893. Messrs Mowlem started work in June 1894 using a Greathead shield. Shafts were dug beside the Thames and excavated material barged to Dagenham Marshes, while construction material was barged in, thus obviating the need to use the streets. As the route was mainly beneath roads, only a very few easements were required. The terminus at Waterloo was 41 feet below the main line platforms, while the City station was 59 feet below the surface. Commuters had to trudge up a slope as the cost of acquiring property to provide lifts was prohibitive. Matters were eased when travolators were installed in 1960. The line opened on 8 August 1898, the cars constructed in the United States had been re-assembled at the London & South Western's Eastleigh works and hauled to Waterloo by a steam locomotive. The cars were powered through a 500V DC central rail from a small generating station at Waterloo. As no deadman's handle was fitted, for safety a crew of two was required in the motorman's compartment. In the event of a signal being passed at 'Danger', a contact arm tripped the main switch on the train. The motor coaches in addition to the low-level buffing gear, had standard buffer beams to facilitate movement on the main line.

Initially tickets were issued at turnstiles but, from 1900, on-board staff used a tramway-style bell punch and tickets. The line was worked as part of the London & South Western and through tickets were available. The London & South Western absorbed the company on 1 January 1907.

Locomotives with inside cylinders required a crank axle and the breakage of one on 16 July 1884 caused the death of 24 passengers when the entire train, apart from the engine, tender and horse box, were derailed at Penistone. Then, at Penistone on 1 January 1885 an axle broke on a coal train and caused a passing excursion to be derailed resulting in the death of four passengers.

On 6 October 1884 the Circle line in London was complete. As part was owned by the Metropolitan and part by the Metropolitan District, traffic was shared by the District trains running anti-clockwise round the inner track of the Circle, while Metropolitan trains travelled clockwise round the outer track.

1885

On 20 July 1885 goods traffic began on the 53-mile long Hull & Barnsley Railway, passenger traffic starting on 27 July 1885. Although engineering had been relatively simple, due to poor management the line cost almost £60,000 per mile making it the most expensive major railway in Britain, the cost being about four times that of similar lines.

1886

The Mersey Railway linking Liverpool with Birkenhead was opened by the Prince of Wales on 20 January 1886 and was open to the public on 1 February. Originally intended to be worked on the pneumatic system, the Mersey Pneumatic Railway Company was incorporated by an Act of 28 June 1866, the name being changed to the Mersey Railway on 31 July 1868. The pneumatic system was not intended to be that of Samuda, as used on the Croydon and the South Devon lines, but a type similar to that which had been demonstrated in the grounds of the Crystal Palace at Sydenham in September 1864. This system, devised by T. W. Rammell, was to close each end of the tunnel with valves and to propel a train, fitting the tunnel like a piston, by means of a strong draught induced by a fan. For the return journey, the fan was reversed to act as an air extractor. The promoters found it impossible to raise the necessary money, especially in view that it was a virtually untried method of propulsion and potential investors remembered the previous failed pneumatic schemes.

It was then decided to use conventional steam locomotives. Work on a test heading was started in December 1879 and completed in May 1881. The original engineer Sir Charles Fox's retirement in 1870 saw James Brunlees and Charles Douglas Fox, Sir Charles' son, become joint engineers. The original contractor fell into financial difficulties and work was delayed, but then on 24 May 1881 John Waddell & Sons of Edinburgh contracted to complete the trial tunnel and build the full-size tunnel concurrently. The railway has three tunnels: the railway tunnel itself, a ventilation tunnel and a tunnel for the drainage system. The two auxiliary tunnels join together and run as one for the short distance at the deepest point, but at the banks their divergence is considerable due to the necessity of having to drain the later downwards on each side from the centre, while the railway rises towards the banks. The tunnel is 3,820 yards in length, 1,300 yards of this being under the river. The tunnel was lighted and in the middle was a signal box and opposite it were two plaques: 'Centre of the Tunnel' and 'Lancashire Cheshire'. Water pumped from the tunnel was used to fill the Birkenhead public baths. The gradient is 1 in 27, the steepest that could be negotiated successfully by steam trains.

A link with the Wirral Railway opened on 2 January 1888 while the Rock Ferry extension which offered a direct connection with the Birkenhead Joint Railway, owned by the London & North Western and the Great Western, opened on 15 June 1891.

The length of the Mersey Railway totalled 4¾ miles and of its seven stations, three were surface stations, two were tunnel stations, one an underground station with a steel girder roof and one station part in the tunnel and part on the surface. The underground stations were reached by hydraulic lifts with 120-foot high towers.

For working such a steep underground line special condensing locomotives were necessary. Beyer, Peacock & Co built nine 0-6-4Ts, and in 1887 six 2-6-2Ts, the latter having a water jet applied to the radial wheels to lessen the grinding action on the tight curves. The carriages had four wheels.

Although the railway was initially well-patronised, it failed to be successful, mainly due to the fact that the frequent steam trains made the atmosphere more and more foul with smoke and soot, despite the latest type of mine ventilating equipment capable of ejecting over 1,000,000 cubic feet of obnoxious gases per minute. The competitive Birkenhead Corporation Ferry was able to claim it was 'the health route'. The company was bankrupt from 1889–1900 and steps had to be taken.

The answer was electrification and in July 1901 a contract was made with the British Westinghouse Electric & Manufacturing Co Ltd for electrifying the whole line, this being the first example of an English steam line so converted. The system was 650 volts DC power collected from an outside third rail and returned through a centre rail. The original American-type motor coaches, with clerestory roofs, matchboard sides and open-ended platforms, the latter later enclosed and fitted with stable-like half doors, were powered by four 100 hp motors. The electric trains were unusual in that they had no compressors to provide air for the brakes but needed the motorman at a terminal station to connect a hose to an air pipe beneath the platform in order to recharge the brake reservoir.

On 3 May 1903 the last steam passenger train left Liverpool Central and, at 6.00 a.m. the same morning, the first electric train ran, thus pre-empting the Metropolitan Railway. In 1902, the last complete year for steam working, the line carried 6.65 million passengers and made a loss of £4,086; in 1935 it carried over 17½ million passengers and made a profit of £85,955. The line survived the 1923 grouping but in 1938 became integrated with the newly electrified Wirral section of the LMS, which introduced some steel-panelled trains and although they had excellent powers of acceleration, rode roughly, so some passengers preferred the old stock, which although jerky in starting and having slow acceleration, glided sedately and quietly. The old stock had a chime whistle rather than a horn.

The North British wished to link its line on the east side of Glasgow to that on the west. An overground line would have meant too much destruction of property, so the answer was an underground line, only the fourth such railway in Britain. It faced several engineering problems, one being the excavation for a four-platform station at Queen Street without disturbing traffic in the main line station above. When excavating, workmen had to contend with patches of wet sand alternating with boulder clay and freestone. The line opened 15 March 1886. At times when Queen Street High Level station was congested, main line trains were routed round to Queen Street Low Level, passengers dropped and then the empty coaching stock taken on to Cowlairs carriage sidings.

Although the Bristol & South Wales Union Railway with its ferry and the Severn Bridge Railway were better than nothing, a faster and more direct route between Bristol and South Wales was required. The advantages and disadvantages of a bridge or tunnel were considered. Bridge spans needed support, which might not be easily available – and at times a strong wind could be a problem, blowing a vehicle off the track. Tunnels needed ventilation and required to be pumped dry. The tunnel method was chosen and in 1872 the Great Western Railway obtained an Act to carry out Charles Richardson's plan. The following year, a shaft was sunk on the Welsh bank and a small heading driven below the Severn to test the strata and prove whether a tunnel was feasible and, if so, the heading would be used as a drain for the full-sized tunnel.

After four-and-a-half-years of work, one shaft and about a mile of 7-feet-square heading was completed. Then on 16 October 1879, when headings driven from both sides of the estuary were within 130 yards of each other, the Great Spring of fresh water broke in under the land portion.

This disaster resulted in Sir John Hawkshaw, the tunnel's consulting engineer, being appointed chief engineer. He only accepted the post on condition that the contract was let to a man he could trust – Thomas Walker.

The workmen started at 6.00 a.m., worked until 9.00 a.m., breakfasted until 10.00 a.m., worked till lunch at 1.00 p.m. and then worked from 2.00 p.m. till 6.00 p.m. On Saturdays they worked for 7 hours, but were paid for 10. Blasting was done immediately before a meal break taken outside the tunnel, as dynamite fumes were dangerous – so dangerous that Walker changed to tonite as fumes from this were so sleight that workmen could return in a minute.

Walker took care of his men. In almost all parts of the tunnel, waterproof clothing was required. He provided this and also drying rooms at the top of the shafts. He made their life easier by providing ponies to haul the spoil skips, instead of them being pushed by hand. Although the work was arduous, pay was good – the average weekly earnings of a miner being £1 18s 0d, almost three times that of the average Chepstow agricultural wage of 13s 0d.

Houses were built for his men, a hall for church services, a hospital and a day school for the children. The houses were either built of stone, timber or concrete – the latter a very early example of concrete houses. Walker was up-to-date and used electricity from generators to provide light through Swan & Brush bulbs for both surface and underground operations.

Returning to the story of the Great Spring, to try to overcome the problem, a shield was lowered down the shaft to cover the spring's entry, but despite efforts, water leaked in. After seven months, when the pumps had at last begun to overcome the water, a pump broke and the shafts refilled. Pump repairs took three months.

Walker decided that an iron door in a headwall had been left open by the panic-stricken men when the Great Spring first burst in. To reach it, a diver had to walk 1,000 feet along the headway, dragging the air hose after him. Then he had to close the valve, pull up two tramway rails, close the door and shut another valve. As one diver was insufficiently strong to draw 1,000 feet of hose, he was given two assistants but due to the weight of the hose, had to give up when he was within less than 100 feet of the door.

Walker heard of Lieutenant Fleuss, RN, the inventor of a pipeless diving apparatus consisting of a knapsack of compressed air making a diver independent of an air hose. Fleuss came, but had insufficient diving skill to traverse the heading. Walker's chief diver, Lambert, donned the Fleuss apparatus, reached the door, lifted one rail but then had to return as his air supply needed replenishment. Two days later, on 10 November 1880, he closed the valve, lifted the other rail and turned the valve the number of times he was told would close it.

The pumps were started and the water level slowly lowered. A month later when the heading was finally pumped clear, pump foreman James Richards walked up the heading and discovered the cause of the slowness – the valve had a left-hand screw and was in fact closed when Lambert reached it, so he had turned it to open!

Troubles were not yet over. On 18 January 1881 a great snowstorm blocked the railway serving the tunnel works and coal was unable to reach the pumps. Messrs Walker had to borrow all possible coal from the neighbourhood and also burn wood. It was three days before the coal could be got through.

Then at the end of April 1881, salt water burst through into the heading on the east bank. At low water, the bed of the pool from which the water came was only about 3 feet deep, the exact site of the hole was determined by the simple expedient of men holding hands and walking in a line through the pool. When the hole was discovered a schooner was loaded with clay puddle and taken to the spot at high tide. When the water subsided the vessel was unloaded and the hole stopped with alternate layers of loose clay and clay in bags. On 26 September 1881, the headings from each side of the estuary joined and then work started on the main tunnel.

No tide had been known to rise as high as the location of the top of the shafts, but on 17 October 1883, a south-west storm coincided with one of the year's highest tides. Waves 5–6 feet high swept through the workmen's houses, extinguished fires in the pump and winding house and cascaded 100 feet down the shaft. Eighty-three men were able to climb to higher workings in the tunnel and were rescued by a boat lowered into the tunnel.

On 27 October 1884 it was possible to walk through the tunnel. The permanent way had to be laid and permanent pumping and ventilating machinery arranged and installed. The line opened to goods traffic on 1 September 1886 and local passenger trains from 1 December 1886, main line trains starting on 1 July 1887. In addition to creating a shorter route to South Wales, it also offered a new route from the west to the north via Abergavenny and Shrewsbury.

1887

On 16 September 1887 a Midland race-goers' excursion from Sheffield was standing at Hexthorpe, the ticket platform for Doncaster where tickets were inspected, Doncaster being an open station with no ticket collectors. A Manchester, Sheffield & Lincolnshire Railway express rounded the curve to see the excursion standing only 360 yards ahead. Driver Taylor applied the simple vacuum brake and flung the engine into reverse but failed to stop before striking its rear. Twenty-five passengers were killed and 94 injured, claims exceeding £30,000. Many of the company employees offered a week's wages to meet these costs, but the directors declined.

Driver Taylor and fireman Davies of the Liverpool express were arrested and accused of manslaughter. It was the first big legal case in which the newly formed Associated Society of Locomotive Engineers & Firemen engaged eminent counsel to defend their members. After hearing the evidence, the jury brought in a verdict of 'not guilty' and the acquittal of these two men boosted union membership by more than 2,000. The Lord Chief Justice said in his summing up that he could not but think that the railway company was seriously to blame for having had in use a brake which not only was not the best in existence, but which was known to be insufficient and liable to break down. Shortly after he made this remark, the Manchester, Sheffield & Lincolnshire adopted the more efficient automatic vacuum brake.

13

The Race to the North

1888

On 1 November 1887 the East Coast partners – the Great Northern, North Eastern and the North British Railway – began carrying third class passengers on the 10.00 a.m. from King's Cross-Edinburgh in 9 hours, the West Coast route carrying their third class passengers in 10 hours. The West Coast lost bookings, so steps needed to be taken. On 2 June 1888 the West Coast partners, the London & North Western and the Caledonian Railway, speeded their London-Edinburgh train to 9 hours, the same time as the East Coast. The East Coast companies retaliated and from 1 July they reached Edinburgh in 8½ hours and on 1 August 1888 both routes reduced the time to 8 hours, the West Coast running a train of just four coaches but the East Coast having an ordinary load. On 13 August the East Coast reduced it to 7¾ hours, but one West Coast train arrived in 7 hours 38 minutes and an East Coast in 7 hours 27 minutes.

Regarding locomotive performance, the best was made by the Caledonian Railway's 4-2-2 No. 123. Daily throughout the racing period with a load of four bogie coaches, she maintained for the 100¾-mile run between Carlisle and Edinburgh a daily average of 107¾ minutes. This included the 10-mile Beattock bank with 6 miles of 1 in 75.

Both sides sensibly came to an agreement before a disaster occurred and racing stopped, the East Coast settling for 7¾ and the West Coast 8 hours. This was an advantage to shareholders as high speeds increased wear and tear of rolling stock; coal consumption increased; the riding qualities of coaches, although acceptable at 60 mph, left something to be desired at faster speeds; slower traffic was disrupted to give expresses a clear run, while running at moderate speeds offered locomotives a better margin for time recovery should a delay have been experienced.

In June 1888 a private railway was opened from Grimsargh, on the Preston-Longridge branch, to Whittingham Mental Hospital. In addition to carrying coal and stores, visitors and staff were also carried free of charge, latterly in old London & North Western Railway brake vans. The line closed on 30 June 1957.

Waverley station, Edinburgh, was highly congested and E. Foxwell, in *Express Trains English and Foreign* gives a description of it in 1888:

> On the platforms of the Waverley station at Edinburgh may be witnessed every evening in summer a scene of confusion so chaotic that a sober description of it is incredible to those who have not themselves survived it. Trains of caravan length come in portentously late from Perth, so that each is mistaken for its successor; these have to be broken up and remade on insufficient sidings, while bewildered crowds of tourists sway up and down amongst equally bewildered porters on the narrow village platform reserved for these most important expresses; the higher officials stand lost in subtle thought, returning now and then to repeated enquiries some masterpiece of reply couched in the cautious conditional, while the hands of the clock with a humorous air survey the abandoned sight, till at length, without any obvious reason and with sudden stealth, the shame-striken driver hurries his passengers off into the dark. Once off, the driver and the engine do much to make us forget the disgraceful rout from which we have just emerged, for the North British engines, especially those which work the Midland trains to and from Carlisle, achieve some of the very best express running in the world – over such hills.

As well as racing to Scotland there was also racing within that country. The Caledonian and the North British each ran a train from Balloch to Glasgow, booked to leave Balloch at the same time and as the line was joint to Dumbarton, each of the two railways arranged to start its train first on alternate weeks. Both trains made the same stops to Dumbarton and the Caledonian had, by agreement with Messrs Denny, the shipbuilders, to stop at Dumbarton East. From Dumbarton to Bowling the two lines crossed each other several times and remained more or less in sight of each other to Clydebank. There was considerable rivalry between the drivers of the two trains and when it was the turn of the Caledonian to leave Balloch first, the extra stop at Dumbarton East allowed the North British train to draw level with it and offer the opportunity of racing. The Caledonian with lighter trains and a 0-4-4T usually did well, except when North British 4-4-0 No. 38 was heading the train.

Manchester also showed an example of railway competition. At 2.00 p.m. expresses for Manchester left Euston, King's Cross and St Pancras and all three arrived within 5 minutes of each other.

1889

On 1 June 1889 a railway and pier opened at Gourock, intended by the Caledonian Railway to be an ocean terminal in addition to a packet station. The pier was larger than Princes Pier, Greenock. The Glasgow & South Western counter-attacked by building a new Princes Pier and station. Thus every weekday morning steamers of the Caledonian Steam Packet Company, the Glasgow & South Western and the North British called at the Holy Loch piers and carried passengers to Gourock, Princes Pier, or Craigendoran for transfer to expresses to Glasgow, while in the evening the process was reversed. The three routes offered excellent services until the start of World War I when most of the steamers were commandeered for war duty. In the 1950s and '60s, Princes Pier was used as a terminal for ships from the USA and Canada, special boat trains ran to and from Glasgow, the last running on 30 November 1965.

Generally goods and passengers were carried in separate trains, but on a lightly used branch line it was sometimes believed to be more economic to combine the two thus forming a 'mixed train'. The Board of Trade was not happy with this arrangement because, for convenience when shunting, goods wagons were placed at the front of the train behind the engine and when continuous brakes were introduced, as these were not fitted to goods wagons, it meant that passenger coaches were without this safety device.

The Regulation Act of 1889 generally prohibited mixed trains but allowed the Board of Trade latitude in enforcing this rule and some mixed trains ran almost to the end of steam.

1890

In 1878 the contractor William Arrol had started work on the Forth Bridge, designed by Thomas Bouch – but following the disastrous collapse of Bouch's Tay Bridge, all work on the Forth Bridge stopped. In September 1881, Sir John Fowler and Benjamin Baker began a new design using three double cantilevers with suspended spans between. The two principal spans were 1,710 feet, at that time the longest in the world. In view of the Tay Bridge disaster, the Board of Trade stipulated that it should be able to withstand a wind force of 56 lb per square foot.

William Arrol was a remarkable man who started his career patching porridge pots. At the age of 29 he owned a construction business and as well as the Forth Bridge, he was responsible for the second Tay Bridge and Tower Bridge. Ingenious, he was able to overcome problems by inventing new techniques. Plates for the tubes of the Forth Bridge were shaped at Arrol's works at South Queensferry, these tubes being only a foot narrower than those used later for the London tube railways. The 1½-mile long bridge contained 54,076 tons of steel. The cantilever towers rose to 341 feet above high water and only Gustave Eiffel had built something higher. Due to the immense weight of the spans, it was impracticable to float them out before being raised so Arrol devised the technique of building the main spans out from the ends of the cantilever arms until they met in mid-channel. When joining girders, it was Arrol's practice to have the ends a short distance apart and let the air temperature expand the girders until they slid alongside each other and bolts could be thrust into the holes already driven.

Some 4,600 workers were employed at peak time. During construction, 63 men lost their lives and 510 were injured. Some of the highly skilled employees came from abroad and cottages were provided for the Belgians and Italians who sank the caissons. British labourers found lodgings in Dunfermline, Edinburgh, Leith, North and South Queensferry and various other settlements in the locality and were carried to the site by train. It was the first major

British bridge to be constructed of steel, as opposed to wrought iron, thus allowing a much greater span.

On the morning of 14 November 1889, when the very last two girders were to be joined, it was a mild day and rising temperatures had been forecast but, just before the historic moment, a cool wind rose and the expected expansion stopped. One of Arrol's men packed wood shavings and oily rags into the girder troughs, lit them and the holes crept into alignment – the bridge was complete.

As the royal train crossed the bridge, a warship fired a salute and sailors, blue with cold and stationed along the bridge footwalk, presented arms as it passed. As it returned across the bridge it stopped in the centre and as top hats were whisked away, the Prince of Wales ceremonially inserted the final rivet. That day the former porridge pot patcher was knighted.

The Forth Bridge was opened by the Prince of Wales on 4 March 1890 and had been paid for by a consortium of several railway companies: the North British contributed 35 per cent, the Midland 30 per cent and the remaining 35 per cent shared equally by the Great Northern and North Eastern. As the approach lines were incomplete, through traffic did not use the bridge until 1 June 1880.

In the first year of the bridge's opening, the North British experienced £22,000's worth of increased passenger and parcels traffic and in that period 20,695 passenger and 8,488 goods trains crossed. Speed over the bridge was restricted to 40 mph, though at least one driver in its early days achieved 62.8 mph.

The Forth Bridge Company received its revenue from tolls paid by the operating companies, crossing the bridge being rated at 19 miles. A staff of 44 were employed, 28 of them painters and until recently, its 145 acres were repainted every three years, this adding 50 tons to the bridge. The bridge has a lifeboat to rescue any workman who falls and when the wind gauge records more than 30 mph, a warning is sent to bridge workers. With the opening of the Forth Bridge, the four goods and two passenger steamers working the Burntisland-Granton ferry became redundant and were scrapped.

During the last-half of the nineteenth century, the Board of Trade inspecting officers fought a long campaign for passenger trains to have continuous brakes. The necessary Act of 1889 had hardly been passed when on 4 March 1890, an accident occurred that was caused by continuous brakes!

The night Scotch express consisting of fifteen vehicles hauled by Webb compound 2-2-2-0 No. 515 *Niagara* was descending from Shap summit but when driver Rumney applied the brakes to control its speed, nothing happened and it ran through Carlisle and collided with a Caledonian locomotive causing the deaths of four passengers.

What had happened? It had been a bitter night and apparently the vacuum pipe between the tender and the first coach had iced up, thus preventing the brakes from working. Francis Webb, the London & North Western's locomotive engineer, had long championed his chain brake and had reluctantly installed the vacuum brake and must have been furious when the jury announced that: 'The London & North Western Railway are incurring a very grave responsibility in using a brake of such an uncertain and unreliable character.'

In due course, the safety of the automatic vacuum brake was vindicated. The London & North Western still used some rolling stock fitted with the old non-automatic brake where the creation of vacuum applied the brake, the exact opposite of the automatic vacuum where the vacuum held it off. No. 515 was converted to work with brakes of either type and when the brake lever was pushed in, the working was automatic, but when a pin was removed and the brake lever pulled right out, it worked simple. Rumney, trying to restore the vacuum to apply the brakes when approaching Carlisle, had pulled the pin out and thus moved it into position for working simple vacuum, which meant for that on this train the brakes were fully released. Although the pipe had iced up, the blockage was only partial and did not seriously affect braking. It was the dual braking operation that was dangerous and Colonel Rich said the London & North Western should speedily equip all its coaches with the automatic vacuum.

Railway companies not infrequently proved antagonistic towards each other and this was demonstrated at Aberdeen in the summer of 1890. The Caledonian Railway disliked the presence of the North British at Aberdeen and created difficulties. On 29 July empty stock for the 3.30 p.m. North British East Coast express to London was delayed from getting to the platform for 40 minutes by the ploy of a Caledonian shunting operation. On another occasion a North British goods train arrived at Aberdeen at 12.30 p.m., stopped at an adverse signal and at 12.35 whistled for it to be cleared. Still there an hour later a Caledonian light engine appeared, whistled for the signal and was immediately given the road. The North

British train was eventually allowed through at 2.43. A week later, a North British engine whistled for the signal at 1.40 p.m. and was not allowed through until 7.08.

The Bristol & Exeter Railway had marvellous accident-free record and claimed that it never killed a passenger, but after it was taken over by the Great Western, a disaster occurred at Norton Fitzwarren on 11 November 1890. A Down goods train headed by Standard Goods 0-6-0 No. 1100 was assisted by a broad gauge pilot locomotive. As only one engine was required for shunting, the broad gauge locomotive was sent a short distance along the Barnstaple line to be out of the way. Shunting complete, the Down goods crossed to the Up line to allow a fast Down goods to overtake. On reaching the Up line, driver Noble correctly changed the headlight from green (then the normal colour of a headlight) to red as a warning to an oncoming train.

When the Down goods had passed, Noble changed the lamp back to green in anticipation of the signalman giving him the road. However signalman Rice had completely forgotten about the Down goods on the Up line and had accepted a special train conveying passengers and mail from a South African Cape liner, which had called at Plymouth. It consisted of two eight-wheeled coaches and a van hauled by broad gauge 4-4-0ST No. 2051. Hurtling towards Norton Fitzwarren at 60 mph, its driver had no warning of the obstructing goods because its lights were green and not red.

Despite the 60 mph impact, the broad gauge locomotive and train remained upright and in line, though the goods train debris made a pile 30 feet high. Unfortunately 10 passengers were killed and nine seriously injured. Signalman Rice carried the blame for accident and the poor man had been unwell since being knocked down by a light engine the previous January when his ribs and skull were injured.

Some good came of the accident. To prevent a repetition, Rule 55 was adopted by all railways in Britain. It ordered that when a train was halted at a signal, the driver was to blow his whistle and if the signalman did not lower his board after three minutes, or immediately in fog or falling snow, he was required to send a fireman, guard or shunter to the signal box to inform the signalman of the train's presence and not leave until a collar had been placed over the relevant signal levers to prevent a conflicting movement being made. Additionally, the person sent was to sign the train register.

In 1890 the GWR produced the first modern type of sleeping car with a side corridor giving access to berth compartments – until then sleeping cars had communal arrangements. Sleeping cars were only available for first-class passengers, the third class having to make do with attempting to sleep in ordinary seats. In 1928 the GWR, LMS and LNER introduced rather basic third class sleepers. Each compartment contained four berths so you might well find yourself sleeping with strangers. The toilet and washing facilities were only at the end of the car and a pillow and rug – no sheets – could be hired if a supplement was paid. After 1948 rather better third-class cars were introduced with two berths, full bedding and wash basins – though you still might have to share with a stranger.

Although carrying minerals was profitable for a railway, the minerals beneath a railway could cause problems. When the working of a coal mine was about to pass under a line, the mine owner notified the railway company which either kept an eye open and built up ground as it sank, or paid the mining company to leave pillars of coal under the line to support it and these stoops had to be paid for. The North British had to pay £1,350 for fireclay below its Castlecary Viaduct and purchase a shale bed under Seven Arch Bridge from Young's Paraffin Light Company. When the North British Cowlairs Works was extended in 1880, the 12½ acres of coal cost £50–60 an acre. A stoop below the signal box cost £473 7s 0d – far more than the box had cost to build.

1891

The Great Blizzard of March 1891 was the worst for fifty years. Eight passengers were trapped in the evening branch train from Princetown to Yelverton and were forced to spend two nights in the train. The storm was so severe than the wind beat snow through closed carriage windows and ventilators, even when they were stuffed with scarves. Snow filled some compartments up to the height of hat racks. The oil lamps went out through lack of fuel and there was no carriage heating.

After a week of being fed salt beef because the blocked line prevented fresh rations being brought to Dartmoor prison, the convicts grew restless and a warder was stabbed in the neck. The governor contacted the Home Secretary who asked the Great Western to clear the line as a matter of urgency so fifty men were sent but were defeated by a 200-yard long drift. The next day eighty men reached the first station and late on the third day eventually got through to Princetown.

On the main line between Plymouth and Totnes two breakdown gangs had just succeeded in re-railing an engine when a train came round a curve at 25 mph and crashed into the stationary train, killing one workman and seriously injuring two others. The Penzance to Plymouth mail due at Plymouth 8.10 p.m. on Monday, did not arrive at Plymouth until 9.30 a.m. on Tuesday.

The Eyemouth Railway, opened on 13 April 1891, owes its foundation to a disaster. On 14 October 1881 a great storm destroyed twenty fishing vessels and cost the lives of 129 men, leaving 107 widows and 351 orphans in Eyemouth. Over the next eight months the remaining fishing crews landed 1,050 tons of haddock and the factories dispatched 67,915 barrels of herring, most being carted by road to Burnmouth and Berwick for onward travel by rail. In 1883 the local MP and a few other prominent citizens decided to build a 3-mile long branch to Burnmouth, but it was all very amateurish: the solicitor had no railway experience; the local bank agent was appointed secretary 'on the footing that no remuneration can at present be promised'; while a local contractor was promised the contract if he subscribed at least £6,000 of the capital and accepted £3,000 of his payment for the work in shares. With the opening of the railway, Eyemouth developed into a family holiday resort enjoying a steady increase in traffic and in 1920, 34,798 passengers booked at Eyemouth.

With the opening of the Forth Bridge, traffic through Edinburgh Waverley grew enormously and the station proved inadequate to cope as its main platform was approached by only double track and the platform was just 4 feet wide. Sometimes through traffic could take an hour to cover 6 miles. *The Times* commented that trains were late in to Plymouth due to delays at Edinburgh the previous day! A letter to the local paper proposed that the motto: 'Abandon hope all ye who enter here' be hung over the main entrance. The *Leith Herald* carried a bogus notice:

New timetable for August. Trains at the Waverley Station will, until further notice, start as soon as they can be got away and will arrive as they can be brought in. It is guaranteed that no trains will arrive or depart more than three hours behind time. Passengers anxious to reach their destinations at a certain hour had better start the day before. All this wonderful acceleration has been brought about by the opening of the Forth Bridge.

Waverley was really two back-to-back stations, one facing east and serving trains to the south, while the other faced west and served the west and north. Between was an administrative block and through trains passed round the sides of this building. The main departure platform was only 4 feet wide – leaving no room for passengers to pass when blocked by luggage – and the waiting room was only 16 foot square. Several platforms were so short that with a train of normal length, some carriages were off the end of the platform. Trains were often late and the station staff had no knowledge of when they would appear.

The expensive solution was rebuilding Waverley and quadrupling the line on each side, including quadrupling three tunnels. Reconstruction took place between 1892 and 1900, with the result that Waverley had more platform accommodation than any in Britain except Waterloo.

The city fathers realised that a strip of Princes Street Gardens had to be sacrificed and an Act of 5 July 1891 authorised the North British to rebuild Waverley and quadruple 6 miles of approach road between 1892 and 1900. The improved station covered 23 acres, had 19 platforms with an aggregate length of 13,980 feet and could accommodate 358 carriages at a time.

On 16 June 1890 the rival 'temporary' Caledonian station at Princes Street, Edinburgh, also encountered problems after it was destroyed by fire. Opened in sections, the new terminus with nine platforms was completed in 1894. On 7 September 1964 the Duff Street connection was upgraded for use by passenger trains enabling West Coast trains and those from Glasgow via the Caledonian to be diverted into Waverley, so on 6 September 1965 Princes Street station closed.

1892

The very first corridor express to run in Great Britain was that from Paddington-Birkenhead, which came into service on 7 March 1892.

The Great Western gradually laid a third rail within the broad gauge of 7 feet 0¼ inches to be able to accommodate standard gauge wagons. Eventually the broad gauge, as opposed to mixed gauge, was only found on lines west of Exeter. It was decided that this should be converted in May 1892. No traffic for Cornwall was sent after 17 May 1892 and on 18 May the first of eight trains carrying 3,400 permanent way men ran to the west. The very last broad gauge train to leave Paddington was the 5.00 p.m. to Plymouth, while the last Up broad gauge train arrived at Paddington early on 21 May.

Thirteen miles of temporary sidings had been laid at Swindon to accommodate the arrival of the redundant broad gauge stock. The conversion of 177 miles in just two days was a most remarkable achievement. Regular standard gauge passenger services started on 23 May and goods the following day.

The conversion caused the 34-year-old ganger-platelayer James Webber to commit suicide. Alternate sleepers had been cut to new length in advance to carry out the conversion quickly. Webber had made good progress with his 2¼-mile section near Torquay but became increasingly anxious about the conversion weekend. The jury at the inquest concluded that he had waded into the sea and committed suicide 'whilst suffering from temporary insanity'.

At Swindon conversion of stock was done efficiently. Convertible engines only needed shorter axles, but convertible coaches were of three types:

1. Bodies designed so that a section could easily be removed to narrow the coach.
2. Standard gauge bodies on broad gauge underframes.
3. Standard gauge bodies on standard gauge underframes.

One coach had its bogies changed from broad to standard in 20 minutes and by 14 January 1893, only twenty-seven locomotives and 145 coaches awaited conversion.

1893

The Liverpool Overhead Railway was the very first urban elevated electric railway in the world. Another world first was that it had automatic semaphore signals and these were replaced in 1921 by colour lights, making these another first. In 1901 the first escalator to be used by a British railway was installed at Seaforth Sands station.

The line was built 16 feet above street level to avoid blocking road entrances to docks. Columns support wrought-iron girders placed at 22 foot intervals. Between the girders was patent flooring consisting of arched plates bent to a radius of 12 inches and riveted to intervening T-bars, the joints sealed with asphalt compound. The flooring, combining water tightness with lightness and great strength, drained into longitudinal gutters, which discharged into pipes fixed to the columns. Longitudinal sleepers laid on this flooring carried 60 lb flat-bottomed rails spiked directly to the sleepers. Three bascule and one swing bridge provided for the passage of outsize road traffic and shipping. The swing bridge was double deck with the Mersey Docks & Harbour Board tracks on the lower deck. The lower deck was also a bascule bridge, which could be lifted to allow low vessels to pass without disturbing traffic on the busy overhead railway. Another curiosity was that although most of the line was carried on a viaduct, the southern terminus, Dingle, was in a tunnel.

The first section of the 6½ miles from Dingle to Seaforth Sands was opened 6 March 1893 and on 2 July 1905 the line was extended to a junction, Seaforth & Litherland, with the Lancashire & Yorkshire lines to Southport and Ormskirk. Through working was regularly provided until 1922 when it was withdrawn due to road competition, though annually on Grand National Day a special service continued to be maintained by the Liverpool Overhead, to and from Aintree. As the Lancashire & Yorkshire used 600 volts DC compared with the Overhead's 520 volts DC, the Overhead drivers were instructed to keep their motors running in series when working beyond Seaforth Sands.

Originally the conductor rail was in the centre, but the link with the Lancashire & Yorkshire made it necessary to move it to the 6-foot, the centre rail retained to reinforce the return, but when colour-light signalling was introduced, the centre rail was discarded.

The first trains consisted of two composite coaches, each seating sixteen first class and forty third class passengers. Later the standard formation became two 45-foot motor coaches with a 32-foot intermediate trailer. Initially two 60 hp motors were provided on each car, but in 1901 competition from Liverpool Corporation Tramways caused them to be replaced by those of 100 hp, reducing the journey time from 32 to 22 minutes.

The line's consumption of electricity proved expensive and in 1908 a more frequent but slower service was introduced with a journey time of 28 minutes. From 1922, 75 hp motors were fitted, reducing both weight and current consumption. Train frequency was every 10, 5 or 2 minutes according the demand. Originally there was a flat fare and third class passengers used a turnstile, tickets only being issued for first class passengers and workmen's returns. In 1905 differential fares were introduced. From 1932, after 6.00 p.m. on weekdays, after 2.00 p.m. on Saturdays and all day on Sundays and Bank Holidays, a passenger could travel to any of the company's stations for 2*d* return, or 4*d* first class. If the full distance of 14 miles was covered, it was the cheapest railway fare in the country. In 1947 a train was rebuilt to a more modern design and a few other trains were similarly converted. There was no goods or parcels traffic, but newspapers were carried.

Between 1900 and 1926, the Liverpool Overhead leased an extension in the form of a street tramway from the ground floor of Seaforth Sands station to Great Crosby. Unusually, the depot at Seaforth had two storeys: trams were kept on the ground floor while the Overhead stock was stabled on the first floor.

Several stations received bomb damage and when sections were destroyed or damaged, a bus shuttle service linked the good sections. So highly did the authorities regard the part played by the railway and its part in the war effort, that every assistance was granted for steel priority to rebuild the wrecked sections. Known as the 'Dockers' Umbrella' the passenger-only line had the double use of daily transport for dockers and offering a bird's eye view of the docks for tourists. For those with an interest in railway locomotives, a bird's eye view was obtained of the Brunswick engine shed and all the locomotives in the shed yard could be seen from Herculaneum station.

The line's closure came in 1956 due to the fact that the system was generally life-expired, had lost traffic to road competition and finance was unavailable for the necessary renewals.

Initially dining cars were just for first class passengers and the North Eastern was the first company to propose providing a third class version. An order was given to the carriage builders who were rather slow at construction and the North Eastern was beaten by a month, the Midland Railway and the West Coast companies, the London & North Western and the Caledonian Railway, coming first.

On 6 November 1893 the Midland opened a 21-mile long line between the Sheffield-Chesterfield and Ambergate-Manchester lines. Its major feature was Totley Tunnel, 3 miles 950 yards in length and the longest in Britain after the Severn. Inundation of water was a severe problem, some days more than five million gallons having to be pumped. It opened to passenger traffic 1 June 1894.

A typical locomotive of the 1890s was a small-boilered 4-4-0 with inside cylinders and if given larger cylinders to cope with the heavier trains, the small boiler was retained to prevent an engine being uneconomically thrashed, as a small boiler could not provide the necessary steam for harsh use.

1894

From 1882 Manchester found that its trade was diminishing due to its inland position; the answer to the problem being a ship canal. The necessary Act was passed in 1885 and the canal opened 1 January 1894, but a railway was needed to serve warehouses and storage ground. The Manchester Ship Canal Railway was incorporated under an Act of 1 January 1894. There were 33 miles of route and 223 miles of track, which spread as far west as Ellesmere Port. It operated a stable of some 70 0-6-0 tank locomotives and more than 2,500 wagons handling about 7,000,000 tons annually. The system did not generally use brake vans but, on the steep bank leading up to the exchange sidings at Ellesmere Port, one was used to provide rear brake power for the heavy trains of loaded tank wagons ascending; normally a train crew consisted of a driver, fireman and a shunter travelling on the engine.

Generally the system was not signalled except at railway swing bridges and exchange points with the main line railways. A control centre was sited at Partington North and before a train entered a single line, permission had to be obtained by a shunter, or other person in charge, from the central control operator. To ensure safety, the shunter was required to give his name and grade and give particulars of the train, its position, destination and state of visibility. In return he was required to obtain the name of the control operator and repeat verbatim to that operator any message received, whether permission to proceed was given or not. In fair weather trains were permitted to follow each other at ten-minute intervals, but drivers seeking permission to enter the single line had to be informed of the presence of any preceding train and the time of its departure. In times of poor visibility, movements were more restricted.

The railway had seven locomotive sheds; locomotives needing overhaul and at isolated sheds travelled to Mode Wheel Road, Weaste, Salford, in a BR freight train or by road on a low-loading trailer. The engines were well maintained, their crews taking pride in shining paintwork and glistening brass. To enable them to round tight curves without derailing, the 0-6-0Ts had flangeless centre driving wheels while the coupling rods were fitted with a knuckle. The leading axles were fitted with Cortazzi sliding axle boxes. The line had three passenger coaches: one for conveying dock labour, one for the engineer's permanent way staff and the third an inspection saloon.

The railway carried such traffic as timber, coal, live cattle, frozen meat, grain and oil. On busy days 120 vans of cotton left the transit sheds while a shipload of bananas required 300 vans, 120 to 150 bunches placed in each van.

In 1923 the railways of the Manchester Ship Canal and those of the Mersey Docks & Harbour Board did not come under grouping.

2 April 1894 marked the opening of the Cathcart Circle line, two 8-mile concentric circles. Its first section had been opened from Pollokshields East to Mount Florida on 1 March 1886 and to Cathcart on 25 May 1886. A service of 89 trains was operated daily and at Glasgow Central the Circle line had its own dedicated platform.

Between Blair Atholl and Druimuachter Summit Down trains on the Highland Railway faced 16 miles of a gradient hardly ever less than 1 in 85. Its locomotive engineer, David Jones, designed some excellent 4-4-0s, but a good deal of double-heading was still necessary. Jones designed the first British 4-6-0 and although designated 'goods', they were used on passenger trains as they were able to handle 200 ton trains as opposed to a 4-4-0's 120 tons.

1895

The summer of 1895 marked the Race to the North. Until the opening of the Forth Bridge the only convenient way from London to Aberdeen was via the West Coast, as the East Coast route involved the inconvenient Granton-Burntisland ferry. The opening of the Forth Bridge meant that it was possible to travel the 512 miles from King's Cross to Aberdeen in the same carriage, whereas the West Coast train ran 540 miles.

Trains by both routes left London at the same time, 8.00 p.m., the East Coast arriving at 7.20 a.m. and the West Coast 7.40 a.m. Suddenly on 15 July 1895, the West Coast speeded its train to arrive at Aberdeen at 7.00 a.m. Managers of the East Coast route, the Great Northern, North Eastern and North British conferred, with the result that from 22 July the 8.00 p.m. from King's Cross was scheduled to arrive at Aberdeen at 6.45 a.m. Drivers and firemen on both routes did their utmost to keep these tight timings. On 25 July the Great Northern believed it sensible to make an agreement with the West Coast, but the North British was adamant that the race should continue.

Although the timetables were revised to give even faster running, they were ignored and the trains went as fast as they could, which in fact proved inconvenient to passengers who arrived at intermediate stations to find that their train had left early, while signalmen had to ensure that the racing express had a clear road and therefore had to shunt slower trains into loops and sidings well before its expected arrival. To solve the problem of intermediate passengers missing the train, both routes ran a relief train sometimes that of the West Coast not carrying a single passenger.

From Kinnaber Junction near Montrose, both routes used the Caledonian Railway to Aberdeen, so the first to Kinnaber Junction was the winner, the signalman gesturing to indicate whether the train had won or lost.

By the third week of August the race was national news, reporters travelled on the trains, relishing the event which provided exciting copy in the 'silly season'. On 20–21 August after a night of racing, the two competing trains only 2 miles from Kinnaber

Junction were within sight of each other, the Caledonian sprinting over the junction a minute ahead of its rival. The following night the North British reached Kinnaber Junction 14½ minutes before the Caledonian, while on the next night the West Coast with a very light train of three coaches made the journey in 8 hours and 32 minutes – 8 minutes fast than the East Coast's best, which had a heavier train consisting of six East Coast Joint Stock coaches and an eight-wheel sleeping car.

The North British became concerned about safety – as well they might as their line was curvaceous and was subject to mining settlements. In the early mornings of 20 and 21 August McLelland, a North British chief inspector, travelled on the train and discovered that speed restrictions had been grossly exceeded: the Forth Bridge crossed at 60 mph and the Tay Bridge at 72 mph and the train had covered the 512 miles in 523½ minutes. John Conacher, the general manager of North British realised the racing should stop before a serious accident occurred, and also questioned the benefit to the public in arriving at Aberdeen at 4.42 a.m. On the night of 22/23 August the West Coast had covered the 540 miles in 512 minutes.

Curiously (or deliberately?), the general managers of the East Coast companies went on holiday: Sir Henry Oakley of the Great Northern to Dublin, George Gibb of the North Eastern to Dornoch and Conacher to Aberdeen, so this meant trying to contact them by telegram.

On the morning of 23 August Conacher had an amazing *volte face*. He asked his locomotive superintendent, Matthew Holmes, if the best performance could be improved on and received the reply: 'Might possibly arrange three ordinary carriages but risky seeing such high speed has to be maintained.' Despite this warning, and the report of Chief Inspector McLelland, Conacher continued his scheme for a 'special effort' run. Then at 2.00 p.m. he received a message from Oakley: 'I think we should wait a few days before running another special and see details of last night's running first.'

Normally the Caledonian would not have issued this information to a rival company, but Conacher had a stroke of luck, McLelland was at Fort William on 23 August attending an inquiry into a derailment on the West Highland and the Board of Trade inspecting officer had a copy of the Caledonian figures and allowed him to make a copy. Conacher tried to persuade the East Coast to pick a quiet night and retrieve the laurels but Oakley was adamant that racing should cease.

Economically the race was poor because as there was no corresponding Race to the South, rolling stock had to be returned empty, while one racing train only carried seven passengers. Before the racing started the East Coast carried the most passengers and this continued through the contest, the East Coast carrying 2,156 and the West Coast 751. Furthermore at the height of the races the East Coast train carried only Dundee and Aberdeen passengers, while mails, parcels and newspapers were taken on the relief train in order to reduce the racer's load.

During the racing period from 16 July to 23 August the East Coast recorded two on-time arrivals, thirteen early arrivals and nineteen late arrivals. Corresponding figures for the West Coast were nil on time, thirty early and nineteen late arrivals. When normal services were resumed in September the 8.00 p.m. from King's Cross carried 608 passengers against the 333 who left Euston.

The general managers had learned their lesson and when in 1900 the North Eastern speeded the Flying Scotsman by 20 minutes over its lines, the North British signalman at Berwick was instructed to hold the train until its scheduled departure time.

Concurrently with the Race to the North, passengers to the south of London were given an extremely slow service and in September 1895 much correspondence appeared in *The Times* under the heading 'The Crawl to the South'. This was largely summarised in its leader of 14 September 1895:

> The Southern managers have no doubt been aware that it would be of little use for them to attempt to rival the magnificent performance of the Great Northern and London and North Western Companies. Their rolling stock and the well-established traditions of their companies put it out of the question that they should try this with success. They have hit accordingly upon another method of distinguishing themselves more suited to their capabilities. They have chosen frankly a very different form of distinction, and the struggle between them now is which of them can claim to have established the slowest, the most unpunctual, and the most inconvenient service of trains. The real rivals are the South Eastern and the London, Brighton and South Coast lines,

and the performance of both are so singular, and their claims to the honour which they are seeking are so nearly balanced, that there are good grounds for a difference of opinion as to their respective merits. Very bad they both are, this at least the most severe critic must admit, difficult as he would find it, on a review of the evidence, to say with certainty which of the two has the better right to call itself absolutely the worst line in the country.

The directors took note of these criticisms and the lines became smart and punctual.

On 22 December 1895 John Hyde, stationmaster at Chelford on the London & North Western, was superintending shunting operations, dusk was falling and a strong wind blowing. A high-sided wagon was shunted into a siding, the engine then drew forward to shunt six wagons into the adjoining road. As these were running back, Hyde noticed that the high-sided wagon was being blown forward to meet them. There was a sideways collision on the points where the two sidings met, the high-sided wagon was derailed and fouled the main line.

Immediately this happened, Hyde heard the roar of the 4.15 p.m. Manchester-Crewe express drawn by 2-4-0 Jumbo class No. 418 *Zygia* and Webb compound 2-2-2-0 No. 520 *Empress*. He ran along the track towards the approaching train waving his red lamp, but both drivers thought he was merely signalling to the shunting engine and made no attempt to stop.

Zygia struck the high-sided wagon, was derailed, fell over on her side, the tender rushing up the platform ramp. *Express* was also derailed but kept upright. The third vehicle of the express struck the signal box destroying the whole of its front. Uninjured by this terrifying experience, signalman Frank Feam in his ruined box tried to send 'obstruction danger' on the block instruments, but finding they were dead, managed to send a warning on his telegraph. The disaster cost the lives of 14 people. In his report Captain Marindin could make little suggestion as to how to prevent a repetition, but said that although it had not been necessary in the past, the brakes of all shunted wagons should be immediately pinned down.

14

Some Unusual Railways; Electric Tramways, Rival Railways in Urban Areas

1896

On 7 March 1896 an accident occurred on the Great Northern at Little Bytham costing two lives. It was the custom in the nineteenth century to have the ballast made up to just below rail level, so it was impossible to see if the packing around the sleepers was correctly maintained. No. 1003, one of Stirling's 4-2-2s, became derailed due to inefficient packing, though the Board of Trade inspector also commented on the axle loading of nearly 20 tons. Subsequently this and other members of the class were rebuilt with a reduced loading on the driving axle. Ballasting was improved by using stone chippings rather than ash and gravel.

On 6 April 1896 the Snowdon Mountain Railway opened. Set at a gauge of 2 feet 7½ inches, it runs from Llanberis to the crest of Snowdon, a distance of 4½ miles. Its steepest gradient is 1 in 5½ and the summit station is 3,493 feet above sea level. Between the running rails was a rack on the Abt system. The bogie coaches were propelled up the gradient, but for safety were not coupled and this fact saved passengers on the opening day. The 0-4-2T locomotive No. 1 *Ladas* mounted the running rails at Clogwyn, thereby disengaging from the rack and plunged into a ravine, smashing herself to pieces. The footplate crew leaped to safety. The coaches, being uncoupled, stayed on the line and were stopped by their brakes, which came on automatically when speed exceeded 5 mph. One scared passenger died jumping from the train. The line re-opened in April 1897 after a beam had been placed on each side of the rack.

The undertaking, originally known as the Snowdon Mountain Tramroad & Hotels Company Limited, was not a statutory company-owned railway. As it was entirely built on the private estate of Mr Assheton Smith, no Act of Parliament was required. The Board of Trade made an unofficial inspection and Francis Marindin reported favourably, but recommended anemometers being placed at breezy spots and the working of trains being subject to a maximum wind speed.

To ensure that the tubes in the boiler were always covered with water, the boiler and firebox tilt forward like a kneeling cow to maintain a horizontal water level. Braking when proceeding downhill is assisted by counter-pressure steam brakes. The original stable of steam locomotives in recent years has been augmented by a diesel locomotive and diesel-electric railcars.

On 10 August 1896 the Caledonian opened the Glasgow Central Railway, which provided a 6¼-mile link between lines in the east and west. The tunnel was made by the 'cut and cover' method and the railway had to guarantee that construction works would not stop tramcars or prevent access to shops. Some tenements had to be demolished and alternative accommodation found within a mile of the displaced tenants' places of employment. Under Kelvingrove Park, trees were not to be disturbed and every blade of grass that was removed was required to be replaced. More than 260 trains used Central Low Level station daily. Locomotive smoke made that station unpleasant and regular passengers used a paper bag as a glove to open the soot-coated door handles. When Glasgow Corporation started electrifying its tram routes in 1898, it was not surprising that some used trams rather than the railway.

1896 marked the beginning of a boom period for newspapers when the *Daily Mail* first came off the press. This was the first popular newspaper and helped fulfil a demand created by the literary improvement brought about by free schooling for all, and an improved standard of living. Its success gave rise to the *Daily Express* in 1900 and the *Daily Mirror* in 1903. The fact that vast quantities could be printed in London and rapidly distributed by rail meant the newspapers were affordable. By the end of the nineteenth century, the vans added to late-night passenger trains had been replaced by special newspaper trains.

England's most curious railway opened at Brighton on 30 November 1896. It came about because Magnus Volk wanted to extend his electric railway opened at Brighton in 1883, along the seafront to Rottingdean without having to construct a viaduct. His solution was to lay on concrete a double rail track along the shore between the high and low water marks. The gauge was 2 feet 8½ inches, the same as for his electric railway, but the big difference was that 18 feet separated the outer rails, the railway's very wide single car running on both tracks at once, as did some dockyard cranes. The car, really a pier head crossed with a ferry, could carry 150 passengers and stood on four legs 24 feet high, each of which had a four-wheel bogie at its base. Unsurprisingly it was nicknamed 'Daddy Longlegs'. Power was supplied from an overhead wire. It covered the journey of 3 miles in 34 minutes. Due to the fact that it sometimes moved through the water, the Board of Trade required it to carry lifebelts and a lifeboat.

Just a few days after opening, severe storms in the first week of December 1896 capsized the car and caused other damage, preventing re-opening until 20 July 1897 and even then it was not a roaring success. The track tended to silt over and by 1900 only short 'fun' trips were given over the Brighton end of the line and these stopped in 1901 when the corporation removed part of the track to create new sea defences. The remainder of the line and 'Daddy Longlegs' were scrapped in 1910.

In 1896 George Jackson Churchward was appointed chief assistant to William Dean, the GWR's chief mechanical engineer who was beginning to suffer from Alzheimer's disease. Dean had already adopted the Belpaire fire-box, which encouraged a smooth flow of gasses and avoided sharp corners which could cause weakness. Churchward improved heating still further by adopting a tapered boiler, the boiler being at its largest diameter adjoining the fire-box, the hottest part, where there was the most rapid circulation of water. Instead of using a boiler pressure of around 180 lb per sq inch like other British locomotive engineers, Churchward chose 225. Although this made the initial cost of a Great Western boiler higher, maintenance charges were greatly reduced. Churchward's successor, Charles Benjamin Collett, although making minor modifications, continued Churchward's designs, which were continued by William Arthur Stanier who moved from the GWR to the LMS and also used modified Churchward designs. On British Railways, Robert Riddles used modified Stanier designs – so Churchward's ideas lasted until the end of steam.

1897

The Glasgow District Subway Company which received its Act on 4 August 1890, was completed in 1896. While it was being built, a tram driver was shocked to see his two horses plunge into a sudden subsidence. Another unfortunate incident was when a visitor to the eastern under-river section, after passing through the air lock, had his cheap hip flask flattened in his pocket by the pressure, to the detriment of his trousers and the loss of his whisky.

The circular 6½-mile long 4-foot gauge line was constructed at an average depth of 29 feet below the surface, varying from 115 feet to only 7 feet. It has no fewer than fifteen stations and passes twice below the Clyde. Due to the variety of soil encountered, constructional methods varied, but sections near the surface were generally made by cut-and-cover. Due to the different geological differences the tunnels are partly cylindrical and partly the more conventional horse-shoe shape. The twin tunnels, nominally 11 feet in diameter, lie side by side at a distance varying from 2 feet 6 inches to 6 feet. At stations the tunnels merge into a single tunnel, 28 feet in diameter. Curves and gradients are generally easy, except the under-river sections that have inclines as steep as 1 in 18.

The line opened for traffic on 14 December 1896, but an accident when 19 people were injured in the rush to travel, caused it to close down the same day and it was not open for regular working until 19 January 1897, [one account says opening 21 January 1897]. Penny tickets allowed admission to the railway through turnstiles. The temptation of the locals to get their pennyworth was too great – on the first day passengers simply rode round and round without getting off. There were two cables, one for each tunnel, driven by a 1,500 hp steam engine at the power station. Each cable was 1½ inches thick and weighed about 57 tons. They were kept in motion at 12½ mph the whole time the railway was open. When the gripper consisting of two steel jaws under the cars was applied to the cable, the cars moved forward, while its release brought them to a stop. To facilitate stopping and starting, the gradient rises 1 in 40 to a station and descends at 1 in 40 from it.

Platforms are of the island type and as the system has no points and train sets kept to the same track, only one side was ever seen by the public. The cars are electrically lit, current being picked up from lateral conductor wires. Rolling stock was lifted in and out of a rectangular well in the centre of the works at Govan. At night the trains, 10 two-car units on each track, were stored in the tunnels below Govan, the grippers and conductors of the last two trains arriving having to walk through nearly half the railways' cars before reaching the open air. The name of the undertaking changed to Glasgow Subway by an Act of 18 July 1914.

Unfortunately the line did not pay and after heavy losses was closed on 25 March 1922, but in August that same year, the concern which had cost £1½ million to construct was taken over by the City Corporation for £381,589. In 1935 it was electrified, the inner circle starting electric working on 28 March and the outer circle in December. The 60 lb rails were replaced with those of 80 lb and the manual somersault signals replaced with automatic colour lights. The original end-gated coaches were retained but refurbished. The livery was red and cream with a grey roof, but the side never seen by those on the platform was a dull red all over. Two 60 hp tramway-type motors were fitted to each bogie on the leading car, the second coach being a trailer. The subway was particularly popular during World War II as it was speedy and brightly lit at a time when surface transport operated in blackout conditions. For the year ending 31 May 1945, it made a surplus of £21,623 while the trams and buses showed a loss. In 1973 ownership passed to the Greater Glasgow Passenger Transport Executive.

The system was scheduled to close on 28 May 1977 in order that it could be modernised, but serious cracks in Govan Cross station roof caused closure on 21 May 1977. Just less than £53-million was spent updating the 6½-mile long line, including the cost of thirty-three cars built by Metro Cammell in orange livery and placed in two-car units. Although not open to the public because the signalling system and the programme of staff training still had to be completed, when Queen Elizabeth and the Duke of Edinburgh visited on 1 November 1979 they were able to ride on it from Buchanan Street to St Enoch. The line was reopened to the public on 16 April 1980, offering a flat rate fare of 20*p* between any of the twenty-three stations. Initially the six-minute frequency service ran 06.05–19.30 Monday to Saturday.

The line has several handicaps, one being the small size of the stations which limit the trains to two cars; another handicap is the absence of crossovers or sidings so there are no facilities for 'laying by' cars during quiet periods. When a car has to be brought to the surface for overhaul it has to be lifted to the surface-level workshops by crane and this can only be carried out during non-working hours.

In 1897 the greatest of the Fife pit owners, Randolph Erskine Wemyss, announced that he was to build and operate a private railway between his newest pits and Methil Docks, this despite the fact that less than twelve months previously he had signed an agreement not to do so. Furthermore, his line was to take revenue from the North British, a company of which he was a director, this act causing its chairman, vice chairman and general manager to resign. The handsome, chocolate-coloured locomotives of the Wemyss Private Railway worked the line until the pits' closure in 1970. Due to legal provisions, the line could not come under British Railways, but was later operated by the Wemyss Estate and the National Coal Board.

2 November 1897 a line opened to the Kyle of Lochalsh thus improving access to the Island of Skye.

1898

The 1-foot-11½ inch gauge Lynton & Barnstaple Railway was formally opened on 11 May 1898. Building it to the narrow gauge, rather than standard gauge, through the hilly and relatively sparsely occupied area was a better economic proposition as curves could be sharper, allowing the line to follow the contours. The company proved just about profitable, generally paying dividends of one-half per cent annually. In 1903 the Lynton & Barnstaple was the first British railway and possibly the very first in the world to run an associated road motor bus service.

Unaffected by Grouping, the line was purchased by the Southern Railway in March 1923, but unfortunately the line was unable to compete with the growth of road traffic and ticket sales dropped dramatically from 72,000 in 1925 to 32,000 in 1934. In 1935 a decision had to be made about whether to undertake the expense of renewing the permanent way or to close the line. The latter course was adopted. A meeting was held at Barnstaple to try to reverse the decision, but the fact that all the railway's supporters had travelled from Lynton by car rather than train, somewhat ruined their case.

The last train ran on 29 September 1935, but this was not the end of the story. Enthusiasts have always been sad that the line had not lingered into the post-World War II era when it might have been saved by preservationists, but all was not lost. In 1979 the Lynton & Barnstaple Railway Association was formed to re-open at least part of the line and subsequently a length opened on 17 July 2004. This proved that it was economically a good thing for the area and it is highly likely that in due course the whole route will eventually be re-opened.

The Waterloo & City Railway opened on 8 August 1898 became amalgamated with the London & South Western Railway from 1 January 1907 and was the only underground system owned and operated by a main line railway company. It was linked to the surface for transfer of rolling stock by a 30-ton hoist. The line had one of Britain's first electric multiple-unit trains. Flat fronted, it pushed air through the tunnel for ventilation. Nicknamed 'The Drain', in 1994 it was sold to London Underground for £1. Since the 1990s it has used modified Central Line stock.

For Barnum & Bailey's Circus's European tour of 1898–1902, four trains totalling 68 bogie vehicles, each 59 feet in length were specially built. They were of the American pattern, reduced to fit the British loading gauge and had small diameter wheels for ground-level loading. Except for the end vehicles, the couplings were of the American buck-eye type. The eight sleeping cars had end-verandahs. After touring Britain for two years, they were shipped to the Continent.

For many years Bertram Mill's Circus used four special trains to move from site to site. The spread of television reduced the circus's appeal and before closing the tented show, en route to Ireland, it used two trains for the journey from Workington to Stranraer Harbour, and then for the return to the winter quarters at Ascot (West).

In 1898 H. A. Ivatt, the Great Northern's chief locomotive engineer, introduced 4-4-2 Atlantics to cope with the heavy corridor stock being introduced. These were the first British Atlantics and he went on to construct this type with even larger boilers: instead of being long and narrow between the frames, they were short and wide over the frames, the wide firebox increasing the evaporative efficiency.

Also in 1898 the locomotive authorities of the Belgian State Railways were so much impressed by the fine work done by the 4-4-0 engines designed by J. F. McIntosh of the Caledonian Railway that they ordered five engines similar to the 766 class to be built. Five were built in Scotland and a further ninety came from the shops of various Belgian makers. When McIntosh enlarged the design, the Belgian authorities followed suit and constructed 140 of this improved version.

Early tank engines had either side or saddle tanks. The introduction of Belpaire fireboxes with their vertical sides complicated saddle tank construction and reduced capacity at the rear where the weight of water was most useful. Saddle tanks with a relatively high centre of gravity and the water subject to surging, were unsuitable for fast running. To obviate these problems, in 1898 the GWR fitted No. 1490 with pannier tanks and in subsequent years a few other pannier tank engines appeared, but standardisation of panniers for all new tank engines dates from about the end of 1909. Although perhaps best suited to shunting and local goods work, they were seen on passenger trains, sometimes even heading expresses such as one in North Somerset, which ran from Frome to Bristol connecting an Up express from Weymouth Quay with expresses to the North. Although pannier tanks were peculiar to the GWR, in the British Railways era some emigrated to bank on the Lickey and Folkestone inclines and to work the Dornoch branch in Scotland.

Most railway companies had their own sheet stores where waterproof tarpaulins for covering wagons were made and maintained. Sheets were laid on the floor and linseed oil and vegetable black brushed on with brooms, five coats being given. Each sheet was numbered and recorded at the Railway Clearing House and subject to demurrage if detained at the receiving station of a foreign railway company beyond the free period allowed for unloading the consignment.

1899

The Manchester, Sheffield & Lincolnshire Railway cast envious eyes at London and in 1892 secured an Act for constructing an extension. Built to the Continental loading gauge – a very forward view at the time – it joined the Metropolitan Railway at Quainton Road and exercised running powers over that line to Harrow from where additional tracks were laid to Finchley Road, independent lines providing access to a new goods and passenger station at Marylebone.

The existing name now being inadequate, on 1 August 1897 it was renamed the Great Central Railway. One very serious problem was that it needed to pass through the grounds of the Marylebone Cricket Club. The difficulty was solved when the railway hid itself in a tunnel and restored the surface to its immaculate condition, and the club rewarded by being given most of the site of the Clergy Orphan School. The line opened for passenger traffic on 15 March 1899 and to merchandise 11 April 1899. The demand for the new line does not seem to have been great as the first three passenger trains from Marylebone only carried a total of 52 passengers. The London extension offered the first buffet cars to run in Britain, these starting in 1899, but they did not come into use on other railways until the 1930s and were frequently converted from ordinary carriages or restaurant cars.

To increase the facilities it could offer, on 2 April 1906 the Great Central opened a line from Ashenden, on the Great Western's new route from Princes Risborough to Aynho, to Grendon, 2¾ miles north of Quainton Road, while another link with the Great Western and Great Central's joint line was from Northolt to Neasden. The use of this joint line offered a relief route for Great Central expresses and was a useful link with the Great Western, which had important connections to railways south of London. As the Great Central largely duplicated other lines, most of it closed on 3 September 1966.

In June 1899 the Great North of Scotland Railway opened a 3-foot-6½-inch gauge electric tramway to connect its railway station at Cruden Bay with its hotel, opened the previous March. The line, 0.66 miles in length, carried passengers to the front door, and goods via a short spur, to the tradesmen's entrance. Hotel guests were carried free, but others were charged. As all the Great North of Scotland's laundry work was carried out at the hotel, the tramway also carried this. The two sumptuous combination cars were built by the railway at its Kittybrewster works. With the 1923 Grouping, the hotel and tramway passed to the London & North Eastern Railway. When the railway branch closed to passengers on 31 October 1932, the tramway passenger service was withdrawn and, like the railway branch, it became goods only. In March 1941 the hotel was requisitioned by the army, the tramway closed and the tramcars sold for use as summer houses.

On 7 September 1899 an amazing excursion carried 15,000 trippers from the Caledonian Railway's St Rollox Works to Carlisle and back in 14 trains each of 18 identical carriages and every locomotive an Improved Dunalistair. The first train left at 5.10 a.m. and the rest followed at ten minute intervals except the last two which were 20 minutes apart and every train kept to the minute. Each engine consumed 1 ton 12 cwt of coal on the journey or 35 lb a mile, or 3 lb 4 oz of coal to carry each passenger from Glasgow-Carlisle which involved a rise to Beattock Summit 1,014 feet above sea level.

In November 1899 the Strathbathie & Blackdog Light Railway, or Murcar Railway, opened from Bridge of Don on the northern outskirts of Aberdeen, to the Seaton Brick & Tile Company's Blackdog brickworks. The 3 foot gauge system carried bricks to within easy carting distance of the city centre and also a passenger service was operated using four ex-city horse cars, while from 1909 a petrol driven car was used built by an Aberdeen firm, J. B. Duff & Company and a Wickham railcar arrived in 1932. As a large proportion of the passengers were those to and from the Murcar Golf Club, when the brickworks closed in 1924 the line was purchased by the club. Regular services were run until 1949 and the Wickham railcar kept for emergency use until October 1951 when the track was lifted. Probably due to Scottish sporting rivalry the trams passed, but did not stop at the neighbouring Balgownie golf course.

1900
By 1900 the rigid eight-wheeler coaches on the Metropolitan, and the District Railways' four-wheelers needed replacement. The two companies decided to electrify the line between Earl's Court and Kensington High Street with DC traction on the fourth-rail system which had been tried and tested on the elevated railways of Boston. With a third-rail system the third rail carries 750 volts in the outer rail, whereas with the fourth-rail the outer is at +420 volts and the inner at

-210 volts, this splitting having the advantage of minimising current leakage. Leakage is more serious underground than on the surface as leakage underground can cause electrolysis to occur in steel tubes and could damage foundations of buildings.

American money was available for investment in British railways and Charles Tyson Yerkes arrived to investigate. He secured control of the District Railway in 1901 and replaced J. S. Forbes as its chairman. Forbes, also chairman of the London, Chatham & Dover Railway died in 1904 and the *Railway Times* wrote an epitaph: 'It is doubtful whether any company, in the long run, benefited materially from his services'.

Yerkes favoured fourth rail DC electrification which had been used for suburban electrification in the States and so in the interests of standardisation, the Metropolitan was forced to follow suit. By 24 September 1905 all the Circle steam trains had been replaced sufficiently early to meet competition from electric trams and tube railways. The southern part of the Circle line became extremely busy and at peak hours no sooner had a train cleared the platform than the following one ran in. In 1911 the first underground escalator was installed at Earl's Court.

In 1900 two accidents occurred on the line between Alton and Winchester – the present 'Watercress Line' – with its significant proportion being on a gradient of 1 in 60. On 1 May 1900 20 wagons of an Up train ran back from Medstead to Alresford, while on 27 December 1900 a horse box which had been uncoupled from a train ran down the bank colliding with its train at Ropley.

Major J. Pringle stated in his report:

The 2.45 pm passenger train from Waterloo to Southampton, on arrival at Medstead station, detached a M&SWJR [Midland & South Western Junction Railway] horse box and started towards Ropley, the next station. The horse box followed the train down the incline and collided with it 300 yds beyond Ropley station. Five passengers complained, but the horse appears not to have been injured.

The mishap occurred due to the horse box being fitted with a vacuum brake pipe, but no hand brake. It was also fitted with solid wheels, so the lack of spokes made it difficult to fit a sprag, so any slight movement of the vehicle would withdraw any pressure on the sprag exerted by the wheel and allow the sprag to fall. The movement in this case was probably caused by the express starting.

Around 1900 many towns and cities opened electric tramways to carry the growing population which was living further from town centres and most tramways were authorised by a Light Railway Order. As these generally ran along streets, they do not really fall within the scope of this book, but some could be considered borderline cases.

One such was the Wisbech & Upwell Tramway which was really a roadside railway, but built by the Great Eastern under the Tramway Acts in order to keep costs low. Opened 20 August 1883 it was worked by steam tram engines with their motion enclosed in order not to frighten horses. Bullhead rail enabled ordinary railway goods wagons to be taken along the line. Passenger traffic was withdrawn 31 December 1927, but goods traffic continued until 20 May 1966, latterly operated by BR with specially adapted diesel shunters.

The Wolverton & Stony Stratford Tramway used grooved rail on street sections and bullhead rail on sleepers on the roadside lengths. It was built to carry passengers, mainly London & North Western Railway employees, to the works at Wolverton. Opened 27 May 1887, its gauge was 3 feet 6 inches and steam tram engines hauled long, double-deck bogie coaches, some seating 100 passengers.

On 17 July 1919 the company went into liquidation and in February 1920 the London & North Western Railway took it over. The General Strike closed the line on 3 May 1926.

Another line which could be considered a railway was the Blackpool & Fleetwood Tramroad. Opened 14 July 1898 it was mainly a single line, sleepered, standard gauge track on its own right of way. Initial services were operated by cross-bench cars with trailers, with saloons being brought into use in the autumn. Blackpool Corporation took over the line on 1 January 1920.

The Kinver Light Railway opened a 3 foot 6 inch gauge electric line from the south Staffordshire village of Kinver to Stourbridge, Worcestershire on 5 April 1905. It was constructed with the object of carrying crowds from Wolverhampton and Birmingham to the delights of Stourbridge and was hugely popular, particularly on Bank Holidays. Grooved track offered street running while sleepered track was used for roadside and on its private right of way through fields and woods. Competition from bus and the private car saw the line's closure on 1 February 1930.

Another borderline case was the Grimsby & Immingham Electric Railway which began life in 1906 as a contractor's line to carry workmen and materials for constructing the Great Central's Immingham Dock project. It opened to the public on 3 January 1910 using a steam railmotor. The Light Railway Order of 1906 provided for an electric tramway to be built alongside the steam line and this opened 15 May 1912 using Brush bogie single deckers, the longest of their type in Britain. In 1948, as traffic demanded more cars, British Railways purchased three single deckers from Newcastle and nineteen from Gateshead. The system closed 1 July 1961.

The Llandudno & Colwyn Bay Electric Railway opened its 3 foot 6 inch gauge line 19 October 1907. Originally single track, eventually most was doubled. It had a long reserved section in the countryside over Penryn Hill. Before closure on 24 March 1956, it was the last 3 foot 6 inch gauge tramway in Britain.

The last of the traditional British electric tramways systems to be opened was the standard gauge Dearne District Light Railways which first ran on 14 July 1924. The line was unusual in that it was laid entirely with sleepered track, ballasted on roadside sections and paved in the street section. As mining subsidence in the area was prevalent, it was believed that this construction would prove easier to repair. It had a short life, closing 30 September 1933.

A few tramway systems, namely Glasgow, Huddersfield and Portsmouth, even in horse-worked days, used the gauge of 4 foot 7¼ inches as it was intended to run ordinary railway rolling stock over the tramway to give through goods services, though in the event, no wagons ever ran on the Huddersfield and Portsmouth systems. Although no connection with the main line network was ever made, in September 1904 two specially built coal-carrying trams came into service running from a siding in Hillhouse goods yard to local mills. This unique service was withdrawn in September 1934. As the depth of the flange on a railway wheel is greater than the depth of the groove of a tram rail, this necessitated railway wagons when using a tramway, running on the tip of the flange rather than the tread, so this necessitated a reduction in gauge of 1¼ inches.

One electric tramway which falls into yet another category is the Seaton & District Tramway. The closure on 7 March 1966 and subsequent track lifting of the Seaton branch was not the end of rail transport along the valley of the River Axe. Modern Electric Tramways Limited, which had operated narrow gauge double-decker tramcars at Eastbourne since the 1950s, had been seeking new location and eventually obtained permission to lay a 2 foot 9 inch gauge line from Seaton to Colyton, the length onwards to the Salisbury to Exeter main line at Seaton Junction having no traffic potential as Seaton Junction station had closed.

When the tramway opened to Bobsworth Bridge, (so called as the return fare was a shilling), on 28 August 1970, as the overhead was incomplete, power was taken from a battery trailer. It was the first tramway to be opened in England since the Dearne District Light Railways opened 14 July 1924. The line was extended to Colyford on 9 April 1971 and power from the overhead first used 23 September 1975. An extension to Colyton opened 8 March 1980. The increased number of visitors to Colyton caused certain problems and in 1980 the *Seaton News*, in connection with parish council meeting, reported: 'The council should write back to say the tram company should provide toilets and also point out that the flow of passengers was not seasonal but all the year round.'

The early 1900s was a great time for railways building cut-offs. As British railways had grown up piecemeal, in some places there was the opportunity and the advantage of shortening some of the routes. Critics of the Great Western Railway claimed that its initials stood for 'Great Way Round' and certainly some of its routes were far from bee lines. Paddington to Taunton was via Bath and Bristol, so the opportunity was taken of creating a shorter route via Westbury; the line from Paddington to South Wales reached the Severn Tunnel via Bristol, so a cut-off was built from Wootton Bassett to Filton to avoid the need to go southwards; a shorter route from Paddington to Avonmouth was via a new link from Filton, while a shorter route to Birmingham than that via Oxford was from Ashendon Junction to Aynho, south of Banbury.

About 1900 new suburban coaches tended to have bogies rather than six wheels, offering a better ride but at the expense of lower capacity per ton. A six-wheel coach weighed 15 tons and held 50 passengers giving 3.3 passengers per ton, but an eight-wheeler weighing 24 tons held 70, giving 2.9 passengers per ton.

15

Fishing & Bananas; Speed to the West; Motor Bus Competition and Steam Railmotors

1901

1 April 1901 the North British line was extended from Banavie to Mallaig thus improving access to and from the Hebrides. Many of the 4,000 men building this West Highland line were crofters and fishermen from the Hebrides. As it would aid the fishing industry the Treasury guaranteed a minimum return of 3 per cent on the capital of £260,000 for 30 years. This proved politically contentious: the Conservatives saw nothing wrong in subsidising a railway which could not be a commercial proposition, but the Liberals objected to taxpayers' money supporting a railway company.

The contractor was Robert 'Concrete Bob' McAlpine who had started as a bricklayer's labourer. The railway expected the line to be completed in five years but Concrete Bob did it in four. The greatest work was the 21-arch Glenfinnan Viaduct 416 yards in length on a curve of 12 chains and maximum height of 100 feet. The bridge over Borrodale Burn had a span of 127 feet, which was at that time the largest concrete span in the world. The fact that when the line was being built police block-houses were set up every 2 miles says something about the peacefulness of the navvies, the Lowlanders and the Irish not always seeing eye-to-eye with the Highlanders and Islanders. With the opening of the line the cost of coal dropped to below that of locally produced peat.

One day as the early morning Glasgow to Fort William goods reached the summit at Rannoch Moor a coupling broke and the brake van with its sleeping guard ran back while the rest of the train continued onwards to Spean Bridge. As no other train was following, the brake van was allowed to continue on its journey until a rising gradient south of Bridge of Orchy stopped it after a 25-mile run. The sleeping guard was woken by the stationmaster to find he had been returned to where he had been 2 hours previously.

The wives of railwaymen at Gorten on Rannoch Moor had passes to allow them to travel on the goods train to Fort William, and if a medical emergency arose, a doctor would be taken from Fort William to Gorten. Primary children from Gorten were taken to Rannoch for schooling and those of secondary age to Fort William. In 1938 when Rannoch School was full, a railway carriage was stabled at Gorten and used as a class room.

In July 1901 the Taff Vale Railway was awarded £23,000 damages against the Amalgamated Society of Railway Servants for loss of business caused by the 1901 strike, for until then it was believed that the 1871 Trade Union Act made it immune from prosecution.

From a junction half a mile south of Elvanfoot on the main Carlisle-Glasgow line, the Leadhills & Wanlockhead Light Railway opened 1 October 1901 to Leadhills and was extended to Wanlockhead on 19 September 1902 for goods and 12 October 1902 to passengers. Worked by the Caledonian, the first train was hauled by the Caledonian Railway's 0-4-4T No. 142 fitted with a cow catcher. This branch was a happy-go-lucky line and trains stopped anywhere to pick up or set down passengers and parcels. Normally one carriage and a van were all that was needed to handle the traffic. The expected revival of the lead industry never occurred and the line closed 31 December 1938.

In 1901–2 bananas started to be imported in large quantities through Avonmouth and Manchester and distributed using vans steam heated to 68 degrees Fahrenheit. These vans needed to be previously strawed and often this material was also brought by rail.

Although the three-link couplings used by railways in Britain until circa 1970 seem quite primitive, they had several advantages. As there was a slack of up to 3 feet between a taut coupling and the compressed buffers when wagons were closed-up, this fact could aid starting. The greatest effort needed by a locomotive was to get a train into motion. If the goods train had its couplings slack, when the driver opened the regulator he could get one wagon moving, then the next and so on until the whole train was on the move, whereas if the couplings were taut he would have to move the whole train as an entity right from the start. On a 60-wagon train the total slack could amount to 180 feet. When a goods train was starting a goods guard listened carefully as the taut coupling grew nearer and nearer to his van because as the engine gathered speed, due to the increased impetus, his van could receive a severe jerk as it was set in motion, so it was wise to brace himself.

A driver had to be careful not to accelerate too quickly or a coupling might break when it snatched, he could only accelerate more quickly when the couplings were taut. Similarly he had to be aware of the gradients: when approaching a dip he could either go quickly making sure that he pulled all the couplings taut or one might snap if wagons had buffered up on the down grade. The alternative was to go slowly down the dip letting the wagons buffer up and then slowly open the regulator for the rise, making sure that the couplings did not have too great a snatch. A skilled goods guard could apply the brakes on his van to help keep the couplings taut. If a coupling snapped in a dip due to a severe snatch, the separated wagons might seesaw back and forth for some while.

Although fitting wagons with vacuum brakes allowed goods trains to run faster due to their superior braking power, because they had to have screw and not three-link couplings, they were not enjoyed by shunters who had to get between the wagons to tighten the screw couplings to bring the buffers together to avoid any slack and then engage the two vacuum pipes. Unfortunately these features were not always scrupulously clean. Some wagons instead of having screw couplings to draw buffers together had Instanter couplings. With these the centre link instead of being oval was triangular, so when two wagons were buffered up, the centre link could be manipulated so that its centre link was facing with the apex down and thus was shorter, keeping the buffers close. If keeping the buffers close was not required, then it could be loose coupled in the normal way.

Some goods trains were fully fitted and others may have only had some vacuum-braked wagons fitted and placed behind the engine to assist in braking. Although normally this was an advantage, it could be a disadvantage, such as an event at Wood Green in June 1963. When D1509 braked and came to a halt, at the rear several loaded steel hopper wagons and bogie bolster wagons loaded with steel piles continued with considerable momentum, the piles shooting off over the adjoining platform.

Coupling wagons was a task which looked easy when carried out by a skilled man, but was not as easy as it appeared. To avoid the danger of actually going between two wagons, a shunter's pole was used. This was a strong pole about 7 feet long and 2 inches thick and at the end was a metal hook having a slight twist. When the buffers of two wagons touched, the end link of the three-link coupling on one wagon was swung up so that it would drop on the hook of the other wagon. As the coupling was too heavy to lift a swing was needed to get momentum. You had to beware that the pole was removed before the coupling fell on the hook.

Likewise, uncoupling was not quite as straightforward as it appeared. The pole was rested on the buffer casting and certainly not on the buffer shank or the pole would be squeezed into matchwood when the buffer was compressed. The hook on the pole was placed under the end of the coupling and when the links were no longer taut, you used the pole as a lever and the coupling was lifted off the hook.

A notice at the head of steep gradients required the driver of a loose-coupled train to stop and pin down brakes. This was done by the fireman and guard dropping the brake lever on a wagon and inserting a pin through a rack to hold the brake down. When a driver believed sufficient brakes were pinned so that he could control the train, he blew the whistle and the fireman returned to the footplate and the guard to his van. At the foot of the incline he stopped for the brakes to be unpinned.

When a wagon was loose-shunted along a siding, a shunter would run beside it to apply the brakes before it hit a raft of wagons too violently. He did this by wedging a brake stick, a strong wooden baton about 3 feet long, between the brake lever and wagon spring, forcing it down and then pinning it into position. It was tempting to steal a ride by sitting on the stick but this was forbidden as it was all too easy to fall and be run over. If you did not have a brake stick conveniently to hand it was tempting to make do with a shunter's pole, but this was dangerous because it was not substantial enough and would probably snap, perhaps even throwing the shunter under the wheels.

Until the end of the nineteenth century most goods wagons had a brake on only one side, which meant that shunters were frequently crossing the line and exposing themselves to danger. In an effort to improve safety, the Railway Clearing House encouraged railways to fit brakes which could be applied and released from either side. Another disadvantage of one-sided brakes was that they could cause a train to run away. At the head of a gradient the guard pinned down brakes as wagons passed him, but if two or three passed him with brakes on the other side, he would be helpless and the train might reach a speed too fast for him to be able to pin any more down. A survey was carried out to determine the number of wagons on average with one-sided brakes to be expected in a freight train. The result was that three in five would have mechanism for brakes on both sides, though in practice, it did not always work out that way.

Originally wagon axle boxes were lubricated with grease and on a cold day added to the resistance of a train until it had moved some distance and the grease had softened. Early in the twentieth century oil boxes were introduced which did not cause this problem. They also avoided another problem which the GWR experienced about 1900 when crows stopped a goods train.

A number of empty goods wagons for the West of England had accumulated in the sidings at Didcot and an engine and brake van were sent to take them on to Swindon. This train of empty wagons steamed out of Didcot, but at Challow, 11 miles further on, was stopped by the signalman who reported that he had seen sparks coming from several hot axle boxes.

The train was carefully examined and it was found that on several wagons the axle box covers were loose and easily lifted, while others were open and lifted right up. The railwayman did not need to be good detective to discover who had sabotaged the train. Crows were responsible and had eaten the yellow grease and left the marks of their feet behind.

The earliest wagon buffers were just extensions of the wooden side frame, later these were replaced with wooden blocks known as 'dumb buffers'. Early locomotives and carriages generally had very thick pads made of horsehair, though by about 1835 coaches had sprung buffers and these were gradually introduced to wagons, though it was 1913 before dumb buffers ceased running on main lines.

In the early 1950s hydraulic buffers became standard on BR freight stock. An hydraulic buffer has oil, which is almost incompressible, within the buffer shank surrounded by a chamber of compressible air. This design was found to reduce shunting impact shocks by 75 per cent. Hydraulic buffers are also found at termini. Another method of protecting fragile goods was the use of shock-absorbing wagons fitted with shock-absorbing underframes.

Traversing a sharp curve, sometimes buffers became interlocked. This was cured by pulling the wagons to a set of points and turning one wagon to one siding and the other wagon on the other.

In the 1960s with faster goods trains, quite a few derailments occurred. Investigation found that some four-wheeled wagons were rigid and that on poor track only three wheels were on the rails, daylight being seen between the tread and rail surface of the fourth wheel! A track testing car would then be run over the line to detect irregularities. The car was loose-coupled as to work effectively it required free movement as any buffing against an adjoining vehicle would tend to keep it steady.

From the 1890s the East Coast companies began using automatic couplers, shocks being absorbed by springs mounted transversely. Retractable side buffers were provided and could be placed in position when the carriage was needed to be coupled to one having a screw coupling. The Pullman Car Company and the SR also adopted automatic couplers as did British Railways. From the 1970s most multiple-units whether electric or diesel were just fitted with automatic couplers and had no side buffers and thus made the fronts aesthetically more pleasing.

Due to the need to be compatible on all railways, buffers were placed at a standard height of 3 ft 6 in above rail level. Some colliery lines used wagons with lower-height buffers, so some companies, such as the Maryport & Carlisle, fitted their locomotives with two sets of buffers, one above the other.

1902

In March 1902 the Great Western took King Edward VII and Queen Alexandra to lay the foundation stone for the Britannia Royal Naval College at Dartmouth. Drawn by the 4-4-0 *Britannia*, it set a non-stop record covering the 229 miles via Bristol to Kingswear in 4 hours and 23 minutes. A year later this achievement was eclipsed when the 4-4-0 *City of Bath* carried the Duke of Cornwall from London to Plymouth 245 miles in 3 hours and 5 minutes at an average speed of 63.4 mph.

The 11½-mile long, 1 foot 11½ inch gauge Vale of Rheidol Railway opened 22 December 1902 with the purpose of serving the district, providing for mineral traffic and providing easy access for tourists from Aberystwyth wishing to visit Devil's Bridge and the Rheidol Falls. It rises 670 feet on a ruling gradient of 1 in 50. The line amalgamated with the Cambrian Railways on 1 July 1913 and was taken over by the GWR 1 January 1922. Winter services were withdrawn 1 January 1930, trains from then only operating in the summer. Freight services were withdrawn 26 September 1937. The line was closed from 31 August 1939 until 23 July 1945. After 1968 it was British Railway's only steam-operated line.

The Glasgow & South Western ran a very lucrative service from Glasgow to the busy ship-building suburb of Govan, but in 1902 due to the electric tramways having siphoned off most of the passengers, the rail service was withdrawn. The same year, a circular service was opened by the Glasgow & South Western to serve the Paisley area, but through tramway competition had to be withdrawn in 1907, while a rival circular line built by the Caledonian Railway with six passenger stations around Paisley, was abandoned before opening!

1903

The 2 foot 6 inch gauge Welshpool & Llanfair Railway opened on 4 March 1903. Worked by the Cambrian Railways it was absorbed by the Great Western on 1 January 1922. Due to bus competition, passenger services were withdrawn on 9 February 1931 and goods traffic ceased 3 November 1956. A preservation society was formed and the first section of the line reopened 6 April 1963. The line now terminates at Raven Square, a mile short of the original terminus at Welshpool, to avoid traffic problems crossing or running along roads in the town. Unlike most British preserved railways, it uses a significant amount of foreign locomotives and rolling stock.

Railways were important in war as they could carry large numbers of troops and their equipment quickly from A to B. Longmoor Camp had been established in Hampshire in 1900 to provide accommodation for soldiers returning from the South

African War. The first railway troops, the 53rd Railway Company of the Royal Engineers, arrived in May 1903 to move huts from Longmoor to Bordon a distance of 5 miles. They were shifted by the ingenious method of laying two parallel narrow gauge tracks about 24 feet apart to carry trolleys on which the huts were transported. The fastest time for a journey was a day.

In 1905 a parallel standard gauge line was laid to connect with the Bordon Light Railway then under construction. Standard gauge traffic began on the Woolmer Instructional Military Railway in 1908, its name being changed to the Longmoor Military Railway in 1933. In addition to carrying supplies to and from the camp, the line had the purpose of training railwaymen for military working. As well as being used for regular soldiers, it was used for the annual summer training of the Supplementary Reserve units recruited from British railway companies. Over 40 trades were taught including those of surveyors, draughtsmen, platelayers, enginemen, signalmen, traffic control staff as well workshop staff comprising such skills as boilermakers, loco fitters and welders. Railway clerical work such as checking and store keeping was also taught. The railway had three departments which dealt with railway construction, operating and workshop practice respectively. Longmoor training was summed up in the remark: 'You can tell a Longmoor-trained Sapper anywhere, but you can't tell him much.'

The line offered the opportunity of experiencing double and single line working with a variety of token instruments and the use of the telegraph line-clear message system. To give staff a chance of enjoying a longer run, Hollywater Loop, 4 miles in length, was surveyed and laid out in 1932 for training purposes, but then lifted. Relaid in 1942 it added an oval to the layout, so that if required, trains could keep going round and round in the style of a model railway in order to give railwaymen the experience of making longer runs.

In 1933 the Longmoor Military Railway was operated by 22 officers and 385 other ranks. Stock that year consisted of 6 locomotives and over 100 coaches and wagons, most of the carriages being ex-First World War Great Western ambulance train vehicles returned from France. To offer further experience, the line had two internal combustion-engined railcars.

During both World Wars traffic was heavy and on some days during the Second World War over 800 wagons were exchanged with the Southern Railway. One unusual fact was that the railway offered free travel to passengers, including civilians, provided they held a ticket stipulating that they travelled at their own risk. The number of train operations declined from 1948 and Oakhanger–Bordon working ceased on 4 April 1966 with the closure of the Bordon Light Railway, and the complete closure of the Longmoor Military Railway came on 31 October 1969.

The Longmoor Railway had an excellent safety record, the only fatalities being on 13 October 1956 when on single track near Liss Forest Road station, War Department 2-8-0 No. 512 collided head-on with 0-6-0 diesel-electric 0-6-0 No. 877. The 0-6-0 was thrust back on top of the brake van immediately to its rear killing six soldiers. The collision was caused by a series of errors.

An example of railway companies being jealous of their territory occurred in the region of the Great Glen. When the West Highland was nearing completion, the North British announced its intention of building a branch from Fort William along the Great Glen to Inverness, hitherto only accessible by the Highland Railway. The Highland countered this proposal with a line from Inverness to Fort William.

Both companies were in financial difficulties and the only successful scheme was a branch from the West Highland at Spean Bridge, to Fort Augustus at the southern end of Loch Ness. The 24-mile long line had four intermediate stations. The financier behind the scheme was Lord Burton and as much of the office work was carried out at Burton-on-Trent by Bass Radcliffe & Gretton, the branch became known as 'the beer line'.

The Fort Augustus branch had no money for locomotives and rolling stock so needed to be worked by a larger company. The North British offered to work it for £3,000 per half year, but the Highland undercut this and offered to carry out the task for £2,000. Opened on 22 July 1903 it had cost £344,000 to build, yet in the first half-year the revenue was only £907. The Highland stopped working it in the spring of 1907, the North British took over and worked the line until 1 November 1911 before it too withdrew. The railway lay derelict until 1 August 1913 when the North British purchased it for £22,500. Never a paying proposition, it closed to passengers on 1 December 1933 and goods on 1 January 1947.

A major bridge completed in 1903 was at Connel Ferry spanning Loch Etive. Strong tidal currents prevented the building of a central pier, so a cantilever design with a span of 500 feet was adopted. The entire length of the bridge and its approaches is 1,044 feet. Construction began in 1898. During working hours a rowing boat was in constant attendance to rescue anyone who fell in. It was used on at least one occasion when it rescued a lad who fell 50 feet.

Connel Ferry Bridge was unusual due to the fact that it was designed for use also by road traffic. Following a contention with the local authority over tolls, for the first few years of its existence road vehicles were carried on a flat truck drawn over the bridge by a tractor adapted for rail use. Eventually a road was laid close to the railway and, when no train was signalled, vehicles crossed under their own power. Gates were provided at each end, interlocked with signals as at a level crossing. Because the bridge saved a 35-mile detour, the toll was be relatively high. When the branch closed in 1966 and the track in due course lifted, it became a single-lane bridge.

One branch affected by an electric tramway was the Southsea Railway jointly owned by the London & South Western and the London, Brighton & South Coast. In 1902 it was found that branch working expenses of £2,149 did not balance well against receipts of only £287. Something had to be done, and that something was singling the line and abolishing signals, unstaffing the East Southsea terminus and having the guard issue tickets. The most important innovation was the steam railcar. It was a novel concept, though not entirely new as *Express* had run on the Eastern Counties Railway back in 1847. The combined coach and locomotive designed by the London & South Western, could be driven from either end, thus obviating the need to run round at the end of each trip, saving both time and the cost of a signalman. The railcar commenced its regular working on 1 June 1903.

The Great Western was threatened by a potential tramway in the Stroud Valley and as the GWR was also designing a railmotor, sought permission to borrow the one built by the London & South Western, though it not really suitable for the Stroud valley being designed for a 1¼-mile long flat branch. With a load of 30 passengers speed did not exceed 8 mph on a gradient and on the two 7-mile runs steam pressure dropped from 150 lb per square inch to 80 and 60 lb respectively. Churchward, the GWR's locomotive superintendent, witnessed the trials and noted particulars of acceleration, running speeds and time occupied in stopping and was confident that his GWR car would be of ample power and steaming capacity for the work.

The GWR railmotors commenced service on 12 October 1903 and by 1905 had become so popular that the GWR was forced to provide a bus service to relieve the demand which exceeded the railmotor's capacity, but this only ran for three months until further cars were available to augment the train service.

Adding additional trailers was not the answer as the power unit was not strong enough to cope with the extra load on gradients. As a result over the years the motors were converted into trailers by the engines being removed to give additional passenger accommodation and were alternately pushed and pulled by tank engines fitted with an apparatus to allow the driver when the engine was pushing, to control the engine from what had been the last coach. The last GWR steam railmotor was withdrawn in 1935.

A locomotive was not allowed to propel more than two loaded carriages due to the fact that with side buffers, when being pushed at speed the thrust line on a curve is displaced inwards creating instability. Modern stock is fitted with centre couplers and this trouble does not arise.

As mentioned on page 218 the first railway in England to be associated with motor buses was the narrow gauge Lynton & Barnstaple. The actual owner of the buses was Sir George Newnes who had been largely responsible for building the line. A keen motorist, he decided to replace the horse-drawn coaches linking the line with Ilfracombe with motor buses and so formed the Ilfracombe Motor Coach Co which purchased two 16 hp 22 seat Milnes-Daimler wagonettes.

The service was inaugurated on 30 May 1903 and all went well until 26 June when the police found one of the drivers travelling at 'a little over' the statutory speed of 8 mph. When on 6 July the driver was fined £3 for the offence, Sir John ruled that the service was to cease at once.

Fortuitously, the GWR was contemplating extending the Helston branch to the Lizard, but before building the line thought it would run motor buses over the route to test the demand. The GWR purchased the two wagonettes from Sir George and they started the service from Helston on 17 August 1903. The service actually operated contrary to the legal requirements, which demanded that a man carrying a red flag should walk ahead of vehicles weighing 3 tons and over. As a bus travelling at walking pace would not have attracted much custom and manufacturers were unable to build a public service vehicle below that weight limit, the difficulty was imaginatively overcome by removing some equipment, painting '2 tons 19 cwts, 2 qrs' on the chassis and then replacing the equipment. The GWR bought more Milnes-Daimlers and the service proved so successful that the GWR decided to extend its bus operations and in October ordered 25 buses from Milnes-Daimler.

Two passengers were allowed to sit in the open beside the driver, but ladies were discouraged from occupying this position in case they distracted the driver's attention. The discouragement was making them 'Smokers only' seats. Some ladies then took up smoking so a 'Gentlemen only' notice was displayed.

If a bus broke down and the driver was unable to repair it, he had to call on a local farmer to provide horses to draw the disabled vehicle back to the depot. Around 1908 a telegram was sent to Slough depot by a driver experiencing problems: 'Mr West, do your best, am in a sewer, down at Clewer.' One short-legged driver had to have wooden blocks fitted to the pedals and could only just peep above his steering wheel, so policemen on point duty believed a driverless vehicle was approaching! Some GWR lorries had their bodies removed in summer and replaced with charabanc bodies for tour use.

Meanwhile the London & South Western Railway purchased two second-hand Milnes-Daimlers and on 1 June 1903 started a service between Exeter and Chagford. In preparation for an inevitable breakdown of one of the buses, arrangements were made with Bickfords of Exeter to supply a horse drawn replacement. The London & South Western gradually introduced bus services to other parts of its area.

In 1905 the London & South Western invested in four Clarkson steam buses. In due course the locomotive superintendent ruled that as the buses were steam powered, they should be sent for maintenance at the Exmouth Junction locomotive shed and it was claimed that they covered more mileage running to and from Exmouth Junction than in running to and from Chagford!

Bus running expenses were high: although petrol was only 4*d* a gallon, rubber tyres were very expensive – about £200 for a set – and they only lasted for about 10,000 miles.

During World War I some buses and parcels vans were converted to run on coal gas stored in a rubber bag on the roof. Sometimes the gas bag became detached and the conductor, conductress or van guard had to chase across fields to retrieve it.

The GWR increased its bus fleet and in 1927 owned 300, whereas in this year the other three main line companies had only about 50 vehicles in service between them.

In 1903 the dead man's handle was brought into use on electric trains operated by the Metropolitan District Railway. This meant that cabs could be single manned because should a driver collapse, the train would automatically stop. It was not quite infallible, as was evident on 6 August 1926 when an electric multiple unit ran through signals and crashed into a freight train near Manors (East) station on the LNER's Tyneside system. Fortunately, passengers received only minimal injuries but the driver could not be found.

A police sergeant walked back and found his body under a bridge not far from the previous station. Marks indicated that he had been leaning out of the door, struck a bridge support and was dragged out, so the train had travelled at approximately 35 mph for 1 mile 96 yards without a driver. But why had the dead man's handle not stopped the train?

A red handkerchief had been looped over the control handle and fastened with a triple knot, and a white handkerchief fastened through the red to tighten it and further depress the handle. The initial pressure needed to depress the handle was 25 lb, while to run the train an additional pressure of 1 lb 12 oz to 3 lb 12 oz was needed. The driver left behind a wife and five young sons. It was not put forward publicly, but the theory was that he had disabled the handle in order to lean far out of the window to spy on a couple in a first class compartment behind him. It may be significant that in October 1926 the LNER distributed a circular to motormen asking them to 'respect the privacy of passengers'.

Railway companies were required to make annual statistical returns to the Board of Trade and from 1856 mineral traffic had to be listed distinct from goods. At first minerals had been those mined such as clay, coal and coke, ore, sand and gravel, salt, stone and mineral fertilizers. From 1903 this classification also included other low-value bulk materials such as basic slag, bricks and tiles, ingots, organic fertilizers, pig iron, scrap metal, slates, sugar beet and tar.

1904

The Great Western's most famous train was the Cornish Riviera Express. In the first decade of the twentieth century there was great rivalry between the Great Western and the London & South Western for traffic between London, Exeter and Plymouth, while in the return direction each company sought passengers from trans-Atlantic liners who had disembarked at Plymouth in order to reach London, or some other destination, faster than if they had waited until the ship docked at Southampton.

As at that time the Great Western route was via Bristol, the London & South Western had the shorter route: 171¾ miles to Exeter compared with 194, and 231 to Plymouth compared with 246 miles. By 1904 the GWR was already running non-stop from Paddington to Exeter, but that year it introduced a non-stop run to Plymouth, the longest in the world.

The *Railway Magazine* was invited to run a competition to determine a name for this new train and prize of three guineas was offered. 1,286 entries were received and the Great Western's general manager, J. C. Inglis, selected the winner. He chose 'The Riviera Express' which had been submitted by F. Hynam of Hampstead and J. R. Shelley of Hackney, the prize being divided. As the train went on to Penzance, it was not long before the title was amended to 'Cornish Riviera Limited Express', which, being rather a mouthful, staff shortened to 'The Limited'.

'Limited' comes in the title because unlike many of the trains of the period it could not be lengthened should traffic be particularly heavy. To run non-stop and keep to its schedule over the steep gradients of South Devon, which in places were 1 in 36, the load was restricted to seven coaches. They were usually hauled by one of Churchward's new City class 4-4-0s, but the French compound 4-4-2 *La France* also appeared.

In due course the Great Western publicity department produced jigsaw puzzles depicting various scenes on the line, including a view of the Cornish Riviera Express. These were sold for 2s 6d and it was a smart move on the railway company to make people pay for its publicity – though to be fair, they were probably sold at cost price, as other similar wooden jigsaws produced by the Chad Valley Company sold at 5s.

In May 1904 4-4-0 *City of Truro* was the first engine to go faster than 100 mph. It did this descending Wellington Bank, west of Taunton, reaching 102.3 mph. The 4-2-2 *Duke of Connaught* took the train on from Bristol to London at an average speed of 71.4 mph.

In 1904 *The Scotsman* had a new building and sidings were laid below the presses in order that papers could be delivered directly to the train, while during the day newsprint and ink could be brought in.

In 1904 the North Eastern Railway introduced petrol-electric railcars while in 1904–5 the Great Northern Railway experimented with two four-wheeled railcars, each powered by two petrol engines. Built by Dick, Kerr & Co they seated 32 passengers. They were returned to the maker's and the Great Northern favoured steam railmotors. In 1905 the London, Brighton & South Coast Railway also tried Dick, Kerr railcars, one working the Brighton to Dyke branch being reported as 'not popular'.

1905

In 1905 the London & North Western and the Great Western had increased bookstall rents to too high a level, causing W.H. Smith to withdraw and instead establish shops as close as possible to stations, and these were manned largely by ex-bookstall staff. These two railways then appointed Wyman & Sons to its station bookstalls. Smith's continued to hold the Midland Railway contract and indeed it was renewed under the LMS, BR, Railtrack and Network Rail – the longest such contract in history.

Some bookstall managers were extremely hard-working. One such was William Vincent at Wyman's bookstall at Taunton. Due to a delayed delivery, he had missed the weekly carrier and was unable to send library books to a subscriber who lived some distance from Taunton. After a day's work he caught the 7.40 p.m. to Wellington and then walked with the books 5 miles to the subscriber. He missed the last train back and stayed overnight at the White Horse Inn where his bed was damp so he slept in his coat. He caught the first train to Taunton and was ready for his day's work. He believed that putting himself out to deliver the books in his own time and at his own cost was better than keeping a client waiting for a week.

Not all bookstall managers were so conscientious, and when porters and carriage cleaners collected used newspapers and ironed them, they sometimes came to an arrangement with an unscrupulous bookstall manager for them to be resold.

A curious line to open on 19 June 1905 was a private railway owned by the Edinburgh District Lunacy Board to serve Bangour Mental Hospital. Leaving the Bathgate line half a mile west of Bangour Mental Hospital, the 2-mile-long branch, with four trains each way daily, was worked by the North British, the line carrying patients, staff, visitors, coal and goods. Passengers could be booked from the North British station at Bangour, the tickets being marked 'Bangour (Private)'. An intermediate station was at Dechmont where many of the staff lived. Competition from road transport caused the passenger service to be withdrawn on 4 May 1921 and goods on 1 August the same year.

On 27 July 1905 two electric trains collided at Hall Road on the Lancashire & Yorkshire Railway and caused the most serious accident to an electric train to date, 20 passengers being killed when a Liverpool–Southport express was switched into a local passenger train standing in a siding.

In 1905 Cecil Paget, locomotive works manager at Derby on the Midland Railway, was appointed to the new office of General Superintendent. He oversaw four senior officers:

Superintendent of Passenger Service
General Passenger Agent
Superintendent of Motive Power
Superintendent of Operation

Serious congestion was experienced on the main line south of Leeds. One would expect such a high-ranking officer to sit in his office and study reports made by others, but this was not Paget's way. He camped out in a saloon coach by the side of the line so that he could take careful notes of passing trains and methods of working. It was not such a spartan life as one might suppose because Paget was a *cordon bleu* cook.

One of the problems was the long hours before footplate crews were relieved. In 1907 at Masborough, one of Paget's principal observation points, an office was set up to record booking-on times of the drivers, firemen and guards and determine where and when reliefs should be made. This work was done using the telephone rather than the telegraph. So successful was the office that although in 1907 there were over 20,000 cases of excessive hours being worked, there was not a single case in 1911.

A further step was when every morning reporting points in each area were required to state the number of wagons being loaded and the number of goods brake vans available. Throughout the day reports on loading were sent to Masborough so that train could only be dispatched when it was likely to be given a fairly clear run on the main line. This system proved so successful that it was extended to the line between Cudworth and Toton.

Where sections of quadruple track existed, two roads were for fast traffic such as passenger trains and parcels traffic, other trains using the two slow roads. Traffic on the fast lines was not usually so intense as on the slow and it would have been advantageous to have switched a freight train to the fast road for some miles before diverting it back to the slow. Such a decision would have been made by the signalman on the spot and he would have been reluctant to make such a decision because further down the line the slow lines may have been congested and there would not have been space to get the goods from the fast back on to the slow to allow an express to pass. The central office, having a wider view, was in a much better situation to make such a decision.

Many railways used the system of showing a day's working on a sheet of squared graph paper, vertical axis representing distance and the horizontal representing time. Paget's men started with a clean sheet of graph paper and plotted the maximum number of trains that could be passed through a section whether or not the existing timetable require that density. This was done for passenger and freight trains and so throughout the day there was a path, whether required or not, for a clear run for a certain class of train. Paths were available for expresses, stopping passenger trains, fast goods, coal trains – in fact for every kind of traffic. This meant that if an extra train was required it was not despatched at someone's whim but allocated to the first timetable path available for its particular class.

This centralised control system required that if a duty was booked for a certain class of engine, then any locomotive of that class must be capable of working it. Paget, with his locomotive training, knew that some engines of a class were better than others, so haulage capacity was based on the minimum rather than maximum haulage power.

Passenger locomotives were placed in four groups – Classes 1, 2, 3 and 4. Maximum loads were established for each class and for each duty. Punctuality was essential or the path system became a nonsense. As Paget had sorted out the long hours problem, he was in railwaymen's favour and they did their best to keep time. If a train exceeded the tonnage laid down for an available engine, then Control was responsible for finding an assistant engine. Depending on gradients, the assistant engine did not necessarily have to travel over the whole of the route and Midland train crews were skilled at detaching a pilot locomotive. In 65 to 70 seconds the fireman of the leading engine climbed down and uncoupled; the engine drew forward, the siding points reversed and the engine set back; the points reversed again and the signal pulled off for the main train to start.

Passengers benefited by Central Control as it resulted in the running of relatively light, frequent trains instead of fewer heavier ones. The only drawback was that as the number of coaches was limited by the available engine power, if there were more passengers than usual it was not possible to add an extra coach. In due course the Central Control system was adopted by the LMS.

The Central Control system affected the appearance of the railway as the small cabside engine numbers were replaced by huge figures on the tender that were much easier for the Control staff to spot, while the locomotive stock was renumbered in 1907, bringing the various power classifications into groups. Freight trains carried letters on the sides of brake vans indicating their origin and destination.

16

Steam Locomotive Improvements and Experiments with Internal Combustion Propulsion

1906

Steam generated in a boiler is saturated, containing moisture which condenses on metal surfaces, creates resistance to movement of the pistons and thus reduces efficiency. If sufficient extra heat is applied steam becomes superheated and will not condense and cause power loss. In 1898 William Schmidt invented a superheater with rows of boiler flue tubes. In 1906 Churchward of the Great Western and Hughes of the Lancashire & Yorkshire, introduced the superheater to England. Churchward used only a moderate superheat as he discovered that superheated steam lacked the lubricant qualities of saturated steam and caused valves and pistons to carbonise. As mechanical lubricators had yet to be introduced, it was common for a driver, while the engine was running, to leave his cab, climb along the running plate and top up the oil boxes at the front end from which the oil was siphoned to the bearings. The cabs were designed narrow so that a driver could climb out without fouling lineside structures. Wing plates beside the smoke box offered shelter to an engineman oiling at speed.

An important advance in safety was made in January 1906 when Automatic Train Control was introduced on the Great Western Railway's Henley branch. This consisted of a ramp formed by an insulated steel bar resting on a timber baulk laid centrally between the rails. A spring contact shoe was fixed on a locomotive so that when crossing the ramp it would be raised. When the adjacent distant signal indicated 'all right', the ramp was electrified and current passing through the shoe rang a bell in the locomotive's cab. If the signal stood at 'caution', or any failure occurred in the apparatus, the ramp remained electrically dead and the raising of the shoe broke a local circuit on the engine and caused a siren to sound in the cab until it was silenced by the driver.

The system was further improved by making the operation that caused the 'caution' signal to sound a whistle additionally open a valve admitting air to the vacuum pipe and thus apply the brakes to the engine and train. One great advantage was that trains could travel at much greater speed in dense fog as they could trust the audible signalling rather than have to rely on visible signals.

In 1927 the Ministry of Transport recommended the system to be adopted by all railways. In 1938 it was demonstrated to senior managers of the London & North Eastern Railway. A 10-coach express travelling at 69 mph approached a distant signal set at 'caution', the driver being instructed to ignore the warning siren sounded. The ramp was 318 yards in front of the distant signal, which was 1,032 yards ahead of the home signal. The train stopped 450 yards before the home signal. The reason that other companies did not adopt his excellent safety feature was that it was a time of financial stringency and also that it had been invented by the GWR and not by them.

The London & South Western's most serious accident occurred on 1 July 1906 when an Up boat train from Plymouth headed by L12 class 4 4 0 No. 421 was derailed on a tight curve at Salisbury, killing 24 of the 42 passengers while additionally four railwaymen died. Although a speed limit of 30 mph was imposed through Salisbury, the train came through the station at 50–60 mph. The driver was killed and reason for the driver's actions remain obscure. One plausible suggestion is that as Driver Robins had come on duty after a rest of only 9½ hours, he may have suffered a 10–30-second micro-sleep. This is particularly likely as his booking-on time moved anti-clockwise, the shift pattern most likely to result in disruption to the Circadian rhythms.

Another mysterious accident happened on 19 September 1906. The 8.45 p.m. semi-fast King's Cross–Edinburgh mail consisted of 12 vehicles, five of which were the heavy 12-wheeled East Coast

Joint Stock, hauled by the Great Northern 4-4-2 No. 276 with Driver Fleetwood and Fireman Talbot on the footplate. Station staff who talked with them confirmed that they were sober. Fleetwood had driven for 18 years and had been in charge of No. 276 since she was new, while Talbot had served a premium apprentice at Doncaster works and working under the district locomotive superintendent, and while firing on different classes, noted their behaviour. It was due to call at Grantham and although the signals were set at danger, it ran through at an estimated speed of 40 mph and the brakes were not applied.

Alfred Day in Grantham South signal box saw the driver and fireman motionless and staring ahead through the spectacle. The road had been set for the Nottingham goods and the engine derailed on the curve. Fires broke out caused by coal from the firebox and gas from the cylinders. Driver and fireman were killed instantly and No. 276 was so badly damaged that it was impossible to tell the position of the regulator and brakes at the time of the accident. Eleven passengers and a postal sorter also lost their lives. The only explanation was that the driver had mistaken his whereabouts, but as both knew the road well and it was a clear night this seems incredible.

The Piccadilly line, constructed like the other tube lines, was opened formally from Finsbury Park to Hammersmith on 15 December 1906. Most of its rolling stock was manufactured in France and Hungary. To overcome the problem of waiting two minutes for a lift, a double-spiral escalator was installed at Holloway Road in 1908, but it was never opened to the public. The first railway escalator linked the District and Piccadilly platforms at Earl's Court in 1911.

Piccadilly Circus began losing passengers because its claustrophobic entrance hall and mandatory lifts meant that it could not deal with the volume of passengers, and rival bus services were siphoning off traffic. Frank Pick completely rebuilt the station, moving Eros. The installation of escalators eased the flow, these being lit by uplighters, not downlighters. The large, bright and new ticket hall opened in 1928 set standards for the future, no longer did passengers have to negotiate dark Edwardian tunnels. Pick wanted to turn the underground into London's biggest art gallery and produced attractive posters. New trains had high-quality fabrics covering sprung seating, while an extra set of sliding doors was placed in the centre of a car to greatly facilitate the flow of passengers getting on or off.

To cater for population growth the line has been extended, many of the new stations being designed by Charles Holden. Today the Piccadilly line has the greatest number of Grade II listed buildings on the underground: 32. 160 million passengers used the Piccadilly in 1960; today the figure is 210 million.

Down Street station in the heart of Mayfair closed in 1932. During WW2 it was used as a control centre by the Railway Executive Committee and being 72 feet below ground level was safe from bombing. Commuters passing inches away on the other side of the wall had no idea it was there.

On 18 November 1987 a fire developed at King's Cross underground station when a discarded match or cigarette ignited fluff and grease behind a wooden escalator. Fifteen minutes later a huge fireball engulfed the ticket hall, killing 31 and injuring a further 100; it took 6 hours for the fire to be extinguished.

1907

Travelling tender-first leads to unpleasant conditions on the footplate as it is cold and draughty and unless the coal is frequently dampened, coal dust blows in your face. To some extent conditions can be ameliorated by fixing a sheet between the cab roof and tender, but it is still unpleasant, especially at speed, so express passenger trains were not usually worked in this manner.

On 28 December 1906, due to freezing snow, the engine of an express for Edinburgh was unable to reach the Arbroath turntable, so it was sent on tender-first. Snow, freezing on the wires, brought them down, putting the telegraph out of action, so to keep trains running the old time-interval was reintroduced. Driver Gourlay was warned by the Arbroath stationmaster to proceed with great caution and keep a good look out for the train ahead – very difficult in a blinding blizzard. At Arbroath South signal box Gourlay was again stopped and cautioned. At a speed of about 30 mph Gourlay crashed into a stationary passenger train standing at Elliot Junction. The last three coaches were demolished and Gourlay's engine mounted and turned over on the wreckage, its wheels furiously revolving for 10 minutes until the regulator was closed by the driver of the local train into which the express had crashed. Gourlay's fireman was killed, as were 21 passengers.

Although one can sympathise with Gourlay for having to drive in such conditions, his speed was certainly reckless and also it was unwise of him to have accepted 'something to keep the cold out' from waiting passengers before leaving Arbroath.

Gourlay was tried at the High Court of Justiciary and imprisoned for five months, provoking a public cry of injustice. On 21 March 1907 the North British board petitioned the Secretary of State for Scotland for the remission of the rest of his sentence and it was reduced to three months. The North British paid his wages while in prison and promised employment on release. The final cost of the Elliot Junction accident was not settled until 26 June 1910 and the bill was £43,637 10s 11d.

It was perhaps due to the Scottish carefulness with money that the North British, realising that gas lamps at some of its stations also lit the public highway, tried to make the local authority share costs. Often a town was responsible for cleaning railway lamps and paying half the gas bill. When the railway installed a clock at Leith Central, in view of the fact that all in the town benefited, asked the council to pay for the electricity that illuminated it; the council complied.

Sorting wagons into various sidings by a locomotive shunting backwards and forwards is labour intensive, time consuming and wearing on both man and engine. A far better method was for an engine to propel a train over a hump, and a wagon, or wagons, being uncoupled and gravity taking them down to the required siding. In April 1905 the Great Central agreed to construct a hump marshalling yard at Wath in the South Yorkshire coalfield. Partly opened on 19 August 1907, on 4 December 1907 it was brought into full operation, the first power-operated gravitation yard in Britain. It contained 110 roads and 15 reception sidings capable of dealing with 5,000 wagons daily. It was shunted by four 0-8-4Ts designed for the purpose.

In 1907 both the North British and the Caledonian were facing financial troubles, so to ease matters formed a joint committee for the purpose of restricting competition, reducing the train service and otherwise lessening the expenditure of the companies, with the special instruction that the board desire that the reduction in the train service and the expenditure should be considered from the point of view of the benefit of both companies and on the lines of what might reasonably be expected to follow a complete amalgamation of the companies. The North British withdrew 107 trains and Sunday services in most areas. The working week at its Cowlairs factory was reduced from five and a half days to four.

Accidents caused by speed are unusual, so it is strange that following the disaster at Salisbury in 1906, another should occur so shortly after, this occurring at Shrewsbury on 15 October 1907. The London & North Western's 1.20 a.m. mail train from Crewe to the West of England consisted of 15 vehicles hauled by the 4-6-0 No. 2052 *Stephenson*. It left Crewe 8 minutes late but between Whitchurch and the outskirts of Shrewsbury had managed to regain 5 minutes.

Before the platforms at Shrewsbury was a tight curve of 610 foot radius with a speed restriction of 10 mph. As the platform already had a train, the penultimate signalman kept his signals at danger and was required to stop and warn the driver before sending him to the next signal box ahead of the platform. Instead of stopping, it ran through the red signals at full speed.

The signalman sent 'Train running away on right line' to the next box, but as the train rounded the tight 10 mph restricted curve at 60 mph, the engine ran for 75 yards over the sleepers and ballast before rolling to the right and falling on its side, the wooden carriages striking the derailed engine and becoming matchwood. The driver and fireman died together with 11 passengers, two guards and three Post Office sorters working in the mail vans.

When the breakdown gang arrived an attempt was made to pull the engine clear of the wreckage by using a steel cable attached to eight locomotives, but the cable snapped and eventually it had to be lifted by crane sent from Wolverhampton.

Why did the accident happen? There has been no answer to this question. The driver knew the road well and was aware of the speed restriction, but perhaps he fell asleep; certainly nothing was found faulty with the brakes, nor the engine. As the accident was inexplicable, the inspecting officer made no recommendations.

Kilbowie station on the Helensburgh line was adjacent to the large Singer sewing machine factory erected on a 46-acre site in 1883 and eventually expanded to 110 acres, being the largest single industrial complex in Scotland. Between 6.00–7.00 a.m., 14 train loads of Singer workers arrived, their carriages unlit unless the workers provided candles. As the firm put so much traffic on the line, the North British Railway provided dedicated wagons with the company's name painted on. As these wagons were restricted to the firm's uses and thus were generally returned empty to Kilbowie, usually making an uneconomic trip, Messrs Singer eventually agreed to give up the special wagons if Kilbowie station was renamed Singer, the change occurring on 3 October 1907.

1908

Interestingly the North British made the decision on 23 June 1908 to abandon the electric lighting of carriages, which had only been introduced two years before, and use incandescent gas light. Perhaps due to the fire risk of using gas, on 30 October 1913 electric lighting was re-introduced.

The Midland Railway had an electricity generating station at Heysham supplying power to the port and inaugurated electric trains between Lancaster and Morecambe on 1 July 1908. It used alternating current at 25 cycles, 6,600 volt DC, and because the line was short and the voltage high, no sub-stations were needed. The trains gave very good value and were not replaced by steam until 12 February 1951 when work started on conversion to 50-cycles at 6,600 volt AC, the Midland's heavy overhead structures superceded by those of much lighter construction. The line reopened with electric power on 17 August 1953 and was the prototype of BR's high-voltage main-line electrification.

1908 saw the appearance on the GWR of Churchward's 4-6-2 No. 111 *The Great Bear* – the first Pacific to run in Britain. Appropriately named, it was virtually a standard Star with a larger boiler. Owing to its weight it was restricted to the main line between Paddington and Bristol. Although a publicity success, it was not deemed sufficiently good for others to be built. Although a few other engineers, such as Nigel Gresley, came to favour Pacifics because the space above the pony truck allowed a wide firebox, the GWR preferred 4-6-0s which although limiting locomotives to a narrow firebox, offered maximum adhesion on the South Devon banks of Dainton, Rattery and Hemerdon.

1909

Quite a number of municipal authorities owned railways, one such being a line to serve the Bradford Corporation's sewage works at Esholt. At its maximum extent about 1931 it had 22 miles of track. The oil recovered from wool-combing effluent was re-cycled as locomotive fuel and also provided grease for wagon axle boxes.

To avoid motorists between the West of England and South Wales having to go north to Gloucester, which was the lowest point at which the Severn could be crossed, in 1909 the GWR operated a car and motor bike carrying service through the Severn Tunnel. This continued until the Severn Bridge opened in 1966.

The first portion of the Brighton & South Coast Railway's overhead electrification scheme, that from Victoria to London Bridge, opened on 1 December 1909.

1910

1910 saw the opening of the 15-inch gauge Sand Hutton Railway on the estate of Sir Robert Walker. In 1920 it was extended to Warthill and Claxton and converted to 1-foot-6-inch gauge in 1922 and extended to Bossall the following year. It opened to passengers 4 October 1924, but closed in March 1932.

On 24 December 1910 Hawes Junction, later known as Garsdale, on the Settle and Carlisle line was the scene of a serious accident. Signalman Alfred Sutton was having a busy night and had five light engines to deal with which had assisted trains up the gradient on each side. Before returning, these assistant locomotives required turning on the famous turntable, stockaded to prevent a strong wind blowing an engine continuously round and round.

After a Down special express had passed, two light engines coupled together moved to the advanced starting signal. In due course it dropped; the drivers sounded their whistles and moved off. The signals did not return to danger. Soon the midnight sleeper St Pancras–Glasgow express appeared, running quickly to take advantage of the falling gradient before the final rise to Ais Gill summit and also passed that signal.

Driver George Tempest of a light engine waiting to return to Leeds spotted that there were now two trains in the section and ran into the signal box asking: 'What have you done with those two engines for Carlisle?' 'They've gone to Carlisle,' Signalman Sutton replied. 'They've not,' Tempest retorted, 'when you pulled off for the Down express them two engines was standing on the Down road behind the advanced starter waiting for it to come off, and when it came off they went.' Sutton laughed and consulted his train register.

He phoned Ais Gill and asked: 'Where's them two light engines I sent on, Ben?' and received the reply: 'You haven't given me any.' Sutton asked: 'Has the Down express arrived yet?' To which Ben replied: 'There's been nothing passed.' Sutton turned to Tempest and said: 'I've done it.' Looking out of the window, the sky towards Ais Gill was crimson.

Drivers Scott and Bath were on the light engines, and when crossing the Lunds Viaduct Bath looked back and saw the headlights of the express. He opened his regulator and whistle and Driver Scott, realising the problem, did the same, but all to no avail. 2-4-0 No. 48 at the head of the express crashed at 65 mph into Bath's tender which was travelling at only 30 mph. Scott's engine stayed on the rails but its tender derailed, while Bath's engine was derailed and proceeded for 350 yards. Unfortunately the second engine of the express, Class 2 4-4-0 No. 549, toppled over against the side of the cutting and the coaches piled against it. The two 12-wheeled sleeping cars had electric lighting, but the rest of the stock was fitted with Pintsch oil gas-lighting, the gas being stored in cylinders at a pressure of 85 lb per square inch. The escaping gas caused the wreckage to catch alight, 12 passengers dying.

In his report Colonel Pringle said that although Signalman Sutton been primarily responsible for the disaster, Drivers Scott and Bath had remained on the Down line for at least 13 minutes and had made no attempt to carry out Rule 55 whereby a fireman should have been in the box to remind the signalman of the presence of the engines. The Midland Railway did not favour lever collars as reminders, but had they been provided and placed over the Down signal levers as soon as the engines were allowed out on the main line, the accident would have been avoided.

Colonel Pringle advocated stronger gas cylinders and automatic cut-off valves to act if the main pipe broke, 'But I still hold that electricity is the more desirable and should be adopted wherever possible.' Unfortunately, as we shall see, the Hawes Junction accident was repeated at Ais Gill in similar circumstances on 2 September 1913 when 14 more passengers lost their lives and two died later.

The Midland continued to build gaslit coaches up to World War I as they were lighter than the heavy batteries and dynamos required for electric lighting. Although gaslit coaches were phased out on the main lines, this form of lighting had to be retained on some branch lines due to the fact that speeds were so low that the dynamos could not keep the batteries charged. The very last gaslit coaches ran on the Culm Valley line in Devon in 1962.

Colonel Pringle's other recommendation was the adoption of track circuits whereby electrically isolating a section of track and passing a low-voltage current through it allowed a train to be detected and signals suitably locked to protect it.

1911

Trams and motor buses drew traffic from the railways and in 1911 another competitor raised its ugly head when Britain's first trolleybuses began a service between Laisterdyke and Dudley Hill.

By 1911 many railwaymen were aggrieved at their pay and conditions of work. The Government offered to set up a royal commission to examine the workings of the conciliation boards which had been set up to enable employers and staff to discuss pay and conditions, but made no promise that any recommendations would be implemented.

The four railwaymen's unions (the Associated Society of Locomotive Engineers & Firemen, the Amalgamated Society of Railway Servants, the General Railway Workers' Union and the United Pointsmen & Signalmen) believed this offer unsatisfactory and on 16 August 1911 sent an ultimatum to all the railway companies stating that unless there was an immediate response within 24 hours, all labour would be withdrawn from the railway industry. This was the first national railway strike.

The Prime Minister, H. H. Asquith, replied:

We cannot allow the commerce of the country to be interfered with in the way it would be by a national dispute, and we want you men to realise in the event of it reaching that stage, His Majesty's Government have decided that they will use all the civil and military forces at their disposal to see that the commerce of this country is not interfered with.

The Home Secretary, Winston Churchill, mobilised 58,000 troops who shot dead two strikers at Llanelli. This aggravated the situation, making the men more inclined to continue the fight, and also caused many members of the public to sympathise with the men.

The strike began on 18 August when many lines, stations and goods yards fell silent. Labour MPs persuaded the Cabinet that mediation and not bloodshed was the way forward and railway companies were told that they must agree to a meeting between their General Managers and the unions, which they had failed to recognise. The companies agreed that if the strike was called off and all strikers reinstated, that the railwaymen's grievances would be examined by a royal commission on which they would accept equal representation with the unions. This offer proving satisfactory, the strike ended on 20 August 1911.

The first railway escalator was installed at Earl's Court in 1911. Early escalators had a diagonal at the bottom and were therefore shorter on the right than on the left. When getting off this moving staircase a special technique was required: you had to start with the right foot leading. It was found that one escalator did the work of five lifts.

1912

In 1912 the London, Tilbury & Southend Railway was absorbed by the Midland. Its terminus was at Fenchurch Street, owned by the Great Eastern which allowed it to use only one platform of the five available. This platform was extended to where all the tracks converged to cross an overbridge immediately beyond the station. Maximum use was made of this platform: tank engines were used exclusively as they took up less space than tender engines; there was room for 13 coaches, but not 14, so the heaviest trains had a 6-wheeler added to the 13 bogies. Trains arrived in the morning at 8.06, 8.15, 8.24, 8.33, 8.44, 8.53, 9.04, 9.10, 9.17, 9.30, 9.34, 9.39, 9.50 and 10.02 a.m. 9 minutes was not long for a 14-coach train to unload 1,000 passengers; a fresh engine to be coupled to its rear, draw the empty coaches out and the points to be set for the arrival of the next train. It meant that drivers, firemen, signalmen, porters and platform inspectors had to be on their toes. The Great Eastern allowed the 8.53 and the 9.34 to use one of its platforms.

In 1912 the Great Western trialled a 4-wheeled railcar on the Windsor branch. Designed by British Thomson-Houston, it was powered by a Maudslay 40 hp petrol engine which drove a dynamo to power two tram-like electric motors on its axles. It proved satisfactory and a contemporary report stated:

> The journey between Slough and Windsor was about 2½ miles in length; the timetable allowed nine minutes and no difficulty was experienced in adhering to it, despite fairly heavy gradients. A maximum speed of 32 miles per hour was obtained. On petrol, the consumption worked out at about 8 miles per gallon with a range of 240 miles, a creditable performance, bearing in mind that the vehicle weighed 14 tons 9 cwts. The overall length was 33 feet 3 inches, which allowed seating accommodation for up to 46 persons. Two staff only were required to run the vehicle – a driver and a guard.

The GWR withdrew this vehicle in October 1919 and sold it to Lever Brothers Ltd for use on their line at Port Sunlight.

In October 1921 the Weston, Clevedon & Portishead Light Railway invested in a railcar built by the Drewry Car Co Ltd. With an overall length of 19 feet it had seating accommodation for 30 passengers with another 12 standing, so on warm days it was just as well that all the side windows could be lowered for ventilation. Petrol consumption was 16 miles to the gallon. Spare cans of petrol were kept in the passenger saloon and there was no bar to smoking.

A larger 4-wheeled petrol-engined railcar was purchased by the SR in 1928 and worked on several branches. It had a 50 hp engine, 20-foot wheelbase and seated 26 until around 1930 when a luggage compartment was added reducing seating to 22. In 1934 it was sold to the Weston, Clevedon & Portishead Railway for £272.

An accident due to the fault of a driver was rare, but one such happened on 17 September 1912 at Ditton Junction on the London & North Western near Widnes. The 5.30 p.m. express from Chester to Liverpool was signalled to cross from the fast to the slow line at Ditton Junction, but the driver, fairly new to the road, misread his signals and believed he had a clear run on the fast line. Consequently he took the 15 mph turnout at 60 mph.

The 2-4-0 turned over and travelled on its side until it struck the pier of an overbridge, breaking its back and bringing down a large section of brickwork. The following coaches leapt over the engine and tender. Gas from the lighting cylinders ignited the wreckage and an inferno erupted. The driver, fireman and 13 passengers died.

1913

On 29 March 1913 the Associated Society of Railway Servants and the General Railway Workers' Union, the latter founded in 1890 to organise workshop staff and the poorly paid workers, together with the United Pointsmen's & Signalmen's Society, united to form the National Union of Railwaymen with a membership of 267,611.

The voltage for the first English electric railways was 600–650 volt DC, but in 1913 the North Eastern Railway adopted 1,500 volt DC with overhead wiring for moving the 1,400-ton mineral trains from Shildon to Newport on Teesside.

On 29 July 1913 the Lancashire & Yorkshire Railway's Bury–Holcombe Brook branch was electrified by Dick, Kerr & Co. of Preston which was considering a tender for an electrification contract in Brazil. It used overhead catenary at 3,500 volts, though due to the expense of the overhead, the Lancashire & Yorkshire Railway chose 1,200 volt DC third rail for its Manchester–Bury line, inaugurated on 16 April 1916. Due to safety considerations this third rail was almost completely boarded in, shoes making side contact with the conductor rail. The Holcombe branch changed to third-rail operation on 29 March 1918.

The Settle to Carlisle line was the scene of another disaster on 1 September 1913. Class 4 4-4-0 No. 993 and Class 2 4-4-0 No. 446 had their tenders filled at Carlisle with Cumberland coal, good-quality steam coal, but had not been screened and thus contained a large proportion of small coal and slack. No. 993 was to work the train from Stranraer and Glasgow leaving Carlisle at 1.35 a.m. while No. 446 would follow at 1.49 a.m. with coaches from Inverness and Edinburgh. Driver Nicholson on No. 993 was further disturbed when he was told that his train was 13 tons over the maximum to Ais Gill and that no assistant engine was available.

Although Fireman Metcalf did his best, it was impossible with the small coal to keep a good fire and the needle of the pressure gauge kept dropping. Between Ormside and Kirkby Stephen they only managed 29 mph instead of the scheduled 40 mph. At Mallerstang steam pressure was so low that Nicholson opened the large ejector, normally used for releasing the brakes after a stop, to hold off the vacuum brakes and 3 miles south of Mallerstang pressure had fallen to 85 lb and No. 993 stalled.

Donelly, the front guard, enquired what was wrong and was told, 'We'll be a few minutes, we're short of steam' and saw Fireman Metcalf using a longer pricker to clean the firebars. Whitley, the rear guard, came up and Donelly called out, 'Only a minute', so Whitley did not go back and place detonators on the track to protect the train.

The signalman at Mallerstang wondered why he had not received the 'out of section' signal from the next box and was told it had not arrived, so when Mallerstang was offered the Inverness and Edinburgh train he kept his signals at danger.

Meanwhile, No. 446 was making rather better progress as it had a lighter train, but the small coal was causing poor steaming. Near Mallerstang Driver Caudle left the cab and went forward to oil an axle box, but due to the very strong wind this took longer than expected; by the time he had returned to the cab the train had passed the Mallerstang distant signal. Back in the cab he found his fireman facing a problem: water was short because the right-hand injector would not start and the left-hand injector was not functioning properly due to the low steam pressure – 140 lbs against the normal 175 lb. Driver Caudle used his expertise to manipulate the steam and water controls to get it started but while doing this failed to observe the Mallerstang signals at danger.

A few minutes later No. 446 crashed through the rear van of the stranded train and into the coach beyond. Gas from the lighting system ignited and set fire to the train, killing 14 passengers and fatally injuring two others, while 38 passengers on the second train were seriously hurt.

Lieutenant-Colonel Sir John Pringle in his report criticised the Midland for not providing good coal and for the fact that, even though it had been stopped for at least seven minutes, those in charge of the first train had not protected it as the rule book required. The accident was principally caused by the failure of Driver Caudle and Fireman Follows to observe the Mallerstang signals, and although Pringle appreciated their problems, he noted that knowing that they had missed the signals they should have proceeded slowly. He also observed that the introduction of wick-type lubricators rendered it unnecessary for a driver to leave the cab while his train was in motion and that the company should have informed its drivers of this fact. He also observed that the Midland should follow other railway companies and have a lever which would allow a signalman to place warning detonators on the track – had the Mallerstang signalman been able to do this when he saw the train running through his signals, the accident would probably have been prevented.

17

WWI and Its Aftermath

1914

The end of the horse-drawn passenger service on the North British Railway's 2½-mile-long Drumburgh–Port Carlisle branch in Cumberland was marked on 4 April 1914. Horses took approximately 25 minutes to complete the journey; the system of horse haulage dated back to 1856, before the North British took over the line. The train consisted of one small, narrow, four-wheeled coach or 'dandy' running on standard gauge track. The branch line being on the English side of the border, the North British considered horse traction quite good enough for these southerners. The horses were not numbered with the company's locomotive stock, but were certainly named. Freight on the line had been steam-hauled until 2 January 1899 when it was closed to goods traffic, but reopened on 1 May 1899 using horse traction. Steam working was reintroduced on 6 April 1914. The last horse-worked passenger service in Britain was the 1½-mile-long Inchture–Inchture Village branch in Perthshire, which closed on 1 January 1917; no goods service was operated.

In 1914 the government controlled the railways through the Railway Executive Committee, consisting of eleven general managers from the principal companies under the nominal chairmanship of the President of the Board of Trade but, in reality, under Herbert Walker, general manager of the London & South Western. The companies were compensated for being taken over by the government on the basis of their net receipts for 1913, suitable adjustments being made for the fact that some railways, such as the

London & South Western, dealt with more army traffic than others as they served military camps on Salisbury Plain and the docks at Southampton.

The War Office gave the committee 60 hours to assemble locomotives and rolling stock to convey the British Expeditionary Force to Southampton. This was achieved in 48 hours and embarkation began on 9 August and was completed by 31 August. During this period, from Southampton had been shipped 5,006 officers, 125,171 men, 38,805 horses, 344 guns, 1,575 other vehicles, 277 motor vehicles, 1,802 motor cycles and 6,406 tons of stores, using 711 trains. The busiest day was 22 August when 73 trains were dealt with, eight timed to arrive between 6.12 a.m. and 7.36 a.m., another eight between 12.12 p.m. and 1.36 p.m. and 21 between 2.12 p.m. and 6.12 p.m. Within a quarter of an hour, each train was emptied of troops, horses, guns and ammunition. This rapid arrival of the British Expeditionary Force in France surprised the Germans.

The London & South Western Railway actually owned Southampton Docks, and by 4 August 1914 practically all of its docks there were taken over by the government and most of the cross-Channel steamers withdrawn. During the war Southampton was so busy that sometimes between 25 and 30 vessels left in a single night. The Military Command believed the army would use Southampton, but then discovered that Dover and Folkestone were nearer the fighting front. Between 1914 and 1918, 5,400,000 men were sent to fight in France and all travelled by train to south coast ports. Trains also carried supplies needed: arms, engineering goods, horses and their forage, food for the troops, mail, road stone and timber for duckboards and supporting the sides of trenches. Just one army division ate half a train's worth of supplies every day. Initially soldiers posted their laundry home and when returned it was often accompanied by cakes and other goodies.

Later in the war, to ease the transport of locomotives and rolling stock to the Continent, a train ferry terminal was made at Southampton. The locomotive building works in Britain were turned over to producing war supplies such as shells, guns and gun carriages, with the resulting neglect of locomotive maintenance. Railway companies loaned locomotives to the government, some for use at munitions factories or rail-served army camps, but most were sent overseas. Some little-used branch lines were lifted in order to provide track for military railways – the Basingstoke–Alton line being one example. Some former running lines were used for stabling – for instance the South Eastern & Chatham's Greenwich Park branch was closed to passenger traffic and used for holding wagons loaded with war material awaiting inspection. The line between Welling and Bexley Heath was worked as a single line while the other road held coal wagons; following the landslip between Folkestone and Dover, the stable section in Shakespeare Tunnel was used for storing more than 100 wagons of explosives.

The South Eastern & Chatham had ordered 10 L class 4-4-0s from the German firm of Borsig. They were delivered in May 1914 and the contract stated that they were on three months' trial before payment. The period expired on 8 August 1914. Payment was not made until 1920, when the bill was settled with interest.

Although at first many railwaymen enlisted, eventually they were not allowed to join the services as they were needed to operate the railways in Britain. To avoid them being given a white feather, which indicated cowardice, railwaymen wore a lapel badge labelled 'On War Service', numbered to prevent forgery.

Hitherto women were not generally employed on the railways except for office, laundry or upholstery work, but with many railwaymen enlisting, female employees handled a much wider range of duties, almost everything except engine driving and firing. This caused a problem because when peace was declared and men returned from the forces and wanted their jobs back, the women were not keen to retire – and the railways enjoyed employing women because their pay was lower. Pre-1914 about 13,000 women were employed on Britain's railways and the figure rose to 46,000 in 1916 and almost 69,000 in 1918. The National Union of Railwaymen did not lift its ban on female membership until July 1915; it was only the Sex Discrimination Act of 1975 that finally gave women the opportunity to drive trains. In WWI, at many key junctions, volunteers maintained refreshment services for servicemen. For example, troops could enjoy a free buffet at Waterloo, paid for by railwaymen whose wives ran it unpaid.

In the early days of the war it was feared that Germans would try to sabotage the railways, so to counteract this threat sentries guarded important bridges and tunnels. After 14 sentries had been fatally injured by trains and two more killed by 'friendly fire', it was realised that it was safer to withdraw most of the sentries.

1915

The Metropolitan Railway's publicity department invented the term 'Metro-land' to encourage the building of housing estates alongside its line, which extended as far as Verney Junction in Buckinghamshire, 50½ miles from London and only 21¾ miles from Oxford. In 1910 the Metropolitan ran a Pullman car from Verney Junction to Aldgate. The first tube line to invade the countryside was the Bakerloo when, in 1915, it reached Queen's Park where it emerged from the tunnel. Eventually it reached Watford Junction, but was cut back to Stonebridge Park in 1982 and then Harrow & Wealdstone. Bull & Bush station, Hampstead, was built because the borough only gave permission for a tube line as long as the station brought visitors to the Heath. At 221 feet it was the deepest station on the tube. Although platforms were installed, no surface building was constructed as insufficient commuters would have used it so it never opened.

When the first Zeppelin raids started in May 1915, underground stations were used as shelters. In February 1918, on one night 300,000 people sheltered there– almost twice as many as would do so in WWII.

Wartime conditions led to reduced standards of maintenance and this resulted in an accident at Weedon, Northamptonshire, on 14 August 1915. The 8.45 a.m. Birmingham (New Street)–Euston express was hauled by George the Fifth class 4-4-0 No. 1489 *Wolfhound*. A taper pin, smaller in size than a pencil, which should have locked the screwed collar retaining the offside coupling rod on its crank pin, fell out. The collar then slowly unthreaded itself, and when this too fell off the coupling rod became detached from the crank pin. The rod struck one of the sleepers on the Down line, pushing the track seriously out of alignment. This happened immediately in front of the fifteen-coach second portion of the Irish Mail, which was approaching at speed headed by Precedent class 2-4-0 No. 1189 *Stewart* piloting Renown class 4-4-0 No. 1971 *Aurora*. The ensuing derailment killed ten passengers and injured sixty-four. Fortunately the two trains did not collide and the Birmingham–Euston express stopped without further tragedy. The Board of Trade inspecting officer recommended that in future the collars should be given left- and right-hand threads so that in the event of a locking pin being lost, they would be unlikely to unscrew themselves.

In 1915, F. G. Smith of the Highland Railway designed a River class 4-6-0, but the company's civil engineer, concerned about the locomotive's high axle weight, stated that he would not permit it to run over the tracks for which he was responsible. Smith refused to make any alterations to the design and his decision was supported by the directors. When *River Ness*, the first engine of the half-dozen ordered was delivered, a representative of the civil engineer arrived at the shed in the early hours of the morning and set up a pair of templates representing the maximum profile permitted. To everyone's consternation she fouled the templates. As the line was vital wartime link to and from the north of Scotland, carrying the Jellicoe Specials taking coal and personnel to Thurso for the fleet at Scapa Flow, the civil engineer could not take any risks so imposed a ban, which the directors supported. Smith was forced to resign and due to wartime inflation, the Rivers were actually sold to the Caledonian at a profit. Ironically in 1928 the Rivers appeared on ex-Highland lines in LMS days and did splendid work on the lines for which they had been designed.

The worst British railway accident occurred on 22 May 1915 at Quintinshill on the Caledonian Railway. As two Scotch expresses were running half-an-hour late, it was decided that instead of running a local train after them, the local would go first and be shunted into a loop at Quintinshill to let the expresses overtake.

Signalman Tinsley was on the day shift at Quintinshill. He lived at Gretna Junction and normally cycled to work, but whenever the local train was to call at Quintinshill he had an unofficial arrangement to be informed of this by signalman Meakin, who was working the night turn. The local did not normally stop at Quintinshill as there were no platforms but when it did, Tinsley liked to use it to avoid a cycle ride. As Meakin officially ended his turn at 6.00 a.m., all train movements after this time were jotted on a piece of paper so that Tinsley could copy them in his own hand into the Train Register, suggesting that he had come on duty at the correct time.

When the local arrived, the Down loop where it would have been placed was already occupied by a goods train, so the local was switched to the Up main line. Meakin failed to use the lever collars provided to remind him of the presence of that train and accepted the first part of the Scotch express. At 6.34 a.m. an empty wagon train arrived in the Up loop just as Tinsley arrived to take over the box. Tinsley was busy copying the entries into the register and the fireman of the local train arrived in the box to carry out Rule 55, signed the register, but failed to check that collars were placed on the Up signal levers.

Either Meakin or Tinsley had sent the 'Train out of section' signal to the previous box and cleared the block section indicator, but failed to send a 'Blocking back' signal to show that the local train was occupying the Up line. Tinsley pulled off his Down signal for the Scotch express and accepted an Up troop train drawn by 4-4-0 No. 121. This was travelling very fast down a gradient of 1 in 200 and crashed into 4-6-0 No. 907 at the head of the local train standing on the Up line. The tender of No. 907 lay across the Down line. The troop train comprised 15 old Great Central coaches and these were smashed to pieces; its length of 213 yards reduced to only 67 yards.

The guard of the local train and the footplate crew from the empty wagon train had the presence of mind to realise the danger of the approaching Down Scotch express consisting of 13 bogie vehicles drawn by two Dunalistair class 4-4-0s No. 140 and No. 48 travelling at approximately 60 mph. The driver of the leading engine saw the guard's frantic waving and made a full application of the vacuum brake, but the distance of 270 yards that the guard had covered offered too little space to stop the train. The two engines killed many of the troops who were trying to rescue their injured comrades.

All the coaches on the troop train were gaslit and before leaving the cylinders had been fully charged. Coal from the overturned troop train engine ignited the gas and the wreckage went up in flames. Attempts were made to douse the fire: extinguishers were used, water taken from tender tanks, a pump and hose connected to a stream and the Carlisle fire brigade summoned but the fire was still smouldering 24 hours later. The death toll was horrific: 8 lives lost and 54 injured in the express, 2 passengers killed in the local train, and as the roll of the Royal Scots was lost in the accident, the exact number of troops killed was not exactly known but it was estimated that 215 lost their lives in addition to 2 railway servants, while 191 soldiers were seriously injured. Out of a battalion strength of 500, only 52 were able to parade in a neighbouring field to answer their names.

The Board of Trade inspector, Colonel Druitt, said that the two signalmen were responsible, together with the fireman who should have ensured that collars were over the levers. Druitt strongly urged the abolition of gas lighting and the introduction of steel rolling stock. Convicted of culpable homicide, Tinsley received three years' hard labour and Meakin 18 months' imprisonment.

The Railway Operating Division was formed as part of the British Army in France and the Low Countries and a large stock of locomotives was immediately required – and the ones needed were those in shortest supply, namely medium and heavy goods. Fortunately, in 1915 the North Eastern Railway had electrified its most heavily worked mineral line, between Shildon and Newport, and was able to spare 50 of its 0-8-0s. The Great Western, London & North Western and the Midland railways were also able to contribute.

These were insufficient, and robust new engines were required. There was no time to design a new class, so a choice was made from existing British engines and the Great Central's rugged and powerful 2-8-0 was chosen.

Coaches and luggage vans were converted to ambulance trains, some of which ran on the Continent to ports in France, while others conveyed the wounded from British ports to hospitals. The carriages were virtually mobile hospital wards and were staffed by service medics and nurses. Carriages for naval wounded had swinging cots, similar to hammocks, whereas army carriages were equipped with bunks. An injured serviceman on board a hospital train had a reasonably good chance of survival.

The London & South Western Railway's third rail electrification between Waterloo and East Putney opened on 25 October 1915.

1916

On 2 February 1916 two arches of Penistone Viaduct collapsed when heavy rain scoured their foundations. A 2-4-2T plunged into the gap and, as it could not be readily recovered, was cut up where it lay, its chimney recycled as a flower pot on Brockholes station platform. The repaired viaduct was reopened on 14 August 1916.

Southampton was one of the principal ports for hospital ships and during WWI dealt with a total of 1,234,248 wounded requiring 7,822 trains. Following the Battle of the Somme, on 1 July 1916 no less than 29 hospital trains were required, and during the week ending 9 July 1916 a total of 151 hospital trains ran. Dover Marine was another important station for the wounded. Two vessels and six hospital trains could be dealt with simultaneously. From December 1914 until February 1919, 4,076 hospital ships containing a total of 1,260,506 wounded, and 7,781 hospital trains, were dealt with at Dover.

During WWI, 14,871 special Forces' leave trains ran from Dover or Folkestone to Victoria and vice versa, while military mail was dealt with at Victoria and carried to Folkestone, usually requiring about 30 covered goods wagons each night. Civil mail to and from the Continent travelled via Southampton.

1917

To cover increased costs due to the war and to deter civilian travel to free seats for troops, at the beginning of 1917 ordinary fares were increased by 50 per cent. To economise on staff, some stations and halts were closed as were some branches.

1918

Fortunately, accidents caused by landslips are rare, but one occurred on 19 January 1918 on the Settle–Carlisle section of the Midland Railway. The 8.50 a.m. St Pancras-Glasgow express was just running into Long Meg cutting, between Little Salkeld and Lazonby, when a slip caused by a sudden thaw suddenly blocked the line ahead. Ironically only five minutes before, a platelayer had walked by the exact spot and seen nothing wrong.

The driver had no time to stop so 4-4-0 Compound No. 1010 ploughed into the clay at nearly 60 mph, fell over on its side and the two leading coaches were telescoped against the tender. No. 1010 received surprisingly little damage. However, she was involved in a further accident at Little Salkeld 15 years later when hauling the Thames–Forth Express on 10 July 1933; she ran into a goods train being shunted.

Approximately 21,000 railwaymen serving in the forces were killed in WWI.

A new military port, which eventually had 65 miles of track, was created at Richborough in Kent, from where 9,644 barges were taken across the Channel right into the French canals serving the battlefields. By 10 February 1918, a roll-on/roll-off train ferry operated from Richborough to Calais and Dunkirk carrying various war supplies including locomotives, rolling stock, tanks and heavy guns on their own mountings. The three train ferries each carried 10 Railway Operating Division 2-8-0s, or 54 wagons.

1919

On 1 February 1919 trade union demands for an eight-hour day were met, and coupled with the higher cost of coal plus rates and taxes this made 1919 expenses double those of 1913. Yet the railway companies had to meet these costs from just a 50 per cent increase in passenger fares, while the goods and mineral rates had been fixed by the Government to those charged in 1913. Rumours spread that the Government planned a £2 0s 0d a week minimum wage compared with the existing £2 11s 0d and a pre-war minimum of 18 shillings. The Government, which was still running the railways, in August 1919 craftily offered a rise to footplatemen in the belief that if a dispute arose over the reduction of pay for some other departments, the footplatemen would not support a strike. In the event, the plan did not work. All railwaymen, including those on the footplate, went on strike from 27 September 1919.

For the first time, both the National Union of Railwaymen and the Government placed advertisements in *The Times* and other newspapers explaining the position. On 5 October 1919 the strike ended when the Government abandoned its plan to reduce wages. The strike had demonstrated the power of the unions and from this date the Government and railway management saw that cooperation, rather than confrontation, was the best policy. Unfortunately for the railways, this strike assisted the development of the road haulage industry, which was boosted by ex-servicemen driving army-surplus lorries. Due to wartime conditions with extra trains being run carrying troops and war supplies, coupled with the fact that the railway works had been producing armaments, locomotive overhaul and maintenance had been sorely neglected.

Old engines, which should have been scrapped, had been kept running and, for example, on 20 December 1919 no less than 22.05 per cent of North British locomotives were unfit for service. There was a coal shortage in December 1919 and several British railway companies experimented with the Scarab apparatus for burning oil.

1920

After four and a half years of war during which only the minimum maintenance had been carried out on Britain's railways, they were worn out. During WWI the army had used 66,000 lorries and many of these were sold to the demobilised soldiers who had driven them during the war. Approximately half the railways' revenue was derived from freight and now, when it was at its weakest, the railway faced a rival. Furthermore, it was a legal requirement for the railways to publish a book of charges, so all the road hauliers needed to do was to look up a charge, undercut it and so secure a load for themselves. To combat this threat, the North British Railway hired a fleet of 20 ex-army lorries from the government and set up as a road haulier.

On 11 November 1920, the second anniversary of the Armistice, a shunting locomotive drew up at Platform 8, Victoria station, with a van containing the body of the Unknown Warrior, which was carried to Westminster Abbey and interred at 11.00 a.m.

The Great Eastern Railway became principally a passenger-carrying railway and in 1891 had been the first to allow third-class passengers to use a restaurant car. It took a pride in punctuality. An American, Henry Thornton, was appointed general manager in 1914 and in 1920 reorganised its suburban services to offer the finest and most intensive steam-operated services in the world. As the first- and second-class carriages carried distinctive yellow and blue stripes, they were nicknamed 'jazz trains'.

The North British S class 0-6-0s with a tractive effort of 25,211 lb were quite good engines, but one was unable to handle the heaviest Dunfermline–Aberdeen coal train without assistance, the maximum for one engine being 27 wagons. In 1920 Major Stemp, the company's traffic superintendent, investigated powerful goods locomotives belonging to other British companies and was impressed by the performance of GWR 2-8-0s, which regularly hauled 28 wagons over the 9 miles 22 chains between Lostwithiel and Doublebois, with its ruling gradient of 1 in 58, in 29 minutes. The same class regularly hauled Welsh coal trains of 38 wagons over 1 in 90 gradients.

GWR 2-8-0 No. 2846 was sent to Scotland and the test arranged for 12 January 1921 over the 6 miles 53 chains of 1 in 75 between the Bridge of Earn and Glenfarg. Unfortunately weather conditions were atrocious, the track covered in snow and a near blizzard was blowing.

On the first test, a North British 0-6-0 set off with 23 loaded 16-ton wagons (437 tons 8 cwt) and two brake vans, but stalled a short distance up the bank and returned to the Bridge of Earn.

In the second test, GWR No. 2846 was given a load of 29 wagons (552 tons 4 cwt) and two brake vans and reached Glenfarg in the scheduled time of 25 minutes.

For the third test, five wagons were added to the load, bringing it to 643 tons 9 cwt. After running for approximately 2 miles, No. 2846 encountered hard packed snow on the rails, slipped badly, came to a stand and was unable to restart.

James Calder, general manager of the North British, wrote a very nice thank-you letter to his GWR counterpart F. J. C. Pole:

> Mr Nicholls [GWR Superintendent of the Line] will no doubt have informed you of the results of the tests. I may say that these were carried out under pretty extreme weather conditions, but they proved the superiority of your company's locomotive over ours, and will of no doubt be of great assistance to us in connection with designing engines in the future for the hauling of mineral traffic over heavy gradients. I should just like again to thank you very cordially for your kindness in giving us the loan of your locomotive.

The North British civil engineer was unhappy about the weight of No. 2846, while the locomotive superintendent was concerned about the high pressure and consequently the high maintenance costs involved.

One observer of the tests was Major H. A. Watson, general superintendent of the North Eastern Railway, who on returning home immediately wrote to C. H. Stemp, the North British operating superintendent:

I am pleased to tell you that we have tested one of our 0-8-0 three-cylinder freight locomotives with a load of 700 tons on a five-mile bank of 1 in 70 and it lifted the load quite satisfactorily. In fact it made up a minute compared with the standard running for the regular mineral service over the same section of line. In view of this Sir Vincent Raven [the North Eastern's chief mechanical engineer] will be very pleased to send the locomotive to be tested on Glenfarg bank if Mr Whitelaw [chairman of the North British] so desires. I may say that on formula the tractive effort of our locomotive is 36,000 lb compared with the Great Western's 33,000 lb so it ought to accomplish what the Great Western engine failed to do.

William Whitelaw agreed to the tests, but the civil engineer said it would be too heavy for general use on the North British. Due to the coal strike, tests were postponed and did not take place until 28 August 1921. The 0-8-0 No. 903 with a load of 617 tons 5 cwt reached Glenfarg in 33 minutes, two minutes late. On the second trip with 703 tons she was on time, as she was on the third with 754 tons 16 cwt. It was estimated that using a T3 0-8-0s on Aberdeen coal trains would save £10 9s 9d per train or £2,250 18s 9d a year, but the civil engineer rejected the proposal.

It was announced that a Great Central 2-8-0 would arrive for testing on the North British but before this could be carried out, grouping had occurred and the Great Central, North Eastern and North British were part of the LNER, the North British chairman, William Whitelaw, becoming chairman of the LNER. Ex-Great Central 2-8-0 No. 1185 arrived in July 1923 and made successful runs. It was believed to be superior to the North Eastern 0-8-0. No. 1185 was of the same class as 125 ex-Railway Operating Division engines which the LNER had purchased from the War Department, and 10 of these went to Scotland.

1921

Although mechanical and electrical gadgets to ensure safety had been introduced with the development of railways, when the human element entered the equation, mistakes could happen. In 1880 Edward Tyer invented a seemingly foolproof method of working a single line that made it impossible for two trains to collide head-on. At each end of a section, metal tablets were held in an instrument and electrically interlocked so that only one tablet could be issued at a time. To avoid the possibility of the tablet from one section being placed in the instrument of another section, the tablets were named with the stations at either end and differently shaped, so it seemed that nothing could go wrong; unfortunately, though, it did on 26 January 1921.

At Abermule on the Cambrian Railways, the stopping train from Whitchurch was scheduled to cross the Aberystwyth–Manchester express, but if either train was late, they passed at the next station either to the north or south. On that particular day, the staff at Abermule consisted of relief stationmaster Lewis, signalman Jones, porter Rodgers and Francis Thompson, a 15-year-old junior clerk who collected tickets and assisted in the booking office. The Tyer's electric tablet instruments were kept in the station building rather than the signal box, and only the stationmaster and signalman were authorised to use them, but in practice everyone could and did.

Montgomery signal box advised Abermule that the stopping train had arrived and was waiting to proceed. Signalman Jones was in the instrument room with Rodgers and Thompson, the stationmaster having gone to lunch, and Jones pressed the release to allow Montgomery to take out the Montgomery–Abermule tablet. He then went to his signal box to set the road and open the level crossing gates. The stationmaster then returned from lunch and went to the goods yard to superintend the movement of wagons, leaving Rodgers and Thompson in charge. Newtown asked permission to send the express on to Abermule and this time Rodgers pressed the tablet release. When the stopping train arrived Thompson collected the tablet from the driver, intending to return it to the instrument, but when he met the stationmaster returning from the goods yard he gave it to him.

Unfortunately, Lewis assumed that the tablet was for the stopping train to proceed and handed it to the driver. Compounding this, the driver assumed it to be the correct token for the section ahead and failed to examine it as the rules demanded. Jones, knowing the express was running to time, was surprised when the stopping train left, but assumed that for some reason the express had been held at Newtown and that the tablet he had allowed to be released had been replaced. Only after the stopping train had set off did they realise that the tablet had not been replaced.

About a mile from Abermule the express was travelling fast on a falling gradient when the driver spotted the stopping train pounding up the gradient. He made a full brake application but the driver of the stopping train failed to spot the express. The engines collided, killing the footplate crew of the stopping train and 15 passengers. The express driver and fireman climbed down the footplate steps, hung on to the last minute and then jumped off, thus saving their lives. At the time of collision both trains were travelling at about 30 mph. Lying seriously injured, the express driver asked his fireman to search for the tablet of the other engine and found it was for the Montgomery–Abermule section.

The inspecting officer, Col Sir John Pringle, recommended that the Tyer's instruments be in the signal box and that the starting signals interlocked with the tablet instruments so that a signal could not be pulled off unless the instrument had been cleared.

When the wartime Railway Executive Committee was disbanded on 15 August 1921, it was believed that rather than return to the pre-1914 competition between railway companies, a more unified system should be set up – thus avoiding some uneconomic duplication of facilities. It was, in fact, a compromise between the pre-1914 situation and nationalisation. Thus the Railways Act of 19 August 1921 amalgamated 120 railways into four main groups – commonly referred to as the 'Big Four': the Great Western (GWR), the London & North Eastern (LNER), the London Midland & Scottish (LMS) and the Southern Railway (SR). The Act came into force on 1 January 1923. Each group consisted of constituent and subsidiary companies. These constituent companies are listed in Appendix 4.

The Railways Act of 1921 stated that, for the first time, charges were to be related to profits and the Big Four were given a standard revenue, roughly their 1913 receipts. Due to the rise in road transport, this did not work; just at the time when the railways needed a large income to pay for the four and a half years of wartime neglect, they were losing money to road haulage.

In 1921 the Great Central, North Eastern and North British Railways, with the Great Western, established a through service between Aberdeen and Penzance, a distance of 785 miles.

Existing trains were used from Aberdeen to York and Swindon to Penzance, a new express being introduced between York and Swindon. Through passengers were allowed to make sleeping car reservations either in the Paddington–Penzance sleepers into which they could change at Swindon if going west, or in the King's Cross–Aberdeen sleepers at York if going north. For most of its history it was not a complete train, but a single through coach with first- and third-class compartments, GWR and North British stock being used alternately and, from 1923, GWR and LNER. In summer the through portion expanded to two or more coaches. In 1939 on the southbound run it left Aberdeen at 10.20 a.m. and arrived at Penzance 7.25 a.m. having taken 21 hours and 5 minutes for the trip.

1922

In February 1922 the Huddersfield Gas Works Railway opened from Newtown Yard and for a quarter of a mile it ran along the middle of Beaumont Street and through the market. The train was proceeded by a flagman and the locomotive's wheels were protected by wooden guards.

18

Grouping and Further Attempts at Improving Locomotive Efficiency

1923

1 January 1923 marked the end of most of the British railway companies, which had been amalgamated to form the Great Western (GWR), London & North Eastern (LNER), London Midland & Scottish (LMS) and Southern (SR) railways. The year 1923 was also when the GWR No. 4073 *Caerphilly Castle* appeared, the most powerful express locomotive in the country and widely advertised as such. It brought to prominence the value of naming passenger locomotives, though sometimes these could be humorous – an LNER Pacific named after a racehorse, *Pretty Polly*, looked inappropriate heading an East Coast express, while the SR's *Portland Bill* suggested a quarryman smoking a pipe.

Although the GWR 4-6-0s of the two-cylinder Saint class and the four-cylinder Star class were doing fine work, by 1923 something even more powerful was required. The result was the 4-6-0 Castle class, this wheel arrangement being better suited to the South Devon banks than a 4-6-2.

By 1926 something even more powerful was demanded to haul heavy passenger expresses at average speeds of around 60 mph. The result was the appearance, in 1927, of the King class 4-6-0 which at 40,300 lb had the highest tractive effort of any 4-6-0 ever to run in Britain.

When working hard, a King could burn coal faster than a fireman could replace it, so the fireman had to be able to anticipate the driver's demands for steam. The grate was as large as the narrow firebox could accommodate. Churchward's and Collett's designs paid particular attention to water circulation, and despite the relatively small grate compared with the size of the boiler, climbs were generally followed by falls where there was less demand for steam and the fireman had a chance of replenishing the boiler. The Kings' 22½-ton axle load restricted them to main lines, known as 'double-red' routes due to the GWR's weight restriction code that appeared on the cabside of its engines. The GWR favoured passenger and goods locomotives with good factors of adhesion and high tractive effort that were capable of short, fierce bursts of sure-footed power, choosing these factors rather than a wide firebox.

Although the South Devon banks caused the GWR problems, the hurdle was partly eased by slipping coaches at Westbury for Weymouth and at Taunton for Minehead and Ilfracombe. Slipping coaches was an interesting procedure whereby coaches were uncoupled from the main train whilst on the move, the main train continuing non-stop through a station while the detached coaches drew up at the platform and passengers either detrained, or the coaches were taken to their destination by another engine. Apart from saving time, it meant that a train could become lighter as it went westwards, thus less weight having to be hauled over the steep Devon gradients.

The slipping coach guard detached the vacuum brake and pulled a lever at a designated spot. The coupling hook fell, his coach was detached and he could control braking into the platform. If he saw any obstruction, he could sound a warning gong. The Western Region was the only BR region to operate slip coaches, the last slip being made at Bicester, 10 September 1960.

1924

A strike of members of the Associated Society of Locomotive Engineers & Firemen (ASLEF) took place between 21 and 25 January 1924 due to the introduction of poorer mileage allowances and special duty rates. Members of the National Union of Railwaymen were instructed to work as normal because all the unions, including ASLEF, had assented to a National Wages Board decision in November 1923 accepting some wage reductions.

Although some local trains ran a regular interval service, which made it easy for passengers to remember when they could catch a train, this did not apply to those running longer distances until, in 1924, the GWR standardised the departure times of nearly all its expresses from Paddington: 10 minutes past the hour for Birmingham, 15 for Bristol, 30 for Devon and Cornwall, 45 for Worcester and 55 for South Wales, though trains did not necessarily run every hour.

The Harwich–Zeebrugge train ferry was formally opened on 24 April 1924 by Prince George. Great Eastern Train Ferries Ltd had acquired the three train ferry ships built for the Government in 1917 and used in WWI for ferrying wagons on the Richborough–Calais and Southampton–Dieppe routes.

The ferry service from Harwich was operated by the LNER, but the Belgian Government gave the company thousands of wagons that had been specially adapted for running on British railways and had been used during the war. The capacity of each ship was 54 10-ton wagons offering a through rail connection from most of Europe – excluding Spain, Portugal and Russia, which had a different gauge. This through running avoided the transshipment of perishable, or fragile, traffic such as eggs, fruit, vegetables and dairy produce.

The former Southampton ferry berth was re-erected at Harwich. Wagons were pushed onto the stern of the ferry across a communication bridge carrying two railway tracks. The bridge was hinged at the land end to enable it to rise or fall with the tide. The twin tracks at the ferry's stern soon branched into four. To maximise interior space, the two parallel funnels at the centre of the vessel were set at the extreme edges. Customs & Excise arranged that goods forwarded in padlocked wagons under Customs seal could be examined for Customs' purposes at inland British railway stations instead of at Harwich. Two steamers made six round trips weekly, the third vessel being held in reserve.

In 1924 the trains that left both Edinburgh Waverley and King's Cross at 10.00 a.m. were named the 'Flying Scotsman' and in 1928 made the journey non-stop. In 1929, the London & North Eastern, keen on publicity, agreed to a film, *The Flying Scotsman*, being made and offered the necessary facilities. Unfortunately, to provide plenty of drama for cinema-goers, the action was not very life-like: passengers climbed in and out of carriages while the express was speeding and there was fighting on the footplate, while Nigel Gresley, the company's chief mechanical engineer, was horrified when a villain uncoupled a locomotive from its train using only a penknife – which, of course, in reality would have been impossible. Gresley insisted on the disclosure: 'For purposes of filming, licence has been taken with the safety features of the Flying Scotsman.'

In 1931 the press was invited to watch the Flying Scotsman race against a speed boat and a De Havilland Puss Moth.

To help the East Coast route gain passengers from the competing West Coast route, the Flying Scotsman had such features as a hair salon, a ladies' retiring room, a vibro-massage parlour and a cinema carriage. A potent special 'Flying Scotsman' cocktail was available in the bar and consisted of whisky, vermouth, Angostura bitters, sugar and ice.

The Flying Scotsman is one of the very few named trains running in Great Britain today. Only running in the Up direction, it leaves Edinburgh, competing with the air service. It is also one of the relatively few passenger trains hauled by a locomotive rather than being a multiple unit. It is hauled by a Class 91 electric locomotive, which holds the British speed record of 161 mph.

1925

At the Southern Railway's AGM in February 1925 the chairman observed that the company used two different electric traction systems – overhead on the Central Section and third rail on the Western and Eastern Sections – and as the systems were not interchangeable, the matter would need to be resolved. The solution, announced on 9 August 1926, was the replacement of the overhead AC system by the DC third rail, on the grounds of the latter's ease of installation and its low cost of construction and maintenance. Alternating current trains were gradually withdrawn, the last running on 22 September 1929.

One of the few English narrow gauge railways opened on 7 April 1925. This was the Ashover Light Railway, running from Ashover in Derbyshire to Clay Cross. Although the termini were only 3½ miles apart, due to the topography the line was 7¼ miles in length and its steepest gradient 1 in 36. As was often the case, a railway opening late was likely to close early; its passenger services were withdrawn on 30 September 1936, the line closing entirely on 31 March 1950. The line had several interesting features: most of its locomotives were purchased from the War Department Disposals Board and had been built by the Baldwin Locomotive Works, Philadelphia, USA, for use on light railways on the French and other fronts during WWI. As they performed most efficiently working chimney-first and it was advantageous for negotiating the sharp curves to have the bogie leading, a turning triangle was provided at each end of the line. Mineral traffic was carried in open bogie wagons purchased from war surplus stocks, the flat-bottomed rail coming from the same source.

Initially its trains were well patronised, 5,000 passengers travelling in the opening week, which included the Easter holiday. Fares were low, with cheap day returns being available for only 6*d*; in fact, initially passenger traffic was heavier than mineral traffic. Although four fully enclosed coaches were purchased for year-round use, eight open-sided roofed bogie vehicles catering for summer traffic were from the 1925 Wembley Exhibition 'Never-Stop' railway.

The 850-ton coal trains required assistance up the 1 in 40 Wentworth Bank near Barnsley. The London & North Eastern Railway solved the problem in 1925 by bringing into service the most powerful steam locomotive in Britain, the U1 class 2-8-8-2 Beyer-Garratt; weighing 178 tons 1 cwt, its tractive effort was 72,940 lbs, but even so it generally took something like 2¼ hours to climb the 19 miles from Wath to Dunford Bridge. The engine worked on banking duties for 20 hours out of every 24. The line called for electrification, and experimental working was carried out between Wath and Barnsley on 2 September 1951; the section onwards to Dunford Bridge opened on 4 February 1952 as part of the Manchester–Sheffield electrification scheme. Just a single electric locomotive at the head (with another at the rear to guard against breakaways) was capable of hauling the heavy coal trains up the bank at 30 mph.

From 1 to 3 July 1925 celebrations were held at Darlington to mark the centenary of the opening of the Stockton & Darlington Railway, with a replica of the first train being hauled by the actual engine *Locomotion*.

In 1925 the LNER took delivery of two Sentinel geared steam railcars. Until this year there had been only two attempts in Britain to popularise high-pressure gear-driven rail motors, one being designed by Col H. F. Stephens in 1905 for the Kent & East Sussex Railway, the other being the *Peebles*, which ran trial trips on the Midland Railway. The maximum speed of the latter was 30 mph compared with the 50 mph of conventional motors. Although the Sentinel patent boiler and engine appeared in 1906, it was initially used for road vehicles; in 1923 the Sentinel Waggon Works and Cammell Laird & Co. produced a light, geared steam railcar for the 3-foot-6-inch gauge Jersey Railway. A version of this car was exhibited at the British Empire Exhibition, Wembley, in 1924–5 and this car was tested on the LNER between Scarborough and Whitby, which had a ruling gradient of 1 in 39. Although rather underpowered for these severe gradients, it was purchased with a sister vehicle. Both had two vertical cylinders and chain drive. In subsequent years more were purchased, later models driven by a cardan shaft and with six-cylinder engines. Most of the cars were named after stage coaches, a framed print of the original being exhibited in the saloons of most of the cars; the final purchase, *Phenomena* in 1930, being a double car carried on three bogies and seating 122 passengers. The LNER Sentinels did excellent work, the last being withdrawn in 1947. No. 220 *Water Witch* was destroyed in a collision with a Leeds–London express at Doncaster on 9 June 1929.

Two joint railways in which the LNER had an interest, the Cheshire Lines Committee and the Axholme Joint Railway, also purchased Sentinels. The LMS purchased a two-cylinder chain drive version in 1925 and, following tests, purchased a further dozen and in 1928, a six-cylinder with cardan shaft.

The very last Sentinel built for a British railway was a special design for the steeply graded Brighton–Dyke branch. Extraordinarily light, it only weighed 17 tons 4 cwt. Its compound engine drove through a cardan shaft. The wheels were fitted with external brake drums with road-pattern inside brake shoes. Supplies of coal and feed water were automatic so the car could be manned by just a driver. Forty-four seats were provided in the bus-type body. It entered service on 1 May 1933. It was quick, economical and comfortable and on test its acceleration was phenomenal and it achieved a maximum of 61 mph. When overloaded in 1935, its frame broke. Following repairs it was transferred to the Westerham branch on 2 March 1936 before being withdrawn later than year.

In 1927 Clayton Wagons Ltd built a railcar similar to the Sentinel-Cammell. It was articulated but differed from the Sentinel in that the engine was on the leading bogie driving direct through gearing to an axle, which was coupled to the other by a normal coupling rod. The first was delivered to the LNER in 1927 and 10 more delivered in 1928. Less successful than the Sentinels, they were all withdrawn by 1937. Like the Sentinels, they were named after stagecoaches.

1926

The General Strike lasted from 4 to 14 May 1926. There was no particular railway issue at stake; it was held in support of the miners. The pitmen's union had said 'Not a minute on the day; not a penny off the pay', but due to the economic circumstances, mine owners said that this could not be. Railwaymen struck in sympathy with the miners, but some trains still ran worked by non-strikers and volunteers. The railway strike was declared illegal and ended on 14 May, the miners' strike continuing throughout the summer and into the early winter, railways having to use some imported coal. The railway strike gave a further fillip to road transport, with the railways not always winning back traffic at the conclusion of the strike. Following the strike, the record cards of men who continued working were marked in red ink with 'Remained loyal', but their colleagues never forgot that they were blacklegs.

1927

On 26 September 1927 the LMS introduced a new sleeper for Euston to Glasgow and Edinburgh, supplementing the existing 11.45 p.m., which only provided sleepers to Glasgow. Leaving at 12.30 a.m., it arrived at Glasgow St Enoch at 9.45 a.m. It enabled passengers from Edinburgh to attend the theatre in London, sleep, and have breakfast on the train, before going about their daily business. It also meant that *The Times* was available at 9.30 a.m. instead of 12.42 p.m., because it could not be printed in time to catch the 11.45. Likewise Dundee received

The Times at 12.36 instead of 3.31 p.m., Aberdeen at 1.56 instead of 5.28 p.m., and Inverness at 3.50 instead of 7.50 p.m.

In 1927 the Kitson–Still locomotive appeared, a 2-6-2 designed with an oil-fired boiler providing steam to the base of the pistons in an eight-cylinder, direct-drive engine, steam being used to start the engine and accelerate it up to about 6 mph. Then the compression ignition system took over, steam was cut off, the oil burner shut down and the heat generated by the diesel engine was used to heat the water. When extra power was required, such as when climbing a gradient, the oil burner was relit and the inner ends of the cylinders worked by steam, diesel operation continuing at the other end. The locomotive was tested on the LNER and proved promising, but the failure of Kitson's business halted any development.

The LNER under Gresley and Bulleid were also trying to make locomotives more efficient. Towards the end of 1927, they planned a locomotive comparable to an A1 Pacific but using a Yarrow-type marine boiler with steam at a pressure of 450 psi. After discussion with the Clyde shipbuilders Yarrow & Co., an order was placed with them in 1928 for a boiler consisting of two parallel water drums at the rear, connected by curved tubes to a single steam drum mounted above. The firebox was situated between the two rear water drums. As the boiler's size prevented the fitting of a conventional chimney, deflector plates and a sloping front allowed air to pass to the top of the smokebox to the rear of the chimney and thus lift the exhaust above the cab.

The boiler was first steamed at Glasgow in October 1929. The remainder of the engine was built at Darlington, the wheel arrangement being a 4-6-2-2, the leading rear axle being a Cortazzi, while the rear axle was within an inside-framed Bissel truck, pivoted in front of the first trailing axle. The two inside high-pressure cylinders drove the leading axle while the two low-pressure outside cylinders drove the centre axle. *British Enterprise* nameplates were cast but never fitted. Trial runs were made between December 1929 and the middle of 1930, and due to practical experience certain modifications were carried out.

No. 10000 worked expresses between Newcastle, York and Edinburgh covering 420 miles daily. On one occasion, the trailing axle jammed against the track and it took two 0-8-0s to move No. 10000. It worked the Up Flying Scotsman and also the Queen of

Scots Pullman. In August 1930 No. 10000 returned to Darlington for further modifications. It entered Darlington Works on 29 May 1933 for its first general repair and more alterations were carried out before it returned to traffic on 13 June 1934. In August 1935 it was decided to rebuild it as a conventional three-cylinder engine as it had proved unreliable and had not fulfilled its economic hopes. It emerged from Doncaster in November 1937 similar to an A4 and in a livery of Garter blue with dark red wheels, but with wheels at 4-6-2-2 configuration. Drivers liked its smooth riding, but firemen disliked the distance from the shovelling plate to the firehole door. Numbered 60700 by BR, she was withdrawn on 1 June 1959, having covered 90,000 miles with the Yarrow boiler and a further 785,000 as a conventional engine.

The Railways Act of 1927 allowed the railway companies to purchase existing bus companies in order to eliminate competition and operate bus services instead of running unremunerative branch lines. In 1928 legislation allowed the speed of buses on pneumatic tyres to rise from 12 to 20 mph and then in 1931 to 30 mph.

An innovation was introduced on 1 December 1927 when the first bulk milk-tank wagons left the United Dairies' siding at Wootton Bassett. Tanks were far more economical than churns. One man could rinse a tank with cold water and scrub it, gaining access through a manhole. It was then rinsed with hot water and finally sterilised with steam, a much easier operation than carrying out these procedures with 176 17-gallon churns that held the equivalent of one tank. The 176 churns needed three vans and weighed a total of 80 tons, whereas one tank was only 22 tons.

The 3,000-gallon enamel glass-lined tanks were manufactured by the Dairy Supply Company and the chassis built at Swindon. Each tank was insulated with a 2-inch layer of cork, which meant that the milk left the factory at 38 degrees Fahrenheit and the temperature rose by no more than one degree on its journey to the depot at Willesden. About 15 tanks left Wootton Bassett daily.

1927 was an important year for locomotive preservation, as the LNER opened a railway museum at York. Locomotives have always endeared themselves to those who worked on them, much as an owner loves his pet. This meant that whenever possible an engine was kept, rather than scrapped and recycled. Back in 1853, Prince Albert persuaded Sir Henry Cole, who had been a leading figure in creating the Great Exhibition in 1851, and Bennet Woodcroft, Professor of Descriptive Machinery at University College London, to form a collection of artefacts. William Hedley's *Puffing Billy* and Stephenson's *Rocket* were discovered and placed in what became the Science Museum at South Kensington.

Some enlightened railway companies were reluctant to destroy old engines. The South Eastern Railway discovered Stephenson's *Invicta*, used on the Canterbury & Whitstable Railway, in a locked shed. Kept as an historic relic in 1908, it was displayed in the open air at Canterbury. In 1875 the North Eastern Railway celebrated the Golden Jubilee of the opening of the Stockton & Darlington and placed its 1825 *Locomotion* on a plinth at Darlington North Road station. In 1900 the Furness Railway placed its 54-year-old 0-4-0 *Coppernob* in a glass case at Barrow-in-Furness. The GWR had preserved two broad gauge engines in Swindon Works, but unfortunately when Churchward was appointed chief mechanical engineer he scrapped them early in the twentieth century because he needed the space.

Initially the collection at York was private, but when much of it appeared for the Stockton & Darlington centenary celebrations in 1925, the public's interest in railway heritage increased. The National Railway Museum at York opened in 1975.

To speed the Royal Mail through London's streets, the Post Office decided to make an underground railway linking some of the principal sorting offices with Paddington. Opened officially on 3 December 1927, and for mail on 5 December 1927, it was the first driverless electric railway and the world's only underground dedicated to moving mail. It measured 6½ miles from end to end. The tunnels are 70 feet below the surface and 2-foot gauge trains are worked at 440 volts DC from a centre third rail.

Initially trains were controlled from a cabin at each of the stations, but in 1993 this was changed to central operation from Mount Pleasant. Trains run at a maximum speed of 35 mph but are slowed to 8 mph approaching station by a rising gradient coupled with a reduction to 150 volts. Mount Pleasant was the hub and contained the railway's maintenance workshops, a battery-powered car provided for rescuing broken-down trains or moving equipment. The first-generation cars for carrying mail had four wheels and as the line had tight curves, wheel and rail wear proved a problem that was solved by introducing cars with power bogies. These second-generation cars were replaced 1980–2 with third-generation cars, while in the line's jubilee year of 1987 their livery was changed from green to red with a yellow front bar, and the undertaking named Mail Rail.

The opening of the postal hub at Willesden in 1996 led to mail ceasing to use the London rail termini and Rail Mail was mothballed in 2003. In July 2017 a new postal museum opened, with new passenger-carrying cars built to give visitors a riding experience on the lines around Mount Pleasant station. Officially opened 13 June 2017, it was not opened to the public until 4 September 2017.

1928

March, Cambridgeshire, was the junction of lines from London, the eastern counties and from coalfields in Midlands and Yorkshire. By the late 1920s, the yards there had become overloaded so in 1928 the LNER opened a new Up yard at Whitemoor, immediately north of March. A yard on the Down side opened in 1933. The Up yard was the first mechanised one of its kind in Britain, remotely controlled points giving access to the sorting sidings and wagon speed down the slope of the hump controlled by power-operated retarders. The two yards contained a total of 68 miles of track and handled 7,000 wagons daily. It was the largest in Britain and the second-largest in Europe. As it was an important target during WWII, a decoy yard was built to the south to divert German bombs and fortunately the yards remained intact. With the growth of train-load traffic, use of the yard declined and they were closed in the 1990s.

This was not the end of the story, for in 2004 Network Rail reopened part of the yards as a distribution centre for permanent-way material and expanded the site even more in 2011 when the National Track Materials Recycling Centre was established. All track materials are returned to Whitemoor to be sorted, graded and recycled. Annually it deals with more than 500 miles of used rail, 800 crossings and switches and 50,000 tonnes of contaminated ballast.

At 10.00 a.m. on 1 May 1928 the train the Flying Scotsman hauled by 4-6-2 No. 4472 *Flying Scotsman* left King's Cross to start the first London–Edinburgh non-stop service, and as it covered 392.9 miles it was the longest non-stop passenger service in the world. Due to a previous agreement with the LMS it had to take 8¼ hours for the trip, which meant an average speed of 47.6 mph. That it was an easy schedule is shown by the fact that the much heavier train following the Flying Scotsman called at all the usual stops and covered the distance in the same time!

As working a non-stop express from King's Cross to Edinburgh would have been too long a stint for one crew, in 1928 Nigel Gresley conceived the idea of a corridor tender for *Flying Scotsman* so that crews could exchange duties midway. In order to check the minimum width required, at home he arranged a row of chairs facing a wall. One of his daughters was surprised to see him on all fours squeezing his great bulk through the narrow space. He remarked that if he could get through, so could his biggest engineman.

The train had new vehicles including a restaurant car and an adjacent coach, which contained a cocktail bar, a hairdressing salon complete with barber and a retiring room for ladies.

In May 1932, 25 minutes was cut from the summer schedule and in July this was reduced to 7½ hours, in 1936 to 7¼ hours and in 1937 to 7 hours, with the average speed now 56.1 mph. Corresponding reductions were made in the winter schedule until in 1938 the Flying Scotsman, with all stops included, covered the distance in 7 hours and 20 minutes.

In 1928 the LMS made an interesting experiment. A four-coach Manchester–Bury electric multiple-unit built in 1916 for the Lancashire & Yorkshire Railway was withdrawn and a 500 hp diesel engine and generator installed. The unit was tested between Blackpool Central and Preston but after nine months running was withdrawn from service in April 1929. Even with one-man operation, costs came out at 19*d* per mile against the 14*d* for a steam train.

The last serious accident involving gaslit coaches occurred at Charfield on 13 October 1928. Signalman Button decided to shunt the Wolverhampton–Bristol freight back into a siding in order not to delay the Leeds–Bristol Mail. From his box he watched GWR 2-6-0 No. 6381 reverse its 49 loaded wagons and brake van into the refuge siding. While this was happening, two other trains were approaching Charfield: an Up empty freight from Westerleigh to Gloucester and the Leeds–Bristol Mail. The Down signals were against the Mail because the interlocking would not permit them to be cleared until the Bristol-bound goods had completely reversed into the siding. As he watched the goods propelling, Button kept glancing at his track circuit indicator for the Mail's approach, eager to change the points as soon as possible and pull off the signals in order not to delay it longer than necessary.

To his horror, he saw that the Mail had failed to stop at the outer home signal! Simultaneously an Up empty freight passed through Charfield station. He knew three trains were about to collide and could do nothing to prevent the catastrophe.

Class 3 4-4-0 No. 714 and its Mail train grazed the last two wagons of the Great Western goods train setting back into the siding and struck the right-hand rear end of the tender of GWR No. 6381. This resulted in No. 714 becoming derailed and coming into contact with the wagons of the passing Up empty freight drawn by Class 3F 0-6-0 No. 3593 and then ploughing to a standstill on its side. Its tender, together with GWR No. 6381, became wedged under an overbridge and, with the wreckage of the destroyed wagons, blocked the forward movement of the Mail's coaches. This resulted in the first five vehicles of the Mail piling themselves on each side of, but chiefly under, the bridge in an inextricable mass of steelwork and timber wreckage, the momentum of the whole train being absorbed in the destruction of the first five vehicles.

The wooden-bodied coaches were lit by gas and so all the ingredients for an inferno were present. Fire started in the wreckage and rapidly grew into a furnace. Fire brigades were summoned, but despite their efforts the blaze continued for 12 hours. Out of a total of approximately 60 passengers on the Mail, 16 lost their lives and 24 suffered injury, while additionally 13 Post Office sorters, as well as the driver and fireman of the GWR goods and both guards of the LMS trains were hurt.

Col J. W. Pringle, inspecting officer for the Ministry of Transport, placed responsibility for the accident on the driver for passing the signals at 'Danger' and recommended that Automatic Train Control be installed, that coaches be made stronger and that gas lighting in coaches be abolished.

1929

From about 1929, due to the rise of road transport for both passengers and goods, some branch lines became uneconomic and had to be closed. In order to combat a threat to rail transport, on 21 May 1929 the Big Four railway companies obtained parliamentary powers enabling them to operate air services. The GWR was the first company to take the initiative and on 12 April 1933 opened a service between Cardiff, Shaldon (sited just inland from Dawlish) and Plymouth.

The plane, a three-engined, six-seater Westland Wessex, was painted in GWR chocolate-and-cream livery and its interior décor similar to a standard first-class railway compartment. Imperial Airways supplied the plane, pilot and ground staff for the twice-daily flights. It took about 50 minutes to cover the 80 miles, compared with almost 4 hours and 140 miles by rail. In 1944 the Big Four published a plan for the development of air transport to Europe, however a change of Government in 1945 altered the ownership plan and brought to an end the railway development in air transport, British European Airways taking over the railway airlines on 1 April 1947.

In an effort to improve the concept of a railway, as early as 1824 H. R. Palmer, engineer to the London Dock Co., instead of using two lines used a monorail to convey merchandise from the Thames to a warehouse at Deptford. Loads were balanced from the axles of wheels running on an overhead rail, the line being horse-worked. A century later, this concept was developed and the George Bennie railplane demonstration track was constructed between Milngavie and Hillfoot near Glasgow. The car, suspended by two-wheel bogies and stabilised by a lower rail, was moved by propellers fitted front and rear. The idea literally did not take off.

1930

There were the makings of a serious accident on 23 January 1930. While hauling the Up Golden Arrow, when approaching Kent House and running two minutes late, the leading and centre driving wheels of Lord Nelson No. E853 *Sir Richard Grenville* became derailed at 50–55 mph. Luckily the middle wheels soon rerailed themselves at a crossing, but the leading set ran 880 yards before getting back onto the track. Its crew were quite unaware of this

The cottage at Wylam where George Stephenson was born.

Henry Palmer's suspension railway of 1823. The gate on the left is for crossing a road. The horse and the man have just forded the stream. (Author's collection)

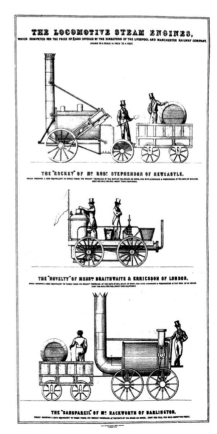

The three principal locomotives, *Rocket*, *Novelty* and *Sans Pareil* which competed for the prize of £500 at Rainhill.

A horse gin: as the two horses walk round, material is lifted or lowered from the shaft seen on the centre-left.

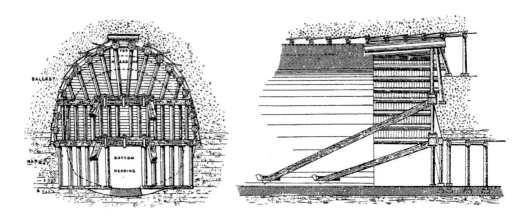

Completed timbering for a full-size tunnel in soft ground.

Hand signal for Stop.

Hand signal for Caution.

LINE SIGNAL "ALL RIGHT."

Hand signal for All Clear.

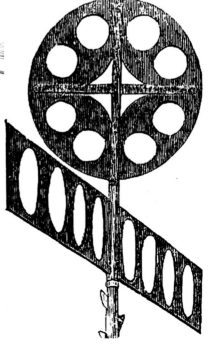

STATION SIGNAL "ALL RIGHT."

A disc-and-crossbar signal. They are set at right angles so one or the other is edge-on. The crossbar means 'Stop' and the disc 'All clear'.

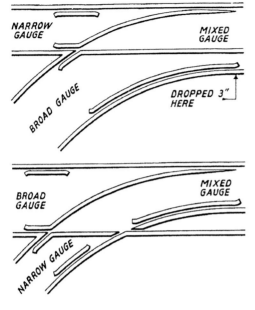

Brunel's clever design for a mixed-gauge junction which required no moving parts – the check rail pulled a vehicle to the correct road.

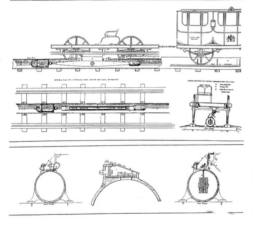

The atmospheric railway: the upper picture shows the haulage carriage with a piston fitting into a pipe, while the lower illustration depicts the pipe and sealing mechanism.

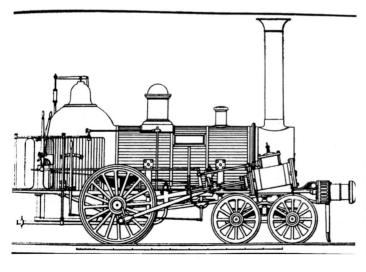

A 4-2-0 American-type locomotive built to work the Lickey Incline south of Birmingham.

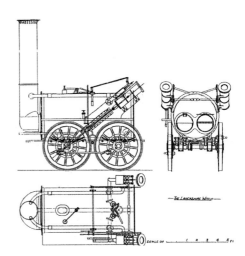

Stephenson's *Lancashire Witch* built for the Bolton & Leigh Railway opened in 1828.

James Edward McConnell, London & North Western Railway's locomotive engineer's 2-2-2 *Eugenie* which was exhibited at Paris in 1855.

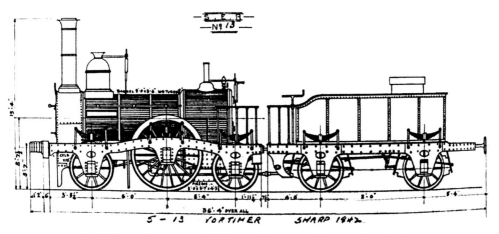

A standard Sharp, Stewart 2-2-2 No. 5 *Vortimer*, built for the South Eastern Railway in 1842. She was re-numbered 13 in 1855.

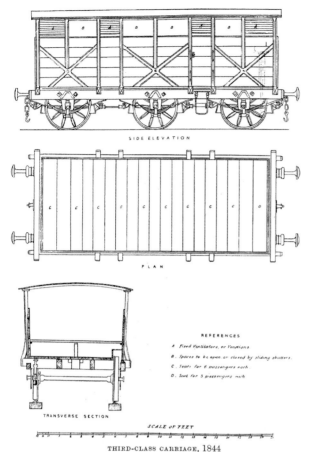

SIDE ELEVATION

PLAN

TRANSVERSE SECTION

REFERENCES

A. Fixed Ventilators, or Ventions

B. Spaces to be open or closed by sliding shutters.

C. Seats for 6 passengers each.

D. Seat for 5 passengers each.

SCALE OF FEET

THIRD-CLASS CARRIAGE, 1844

A third-class carriage of 1844. Unlike the earlier third-class coaches, passengers were enclosed so there was no danger of being thrown out; the problem was gaining access through the 2-foot-wide doorway. The only view was through the ventilators. Seating 49 passengers and a guard in an area 20 feet by 8 feet must have been cosy.

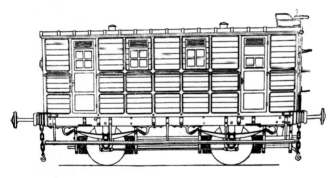

A four-compartment third-class carriage on the Leeds & Thirsk Railway. The guard had plenty of fresh air sitting on the roof.

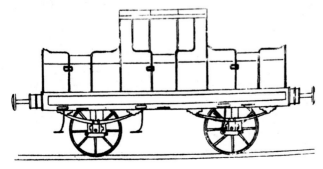

A first- and second-class composite carriage built in 1842 for the Grand Junction Railway. The former class were enclosed, while the second class enjoyed a more lively ride over the axles in the open air.

RAILWAY PASSENGERS IN 1848

as portrayed in "The Comic Bradshaw, or Bubbles from the Boiler," by Angus R. Reach, illustrated by H. G. Hine, and published by E. Bogue

The First-Class Passenger	The Second-Class Passenger	The Third-Class Passenger
"He hath an infinity of luggage, and no end of cloaks, wrappers, plaids, and pilot-coats. He is particular about a brass-bound dressing case and he deposits one of his outer garments in a compartment of the carriage, so as to take possession"	"Sometimes he walks to the station baggageless—at others, he comes in company with a carpetbag on the top of the omnibus. When he wears a pair of gloves, he sticks his ticket into one of them"	"If his luggage does not consist of a bundle tied up in a blue spotted cotton handkerchief, it is sure to be comprised in a ponderous wooden chest. He sticks his ticket in the band of his hat, as a visible sign that he has paid his fare"

Railway passengers in 1848 as portrayed in *The Comic Bradshaw* by Angus R. Reach.

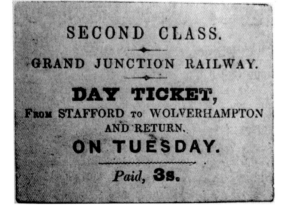

SECOND CLASS.

GRAND JUNCTION RAILWAY.

DAY TICKET,

FROM STAFFORD TO WOLVERHAMPTON AND RETURN.

ON TUESDAY.

Paid, **3s.**

Above: A return ticket issued by the Grand Junction Railway in 1842.

Right: Bradshaw's Railway Time Tables for 25 October 1839. Being a member of the Society of Friends, he was unhappy at printing months named after heathen gods, so, for example, used '10th Mo.' for 'October'.

BRADSHAW'S

Railway Time Tables,

AND ASSISTANT TO

RAILWAY TRAVELLING,

WITH

ILLUSTRATIVE MAPS & PLANS.

AUTHOR OF

BRADSHAW'S MAP AND SECTION OF THE RAILWAYS OF GREAT BRITAIN, 5FT. 4IN. BY 3FT. 4IN.

PRICE IN SHEETS . . . 1 11 6
MOUNTED 2 10 0

AND SOLD BY G. BRADSHAW, BROWN-STREET, MANCHESTER; AND WYLD, CHARING CROSS, LONDON.

PRICE ONE SHILLING.

LONDON :

SHEPHERD AND SUTTON, AND WYLD, CHARING CROSS.

AND SOLD BY ALL BOOKSELLERS AND RAILWAY COMPANIES.

10*th Mo.* 25*th*, 1839.   (**No. 3**)

A lithograph by George Measom of the interior of the first engine shed at Paddington *circa* 1852. Leo class 2-2-2 *Elephant* is on the left and Iron Duke class 4-2-2 *Rover* on the right. The short turntable required engine and tender to be turned separately.

Excursion Ticket.

LEICESTER TO FRANCE.

SECOND CLASS.

This Ticket to be given up at the Camden Station.

JUNE 16th.

Excursion Ticket.

LEICESTER TO FRANCE

SECOND CLASS.

This Ticket must be given up either at Dover or Folke-stone, and exchanged for a Steam Packet Ticket.

JUNE 16th.

Excursion Return Ticket.

FRANCE TO LEICESTER

SECOND CLASS.

This Ticket to be given up at the Bricklayers' Arms Station.

JUNE 19th.

Excursion Return Ticket.

FRANCE TO LEICESTER

SECOND CLASS.

This Ticket must be given up on arrival at Leicester.

JUNE 19th.

19-

FIRST EXCURSION-TICKET TO THE CC

Above left: A metal ticket issued by the Leeds & Selby Railway, 1832.

Above right: A press to stamp a date on a ticket.

Left: A four-part ticket for the first Thomas Cook excursion to the continent.

Below: Plan of Taunton station, an example of Brunel's one-sided designs to obviate the need for passengers to cross the tracks. Logically the Up station is at the Up end of the layout.

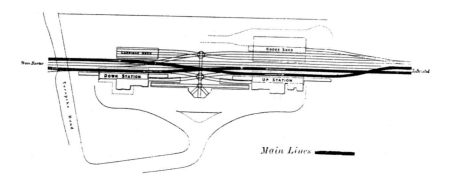

Main Lines

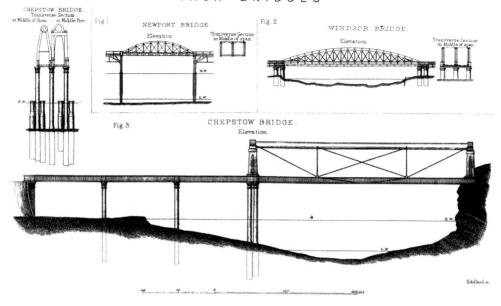

Brunel's bridges at Chepstow, Newport and Windsor; the latter was the basis for his Royal Albert Bridge at Saltash.

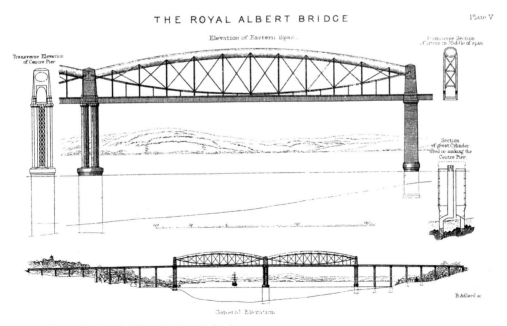

Brunel's Royal Albert Bridge, Saltash.

Wagons being loaded on the train ferry *Leviathan*, to cross the Forth between Granton and Burntisland. It opened 7 February 1850.

Constructing the Metropolitan Railway in 1862. Notice the disruption to street traffic.

Some advertisers took advantage of the smoky conditions of the Metropolitan Railway. The guard tells a choking and coughing female: 'Here, take a Geraudel's Pastille and welcome. The Company provide 'em. I've never been afraid of damp fog, or cold since I carried a box of Geraudel's.'

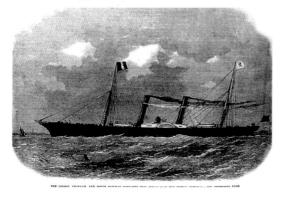

The London, Chatham & Dover Railway's cross-channel paddle steamer *Princess Imperial* when new in 1864.

The interior of a Midland Railway Pullman car.

The Staplehurst accident of 9 June 1865 in which Charles Dickens was involved.

Above left: An ambulance for injured workmen on the Settle & Carlisle Railway.

Above right: The contractors' hotel, Blea Moor, for Settle & Carlisle navvies.

Right: The bog cart used in building the Settle & Carlisle Railway; the weight is spread over a large surface.

Above: The Britannia tubular bridge.

Below: View downstream to the Severn Bridge, 1869.

Above left: Digging Baker Street Junction for the Metropolitan Railway's Uxbridge line, 1868.

Above right: A 'padded cell' – the interior of a City & South London Railway car.

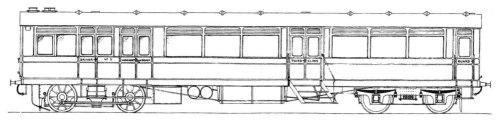

A London & North Western steam railmotor. The boiler is at the left-hand end.

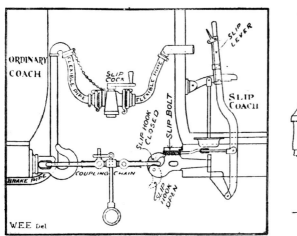

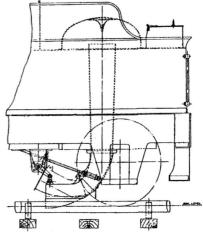

Above left: Drawing of the Great Eastern Railway slip coach apparatus.

Above right: Diagram of an apparatus to enable a locomotive to pick up water without stopping.

Below left: 1911 rail strike: Great Western Railway poster.

Below right: 1911 rail strike: London & North Western Railway poster.

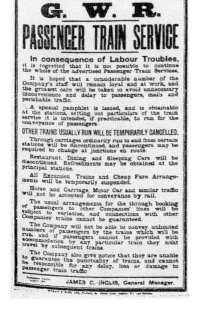

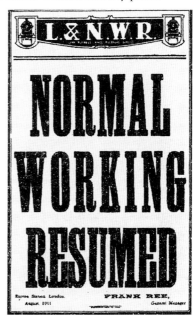

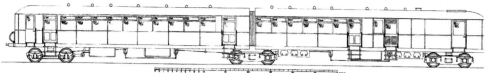

L.N.E.R. Sentinel. "Phenomena".

The London & North Eastern Railway's articulated Sentinel steam railcar *Phenomena*.

Above left: An advertisement for the Highland Railway's Inverness Hotel.

Above right: A Metropolitan Railway advertisement to persuade people to live in Metro-land.

Below left: A poster issued in September 1939 announcing necessary alterations to the passenger service during the evacuation.

Below right: Poster issued by the Railway Executive Committee on 11 September 1939 warning of reduced services due to the war.

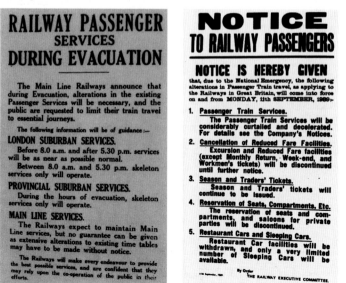

2 - 6 - 0 FREIGHT LOCOMOTIVE Cl. 2F

Designed by H. G. Ivatt, 1946

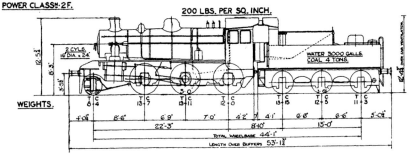

BOILER Barrel 10' 9⅞". Dia. outs.
4' 3" increasing to 4' 8"

FIREBOX Outside 5' 11" × 4' 0⁷⁄₁₆"

TUBES
Superheater Elements 12-1⅜" dia.
outs. × 11 s.w.g.
Large 12-5¼" dia.
outs. × 7 s.w.g. } 10' 10½"
between
Small 162-1⅜" dia. } Tubeplates
outs. × 12 s.w.g.

HEATING SURFACE Tubes 924·5 sq. ft. } Total 1,025·5
Firebox 101 „ } sq. ft.
Superheater 134 sq. ft.

GRATE AREA 17·5 sq. ft.

TRACTIVE EFFORT at 85% B.P. 17,400 lbs.

WEIGHTS	Engine T. c.	Tender T. c.	Total T. c.
Light	43 5	19 15	63 0
Loaded	47 2	37 3	84 5

Above: Diagram of a Class 2 2-6-0 freight locomotive designed by H. G. Ivatt for the London, Midland & Scottish Railway in 1946.

Right: A handbill issued in April 1956 giving details of holiday runabout tickets in Cornwall, Devon and Somerset.

Below: If he experienced no mechanical problems, a London, Midland & Scottish Railway driver would complete this form at the end of his turn.

(Form referred to in Rule 183, clause (g)).
BRITISH RAILWAYS

.... Region

(A supply of these Forms must)
(be kept by each Driver)

WRONG LINE ORDER FORM
DRIVER TO SIGNALMAN **B**

To the Signalman at .... signal box

Allow an engine or breakdown van train to proceed in
the wrong direction to my train, which is stationary on
the * .... line at ....

I will not move my engine in any direction until the arrival
of the engine or breakdown van train.

Catch points, spring or unworked trailing points exist
at ....

Signed .... **Driver**

Date .... 19 ..... Time issued ....m.

† Countersigned ....
Signalman

at .... signal box

* Insert name of line, for example, Up or Down
Main, Fast, Slow or Goods.
† If necessary.

BRITISH RAILWAYS

....19

From...

SHIPPING TRAFFIC

To ....

....

.................Region.................Section

VIA ....

3

Owner and
No. of Wagon

Sheets in or
on Wagon

....

....

Consignee ....

....

100,000 10/49.

O. 6074 (B)

BR. 29102

LADIES ONLY

Above left: A British Railways
form to request a signalman
to allow a driver to proceed
'wrong line'.

Above right: A British Railways
wagon label.

Left: British Railways label for
the window of a Ladies Only
compartment.

BRITISH RAILWAYS **DRIVER'S REPORT** B.R. 32841

Bristol 82E Depot Barrow Road M.P. Area Western 19 59

7 40ᵐ.m. 86 Train from Bristol Bridge to Bristol Meads 12/12/ 19 59

Load (Reg.)............... Train Loco. No. 73054 Asst'g. Loco. No. ....

(Act.) E Flowers Class 5 MT (BR) Class ....

Driver E. Flowers Fireman L H Gole Guard ....

Depot Barrow Rd 82E Depot Barrow Rd 82E Station ....

Reg. No............... Reg. No............... Weather...............

SUBJECT Loss of Time

Driver Reports:– The wind was high the steam was low the
train was heavy, she would not go the coal was
small and plenty of slate that's the reason why
we were late

copy 18/2

Driver's Signature E Flowers

A Bristol driver submitted this report to explain lateness of an empty carriage
train on 12 December 1959: 'The wind was high, the steam was low, the train was
heavy, she would not go, the coal was small and plenty of slate, that's the reason
why we were late.'

THE FIRST RAILWAY TUNNEL IN THE WORLD!
Tyler Hill Tunnel, Canterbury and Whitstable Railway, from the Whitstable mouth.

Above left: Tyler Hill Tunnel on the Canterbury & Whitstable Railway – the first purpose-built railway tunnel in the world. (Author's collection)

Above right: A horse drawing wagons of china clay. The sleepers are covered with ballast to prevent the horse tripping. (Author's collection)

Right: Robert Stephenson's business card depicting Newcastle high-level bridge. (Author's Collection)

Above left: Timothy Hackworth's business card *c.* 1830, depicting a locomotive with rear cylinders. (Author's collection)

Above right: Robert Stephenson's erecting shop in 1864. (Author's collection)

Right: Stephenson's *Rocket*. (R. J. Cannon)

Above left: An early first-class coach. (Author's collection)

Above right: An early second-class coach – its compartments not as wide as first class. (Author's collection)

Above: An early third-class coach – plenty of fresh air and smuts in your eyes. (Author's collection)

Left: Outside the Board of Trade offices on 30 November 1845 when many railway companies were trying to deposit their plans before midnight. (Author's collection)

Below: The Doric arch at Euston. (Author's collection)

Above left: George Hudson, the Railway King. (Author's collection)

Above right: The opening of Birmingham, New Street station in 1854. (Author's collection)

Right: Collapse of the bridge over the River Dee, Chester, 24 May 1847. (Author's collection)

A photograph of the Staplehurst derailment on 9 June 1865. Charles Dickens was a passenger. (Author's collection)

The Royal Albert Bridge, Saltash. (Author's collection)

Artist's impression of the proposed station at Baker Street. The street is shown above. (Courtesy *Illustrated London News*)

The opening of the Metropolitan Railway on 10 January 1863. Notice the mixed-gauge track capable of accommodating broad- and standard-gauge rolling stock. (Author's collection)

The pleasantly designed Metropolitan stations at Paddington, Edgeware Road (*sic*), Baker Street and Portland Road. (Author's collection)

King's Cross Junction: Midland Railway; Great Northern Railway and the Metropolitan Railway. (Author's collection)

Metropolitan Railway 4-4-0T No. 11 in its original condition with unroofed cab. Notice the condensing apparatus which carries used steam from the cylinders back into the side tanks. (Author's collection)

Metropolitan Railway 4-4-0T No. 3 having been given a roofed cab. The destination board reads 'Harrow'. There is a brass number on the chimney. The rural setting is striking. (Author's collection)

The Irish Mail disaster at Abergele, 20 August 1868. (Author's collection)

London & North Western Railway Precedent class 2-4-0 No. 1211 designed by Francis Webb and named *John Ramsbottom*, his predecessor. (Author's collection)

An official London & North Western Railway postcard showing Queen Victoria's saloon. Notice that the carriages are close-coupled and have a corridor connection. (Author's collection)

Above left: The Tay Bridge disaster of 28 December 1879. (Author's collection)

Above right: The tender of the engine concerned in the Tay Bridge disaster. Despite falling into the water, it looks in good condition. (Author's collection)

Left: Brighton *c.* 1880 showing the old custom of mounting signals on a signal box. (Author's collection)

Above left: Porters handling milk churns. (Author's collection)

Above right: The derailment at Chelford 22 December 1894. (Author's collection)

Entrance to the Necropolis station, Waterloo. (Author's collection)

Above left: The Necropolis platforms. (Author's collection)

Above right: A coffin is about to be placed in the hearse van at the Necropolis station. (Author's collection)

Right: The Necropolis platform following bombing in WW2. (Author's collection)

Above left: Two North British Railway 4-4-0s are assisted up Cowlairs Incline by a cable which can be seen between the buffers of the leading engine No. 595. (Author's collection)

Above right: A City & South London Railway electric locomotive and train on the opening day, 18 December 1890. (Author's collection)

Below: Central London Railway electric locomotive. Notice the low-slung tube car. (Author's collection)

Above left: Bank station on the Central London Railway on the opening day, 30 July 1900. Notice the timber platform. (Author's collection)

Above right: An early electronic device on the District Railway, 1905. Numbers are illuminated alongside the station names to indicate whether they will be served by the first, second, or third train. (Author's collection)

Liverpool, Lime Street station at the end of the nineteenth century. (Author's collection)

A Great Eastern Railway official postcard depicting Liverpool Street station. The vehicle on the left is a horse box. (Author's collection)

Above left: The Great Eastern Railway 0-10-0T No. 20, designed to show that a steam-hauled train could accelerate as fast as an electric train. (Author's collection)

Above right: A London & North Western Railway engine at full speed picks up water from troughs. Against regulations, the engine carries no headlamps. (Author's collection)

Above left: The sumptuous luxury of a Midland Railway corridor train in 1899. (Author's collection)

Above right: London & North Western Railway 2-4-0 No. 1682 *Novelty c.* 1902. (Author's collection)

Below left: A London & North Western Railway train picks up mail at speed. The net at the foot of the post collects mail dropped from the train. The hut on the right offers the postman shelter while he is waiting for the exchange. (Author's collection)

Below right: The accident to a Lancashire & Yorkshire Railway electric train at Hall Road 27 July 1905. This was the first major accident to an electric train in Britain. (Author's collection)

Above left: London & North Western Railway compound 2-2-2-2 No. 1512. The driving wheels are uncoupled: the rear set is driven by the small, external high-pressure cylinders, while the leading set has a large low-pressure cylinder just visible below the buffers. (Author's collection)

Above right: Ex-Mersey Railway double frame 0-6-4T No. 3 *Duke of Lancaster*. Notice the pipe carrying used steam from the cylinders to the water tank where it could condense. The roofless cab would help to keep the crew cool. Built by Beyer, Peacock & Co. in 1885 and sold to the Alexandra (Newport & South Wales) Docks & Railway when the Mersey Railway was electrified. Alexandra Docks No. 23, it was withdrawn by the GWR in June 1923. (C. Roberts collection)

London & South Western Railway's E10 class 4-2-2-0 built in 1901 and withdrawn in 1926. The design was not a success and the conventional T9 class 4-4-0 proved more reliable in addition to being easier on fuel, oil and water. (Author's collection)

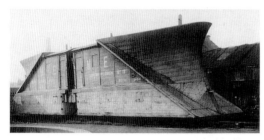

North Eastern Railway snow ploughs Nos 11 and 12 at Blyth locomotive depot. Each weighs 23 tons. Notice the wooden dumb buffers. (Author's collection)

Space in industrial premises was often limited, and to maximise that available wagon turntables were used. As these were too short to accommodate a bogie wagon in its entirety, it was turned one bogie at a time. The wagon is fitted with vacuum brakes. (Author's collection)

A dramatic sight at Rugby *circa* 1897. Each signal is doubled to allow clear sight lines past the Great Central Railway overbridge being built beyond the gantry. (Author's collection)

Great Central Railway 2-4-0T No. 24 at Aylesbury *circa* 1909. It is a push-pull train: the engine draws it one way and then for the return journey the driver goes to what was the rear of the coach and drives the locomotive from a control compartment, the locomotive propelling. (Author's collection)

 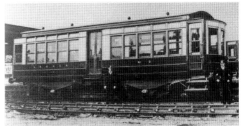

Above left: Police guard Pouparts Junction signal box, Battersea, on the London, Brighton & South Coast Railway during the 1911 strike. (Author's collection)

Above right: London, Brighton & South Coast Railway petrol railcar No. 3 built by Dick, Kerr & Co. in 1905. It was reported 'not to be popular'. (Author's collection)

Below left: The French-built Great Western Railway compound 4-4-2 No. 103 *President*. It was compared with similar Great Western 'simple' engines and found to be no better. (Author's collection)

Below right: The first Pacific to run in Great Britain, the Great Western Railway's 4-6-2 No. 111 *The Great Bear,* seen here in handsome grey livery, was a one-off. Due to its weight and length it was restricted to the line between Paddington and Bristol. It was really a Star class engine with a longer boiler. In 1924 the front part of its frames was used to turn it into a Castle class 4-6-0 No. 111 *Viscount Churchill.* (Author's collection)

From 1914, railway factories turned to war work in addition to keeping stock in repair. Here on 25 October 1916 6-inch naval guns and limbers are on wagons outside the factory at Swindon. The guns will need to be lowered as they are out of gauge. (Author's collection)

In World War I troops on the continent required engines to haul supplies. In addition to locomotives loaned by various British companies, 2-8-0s of Robinson's Great Central Railway design were specially built for the Railway Operating Division, one of which was No. 1928. The board on the top lamp bracket indicates the depot to which No. 1928 was allocated. (Author's collection)

Above left: An ambulance train at the Royal Victoria Military Hospital, Netley. It consists of London & North Western Railway 48-foot-long fruit vans suitably converted. (Author's collection)

Above right: The London, Brighton & South Coast Railway's war memorial locomotive 4-6-4T No. 333 *Remembrance*. (Author's collection)

Below left: A Harwich-Zeebrugge train ferry at Harwich in 1924. (Author's collection)

A wagon-lit London–Paris through sleeping car, on board a train ferry being jacked and secured to the deck to prevent oscillation. The noise seems to have woken at least one sleeper. (Author's collection)

K class 2-6-4T No. 800 *River Cray* derailed near Sevenoaks on 24 August 1927. The accident occurred due to poor track drainage. As rolling was more serious with tank engines, the class was rebuilt as 2-6-0 tender locomotives. (Author's collection)

UU 975 Great Western Railway coach fleet No. 1651. Seating 20 passengers and with luggage space on the roof, it carried passengers booked through from Paddington to the continent. It has a Guy chassis and a Duple body. It was first licensed 11 June 1929. (Author's collection)

Above left: London, Midland & Scottish Railway 2-6-0+0-6-2 Beyer-Garrett articulated locomotive No. 7973 at Crewe works. The introduction of this class avoided the expense of double-heading Toton-Brent coal trains. To aid the fireman, the bunker rotates to bring the coal forward. No provision is made for the engine to work vacuum-braked trains. Notice the fresh '7' on the leading water tank – in 1938 it was re-numbered from '4973'. The engine cost about £44,000. (C. Roberts collection)

Above right: Ex-Lancashire & Yorkshire Railway 0-6-0 as London, Midland & Scottish Railway No. 12615 heading an excursion train. Although engines of this wheel arrangement were really goods engines, railway companies used them at weekends, when there was not so much goods traffic, to haul excursions. (Author's collection)

Below left: Princess Coronation class 4-6-2 No. 6230 *Duchess of Baccleuch c.* 1939. In order to maximise the size of the boiler, the mountings have to be low to avoid fouling the loading gauge. (Author's collection)

Below right: K4 class 2-6-0 No. 3441 *Loch Long* at Fort William in September 1939. (E. J. M. Hayward)

Above left: Enthusiasts board the preserved Great Western Railway railcar No. 4 at Swindon. Brought into service in 1934, a joint effort between AEC and the GWR, it cost £6,541, had two 130 bhp engines (almost identical to those used on contemporary London buses), incorporated lavatories and a small buffet and was designed for high-speed cross-country service. Its maximum speed was 75–80 mph. It was withdrawn 12 July 1958. (R. J. Cannon)

Above right: With many men enlisted in the forces, women took on what had been considered men's work. Here women are working on the permanent way at Coley Yard, Reading in March 1943. The woman on the right is the gang's look-out. (Author's collection)

In 1940, as the Germans were expected to invade Britain, armoured trains were prepared, motive power provided by loaned LNER F4 class 2-4-2Ts suitably strengthened. When completely closed, the cab must have become very hot. (Author's collection)

To make matters more difficult for invaders, in 1940 identification signs were removed. Here the plate from Esher West signal box is being taken down. (Author's collection)

In order to prevent the fire glow being spotted at night from any aircraft, a canvas screen was placed over the gap between the cab roof and tender. (Author's collection)

A bombing raid damages the Great Western Railway at Newton Abbot. (Author's collection)

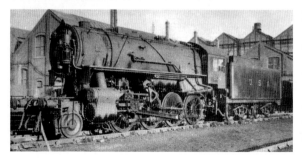

In preparation for the invasion of Europe, 2-8-0s were sent over from the United States. Class 160 No. 1604 built by the American Locomotive Company stands outside 'A' shop at Swindon. It was on loan to that company from January 1943 to September 1944. (Author's collection)

In 1946 the Great Western Railway ordered a gas-turbine locomotive from the Swiss firm of Brown-Boveri, only the third such machine in the world. It did not arrive in England until 1950. No. 18000 is seen here at Swindon on 31 October 1954. (Author's collection)

With nationalisation of the railways having taken place, this ex-LMS compound 4-4-0 is being re-numbered and the 'LMS' painted over. (Author's collection)

Ex-North British Railway J36 class 0-6-0 No. 65257 at Bo'ness in August 1959. (R. E. Toop)

Ex-War Department 2-8-0 BR No. 90066 at Woodford Halse, 18 May 1961. (Rev'd Alan Newman)

The very versatile BR Class 9 2-10-0 No. 92207 at Oxford 4 September 1962. Although designed as a heavy freight locomotive, it was found that it could haul express passenger trains up to 90 mph. (Rev'd Alan Newman)

Above left: BR Class 5 4-6-0 No. 73001 approaches Bradford-on-Avon with an express 29 August 1964. (Rev'd Alan Newman)

Above right: Newly ex-works Hymek diesel-hydraulic D7001 at Bradford-on-Avon 18 July 1961 heading a stopping train to Bristol. (Rev'd Alan Newman)

Above left: Westbury 26 February 1966: West Country class 4-6-2 No. 34013 *Okehampton* at Westbury meets a diesel-multiple unit bound for Weymouth Town. (Rev'd Alan Newman)

Above right: A diesel-electric Class 47 heads a merry-go-round coal train at Aberthaw power station in 1982. Built by Brush Traction 1963–1967, examples are still in use over 50 years later. (Author's collection)

Above left: Two 3-car Gloucester Carriage & Wagon Works diesel-multiple units leave Westbury with an Up train 29 September 1969. (Rev'd Alan Newman)

Above right: Tommy shunts a horse-box at Newmarket in September 1961. (Author's collection)

event and it was only revealed by damage to the permanent way. The Golden Arrow arrived at London Victoria at the right time.

The Road Traffic Act of 1930 and the Road & Rail Traffic Act of 1933 to a certain extent controlled road competition by restricting growth through licensing.

1931

In 1931 Harry Beck, working as a draughtsman for the Underground, realised that the growing network made a map of the system a tangle of lines that was not easy to read. Using the principles of electrical diagrams, he produced a revolutionary map. Ignoring geography, he emphasised connections using only straight horizontal, vertical or diagonal lines. Station names were always proportionally the same size as each other, no matter the size of the map. At first his map was rejected, but then its value was realised and 750,000 copies of the pocket map were printed in January 1933; poster versions were printed later that year. He received £5 5s 0d for his pocket map and £10 10s 0d for the poster. In due course, his map scheme was adopted by underground railways abroad and also by British Railways.

In September 1931 the GWR cut the time of the Cheltenham Flyer from 70 to 67 minutes for the 77.3 miles between Swindon and Paddington, giving an average speed of 69 mph. For the first three days, drivers were encouraged to improve on the timing and the best was 58¼, an average of 79.6 mph, a world record, while on 5 June 1932 the time was reduced to 56 minutes and 47 seconds, an average of 81 mph.

An interesting and curious innovation in 1931 was the petrol road-rail car built by Karrier for the LMS. It was a 22-seater bus capable of running on either rail or road. Its body was like an ordinary contemporary road bus, except that it had a passenger door on both sides. Like the coaches of the period, provision was made for carrying luggage on the roof. Powered by a 37.4 hp petrol engine it had a top speed of 75 mph on rail and 60 mph on road, though in reality the Ministry of Transport restricted its speed on public roads to 30 mph as it did with all heavy vehicles. Petrol consumption was 8 mpg on road and 16 mpg on rail.

Flanged wheels were fitted to the vehicle's axles and on the outside of these were pneumatic-tyred road wheels, each of which was mounted on eccentrics fitted to an axle extension through the rail wheels. When on the road, the road wheels were locked concentrically to the rail wheels, which, being of a smaller diameter were clear of the ground.

For road to rail transfer the Road-railer was driven to any place where the rail surface was flush with the road. Then, with the rail wheels directly above the tracks, it was driven forward a few yards until it reached a spot where the road surface tapered off. This caused the rail wheels to gradually come into contact with the rails and took the vehicle's weight off the road wheels. The latter, mounted on an eccentric, were raised above rail level by the driver who turned them on their eccentrics and locked them to the chassis by means of a pin. The road wheels did not rotate when the coach was on the rails. The rear wheels were driven by a shaft in the same way as an orthodox road vehicle and were provided with sanding gear. The average time for changeover road to rail or vice versa was about four minutes.

The LMS had opened the luxury Welcombe Hotel at Stratford-upon-Avon on 1 July 1931 and from 23 April, Shakespeare's birthday, until 2 July 1932, the Road-railer ran from the hotel to the station and then onwards by rail to Blisworth where passengers could change to a London train. It then returned to Stratford with fresh passengers. Although a mechanical success, at 7 tons 2 cwt it was too heavy for its power and seating capacity and was withdrawn after the front axle broke.

1932

The year 1932 marked the beginning of the end of the steam locomotive in Britain. In 1930 the LMS purchased its first diesel shunter, a 0-4-0 diesel-mechanical for use on the 1-foot-6-inch gauge lines in Crewe Works. Proving a success, in 1932, at a cost of almost £6,000, and using the frames of ex-Midland Class 1F 0-6-0T No. 1831, a diesel engine supplied by Davey Paxman & Co. was fitted. The hydraulic transmission was manufactured by Haslam & Newton. In addition, eight more diesel locomotives, mostly 0-4-0s, were bought from manufacturers and although reasonably successful, as the output was mechanical, they necessarily had limited power.

R. & W. Hawthorn-Leslie & Co. Ltd lent the LMS a 300 hp 0-6-0 diesel-electric shunter. It became No. 7079 and was the prototype for the future. Designed for local passenger train duties in addition to shunting, it was fitted with automatic air brakes with a vacuum brake valve and exhauster for working fitted stock. Its maximum speed was 35 mph. The LMS eventually settled on a diesel engine producing 350 hp at 680 rpm. In 1935, 20 diesel-electric shunters were ordered at a cost of £6,500 each. They proved economical and when it came to shunting duties of more than 6,000 hours a year with single manning they offered a saving of 4s 6d per shunting hour, or with double manning saved 1s 9½d an hour. The first British Railways shunter was based very closely on the final LMS design.

Early in 1932 a Micheline unit was tested by the LMS between Bletchley and Oxford. The first rail vehicle in Britain to use pneumatic tyres, it was carried on a six-wheeled bogie (six wheels were required due to the comparatively narrow tread of a standard rail) at the front and a four-wheeled bogie at the rear. The centre pair of front bogie wheels were drivers, chain-connected to the front pair. The pneumatic tyres had a metal flange on each inside rim. A gauge on each wheel monitored the air pressure and if it fell in excess of 14 lb per sq inch below the normal 85 psi, an audible warning system sounded. In the event of a burst tyre, a wooden hoop within took the load. A tyre lasted for approximately 20,000 miles. The spare wheel and tyre carried on board could be fitted in about 5 minutes. A 27 hp engine drove through clutch and gear box. Separate reverse gears permitted four speeds in either direction, but as the railcar could only be driven from the front, reverse was only used when shunting. From a standstill and with a full load, the car reached 60 mph in 2 minutes. It ran almost silently and had a petrol consumption of 12 mpg.

LMS authorities disliked its almost silent operation, considering it a danger to staff on the line; rubber tyres also caused problems with track circuiting. It had no drawgear so could not be hauled 'dead' or used to haul a horse box. In May 1932 it was tried by the SR, which also failed to place any orders.

In 1932 an AEC Regal single decker bus was fitted with railway wheels, making its initial trip on the GWR between Slough and Reading. Its next outing was on the LNER at Hatfield. It was not a success as at speed the springs were 'sloppy' and the axles unsuitable so trials ceased.

1933

When the Labour Government came into power following the General Election of 1929, more than a million men were out of work. To alleviate this situation, the Loans & Guarantees Act was passed, the Government undertaking to guarantee and pay interest on large public schemes. The SR took advantage of this legislation and electrified its suburban lines, including to Brighton.

The London, Brighton & South Coast Railway in 1908 had inaugurated the Southern Belle, a Pullman train that ran the 50½ miles from Victoria to Brighton in exactly an hour. With the line being electrified, the Southern Railway decided to introduce an electric multiple-unit Pullman to operate part of this service. Launched on 1 January 1933, it was the flagship of their electric service – which at that time was the largest suburban electric service in the world. The result was the Brighton Belle, which consisted of three units of five cars. Although the Pullman Company made a supplementary charge for passengers to use the train, demand was sufficient to offer six departures daily from London, which covered the distance in an hour.

Each Pullman car, in umber-and-cream livery and named after a girl, was a work of art, individually designed by one of the leading design houses of the day – Heal's, Maples and Waring & Gillow – so a different experience was offered in every car. Keith Waterhouse, who lived in Brighton and travelled on the train, said that the Brighton Belle resembled a string of sausages pulled out into the Palace of Versailles. The toilet walls were *eau de Nil* with black beading, the wash basins of black porcelain, the soap dispensers iridescent and the floor was marbled mosaic flecked with mother-of-pearl.

The last Brighton Belle of the day left Victoria at 11.00 p.m., and because it was used by actors and actresses who had performed on the London stage and were returning home, it was referred to as the Equity Express. It was used by such personalities as Dora Bryan, Jimmy Edwards, Peter Jones, Moira Lister, Laurence Olivier, Terrance Rattigan and Flora Robson.

In the mid-1970s the Brighton Belle was repainted in the standard BR livery of blue and grey, had become rather rough-riding and made its last run on 30 April 1972. Fortunately two driving cars are being restored and will be run with their coaches on special trips.

An Act of 13 April 1933 set up the London Passenger Transport Board to provide a co-ordinated transport system for the capital for all rail and road transport in partnership with the main line railways, which continued to retain control of their London suburban services.

The London Passenger Transport Board covered an area of 1,986 square miles. The board was under the chairmanship of Albert Stanley, of the London Passenger Traffic conference, who had now become Lord Ashfield. The board took over five railway companies, 14 municipal tramways, three private tramway companies and 61 bus companies.

In 1934 it owned 174 route miles of railway, 3,072 electric cars, 84 locomotive-hauled coaches, 51 electric and 38 steam locomotives. It did not just deal with passengers – in 1934 it handled 3-million tons of goods and coal and 56,000 head of cattle. All passenger receipts between stations in the Transport Area were pooled and divided in proportion:

London Passenger Transport Board	62 per cent
Southern Railway	25.6 per cent
London & North Eastern Railway	6 per cent
London Midland& Scottish Railway	5.1 per cent
Great Western Railway	1.3 per cent

William Stanier, locomotive superintendent of the LMS and one-time assistant on the GWR to Charles Collett, in 1933 produced the Princess Royal class 4-6-2, virtually a Pacific version of a GWR 4-6-0 King. In 1937 Stanier's Princess Coronation class appeared, an improved version of his Princess Royals. Twenty-four of the Coronations were brought out with streamlined casings, but these casings were eventually removed to ease maintenance.

One innovation by the LNER in 1933 was the Northern Belle train cruise. The 15-coach train provided accommodation for 60 passengers and a staff of 27. Where convenient, the night portion of the train, including six first-class sleeping cars, was detached and worked separately. The day coaches provided quarters for the staff, a kitchen car, two restaurant cars, a hairdressing salon, ladies' retiring room, buffet and office, and writing and smoking rooms.

On the first day it left King's Cross at 9.00 p.m. and travelled to Barnard Castle. On Sunday it reached Penrith, where a motor coach took passengers to the Lake District. The next day was devoted to excursions in the Edinburgh area, while the following day Royal Deeside and Braemar were visited by motor coach from Aberdeen. The overnight journey to Balloch Pier was followed with a steamer trip on Loch Lomond. Passengers joined the day portion of the train at Ardlui before travelling to Fort William, where the night portion had been sent ahead from Balloch Pier and was awaiting them.

The day coaches travelled to Mallaig and back over the scenic West Highland line and as the Northern Belle stopped on Glenfinnan Viaduct to allow passengers to enjoy the view, it may have explained why the majority of passengers preferred to take that option, rather than the alternative of a motor coach trip to Fort Augustus with the problematical view of the Loch Ness monster.

The next morning the day portion proceeded to Craigendoran where passengers embarked on the *PS Waverley* for a cruise down the Firth of Clyde and round the Kyles of Bute. After their return to Craigendoran, passengers were taken to Edinburgh before the overnight journey back to King's Cross.

As a variant to meals on the train, dinner was served at LNER hotels during the visit to Edinburgh and Aberdeen. On three nights out of the seven, the train was stationary and on the other four, it was at rest for part of the time. These land cruises were usually fully booked.

Another innovation made by the LNER in 1933 was when in July it offered holidaymakers the first camping coaches. Ten old carriages had been converted to provide overnight living and cooking facilities and one of these, accommodating six people, could be hired for a week for £2 10s 0d, the company insisting that the vacationers travelled by rail. The LMS and the GWR followed suit in 1934 and the SR in 1935. In 1935 there were 215 coaches at 162 stations in Britain and 439 in 1939. Demand decreased in the 1960s partly due to the closure of branch lines where many were situated and partly due to holidaymakers wanting more satisfaction, perhaps with holidays abroad. BR's last camp coach was in 1971.

In July 1933 Hardy Motors Ltd, of Southall, were putting the finishing touches to a diesel-driven railcar chassis before being taken to the Park Royal factory to have a body to be fitted. Completed, it was exhibited at the Commercial Motor Transport Exhibition, Olympia, that October and it was announced that the GWR had purchased it for £3,249. The streamlined design allowed a standard 130 hp bus engine to be fitted. Aerodynamics ensured that even the steps from rail level to the cab were automatically covered with a flap when the door closed. Wind tunnel tests on models had been carried out at the Chiswick Laboratory of the London Passenger Transport Board. A fluid flywheel replaced the clutch; the pre-selective gearbox had four gears. It began a regular daily roster of 218 miles. It weighed 20 tons empty and seated 69 passengers. Maximum speed was 60 mph and acceleration was not of the highest order. The vehicle performed superbly from its introduction until its withdrawal in 1955. In its first year it covered in excess of 60,000 miles and a railway official stated that many people took trips on the GWR main line for the sole purpose of riding in the car and watching the track ahead for the first time.

On 19 December 1933 the retired Great Western locomotive engineer George Jackson Churchward was killed by *Berkeley Castle* heading a Paddington-Fishguard express, which he failed to see in the fog when he was inspecting a possible fault in the track. Nigel Gresley, who had designed *Mallard*, the world's fastest steam locomotive, said of Churchward: 'Locomotive engineers owe more to his ingenuity, inventiveness and foresight than to any other engineer.'

19

Further Development of Internal Combustion Propulsion; the Streamline Craze

1934

In addition to running the Cheltenham Flyer, the fastest train in the world, the GWR operated the 12.50 a.m. Paddington–Plymouth newspaper train which, headed by a King class 4-6-0, only took 140 minutes to run the 143 miles to Taunton, giving an average speed of over 60 mph. The initial diesel railcar proving a success, the GWR decided to order a further three at £6,541 each. Designed for express service, the cars seated 40 passengers and were equipped with toilet, cafeteria and kitchen. A flat-rate supplement of 2s 6d was charged. July 1934 saw the start of the first long-distance diesel railcar service in Britain, from Birmingham to Cardiff. To cope with speeds of 75–80 mph two engines were fitted in each car.

By 1936, 17 railcars were in use, most being without buffets and some with, and others without, lavatories. No. 17 was a departure, being a van with hinged shelving to deal with the growing suburban parcels traffic.

The 8.30 a.m. Plymouth–Paddington slipped a coach at Reading, and one day during the 1948 locomotive exchanges a Southern engine and crew were in charge. The slip took place satisfactorily and while the enginemen and inspectors were talking on the platform at Paddington, a Southern inspector glimpsed railcar No. 17 running into the parcels platform. He remarked: 'We must have been going some at Reading as our slip coach has just followed us in!'

An important event took place at the bookstall at Exeter St David's in 1934. Allen Lane was perusing the stall for reading material and was peeved to find that there was a shortage of good-quality books at a reasonable price. This encouraged him to launch the affordable paperback imprint that became Penguin Books.

Gresley of the LNER was interested in the locomotive developments of André Chapelon. He was keen on internal streamlining to ease the flow of steam and thus increase power and maximum speed. The result was Gresley's 2-8-2 *Cock o' the North*, which easily reached 85 mph.

To avoid the long drive from the south of England to Scotland, an increasing number of motorists travelled in a sleeping car with their vehicle on a carriage truck; by 1934, 505 cars were being carried annually from King's Cross, 70 per cent of these in the summer.

In 1934 the LMS took delivery of three four-wheeled Leyland diesel-hydraulic railcars, basically of bus-type construction. They could be driven from either end, the driver sitting in a small compartment on the left-hand side, so passengers on the right-hand side enjoyed an excellent view. Although fine initially, when wear and deterioration set in, coupled with having to be maintained in a dirty environment of steam and smoke, riding and reliability suffered. All were withdrawn in 1951.

1935

Railway engineers were interested in the German diesel-powered multiple-unit Flying Hamburger. The London & North Eastern invited its German builders to study the idea of a high speed service between London and Newcastle and London and Leeds. The speed projected was not as high as had been anticipated and the accommodation rather cramped; the LNER believed that a steam engine and standard stock could do the task just as well.

In March 1935 4-6-2 No. 2750 *Papyrus* ran the 536.6 miles from King's Cross to Newcastle and back at an average speed of 68.7mph reaching a maximum of 108 mph – a world record for steam traction. Gresley felt that at speeds of over 70 mph, streamlining would reduce air resistance and so introduced a modified design for engines to work this Silver Jubilee train. To reduce air resistance, the gangway connections between the seven coaches were full-width and shrouds between the bogies smoothed the spaces below the frames. Engine and train were finished in silver-grey with stainless steel lettering. The four engines dedicated for the train were: *Silver Link, Quicksilver, Silver King* and *Silver Fox*. The trial run for the Press was made on 27 September 1935, exactly 110 years after George Stephenson had driven *Locomotion No. 1* over the Stockton & Darlington Railway at the opening of the first public railway.

Leaving King's Cross up the 1 in 200 gradient to Potter's Bar, speed was increased steadily to 75 mph, while following the summit near Knebworth 100 mph had been attained at milepost 25, and for the next 30 miles speed remained in three figures. Twice a maximum of 112½ mph was reached, the highest in Great Britain until that date. From King's Cross *Silver Link* passed Peterborough, 76.4 miles in the unprecedented time of 55 minutes, 2 seconds, or 8½ minutes less than the schedule for the train's regular running.

The Silver Jubilee began a regular service on 30 September 1935. A highly popular train, a supplement of 5s first class, or 3s third class, was charged for each seat and it was unusual for a seat to be vacant. Despite the fact that the Silver Jubilee did not run on Sundays, in two years these supplementary charges raise a sufficient sum to pay for the entire cost of constructing the train. For safety, the engines were fitted with speed recorders and one of the first duties of the day in the running superintendent's office was to examine the charts to ensure that all speed restrictions had been observed. In return for his work on improving locomotives, Gresley was rewarded with a knighthood.

In the 1940s, for ease of maintenance, the skirt hiding the wheels was removed. When the streamliners were eventually replaced by BR diesels and withdrawn from the East Coast main line, they were cascaded to the Glasgow-Aberdeen service.

In reply to the London & North Eastern's Silver Jubilee, the London, Midland & Scottish fought back when a Stanier 4-6-2 worked a special from London to Glasgow at a non-stop average of 68.2 mph, increasing this to 70.0 mph when it returned the following day.

In 1935 the LMS built No. 6202, nicknamed *Turbomotive*. It was a standard Princess Royal class 4-6-2 but with the four cylinders replaced by forward and reverse turbine. It proved efficient and marginally more frugal in water and coal consumption compared with her four-cylinder sisters. She was smoother running and gave less hammer blow – the thrust of the connecting rod on the crank, transmitted through the driving wheels to the rail. The main drawback was that being a one-off, spare parts were not readily available; indeed she was out of service for periods awaiting them. She was withdrawn in 1949 and emerged on 15 August 1952 as an ordinary four-cylinder Pacific, but unfortunately was destroyed in the Harrow & Wealdstone disaster of 8 October that year. (*See* page 331)

In 1935 the Central Line was planned to be extended east into the Essex countryside. The new stations were to become the centres of new communities and each station was of a unique design. After four years of construction the extension was almost complete, but World War II began before it could be opened and the project was kept in abeyance. Gants Hill station and 5 miles of tunnels were converted to a secret armaments factory. Bethnal Green station become one of the largest air raid shelters, where 10,000 East Enders sought refuge. It was the site of a tragedy on 3 March 1943 when among the folk rushing down into the shelter a woman and a young child slipped, created a domino effect in which 173 people died through being crushed, 92 of them children. It was the greatest loss of life in the history of the underground. The extension to Woodford Park opened in December 1947.

In the mid-1930s road began to seriously challenge short-distance passenger, and short-to-medium distance freight, while the slump in the world's trade caused coal traffic 1934–1938 to fall 16 per cent from the 270 million tons carried by rail annually 1909–1913.

In 1935 a larger Micheline railcar was tested on the LMS. Carried on two eight-wheel bogies of light construction, each wheel had a pneumatic tyre. One of the bogies was driven through mechanical transmission. A maximum of 66 mph was obtained and running was silent and very steady. The LMS considered the idea to have a future and ordered two cars of a British version from the Armstrong-Siddeley Motor Co, Coventry, which developed a 13 litre engine that although initially successful when delivered in 1936, developed crankcase trouble and was replaced with an Hispano Suiza engine. Drive was through a four-speed gear box and on a Press run achieved 72 mph. The driver sat in a raised conning-tower in the No. 1 end of the car and from this position could drive in either direction. Track circuiting problems were solved by the Westinghouse Brake & Signal Co supplying a generator supplying a 66 volt 300 cycle current across the rails acting as a carrier for the track circuiting current. The excellent adhesion allowed 50 mph to be reached in 30 seconds or 900 yards, while it could be stopped from 50 mph in about 9 seconds or 250 yards. Although liked by passengers, railwaymen showed little interest and because Armstrong-Siddeley was busy with the re-armament programme it, too, showed little interest; late in 1937 the two railcars were returned to the works at Stoke-on-Trent and broken up in 1945. Railcars did not meet with everyone's approval, one farmer living beside the line complaining that its horn scared his horses.

The first 17 GWR railcars lacked substantial buffing gear, but in 1935 No. 18 was designed for the Lambourn branch to haul loads of either passenger or goods vehicles up to 60 tons. To allow it to be coupled to other units, standard jumper couplings as used on electric trains were adopted. By March 1937 the GWR operated 72 per cent of Britain's diesel railcars.

1936

On 29 July 1936 a comedy of errors was acted out on the Somerset & Dorset Railway. Driver Rawlings and fireman Parker were on Class 3F 0-6-0T No. 7620 shunting at Writhlington, formerly named Foxcote, which had played an important role in the accident of 7 August 1876 – almost exactly 60 years previously. They were standing on the main line facing Radstock with eight empty wagons behind them. Suddenly driver Rawlings was horrified to see Class 7F 2-8-0 No. 13803 approaching on the same line with a train of 37 wagons: it had run through signals.

Rawlings noticed that there was no one on the footplate because both the driver and fireman had jumped off and were busy pinning down wagon brakes. Swiftly thinking how a collision could be avoided, Rawlings flung the reversing lever over, opened the regulator and when the eight wagons in front were safely buffered up, he opened it fully. By this time the two engines were almost buffer to buffer. Quick as a flash he jumped off No. 7620 and as No. 13803 lumbered by, swung on to the footplate, fully closed the regulator and brought the runaway to a halt within three engine lengths.

But pride comes before a fall. As he leapt from his side of the cab, his fireman, not hearing his driver's shout to stay on the footplate, jumped off the engine, so no-one was now on board No. 7620 to close its fully open regulator. When he realised he had mistaken his driver's intentions, fireman Parker ran after his escaping engine, but to no avail.

The runaway roared through Wellow at a speed the signalman estimated at 50 mph and continued on to Midford. Here the double track became single and seven of the eight wagons derailed – felling signals, telegraph poles and the signal box – fortunately not harming the signalman. The stationmaster, hearing the loud crash, lay on the floor of his office. Six wagons shot down over the 40 ft high retaining wall into the garden of the Hope & Anchor – the public house where the unfortunate Wellow stationmaster had been quenching his thirst 60 years previously.

No. 7620 kept to the rails and careered on her way, pushing before her like a coster's barrow the remains of a wagon running on only two wheels. Remarkably this curious vehicle succeeded in negotiating the mile-long, single-bore Combe Down Tunnel. It then passed through Lyncombe Vale and Devonshire Tunnel, but at Claude Avenue Bridge, about midway between the north portal of Devonshire Tunnel and Bath Junction, the end door of the wagon fell off, derailing the locomotive's rear wheels and bringing it to a halt. About the same time, owing to a shortage of water, the fusible plug on the firebox crown melted and put the fire out.

Why did No. 13803 run through the signals? The driver was instructing his 19-year-old mate in firing and missed seeing the distant signal at caution and noticed the home signal only when he was almost upon it. Unfortunately the error was compounded by the fact that the Writhlington signalman had misunderstood his clearance point and accepted the goods when he should have refused due to the position of the shunting engine and wagons.

No. 13803's driver, seeing the signal at danger, immediately threw the engine into reverse and opened the regulator. In his panic he omitted to use the catch to secure the reversing handle which, owing to the weight of the valve gear, spun back into full forward gear. He tried to close the regulator, but it jammed. By the time he jumped, speed had been reduced to 10 mph.

Signalman Larcombe at Midford showed great presence of mind. The derailment had wrecked the telegraph wires, so he sped to a nearby house and used its telephone to warn Bath Control, which made arrangements with the Bath Junction signalman that if the runaway appeared, to direct it into the goods yard. Staff in the Bath locomotive office were ordered to leave immediately as the runaway would have been diverted beyond the yard down a siding only inches from the office wall.

On 14 October 1936 a sleeper service was inaugurated between London and Paris. Each of the three steamers, *Hampton Ferry*, *Twickenham Ferry* and *Shepperton Ferry* could carry either 12 sleeping cars, or 40 goods wagons spread over four tracks. The trains left Victoria and the Gare Du Nord each night at 10.00 p.m. and 9.50 p.m. respectively, the corresponding arrivals being 8.55 a.m. and 8.30 a.m. The aim was not to produce a fast service, but a comfortable route allowing a passenger to go to bed on leaving Victoria and then wake up in France in time to dress and have breakfast on the train before reaching Paris. As the coaches had to be chained to the deck and then unchained on the other side of the Channel, passengers did not enjoy an undisturbed rest. On board, passengers were locked in the cars, which could have proved dangerous had the ship struck a rock or another vessel. As the toilets at the end of the cars discharged straight onto the track, on board the ferry sumps were placed in strategic positions collected the waste.

For the first time in history the blue liveried sleeping cars of the International Sleeping Car Company could be observed in England, though they were slightly smaller than the usual Wagon-Lits vehicles as they were designed to fit the British loading gauge. The compartments were unlike most others as they contained a seasickness bowl, a lifebelt and a net for securing luggage. The *vase de nuit* often proved useful. Only the sleeping cars and the brake van ran through to Paris, passengers in ordinary first and second class compartments had to change at Dover and Dunkerque on and off the ferry steamers just as they had to do in the day time. Due to the fact that the class of passenger using this service defected to air travel, the Night Ferry last ran on 31 October 1980.

The long, steeply-graded Manchester- Sheffield route through the Woodhead Tunnel called for electrification and in 1936 the London

& North Eastern began work on Britain's first electrification scheme for goods as well as passenger trains. It was to be on the overhead system at 1,500 volts DC. World War II interrupted work and in 1948 work on a new double-track tunnel was started as the existing tunnels had insufficient headroom for the overhead wires. The new tunnel took six years to cut and cost six lives. The 1,100 men needed for its construction were accommodated in a shanty town at Dunford Bridge, which was provided with a cinema, inn, hospital and shops. The new Woodhead Tunnel, 3 miles 66 yards in length, opened on 14 June 1954. Due to a decline in coal traffic, electric trains were withdrawn on 20 July 1981 and Woodhead Tunnel closed after a life of only 27 years. The former Up tunnel was utilised to carry high voltage electric cables when permission for an overhead route through the Peak District National Park was denied. For maintenance purposes a 2 foot gauge railway was laid in June 1969.

On 16 November 1936 the West Coast route assembled a seven coach train – the same length as that of the Silver Jubilee – and with 4-6-2 No. 6201 *Princess Elizabeth* at its head, reached Glasgow from London in 6½ minutes less than 6 hours. The return run of 401.4 miles on 17 November was made in 344½ minutes at an average speed of 70 mph and with a load one coach heavier. Not having a corridor tender, a third man, a passed-fireman, was carried who could help with the firing or take over the regulator.

1937

The Silver Jubilee had shown that time could be maintained regularly on a 4-hour schedule over the 268.4 miles between King's Cross and Newcastle, while an additional 2 hours for the 124.5 miles to Edinburgh would place the Scottish capital within 6 hours of London. This would be the fastest time since 1895 when, in the Race to Aberdeen Edinburgh, Waverley had been reached in 6 hours and 19 minutes, but that train weighed only 105 tons whereas the new train, the Coronation, would weigh 312 tons, which was 42 per cent more than the Silver Jubilee.

The train set had a striking appearance. The exterior was enamelled in two shades of blue: light blue upper panels and garter blue lower panels. The rear coach was given a beaver tail, reversing the front wedge of the streamlined locomotive and designed to reduce the air resistance caused by the suction of a normal square coach-end. This carriage was designed as an observation car and fitted with loose armchairs available to both classes of passenger for a shilling for an hour's viewing.

For the first time in Great Britain, air conditioning was provided – the air in each coach being changed every three minutes. Each carriage had double-glazing, the windows being permanently closed. The cutlery had flat handles in order that the quietness would not be disturbed by rattling when the tables were laid! Every first class seat was arranged in an alcove with a swivelling chair and a table tapering towards the window allowing the passenger to swing the chair towards the window, the better to enjoy the view.

The Down Coronation left King's Cross at 4.00 p.m. allowing a businessman almost the whole day in London, yet it arrived in Edinburgh at 10.00 p.m. In winter, as most of the journey was made after dark, the observation car was removed giving a welcome reduction in weight when weather conditions were at their worst.

Since the days of the Race to Edinburgh in 1888 (*See* page 194) and the Race to Aberdeen in 1895 (*See* page 209) the West and East Coast companies informed the other of any plans for improvement. In 1936 the LNER informed the LMS that it was to introduce the Coronation.

As expected, the LMS made a reply on 7 November 1936 when No. 6201 *Princess Elizabeth* hauled a seven coach train over the 401.4 miles from Euston to Glasgow Central in 5 hours and 53½ minutes, returning the next day with one coach more in 5 hours and 44¼ minutes, thus completing the entire trip at an average speed of exactly 70 mph. This feat involved lifting the train to the summits at Beattock and Shap, respectively 1,015 feet and 915 feet above sea level.

As it was believed that a timing of 6 hours would be too tight for everyday use, the new train, the Coronation Scot was to take 6½ hours and would call at Carlisle for a crew change.

On 29 June 1937 a Press trip from London to Crewe and back with the first Princess Coronation streamlined 4-6-2s achieved a speed record of 114 mph. The fact that 25 minutes were gained on the Coronation Scot timing from Crewe demonstrated how ample a margin of time the new train would have in its day-to-day running.

Unlike the LNER, the train did not comprise specially-built coaches but was ordinary stock, painted blue with horizontal white lines continuing the white lines carried by the streamlined blue engine. In 1939 a new train was built for the service with coaches in the standard LMS red, with horizontal gold lines, most of the streamlined Pacifics being painted to match.

In 1939 this train, with the locomotive *Coronation*, was sent to the New York World's Fair. With the outbreak of World War II and the risk of shipping being sunk by the enemy, *Coronation* was returned, but the coaches loaned to the United States were to serve as a rest train for officers until the end of hostilities, when they were returned.

1938

In 1938 the GWR decided to increase its fleet of 18 diesel railcars by a further 20, but stipulated that it would construct the underframes, bogies, brake gear and bodywork, which was to be more angular. The design, although monitored by the GWR, was to be to the AEC specification. Controls were electro-pneumatic so that two or more cars could run coupled. Four of the new cars would be in pairs with vestibule connections and would have a speed of 70 mph but the others, intended for branch line use, would be geared for a maximum of 40 mph but able to haul up to 60 tons. Two branch cars would be fitted with dual-range gear offering a maximum of either 40 or 60 mph. Maintenance of all the GWR railcars was carried out on a mileage basis by the makers, AEC. These GWR diesel railcars formed the basis of British Railways DMUs introduced about 20 years later.

Having benefited from the experience of the Micheline cars and the Coventry version, the LMS designed a three-car unit of rather more robust character. Early in 1938 Derby Carriage & Wagon Works completed the train, which ran trials between Oxford and Cambridge. It was driven by six Leyland 125 bhp diesel engines through Lysholm-Smith torque converters. Axles turned on SKF roller bearings and brakes were Westinghouse compressed air. Its maximum speed was 75 mph and total weight of 73 tons. It was rostered to cover 462 miles daily between Bletchley (where it was based), Cambridge and Oxford. Air-operated sliding doors were controlled by the guard and interlocked with the engine control so that a driver could not start a train with a door open. Buffers and drawgear were for emergency use only – the unit was not intended to work in multiple. Detachable oval buffer faces were carried and could be secured by pins to the existing tube-shaped buffers to enable the unit to be coupled to an ordinary locomotive or rolling stock. These buffer heads were removed in normal service to reduce wind resistance.

Trials led to several modifications: the streamlined panels between the bogies were removed and a wire grille fitted in front of the driver's window to prevent shattering by, for example, a lump of coal falling from a passing tender. Withdrawn at the outbreak of World War II, the train was stored until 1949 when it was converted to a two-car maintenance train for the Manchester South Junction & Altrincham electric line.

In the mid-1930s, streamlining was all the rage. The London & North Eastern produced the A4 class 4-6-2 in 1935, the LMS produced the Coronation class 4-6-2 in 1937, while the Great Western directors feeling that they must join the fad, persuaded the reluctant Collett to streamline a Castle and King 4-6-0. He did this by smoothing Plasticene over a model and the result was as unpleasant as you would expect it to be. Within a few years, all the superficial additions were removed from this particular Castle and King.

In 1938 the first tube stock appeared with motors below the coach body, instead of within it, leaving more room for seats.

On 29 June 1938 the LMS achieved a record of 114 mph, while on 3 July the London & North Eastern's *Mallard* achieved 126 mph descending Stoke Bank, a record unlikely to be surpassed by steam.

Bus competition led the railways to adopt competitive fares – for example the cost of a day return from Leeds to Castleford fell from 2s 3d in 1923 to just 9d in 1938.

Road haulage had siphoned off a significant proportion of goods traffic. In addition, income from carrying such heavy goods traffic as coal had declined, so in November 1938 the railways launched a Fair Deal campaign to release them from statutory control over charges. Although the government agreed to this in principal, Britain was plunged into World War II before any practical moves could be made.

With the threat of war on the horizon, the Railway Executive Committee was formed on 24 September 1938. It consisted of the general managers of the Big Four plus Frank Pick representing London Transport. Although nominally the committee was chaired by the Minister of Transport, in practice his function was fulfilled by Sir Ralph Wedgwood, a former manager of the LNER. The committee's headquarters was in a bomb-proof shelter at the former Down Street station on the Piccadilly line. The wall built along the platform edge had a small gap to allow the 'top brass' to step out of the driver's cab in secret. In May 1941 railways came under the Minister of War Transport, but operational management was still retained by the Railway Executive Committee of railway managers.

The war in Spain had shown that a new aspect of hostilities was aerial bombing. With the rise of Hitler and the prospect of war with Germany a very great possibility, it was realised that it would be prudent to evacuate major British cities – Operation Pied Piper – and this would be largely carried out by the railways.

20

World War II

1939

On 1 September 1939, three days before war was declared, the mass evacuation from British cities began, the biggest movement of people in British history – moving a million children from cities to the country where host families were found. From London, 2,000 trains left with children. Valuable art works were evacuated from London galleries and sent to safe places such as slate mines in North Wales, and animals were evacuated from London Zoo.

To avoid being seen from the air, during black-out hours no lights were to be shown externally, so windows had to be screened and blue 15-watt bulbs fitted to give the very minimum illumination. Carriage windows were covered in mesh so that if they were shattered by bomb blast, glass shards would not injure passengers. It was very tempting for small boys and others with a curious nature, to pick at the mesh to discover how firmly it was attached. Platform lighting was limited to blue electric lights, or enclosed gas lamps below verandahs. Colour light signals were fitted with long hoods and anti-glare sheets were fixed between a locomotive cab and tender to obscure firebox glow, but made the footplate very hot.

The Big Four released 110,000 men for military service and provided the War Department with 298 steam and 45 diesel locomotives.

1940

The evacuation of 319,000 troops from Dunkirk between 27 May and 4 June 1940 required the SR to provide 327 trains from Dover, 82 from Ramsgate, 75 from Margate plus 75 ambulance trains, as well as 64 troop trains from Folkestone and 17 from Sheerness. The efforts of the 'little ships' rescuing soldiers has been well-publicised, but the sterling efforts of the railways almost neglected.

For the first nine months of the war, the Channel Islands was almost unaffected, railway ships carrying potatoes to England as usual. With the fall of France, it was obvious that the Channel Islands would be almost impossible to defend, so evacuation was offered to women, children, and men willing to join the armed forces. From 17–28 June 1940, five SR cargo ships carried 8,000 people from Jersey and 17,000 from Guernsey.

The Defence Volunteer Corps, later to become the Home Guard, was established to protect vulnerable railway facilities such as goods yards, tunnels, and major bridges and viaducts. Initially managing with make-shift weapons, they were later supplied with guns and ammunitions, other railwaymen manned anti-aircraft batteries near marshalling yards and major stations. Some major marshalling yards had decoy yards in the nearby countryside to try to deceive German aircraft.

Following the evacuation of Dunkirk, a German invasion was a real possibility so in order to make an invasion more difficult, 283 rail blockades were prepared for setting up on SR territory. Twelve armoured trains were deployed in areas where they might land. At Martin Mill, near Dover, several spur lines were constructed for use by heavy long-range rail-mounted guns, while the Elham Valley line was taken over for their use. It was the custom to fire a few rounds before moving on to a new firing point before enemy plotters could get the range.

The original proposal for using armoured trains in World War II had been put forward by Lt Col Alan Mount, Royal Engineers, Chief Inspecting Officer of the Ministry of Transport. He outlined his ideas to William Stanier and Sir Nigel Gresley, chief locomotive engineers of the LMS and LNER respectively, so they could work out the means of implementation. The final design was decided at a meeting held in the coal yard at King' Cross towards the end of

May 1940. An LMS 20-ton coal wagon was brought as the possible basis for an armoured truck and accepted for the purpose.

This all-steel vehicle had a 12 foot wheelbase and 21 foot long body. For a distance of 4 feet, the sides were to be lowered from 5 to 3 feet to provide a complete circle of fire for the six-pounder, 6 cwt Hotchkiss Mark II gun. Originally used by the navy in 1885, this particular variant of the weapon had been introduced in 1917 as the main armament for a tank. At this stage in World War II, it would have been effective against a German tank or armoured car at anything up to 800–1,000 yards.

To avoid using steel, which was in short supply, Stanier, responsible for the armoured train's rolling stock, proposed that a strengthening layer of concrete be applied to the coal wagon's interior. When the War Office observed that a bullet striking the exterior could cause a fragment of concrete to fly off and kill those inside, a revised plan was adopted. This used an outer skin of ³/₁₆ inch mild steel plate welded to the wagon's exterior framing, the intervening 4 inches filled with concrete. A transverse partition of similar construction was inserted, dividing the wagon into two compartments: a section just under 9 feet in length containing the gun, and a main compartment 12 feet 3 inches long. The latter had the additional protection of ¼ inch mild steel plates fixed above the wagon sides and angled inwards at 30 degrees from the vertical to deflect bullets or splinters. Each sloping plate had three loopholes for rifles and Bren light machine guns, each armoured wagon having three of the latter. When not in use, the slits could be closed by sliding steel shutters. One armoured wagon in each train was in wireless communication with headquarters. A steel guard protected each axle box, while the substitution of screw couplings for the three-link type demanded 2½ inch packing between the wagon frame and buffer beam. As the gun end formed the leading part of the train, T-section guards projected down from the underframe at the outer end of the wagon to thrust any obstruction off the track. Four brackets, also fitted at this end, allowed the necessary head or tail lamps to be displayed. A removable ladder gave access to the wagon's interior.

Motive power was provided by LNER F4 class 2-4-2Ts on loan. Armouring consisted of external plating over the tank sides, and the lower part of the bunker, which also contained water. Plates screened the Westinghouse brake pump, boiler feed pipes, whistle and safety valve. Sliding plates covered the spectacle spaces and side openings, separate upper and lower doors enabling the cab to be fully enclosed. When in that state, the driver could be given instructions by a bell signal from the leading wagon. Armouring raised the weight of the locomotive from 53 tons 19 cwt to 59 tons 18 cwt. Initially the trains were painted in camouflage, but later repainted black.

The army footplatemen were required to pass the relevant railway company's rules and regulations to the satisfaction of the district locomotive superintendent. One suggestion was adopted in July 1940: 'On cold or misty mornings it will be possible under favourable conditions to use exhaust steam from the cylinder cocks to blind a position or cover a withdrawal. This should be practised.'

In the late summer of 1940, an armoured train was returning to Barnstaple from an early morning patrol and travelling at about 30 mph when the crew was horrified to see the signal protecting Duckpool Crossing fly to Danger. Although the driver applied the brakes – the only brakes were on the engine – it was not possible for him to stop before smashing into a lorry killing the driver of the latter. To prevent a repetition, a braked vehicle was added behind the bunker.

The LMS had some redundant ex-Caledonian Railway high-sided bogie tenders, designed to carry 4,600 gallons of water on a system with no water troughs. These tenders were prepared for the armoured trains at the LMS St Rollox Works, Glasgow. The War Office specification was for a limit of 3,400 gallons in order to preserve acceptable axle loading, but with armour plating a tender weighed 59¾ tons. The tender had the advantage of augmenting the locomotive's water supply, as in the event of an invasion it would have been a pity to have had to break off an engagement with the enemy in order to refill the tanks. A further modification was a grenade net to fit over the armoured wagons as it would have been easy to lob a grenade down into a train from an overbridge.

At Dunkirk, 79 British locomotives fell into German hands. As these needed to be replaced and more engines were required to assist the war effort, the Railway Executive Committee ordered

400 LMS Class 8F 2-8-0s from the Big Four. To avoid air-raid damage to engines and rolling stock, some was dispersed overnight to safe places – to a tunnel, or out to a country station.

In the event of an air raid, on receipt of a Red warning, passenger trains were required to stop at the first station, allow any passengers who wished to step out to do so and perhaps enter a shelter. The train was then required to proceed at not more than 15 mph.

Goods trains were expected to stop at the first signal box to receive instructions and then continue not in excess of 10 mph. As so many warnings were given in the summer and autumn of 1940, rail transport was chaotic. In July 1940 an extra warning, Purple, was added to indicate that enemy aircraft were in the vicinity and that all lights should be extinguished. Speed restrictions were eased in November 1940 and only at night were trains stopped and drivers instructed to proceed at not in excess of 30 mph.

Tube stations made fine air raid shelters and some were equipped with three-tier bunk beds; tickets were free, but space had to be booked in advance. Food and tea were supplied by a catering train. There were two peaks for shelter use: in 1940 during the blitz and 1944 when the V1 and V2 rockets threatened. Unfortunately on 14 October 1940 a 3,000 lb bomb dropped through the road into Balham station where 600 were sheltering. Broken water mains brought hundreds of tons of rubble into the station and 68 people died. The station clock stopped at 8.02 p.m. when the incident occurred.

Laying concrete runways at airfields required almost 750,000 tons of rubble from London's bomb damage to be transported by rail. Each 1,000-bomber raid needed eight trains of bombs and 28 trains of aviation spirit.

Unlike during World War I, British railways suffered far more bomb damage, but were extremely efficient in repairing even serious damage. Bus replacement services were set up within minutes and craters filled, track replaced and train services restored – often within 24 hours. The highly-adaptable railway engineering works produced tanks, munitions, landing craft, midget submarines, aircraft parts etc.

To discourage rail travel during World War II in order to leave locomotives and stock available for essential supplies and troop movements, Cheap Day Returns were discontinued, but re-introduced in 1948. These tickets were approximately the same as a bus fare between the stations, sometimes even undercutting them.

1941

Under an agreement of January 1941, the government gave the railways an annual guaranteed income of £43.5 million, the government taking any surplus receipts above this figure. With the shortage of imported petrol and diesel oil curtailing road transport, the railways did very well as in World War II freight increased by 50 per cent and passenger traffic by 67 per cent – without any significant increase in basic equipment. Post-war earnings fell from £62.5 million in 1945 to £32.5 million in 1946.

In 1937 Oliver Bulleid had become the SR's locomotive superintendent, a man with startling new ideas. His aim was to build a locomotive capable of hauling a 600-ton train at 70 mph. The result was the 4-6-2 Merchant Navy class, which appeared in 1941 with many innovations. The exterior was air-smoothed and they had patent disc wheels, chain-driven valve gear, a steel firebox rather than copper, and electric lighting. Other innovations were a multiple-jet blast giving a comparatively soft exhaust; a boiler pressure of 280 lb per square inch, the highest to date on a British railway using a normal boiler and firebox; the firebox was welded steel with two Nicholson thermic syphons; the fire-hole door was steam-operated from a treadle, thus making life much easier for a fireman, while the cab and tender were built to the same external contour as the coaches.

The numbering system of the Merchant Navies was different: 21C1 indicated two leading axles, a trailing axle while the C showed three driving axles, the last numeral being the engine's number in the class. To overcome the wartime restriction on building express locomotives, it was classified 'mixed traffic'.

Being revolutionary, it was not without faults: the oil bath tended to leak and the lubricant ran onto the rails and caused slipping and occasionally fire; the steam reverser suffered steam leakage and could accidentally move from 25 per cent cut-off to 75 per cent. From 1956 they were rebuilt with Walschaerts valve gear and modified details, the air-smoothed casing being removed to make it look like a conventional locomotive.

In the poor visibility of the blackout it was impossible to ensure that first class passengers obtained the accommodation for which they had paid so, as a result, trains in the London area became third class only from 6 October 1941. This move had the additional advantage of making maximum use of the available accommodation. Indications on the doors were painted out and rugs removed from first class compartments. Knowledgeable travellers then sought out ex-first class compartments where they could avail themselves of more luxurious accommodation and greater leg room.

As it was anticipated that bombing could sever important rail links and thus halt vital wartime traffic, several new links were made between the GWR and the SR to provide alternative routes should one be blocked or overcrowded. These connections were built at government expense and were government, and not railway, property – although they were managed by the railway companies. A new junction was put in at Reading; another at Staines; in the West Country new links were provided at Launceston, Lydford, St Budeaux and Yeovil. On the GWR itself, a connection was restored at Thingley, south of Chippenham, while a new spur was laid at Westbury. At Oxford a new link was made with the LMS.

As timber was in short supply and second-hand sleepers were required for government work and army operational purposes, new timber was only used for main line sleepers and block-type concrete sleepers were developed with a steel tie bar for use in sidings and goods loops. Although they could be used with stone ballast it was found that pot sleepers got a better bearing on ashes. By the spring of 1943, the GWR was making 5,000 pot sleepers every week.

To speed parcel traffic and avoid over-carrying, short-carrying, missed connections or delay in unloading because parcels were far from the door, female travelling porters started from principal stations and travelled on trains ensuring that every package went into the right van on the right train and was at the most convenient door for unloading. Between stations this porter passed through the connecting gangway adjusting stowage.

1942

One development in 1942 was that Ian Allan, a clerk on the Southern Railway, published an *ABC of Southern Railway Locomotives,* listing all that company's engines. Hitherto such lists had only been available to member of an enthusiasts' society, whereas his booklet was sold on railway bookstalls and easily available to boys keen on collecting engine numbers. It proved a success and was followed with similar books on the GWR, LMS and LNER. He also developed the Locospotters Club, which at its height had 150,000 members. Then, within the 10 years between 1958 and 1968, most of the 20,000 steam locomotives were withdrawn and spotting became less popular, especially as modern youth had more opportunities and more money to spend on entertainment. Locomotive spotting in steam days had a lot in its favour by enlarging the exponents' knowledge of English kings; the names of Commonwealth countries; wild life, and so on, in addition to giving them a knowledge of areas and towns in Britain.

In 1943 Oliver Bulleid produced the austerity Q1 class 0-6-0; not very attractive to look at but the most powerful British 0-6-0 and a useful workhorse.

On 26 November 1942 SR D3 class 0-4-4T No. 2365 shot down a German plane. Its boiler had been punctured by enemy bullets and the escaping jet of steam caused the attacking aircraft to crash, its pilot flung out and drowned in a ditch. The plane was destroyed but No. 2365 was repaired.

1944

In 1944 German flying bombs caused a certain amount of havoc on the railways. At Cow Lane Viaduct, Peckham, a viaduct collapsed. On another occasion a V2 rocket fell in front of a Kent Coast express killing several passengers.

By the end of 1944 a million United States troops had sailed from Southampton and between D-Day and VE-Day no less than 2,840,346 personnel had been embarked or disembarked. With the advent of peace, it was revealed that during the war a Pullman train had left Victoria every night at 7.08 p.m., to Hurn Airport and the Poole flying boat base. Between 1941 and 1945 this train had carried 30,000 passengers.

1945

In 1945 Oliver Bulleid produced a slightly lighter version of the Merchant Navy class. Weighing 86 rather than 92½ tons, it was able to run over most of the SR's lines. The class had two groups of names: those for use in the West Country were named after places in the area, while those for use in the rest of the SR territory were named after fighter squadrons and persons associated with the Battle of Britain in 1940. In due course, these Pacifics were used over the steeply-graded and curvaceous Somerset & Dorset line between Bournemouth and Bath. Leakage of oil from the bath containing the chain-driven valve gear occurred on sharp curves, the oil being thrown on the ballast. On long down gradients, the heat generated by the brakes sometimes ignited the oil thrown out over parts of the engine. Like their sisters in the Merchant Navy class, these lighter Pacifics were rebuilt and modified from 1957 to a more conventional design.

1946

Due to the very minimum number of repairs and replacements carried out during World War II, by 1945 there was a very serious backlog of work that needed to be done.

Rolling Stock Under/Awaiting Repair

	31.12.38 (%)	31.12.46 (%)	Increase (%)
Locomotives	6.04	7.98	32
Coaching stock	6.52	12.92	92
Wagons	2.82	10.79	281

On 31 December 1946 as many as 7,981, or 39.3 per cent, of the locomotives were more than 35 years old; as were 28 per cent of the wagons and 21.6 per cent of the coaching vehicles.

To try to obviate the coal shortage in 1946, the Ministry of Transport ordered the railways to convert 1,200 steam locomotives to oil firing. Three million pounds had been spent on plant and only 93 had been converted when, in September 1947, the Treasury said foreign currency was unavailable to buy the fuel and so the scheme was abandoned. It was just as well because oil-firing locomotives were uneconomic and cost two-and-a-half times more to operate than using coal.

The wide disparity in dividends paid by the Big Four are interesting:

Main Line Railway Companies' Ordinary Dividends 1929–1947
(averages)

Stock	1929–34 (%)	1935–39 (%)	1940–45 (%)	1946–47 (%)
GWR ord. £42,929,800	4.17	2.80	4.42	6.14
LMS ord. £95,202,450	1.13	0.85	2.67	3.82
SR deferred ord. £31,490,200	0.63	0.65	1.79	3.54
LNER preferred ord. 5% £42,361,000	0.54	0.00	0.00	0.41

The post-war shortage of materials meant that rolling stock was patched rather than replaced. New works were curtailed, the only significant ones being electrification Liverpool Street-Shenfield at £8 million and Manchester-Sheffield-Wath at £9.1 million, inherited from the 1935–1940 New Works Programme.

In October 1947 passenger fares and freight rates were increased to 55 per cent above those of October 1937, though railway costs had risen by at least 80 per cent, while the average weekly earnings of railwaymen had doubled and they had enjoyed a reduction in the working week from 48 to 44 hours in June 1947.

The year 1947 was a serious one for accidents with 121 passengers being killed – the second-highest year in railway history. Certainly some of these accidents were due to arrears of track maintenance and the postponement of the introduction of colour-light signalling. On nationalisation, the backlog of maintenance was £210 million.

21

Rationalisation and Nationalisation; The Railway Preservation Movement

William Gladstone's Act of 1844 gave the Government the option of acquiring, after 1865, post-1844 railway companies on a basis of 25 years' purchase of the annual profits for the previous three years. As we have seen, during World War II British railways had been run by the Government's Railway Executive Committee. Since 1908 the Labour Party had committed itself to the nationalisation of railways and when it came into power in 1945 with a majority of 145, it seized the opportunity to nationalise not just the railways, but virtually all public transport.

It is interesting to record that another project of the Labour Government was the National Health Service and that this was largely based on the Great Western Railway's medical service, which had proved that a medical health service, free at the point of use, was possible.

During World War II the railways had carried 50 per cent more freight and nearly double the number of passengers than in 1938, with almost no investment or maintenance. Something needed to be done. The Transport Act of 6 August 1947 required railways, canals, ports, harbours, bus companies and long-distance road haulage to be owned by the Government under the British Transport Commission (BTC). With nationalisation three options were open:

Functional – base on transport mode
Territorial – based on the existing Big Four
Regional – non-railway based areas incorporating all modes of transport.

The functional form was selected, each form of transport was under its own executive committee, railways coming under the Railway Executive. Although in theory, all land transport were integrated, in reality, they were not.

Part I of the Transport Act established the British Transport Commission with a 'general duty ... to provide ... an efficient, adequate, economic and properly integrated system of public inland transport and port facilities.' There were five executives: Docks & Inland Waterways; Road Transport; Railways; London Transport and Hotels – including railway catering services. The Southern was angry at the loss of its Southampton Docks. Most members of the Railway Executive had entered the industry straight from school and had worked for just one company. Although at the top level all of the Big Four were represented, lower down it was not so – ex-LMS employee R. A. Riddles, appointed mechanical engineer for British Railways, chose four of his officers from the LMS, while the civil engineer, J. L. Train, ex-LNER, selected two of his staff of four from the LNER.

On 31 December 1947 the Big Four ceased to exist and became part of British Railways: the Great Western Railway became the Western Region, the Southern Railway, the Southern Region, while the English lines of the London, Midland & Scottish became the London Midland Region. Its Scottish lines, with those of the London & North Eastern Railway in that area, became the Scottish Region, while the remainder of the LNER was allotted to the Eastern Region and North Eastern Region. The more important minor railways were taken over, but smaller ones, including industrial lines, remained independent. The London Transport, including the underground, was taken over by the London Transport Executive. Private owners' wagons were also taken over by the British Transport Commission.

Each region had its colour code for station name boards, timetables and other publicity material: Eastern, dark blue; London

Midland, maroon; North Eastern, orange; Scottish, light blue; Southern, green; and Western, brown.

Ex-GWR locomotives retained their original number, those of the SR had 30,000 added; the LMS 40,000 and 60,000 for those of the LNER. BR adopted the LMS shed code system, with the main shed in an area being given a number followed by the letter 'A', with sub-sheds bearing suffixes B, C, D and so on. The number and letter were generally carried on a plate on the smoke box door.

The Big Four shareholders received British Transport Stock bearing an interest of three per cent guaranteed by the Treasury.

On 1 January 1948 the British Transport Commission owned 19,639 route miles, 20,023 steam locomotives, 36,033 passenger vehicles, 4,184 emus and 1, 223,634 wagons.

In December 1948, 558 second-hand Austerity freight engines were bought from the War Department for £1.5 million, about half the price paid by the LNER for 200 in 1946. It is interesting that Riddles, who designed them during WW2, said that they could be 'thrown into the sea' after the war. When built, they were only designed to have a life of seven years. They proved expensive to maintain and lacked operational flexibility.

Engineers found that a diesel engine has advantages: it can be started immediately, it does not require special track or wires and can be driven by one man. It cannot drive the wheels directly and as a gear box for an engine large enough for a locomotive is impractical, a diesel engine drives a generator and the electricity drives the wheels and offers control of power. The maximum thermal efficiency of a steam locomotive was about seven per cent, as compared the 15 per cent of a diesel locomotive.

In 1945 Charles Edward Fairburn had proposed that the LMS build a diesel-electric and introduced the first main-line diesel-electric to run in Britain, a 1,600 hp Co+Co. (As the Whyte system is not quite suitable, it is modified and powered axles are indicated with a letter – Co-Co indicating that each bogie has three powered axles, and there are no idle axles).

Mid-December 1947 saw the appearance of LMS No. 10000 built by the LMS at Derby with power equipment supplied by English Electric. The engine was a 16-cylinder Vee-type, four-cycle turbo-charged unit. It was started by using the main generator as a motor on receiving current supplied from batteries. A driver's compartment was situated at each end of the 60-foot long machine. Warning lamps indicated if anything untoward was happening. The controller had eight notches and, in normal conditions, could be fully opened within about 150 yards from the start. Normal practice was to use full power on the level, or rising grades, and ease back to the sixth notch when running within schedule, or when speed approached 75 mph. A passageway offered access throughout the locomotive. No. 10000 was designed to work either independently or in tandem with a second unit to form a 3,200 hp locomotive capable of working the heaviest long-distance expresses. Doors were provided in each nose to enable the crew to gain access to either whilst on the move.

The SR placed an order in August 1947 for three 1-Co+Co-1 diesel-electric locomotives a joint design between Oliver Bulleid and English Electric, the engine being 1,750 hp. The third, No. 10203 uprated to 2,000 hp, became the prototype for the BR Class 40.

The GWR being a very individualistic railway; rather than invest in diesel power, tried the gas-turbine-electric. A gas turbine functions by sucking air into a compressor, where it is heated by oil, the air then emerging at high velocity to drive a turbine, which in turn drives a generator to power the electric traction motors.

In 1946 it decided to order such a locomotive from the Swiss company Brown-Boveri, which had experience of this power having built one in 1941. The GWR also ordered a British machine from Metropolitan Vickers. Delays in the completion of the order meant that the Swiss engine, only the third such machine in the world, did not arrive at Harwich until 3 February 1950 and arrived at Swindon two days later. On 22 February 1950, No. 18000 made a test run between Paddington and Plymouth, but on 9 March 1950 it failed, necessitating the replacement of the main compressor turbine blades. Repaired, it took up duties between Paddington-Bristol and Paddington-Plymouth. It suffered frequent failures and spent quite a time in the Swindon works. In 1955–6, No. 18000 received an extensive overhaul but then early in 1957, one of its traction motors failed. It was decided to continue using the engine utilising the remaining three operational motors and as its load and speed capabilities were reduced, it was downgraded from the prestigious Bristolian and Merchant Venturer expresses to more humble workings. It operated such trains until its withdrawal in September 1959. It was eventually returned to Switzerland and used for adhesion tests until 1975 when the shell was displayed at Vienna until 1993, when it was returned to Britain, exhibited on several sites before arriving at the Didcot Railway Centre in July 2011. It is in the care of the Waterman Railway Heritage Trust.

No. 18100, the Metropolitan-Vickers British-built gas-turbine, was delivered to Swindon in December 1951 and tests showed that it was very suitable for climbing the South Devon banks with gradients as steep as 1 in 36. Following these tests it was placed on the Bristol run, working the Down Merchant Venturer and returning with the Up Bristolian.

An interesting incident occurred with this working on 31 May 1952. When it was time to return with the Bristolian, the engine failed to start. The station pilot replaced No. 18100 at the head of the express and left for Paddington via Bath and Chippenham. Meanwhile efforts to start No. 18100 had succeeded and it was decided to run it light engine to Swindon via the shorter Badminton route where it would regain its rightful place at the head of the train. No. 18100 speeding through South Gloucestershire and Wiltshire carrying the Bristolian headboard must have been a sight indeed!

In September 1953 it was decided to convert it to use heavy fuel oil, rather than the light oil for which it had been designed. Back at the manufacturers for three years, the conversion was not achieved and the decision made to convert it to normal electric locomotive for training Manchester Longsight crews ready for the electrification of the West Coast main line. Latterly it was used over former Great Central lines to evaluate various pantograph designs before being scrapped in 1972.

Both gas turbine locomotives suffered from the defect that they consumed almost a much fuel when idling as when hauling a train, so diesel-electric, rather than turbine-electric proved more efficient. With a light load, the Metropolitan Vickers locomotive consumed 2.97 gallons a mile, approximately three times the consumption of a diesel-electric.

On 2 April 1950 regional boundaries were redrawn on a more geographical basis, but operating and motive power was exempt from strict geography so 'penetrating lines' were designated for operating purposes such as Birmingham-Bristol, Manchester-Sheffield and Nottingham-Aylesbury. The Western Region was given all lines west of Exeter, while the Southern being given the ex-GWR facilities at Weymouth caused a certain amount of anger. Nationalisation did not mean that everything became the same – Keith Grand, chief regional officer of the Western Region, refused to accept standard upper quadrant signals, the Western continuing to use lower quadrants.

The initial emblem was a lion astride a wheel – patriotic perhaps, but not giving a modern image. The most powerful express engines were painted dark blue, other express engines were dark green, lined out in black and orange; other passenger engines and mixed traffic engines were black, lined in red, cream and grey; while freight and shunting classes were painted black. In practice the blue livery did not wear well becoming almost black, so all express engines were painted green.

Corridor coaches were cream and red, commonly referred to as 'blood and custard'; non-corridor coaches were red; while electric stock appeared in a green livery. The Southern Region having a goodly number of electric coaches and plenty of green paint, took advantage of this, and quite a number of its steam-hauled stock continued to be painted green.

Standard designs of steam locomotives had not been prepared in advance, so those of the old companies continued to be built until new ones appeared in 1951 – the Festival of Britain year, when, for the first time, Britain was beginning to throw off the austerity of war and the post-war years. As many as 1,538 locomotives were built to pre-BR designs between 1948 and 1956: 452 to GWR designs, 640 to LMS, 396 to LNER and 50 to the SR. Several of the LMS types were constructed and used in other regions.

Although diesel traction was proceeding apace in the USA, it was believed that with large coal reserves, and the fact that little oil had been discovered in the United Kingdom, it was better from the foreign currency point of view to continue using steam traction. Although diesels were more expensive to build than steamers, they were cleaner – an important factor when shortage of labour meant that the workforce could be more selective about the job desired; the diesels' maintenance and running costs were lower and a greater range was possible.

Robert Riddles was appointed the chief mechanical and electrical engineer to BR. Starting his career on the London & North Western Railway at Crewe in 1909, in 1935 he became Stanier's deputy on the LMS and during World War II served with the Ministry of Supply and, rejoining the LMS, became Vice-President in 1946. His principal assistants were R. C. Bond as Chief Officer (Locomotive Construction and Maintenance) and E. S. Cox Executive Officer (Design).

The first steps towards the creation of Standard locomotives were:

1. A series of exchange trials to compare the performance and efficiency of the principal locomotive classes over selected main lines.
2. The setting up of a locomotive standards committee under Western Region chairmanship to make recommendations on such matters as whether a limited range of existing types could be selected for construction until standard types were developed.

Thirteen locomotive types were tested, passenger engines being:

Eastern Region: A4 4-6-2; London Midland Region Duchess 4-6-2, Royal Scot 4-6-0; Southern Region Merchant Navy 4-6-2; Western Region King 4-6-0.

Mixed traffic engines: Eastern Region B1 4-6-0; London Midland Region Class 5 4-6-0; Southern Region West Country 4-6-2; Western Region Hall 4-6-0.

Heavy freight engines: Eastern Region O1 2-8-0; London Midland Region 8F 2-8-0; War Department Austerity 2-8-0; Western Region 2800 2-8-0.

In each category no single engine emerged as obviously superior and this demolished the belief that locomotives needed to be designed for a particular tasks – the SR light Pacifics carried out some of their finest work between Perth and Inverness.

To make steam locomotives pleasanter to maintain, Cox was a believer in the self-cleaning smokebox, rocking grate and self-emptying ashpan, coupled with high superheat, long-travel valve gear and outside cylinders. They were to be built incorporating standard boilers, flanging blocks, cylinder patterns, wheel and tyre sizes and use a standard range of fittings. They would comply with either a locomotive gauge L1 permitting running over almost all main lines, or L2 covering more powerful locomotives used on trunk routes. They would have wide fireboxes to improve combustion and ease problems when using small coal.

Three basic sizes of 6-wheeled tenders were built, originally with the sides of the coal bunker inset to offer improved visibility when running backwards, but when a greater capacity was required, two larger types were designed with straight sides curved at the top to make full use of the loading gauge.

To be fair to the drawing offices of the previous Big Four, design work was shared, but when the new locomotives appeared, most were basically modified LMS designs. One design which did not appear was a steam shunter, it having been discovered by the Big Four that diesel-electrics were more economic for such a duty.

The smallest Standard engine was a Class 2MT (mixed traffic) 2-6-2T introduced in 1953 and designed at Derby; the next was a Class 3MT 2-6-2T which appeared in 1952 and designed at Swindon, while the Class 4MT 2-6-4T introduced in 1951 had been designed at Brighton.

The smallest tender engine was a Class 2MT 2-6-0 designed at Derby, then a Class 3MT designed at Swindon, a Class 4MT 2-6-0 designed at Doncaster, a Class 4MT 4-6-0 designed at Brighton – it could be argued that one of these latter two classes were superfluous, a Class 5MT designed at Doncaster, a Class 6P5F (passenger/freight) 4-6-2 designed at Derby, a Class 7P6F designed at Derby and a Class 9F 2-10-0 designed at Brighton. Riddles ex-Ministry of Supply War Department 2-8-0 and 2-10-0 locomotives purchased by BR in 1948 were also considered Standard locomotives and numbering 587 formed the largest class.

The Standard locomotives were constructed at Brighton, Crewe, Darlington, Derby, Doncaster, Horwich and Swindon. It is interesting to note that during and in the post-World War II period, all these works had constructed Stanier Class 8F 2-8-0s or other types of LMS engines and so were familiar with many of the design features of the BR locomotives.

In order to evaluate certain features, some Standard locomotives were non-standard due to experiments being carried out! It was found that engines having plain bearings were no worse than those with roller bearings and due to favourable results using the Caprotti valve gear, the last 30 Class Fives were constructed with this gear. Ten Class 9F 2-10-0s were equipped with Crosti boilers, one being fitted with a Giesel blastpipe and chimney, and three with mechanical stokers. None of these was found of sufficient benefit to warrant their adoption. Double blastpipes and chimneys were added to some engines.

Although 999 BR Standard locomotives were constructed between 1951 and 1960, it is arguable whether it would have been better to have continued building the old company standard designs – the 1948 trials had shown that they were flexible and could be used on routes other than those for which they had been built – so perhaps keeping them would have been the way forward rather than introducing yet another standard, with yet more spares to be kept. Developments overseas had proved that electric, or at least diesel-electric, was the way forward and existing designs could have coped in the interim. Although steam locomotives were thermally inefficient, their first cost was low and due to restriction on capital investment it made sense to continue building them in Britain in the 1950s. Keeping miners employed made the choice in Britain either steam or electric propulsion and not diesel, as well as the shortage of foreign currency needed for imported oil. The WR decision to build 343 steam shunters between 1948 and 1956, when diesel-electric shunters had already proved more efficient was a very poor judgement. A further argument in favour of diesels was that they were pleasanter to maintain – there were no choking ashes to be shovelled out or parts to be oiled in awkward places, while full employment meant that it was increasingly difficult to attract labour to maintain steam locomotives.

Arguably the best of the Standard engines was the Class 9F 2-10-0. Very capable of handling heavy freight trains, it proved remarkably good at hauling express passenger trains, being highly popular with crews on runs between Cardiff and Paddington where examples of the class attained speeds of 90 mph. As the driving wheel diameter was only 5 feet and it was not intended for running at such high speed, engineers frowned on such use. Another passenger turn where they proved valuable was over the Somerset & Dorset line between Bath and Bournemouth.

Long climbs at 1 in 50 over the Mendips meant that passenger trains of any length needed to be double-headed and apart from the expense of an additional locomotive and crew, a shortage of locomotives at Bath could mean that it was a severe problem finding enough engines. The introduction of the Class 9F to the Somerset & Dorset in 1960 meant that one engine and one crew could handle the longest expresses over the line as it proved to be the ideal locomotive for the difficult terrain. Unfortunately having discovered the perfect engine to work these trains, the through expresses were withdrawn in 1962!

In 1937 the LMS and the LNER decided jointly to build a locomotive testing station at Rugby. Inspiration for the design came from a plant in France and another in Pennsylvania, but the outbreak of World War II meant that the project had to be suspended. After the war, work was resumed and the plant opened in October 1948. The last steam locomotive tests are believed to have taken place at Rugby in 1959, but the testing of diesel locomotives continued until 1965. The testing station closed in 1970.

The British Transport Commission set up a film unit with three aims: to promote the use of public transport; to use film for internal communication purposes such as up-dating staff on working practices and to communicate to the public and staff railway development, particularly the technical side. British Transport Films was disbanded in 1982.

On 2 November 1949 Oliver Bulleid's two double-deck four-coach trains were placed in service. Weighing the same as a normal set, they seated 508 passengers rather than the 386 capacity of a conventional design. They were really half-decks, compartments being interlocked at two levels, as the feet of the upper passengers were between the backs of those sitting lower. The restrictions of the loading gauge prevented windows in the upper deck being opened, but pressure ventilation was provided. An entrance to each upper deck compartment was provided from a lower deck compartment. Due to the fact that access to the upper compartment meant pushing through a lower compartment, the coaches were unpopular with passengers; the railway staff did not like them as they needed a longer time at stations for passengers to get in and out. The double-deck train had one door for every

22 seats, compared with 10 or 12 in ordinary compartment stock, moreover the double-deck coaches provided less cubic capacity per passenger and had smaller and less comfortable seats. They were withdrawn in 1971.

1951

On 9 January 1951 the Fell diesel-mechanical locomotive made its first run. It had been authorised by the LMS in October 1947. Instead of being powered by one large engine, it had four 500 hp engines, which could be cut in and out as required to adjust power and speed demands. Transmission was via differentials. Although it appeared to be a 4-4-4-4, in reality, it was a 4-8-4 as the two centre axles were coupled by internal gearing. Popular with drivers, it offered excellent power and smooth starting, but proved difficult to service and its end came on 16 October 1958 when a train-heating boiler caught fire.

1951 brought the Festival of Britain aimed at giving the country a new start after the austerity suffered in war and post-war conditions. British Railways helped this spirit of freshness, and the new Elizabethan era of the Coronation of the new queen in 1953, by introducing many new named trains and named with special headboards at the front and roof boards on the coaches – not just cheap paper labels stuck on windows as is the case today.

Several railway enthusiasts were disappointed at the closure of the narrow gauge Lynton & Barnstaple Railway in 1935 and in the late 1940s L. T. C. Rolt was concerned about the future of the 2 foot 3 inch gauge Talyllyn Railway owned by the elderly Sir Haydn Jones. Acting on a suggestion of O. H. Prosser, the Talyllyn Railway Preservation Society was established and in 1951 his widow Lady Haydn Jones handed the line to the society, which ran its first trains that year. This success encouraged others and also led to a film being made on preservation: *The Titfield Thunderbolt*.

The narrow gauge Ffestiniog Railway had lain derelict since closure in 1946 and this was bought by Alan Pegler in 1954 and later transferred to a charitable trust. These two lines were narrow gauge with relatively small rolling stock and locomotives, light track and thus relatively easy to maintain, but then in 1960 two standard gauge lines came under preservation: the Middleton Railway at Leeds and the Bluebell Line in Sussex involving heavy track, rolling stock and locomotives, far more difficult to maintain. They led the way to many branch lines being preserved so that most people in Britain now live within easy distance of such a line. Some main lines have been preserved: the Great Central's Loughborough-Leicester being one and the Gloucestershire Warwickshire Railway another.

One very daring example of preservation was relaying the Welsh Highland Railway. It was closed to passengers in 1936, freight in 1937 and the line dismantled in 1941. Today the track has recently been relaid, bridges replaced and suitable locomotives and rolling stock found or made. It is now a superb tourist attraction, keeps visitors off the roads yet brings them to the area to spend money. The Lynton & Barnstaple Railway in North Devon is similarly being relaid and will produce a similar result. Preservation societies usually began by carrying out all the work with volunteers, but then as traffic grew, generally find they need to employ a few staff.

British Transport Historical Records was established by the British Transport commission in 1951 and ensured that valuable documents such as company minute books and time tables were preserved for the use of future historians. In 1973 they were transferred to the Public Record Office, now known as the National Archives.

In October 1951 a confidential memorandum, *A Development Programme for British Railways,* supported electrification of 2,900 route miles of main lines, including Euston-Glasgow, King's Cross-Newcastle, Paddington-South Wales, St Pancras-Manchester, Liverpool Street-Cambridge and Ipswich, and the Southern Region's steam lines to Dover, Bournemouth and Hastings. The thinking was that electrification would be 'the most effective means of harnessing atomic power for railway purposes'. It was envisaged that diesel power would be used for inter-urban, cross-country and local lines.

1952 saw a shortage of track maintenance workers and this was cured by importing Italian labour and also recruiting women and by February 721 Italians and 488 women were working on the permanent way. Employing the Swiss-made Matisa tamping machine eased work compacting and consolidating the ballast, though the paucity of foreign currency led to difficulty in obtaining import licences. The steel shortage continued so only 300 locomotives, 1,000 carriages and 28,500 wagons were built compared with the original plans to build 400, 2,500 and 50,000 respectively. BR had to buy 9,000 second-hand 16-ton mineral wagons from French Railways. These had been built in Britain in 1944–1945, but acquiring them was a backward step as plans were well advanced for introducing the more economical 24.5 ton capacity wagons.

Carriages were originally built of timber; then steel was used, first for the frames and then for sides; then in 1951 at the Festival of Britain, London Transport displayed the first aluminium car. In 1952 the first aluminium train ran on the District Line. Originally it was left unpainted, thus saving cost and weight; it was found that when graffiti was cleaned off, a trace still remained so painting is now back in favour.

Mechanical failure causing an accident was rare. One such instance was on 21 September 1951 when the Liverpool-Euston express comprising 15 coaches hauled by 4-6-2 No. 46207 *Princess Arthur of Connaught* rounded the curves at Weedon at about 65 mph, then passed on to straight track and ran through Stowe Hill Tunnel. Suddenly the driver felt a shake at the front. He applied the brake but the whole engine derailed and fell down the 12 foot embankment; the fact of the engine stopping from about 60 mph in less than 100 yards derailed and smashed many of the coaches killing 15 passengers. The investigation showed that the bogie had derailed on the Weedon curve and had run for about 1,200 yards off the rails of the flat-bottom track, but when reaching the bullhead rails the wheels smashed the chairs, instantly throwing the track out of gauge causing the driver to feel shaking at the front. During a visit to the Edge Hill sheds, Liverpool on 19 September, it had been decided to transpose the front and back sets of bogie wheels to even out wear because sharp leading flanges could, and did, split points. To enable the axle boxes to move up and down to cater for varying track levels, the axle boxes were able to move in horn slides. The fitter carrying out the work unfortunately made a miscalculation and as the engine went round the curve the axlebox rose, became jammed, failed to lower and thus No. 46207 became derailed. Fifteen passengers lost their lives because it lacked the clearance of a 20 thousandths of an inch.

In 1952 when debating the future of the Railway Executive, Lord Leathers suggested:

Why not restore the old names and titles? For instance, Western Region should be called the Great Western Railway. The head of it should be called the General Manager, as he always was. It would also give great pleasure if the old colours were restored. Our men used to be proud of their chocolate and brown suits and all the rest; the Great Western institutions such as the Operatic Troupes, Concerts, Boy-Scouts and all the rest should go back to their old names and become distinctive. The regimental system is a great one with the British and it is always a mistake to destroy tradition. I am quite sure from my own talks with old friends in the G.W.R. that they would welcome recovering their identity. They don't care about who owns the shares, what they care about is their own individuality.

History showed that regional managers tended to resist change, while centralised control facilitated change.

The horrific accident at Harrow on 8 October 1952 was the second worst railway accident in Britain. The Watford-Euston was calling at Harrow & Wealdstone fully protected by signals when the Up Perth-Euston sleeping car express, 1½ hours late, headed by 4-6-2 No. 46242 *City of Glasgow,* struck its rear at full speed. Almost immediately the 7.55 a.m. Euston-Liverpool and Manchester headed by 4-6-0 No. 45637 *Windward Isles* piloting No. 46202 *Princess Anne,* entered the station at about 60 mph and crashed into the wreckage. The death toll totalled 112 and as it included the driver and fireman of No. 46242, there was no means of establishing why they ran through the signals. Not all the casualties were actually in the trains – some were walking over the footbridge when its girders were swept away, while others were waiting on the platform. The public demanded to know why the Automatic Train Control system, first installed by the GWR in 1906, was not in place at Harrow & Wealdstone as it would probably have prevented the disaster. The British Transport Commission said it was prepared to consider financial authority for a scheme that would eventually cost £17m and in due course this Automatic Warning System was installed.

In the first five years of BR, 1948–1952, it made a loss of £28.8 million. Gerard Fiennes, general manager of the Eastern Region wrote: 'It is one of the disasters about British Railways that in the years between 1947 and 1955 no one had done the basic work on what we were there for at all; what traffic should be carried by what methods in what quantities, where from and to, at what rates.'

Running Costs 1951

Main line passenger service cost per passenger mile: less than 1*d*
Stopping service on main line cost per passenger mile: 14*d*
Cross-country service cost per passenger mile: 3*d*
Branch line passenger service cost per passenger mile: 25*d*

For the equivalent bus or coach services the cost was less than 2*d* a mile.

In the early 1950s differential fares existed for a bizarre miscellany of special groups such as patients, escorts and visitors travelling to and from convalescent homes; anglers' day returns; members of the Commonwealth Parliamentary Association; shipwrecked mariners; entertainers and music hall artistes; and relatives and guardians visiting children in approved schools.

Between 1948 and 1952, 253 miles of line were closed to both passenger and freight traffic, 1,167 miles to passenger traffic only and 359 to freight only. These closures were only a drop in the ocean, reducing the mileage by only one per cent from 52,190 in 1948 to 51,608 in 1953. Closures included such gems as the London Midland Region's Swannington Incline worked by a stationary steam engine installed in 1833 and the Western Region's narrow gauge Corris Railway worked by horse and gravitation.

In 1952–53 Swindon carried out experiments to restore pre-war standards using 1950s coal. This was done initially by the introduction of high-degree superheating and by the even more important modification of draughting arrangements in the smoke-box. These modifications improved the King class 4-6-0s by up to 20 per cent, sufficient to offer an adequate margin to cope with the worst coal.

In 1953 the Lancaster-Morecambe-Heysham line was experimentally converted to a 50-cycle AC overhead electric system.

In 1954 Class 8P 4-6-2 No. 71000 *Duke of Gloucester* appeared from Crewe Works. More powerful than the Britannia class Pacifics, it was designed for hauling the heaviest and fastest express passenger services and the only BR Standard locomotive not designed for hauling freight. Due to the decision to change to diesel and electric power, it was the only representative of its class.

The London Plan Working Party, set up in 1948, suggested five new underground railways, the only one of which to come to fruition was the Victoria Line between Walthamstow and Victoria via King's Cross. In addition to improving the link between north-east London and the West End, it would supplement the overcrowded Central Line. Powers were obtained in 1955 for the first new tube line across central London since 1907, but finance was not available until 1962 when work started. The Victoria Line opened from Walthamstow to Highbury on 1 September 1968, to Warren Street on 3 November 1968, and Victoria on 7 March 1969; interchange with London Transport or British Railways lines was available at all except one of the twelve stations. Trains were controlled automatically, requiring a one-person crew. An extension to Brixton crossed under the river at Vauxhall and opened in 1971.

In 1954 the catering services of the British Transport Commission took 3s 1d for every £1 of main line railway passenger train receipts. Most of the railway refreshment rooms at some 350 stations were modest establishments of a single room with the policy of giving the maximum service to the maximum number of passengers. For the minority who required something better, there were railway hotel restaurants, grill rooms, lounges and so on attached to some of the larger stations. Fully-licensed cafeteria cars had recently been brought into service doing excellent work on specials, reliefs, excursions and troop trains. The outstanding example of this service was on the Starlight specials between London and Scotland; in the peak of the 1955 season, they provided all-night catering services on 44 trains for more than 20,000 passengers in one night. At that time British Railways had by far the most intensive restaurant car service of any European railway and the prices charged were well below those charged on major European railways.

22

Modernising British Railways

Yorkshire economy was at work when, in October 1954, the Queen and the Duke of Edinburgh visited Dewsbury Central and the station had been repainted only on the side they would see.

In November 1954 H. P. Barker, a part-time member of the BTC, had wisely challenged the obsession with railway *equipment* rather than *operation*:

> The report seems to me to accept implicitly a proposal which I deny, namely that the present operational conceptions of British Railways are viable in the long run, given modern equipment. Evidence is now forthcoming and will be forthcoming in increasing quantity in the next two years to show that a solid proportion of our movement operations as carried today are grossly uneconomic, and by inference that no amount of improvement in equipment would make them viable in the conditions of 1970.

The British Transport Commission's Report *Modernisation and Re-equipment of British Railways* was published on 25 January 1955, aiming to invest £1,240 million over the coming 15 years in order to reduce costs, make rail services more attractive and recover traffic lost to road. This was to be done by concentrating on five areas:

1. Improvement in track and signalling to allow higher speeds over trunk routes; increased use of colour-light signalling;

more power-operated signal boxes; centralised traffic control. Cost £210 million.

2. Steam must be replaced as a form of motive power with electric or diesel traction being rapidly introduced; electrification of large mileages of route and the introduction of several thousand electric or diesel locomotives. £345 million.

3. Replace existing steam-drawn passenger rolling stock largely by multiple-unit diesel or electric trains; remaining passenger stock must be modernised; modernisation of stations and parcel depots. £285 million.

4. Freight services must be drastically remodelled; continuous brakes will be fitted and smoother operation of freight services; marshalling yards and goods terminals will be resited and modernised, with a number of the former being greatly reduced; larger wagons will be introduced particularly for mineral traffic; loading and unloading appliances will require extensive modernisation. £365 million.

5. Improvements at ferry ports; staff welfare, office mechanisms; development and research work associated with the plan. £35 million.

The Modernisation Plan envisaged five types of diesel locomotives:

Type 1	800–1,000 hp
Type 2	1,001–1,499 hp
Type 3	1,500–1,900 hp
Type 4	2,000–2,999 hp
Type 5	Over 5,000 hp.

General Sir Brian Robertson was placed in charge of these developments and was a man who liked to get things done quickly – he had been responsible for the 1948 Berlin Airlift. Almost overnight BR ordered 3,000 main line diesel-electric locomotives and the government insisted that they be British-made. United States and German diesel-electric locomotives had been tried and tested in their homelands, but many of the diesels produced by British builders had not. No less than 26 different types were ordered, whereas for economy, it would have been cheaper to have built fewer types, thus the number of spare parts required for the large variety of engines, transmission and braking systems would have been far fewer and technicians would not have required the knowledge of how to maintain so many classes of locomotives. When built, many of the prototypes were hard to maintain and breakdowns were frequent.

Another serious error was to waste money purchasing small diesel shunters for working dock lines and other sharply curved lines, which were then closed leaving these shunters redundant. Many 0-4-0 shunters were ordered from North British, the Yorkshire Engine, Hunslet, Barclay, Brush and Ruston & Hornsby, and these only just outlived steam. A lack of standardisation on just a few designs meant that many spares had to be carried for diesel-electrics, diesel-hydraulics and diesel-mechanicals. Some diesel classes proved unreliable – for instance the Metropolitan-Vickers Type 2 with the odd Co-Bo wheel arrangement, new in 1958, were all withdrawn by September 1968. The 16 Clayton Type 1 Bo-Bo diesels with a very large central cab were purchased from a firm which had never built any before, had poor reliability and only worked for about eight years. North British Class 22 diesel-hydraulics were purchased for working West Country branch lines, which were soon closed leaving no work for them. Similarly, Class 15 0-6-0 'Teddy Bears' were purchased for local trip freights and then, due to the sharp decline in such traffic, were sold to the National Coal Board and British Steel for internal shunting.

The British Transport Commission can be criticised for purchasing without testing prototypes and settling long-term contracts without a full examination of prices. A reason was given in February 1957. 'By the end of the century the need for a big fleet of diesel locomotives would have disappeared; the need for diesel locomotives was immediate, in order that the commitments contained in the White Paper of 1956 [a promise to break even by 1961–2] might be fulfilled. If their purchase were delayed until full experience was available, many of them would be redundant before their life was expired.'

As *The Economist* wisely pointed out: '... the mere spending of money does not ensure efficiency; it can be a convenient device for ensuring that inefficiency is chromium-plated... Sober analysis suggests that a scheme of this sort is necessary. Grim experience suggests that there are at least three ways in which it could go wrong.' This proved to be true as the modernisation Plan foundered on unimaginative railway management, competitive road transport and a poor response to productivity by railwaymen.

One serious mistake was that the new locomotives were not sufficiently powerful. To compete with air travel up to 300 miles and with road over 70 miles, end-to-end timings at 70–75 mph should have been achieved and for this locomotives of a minimum of 3,000 hp were needed. The only really suitable locomotive was the English Electric Co-Co Deltic, which appeared on trial in late 1955. It was powered by two 18-cylinder Napier 1,650 hp engines designed for a gunboat and could run at 100 mph. A contract to build 22 was placed in 1958. They appeared on regular service on the Eastern Region from early 1961. Perhaps foolishly, other regions did not want them, yet they were 25 per cent more powerful than any others, were running double the mileage of any other and their availability was the best in the country. With the introduction of the HST 125s on the East Coast expresses from 1979, the Deltics were gradually withdrawn and by early 1982 none were left.

Just as the GWR went out on a limb with gas-turbines, so its successor, the Western Region, favoured diesel-hydraulic rather than diesel-electric transmission. This had been tried in Germany and Western Region engineers were impressed by the fact that it was lighter and thus gave an excellent power/weight ratio. With this system, power from the engine is transmitted to the wheels through a torque converter. Based on the success of German lightweight V200 diesel-hydraulic locomotives, which had been in service since 1953, the system was lighter than using electric transmission and so seemed advantageous. In 1956 the Western Region ordered five Type 4 A1A-A1A 'Warships' D600-604 to be built by the North British Locomotive Company using German engines and transmission made under licence. Delivered in 1958/9 they proved unreliable, as did subsequent batches built at Swindon. German track was better than the British and could better withstand pounding from an axle with a heavy weight of transmission. The British problem of smashed rail-joints partly disappeared when 400-foot lengths of continuous welded rail replaced 60-foot lengths.

When one 'Warship' was being tested, its engine caught fire. The locomotive inspector in the cab was informed and ordered: 'Open all the side windows and the wind will blow the flames out.' The suggestion was acted upon and it worked! For the first three years the Warships performed well, but then expensive troubles started. In 1961 the larger and more colourful Western class diesel-hydraulics appeared, but by then diesel-electric designs had improved, were cheaper to build and weighed only very little more.

One of the reasons for changing to diesel power was that it was less labour-intensive: steam locomotives require a lot of maintenance and time spent in preparation, whereas with a diesel engine you just switch on and go. After World War II unemployment had dropped to less than two per cent and it was difficult to find men seeking the dirty jobs essential to running steam locomotives. Although in theory all steam locomotives of a certain class should produce identical work, in practice some were sluggish, while others were eager to take almost any load. If a steam locomotive developed a fault, the driver could often do something to get it to the nearest shed, whereas with diesel and electric propulsion there are no half measures, you either get the standard performance or they fail outright and need towing.

Another fault with the January 1955 Plan was that it proposed 20 to 30 new marshalling yards to reduce costs by gravity-shunting, but modern marshalling yards were not the saviour of the wagon-load business. If management had done some thinking, it would have realised that the future of rail freight was with full train loads running from A to B, preferably of the merry-go-round type where an engine does not need to be uncoupled at the end of a journey but the wagons can be loaded/unloaded on the move. Most other traffic should be in containers that can be mechanically lifted on and off a train. The avoidance of shunting would mean that a journey would be far quicker, fewer wagons would be needed as they would have more intensive use and the economics would be better. The railway's wagon-load traffic was challenged by faster and larger lorries on the motorways being built at the time.

The block load concept was excellent for heavy industry – coal, steel, iron ore and oil – and it was block loads that produced profit, not small barrow-loads. The 1960s saw a great increase in the demand for petroleum – more people were aspiring to car ownership, central heating was becoming popular, some power stations were turning to oil, and oil was needed for plastics. BR was able to win lucrative contracts from the major oil companies and large 45-ton tankers were used to carry it from refinery to distribution depots. Unfortunately for rail, in due course pipe lines were laid and rail lost much of this traffic.

An innovation in the early 1960s was merry-go-round trains supplying coal to the new large electric power stations. A permanently coupled train of air-braked hopper wagons was loaded at ½ mph passing under a hopper at a colliery; it then travelled to its destination where on a circular loop each wagon was discharged on the move into the power station's hopper. This efficient method reduced the number of locomotives, wagons, sidings, train and ground staff required, making rail very competitive. The same principle was extended to cement and steel works operations as well as iron ore. The problem with merry-go-round trains was that terminals at both ends of a journey required re-designing and re-equipment and the terminals were not owned by the railway, but by the National Coal Board or a steel company. When the economics were explained, the proposal made sense and the idea was accepted. In the 1960s, new power stations were built that required up to 20,000 tons of coal each winter day. The efficient way to transport the fuel was to use merry-go-round trains, which could be loaded and unloaded on the move. These trains were hauled by a Class 47, which had a slow control enabling them to run at ½ or 1 mph. For example, on a winter's day, Didcot power station would receive 20 such trains.

Another advantage of rail was that it could carry steel coils at a temperature of 400 degrees and on arrival they would still be at 200 degrees. Road could not possibly deal with such a load.

Rather than spending millions on new marshalling yards, the money would have been better spent on modernising freight rolling stock with larger capacity vehicles and through brakes to enable trains to run at faster speed, the better to compete with road transport. It would have been wiser to have changed from vacuum to air brakes with the introduction of diesel power rather than wait until the late '60s. Stock should have had roller bearings to enable trains to run faster and not having to stop every 150 miles for wagon examination to ensure that there was no hot box.

The Associated Society of Locomotive Engineers and Firemen held a national strike from 29 May until 14 June 1955, the dispute being about pay differentials. In most areas a skeleton service was run and as members of the National Union of Railwaymen were not involved, about a quarter of passenger and a third of freight trains ran. The strike did irreparable harm as it encouraged passengers to seek alternative transport – often the regular use of a car, whereas until that year, the relatively few car owners tended to use them for pleasure, rather than for commuting. Commercial firms purchased their own vans and lorries so that they would not be at the mercy of striking railwaymen. Unfortunately, most of the railway staff did not foresee this outcome.

Although trains have always carried road vehicles, it was not until 1955 that BR started its first long-distance car and accompanied passenger service; by that year more cars were in private ownership, people had money for longer holidays and had the desire to travel longer distances. Motorways were still in the future, so travel from the south of England to Scotland wasted time when you could be enjoying it at the destination, and could be exhausting. The answer was to introduce a twice-weekly overnight service between King's Cross and Perth, passengers travelling in sleeping cars. A daytime service began in 1960. From the mid-1950s trains ran from the provinces such as Newton-le-Willows and Sutton Coldfield to Stirling and York to Inverness. In May 1966 a car reception and loading facility was opened at Kensington Olympia and the car-carrying service was named Motorail.

Olympia had four platforms, all able to cope with handling either single decker or double deck car wagons, a parking bay and a passenger lounge. In due course trains left here for Inverness, Perth, Stirling, St Austell and Fishguard. Peak loads of 100,000 were carried in the early 1970s, but declined as new motorways were opened and Motorail trains were withdrawn in 1995, leaving only Le Shuttle through the Channel Tunnel.

In December 1955, except for the Southern Region, it was decided to standardise on the 25kV AC system as had been used successfully in France, rather than the 1,500 V DC under construction elsewhere in England. Electric traction was more reliable and cleaner than diesel and more popular with the public.

The British Transport Commission was willing to experiment with alternative strategies to closure and in June 1956 ordered 22 light-weight diesel-powered four-wheeled railbuses for trial on lightly used branches. Examples were built by AC Cars; Bristol/Eastern Coach Works; Park Royal Vehicles; Waggon und Maschinenbau and D. Wickham & Co. Although they increased rail use, this was insufficient to keep the branches open. Some of these lines built new low-level halts at places where a full-height platform would have been uneconomic. Another effort was a 2-car battery-electric railcar jointly built by BR Derby and Cowlairs Works. In the event, these reduced losses but none produced a margin of revenue over movement costs and when track and signalling was taken into account, made a significant loss. The Ministry of Transport regulations forbidding them to be one-man-operated helped to give disappointing results.

As it was unnecessary for two men to be in the cab of a diesel or electric locomotive, a single manning agreement was made in 1957 but then could not be implemented on passenger trains because a second man was required to operate the boiler for steam heating the carriages!

Baildon station, near Bradford, had an interesting history. It closed on 5 January 1953, but then with the 1957 Suez crisis causing a petrol shortage, it was reopened 28 January 1957 – only to be closed again 29 April 1957. This was not the end of the story as housing developments caused it to be reopened as an unstaffed halt in 1973.

Between 1954 and 1962, almost 3,500 diesel locomotives were placed in service, half for main-line working, 4,000 diesel multiple-units (DMUs) and 3,800 electric multiple-units. More than half of them were introduced in only three years 1959–61, or 1958–60 for DMUs. Under the Modernisation Plan, steam locomotives that had been expected to be used for many years were rapidly phased out and fleet numbers had halved by the end of 1962 from 18,160 at the end of 1953 to 8,800. The 744 steam locomotives acquired between 1954 and 1960 with a 'useful life in service of some forty years' according to the Modernisation Plan, were scrapped by 1968. The frantic rush to use diesels meant that more locomotives had to be purchased from outside contractors while from 1923 to 1947, the railway companies had built 70 per cent of the locomotives in their own workshops, and from 1954 to 1962, 48 per cent were purchased from outside.

Type 3 B-B Hymeks built by Beyer-Peacock for the Western Region looked attractive and proved reliable. The penultimate diesel-hydraulic design were the Type 4 C-C Westerns, some built at Swindon and the rest at Crewe. The final diesel-hydraulic design were Type 1 0-6-0s for shunting and short trips and nicknamed Teddy Bears. Built between 1964/5 they were withdrawn between 1968 and 1970 (*see* page 336). As the diesel-hydraulics used faster-running engines, maintenance costs proved higher than on diesel-electrics of comparable power, so all the diesel-hydraulics were phased out by the mid-1970s.

The government exerted pressure to buy diesels from private British firms, but even diesels built in BR's workshops had engines and transmissions supplied by specialist firms. The government wished to support contractors and boost their exports, thus the rejection of purchasing locomotives from the United States, particularly those made by General Motors – the restriction on the availability of dollars prevented this. By the time Leyland came forward with a proposal to build General Motors locomotives under licence, the policy of purchasing British was underway and the chance was lost for having reliable, standard designs. In 1960 the government ruled out wholesale electrification and the railway was left with 41 different design diesels, many defective.

Locomotives built by North British of Glasgow were expensive, technically deficient and delivered late, but the firm was chosen for political reasons – to give Scottish workers employment. The North British Type 2 diesel proved to be so poor that they were never let out on the line except in pairs, and not infrequently three at a time were used; eventually steam had to be reintroduced on Glasgow-Aberdeen trains. Shortly before the company went into liquidation in April 1962, BTC contemplated seeking action to recover £300,000 compensation for late delivery. Other diesels were not trouble-free: the London Midland Region Sulzer Type 4 had weak crankshafts, while Deltics were expensive to operate costing £150,000 rather than the £100,000 of other diesels and required careful maintenance.

Steam-hauled passenger trains were replaced by DMUs in the late '50s, which proved a popular move, especially as from many a good view forward could be obtained from the front seats. Unfortunately, instead of keeping to one design, which would have been the most economical choice, different builders were allowed to use their own designs in order that BR could become a shop window and it was hoped that railways abroad might purchase them. Thus there was such a multiplicity of DMUs. Of the 3.600 DMUs placed in service by BR in those early days, there were no less than five main coupling types, each of which was mutually exclusive and could not work in multiple if longer trains were required. DMUs were liked by the public and the first 3½ months of diesel working between Leeds and Bradford attracted 80,000 extra passengers.

But was the decision to purchase DMUs hasty? Would it have been better to have foreseen that as within a few years many branch lines, or rural stations on main lines would be closed, rendering many of the new DMUs superfluous, it would have been more economic to have soldiered on a few more years with steam?

Then there was the Southern Region. As it had wide experience of electric multiple-units (EMUs) it was allowed to build diesel-electric multiple units, basically an EMU with a diesel engine and generator in its body, and the fact that the motor was *in* the body rather than slung *beneath* it as with a DMU, meant that there was less seating capacity. Was this lack of standardisation on BR wise?

The change to DMUs was particularly useful on short, or relatively short, services as it meant that at the end of a journey the driver could simply walk from one end of the train to the other ready for the return trip and that there was no need to run the engine round its train, taking up time and line capacity. For example in 1958, 6-car DMUs took over the Glasgow-Edinburgh service offering a train every 30 minutes.

In February 1956 the decision was made to fit freight rolling stock with vacuum, rather than the more efficient air brakes, the choice made by regional general managers who placed current operating reasons above planning for the future. Another mistake was that *all* wagons should be fitted, yet at the time there were still many wagon-load or pick-up trains that did not allow vacuum-braked vehicles to be actively used with non-fitted wagons. Braked wagons were only useful when used in a train that avoided intermediate shunting.

The three-link couplings of braked wagons had to be replaced with instanter link couplings or screw couplings – an intermediate step until an automatic coupling was developed. Heavier mineral and steel wagons required the heavier Continental screw coupling, but this made more work for the guard or shunter. The British Iron & Steel Federation and the National Coal Board refused to accept the new vacuum-fitted mineral wagons and tipplers, which unloaded wagons by tipping them on their ends or sides, as it was found that the brake gear was fouled. In May 1960 the policy of fitting the entire fleet was abandoned with the result that firms with contracts for making the brakes charged a penalty for cancellation.

The third most serious British railway accident occurred on 4 December 1957 at Lewisham. Due to fog and late running, the driver and fireman of the 4.56 p.m. Cannon Street-Ramsgate had not had time to take on water and so 4-6-2 No. 34066 *Spitfire* was being 'nursed' until its first stop, Sevenoaks. Ahead was an electric train from Charing Cross-Hayes (Kent). No. 34066 gradually caught up the suburban train and met first a double-yellow and then a single yellow warning, but the driver did not reduce speed and it was only when actually passing the red signal that the brakes were applied. It was too late and 138 yards beyond, *Spitfire* ploughed into the back of the electric train, unfortunately where the Nunhead flyover crossed the main line and this 350-ton bridge collapsed on the wreckage. The death toll was 90. Remarkably, *Spitfire* was not derailed and damage to it was relatively light. The inspecting officer placed the blame on driver Trew and recommended the installation of the Automatic Warning System. Trew was tried on a charge of manslaughter but the jury failed to agree and at a second trial he was found not guilty.

BTC's Annual Reports showed that raised levels of spending under the Plan failed to change financial deficits into surpluses, or even halt increasing deficits. Governments had two views on railways: some believed that they should make a profit, or at least break even, while others believed that they should provide a social service and should be run even though they may make a loss.

Track renewals were at the rate of about 1,500 miles annually, with the installation of 1,000 miles of continuous welded rail and the application of the newly developed continuous warning system to 1,200 route miles. Replacing mechanical semaphore signals by electric colour-light was accelerated and about 1,300 track miles were re-signalled 1959–1962.

The Euston-Birmingham-Liverpool/Manchester electrification was originally costed at £75 million, but by 1959 had cost £161 million and the expected yield of £8 million net was a return below the then current interest rate.

One highly important innovation in 1959 was the inauguration of the Condor (containerisation door-to-door) express container train running between London and Glasgow. It captured traffic from customers without private sidings and offered a direct service without delays caused by shunting. This was a successful attempt at attracting road traffic back to rail. The London-Manchester Speedfreight followed in 1963 and the first Freightliner service in 1965, which by 1969 had 33 terminals. Freightliners used standard intermodal containers. Initially the container traffic was just within the United Kingdom and it was not until much later that deep sea containers were carried.

Freight was very important to BR in 1960 as for every £1 earned by passenger carrying, £2 was earned by freight, and two-thirds of the latter was coal. Today, freight earns less than 5 per cent.

In 1954 gross revenue was £449.3 million, operating costs £432.9 giving a net operating revenue of £16.4 million but in 1962 these figures had altered to £465.1 revenue, £569.1 operating costs with a net loss of £104 million. The railway's financial difficulties were so serious that the British Transport Commission's other activities – London Transport, bus services, British Road Services, ships, property transactions, hotels and catering, inland waterways and docks – were unable to reduce much of the railway's shortfall. Inland waterways made a small loss, but the other businesses only produced a small profit.

Traffic Carried by British Railways, 1948–1962 (£m)

Year	Passenger-miles	Freight net ton-miles	Freight index	Coal/coke Merchandise/ livestock	Minerals	Total 1953=100
1948	21,022	9,662	7,041	4,959	21,622	95.2
1954	20,712	10,489	6,542	5,059	22,089	97.0
1956	21,133	10,248	6,008	5,217	21,473	94.3
1958	21,275	8,927	5,231	4,268	18,426	80.9
1962	19,392	7,304	5,200	3,601	16,104	70.7

In 1954 the average goods wagon load was 4.3 tons, which compared unfavourably with 12 tons for mineral traffic and 11.6 tons for coal.

Receipts and costs in passenger and freight traffic, 1959 (£m)

Traffic type	Gross receipts	Direct costs	Operating margin	Joint costs	Profit/ loss
	(i)	(ii)	(i) - (ii)	(iii)	(i) - (ii) + (iii)
Passenger:					
fast/semi-fast	89.3	58.0	31.3	-*	-
stopping	23.3	62.3	-39.0	-	-
suburban	31.3	30.1	1.2	-	-
Total	143.9	150.4	-6.5	74.7	81.2
Freight Merchandise/livestock:					
wagon-load	61.1	73.7	-12.6	17.9	-30.5
smalls (under 1 ton)	39.9	50.9	-11.0	7.6	-18.6
Total	101.1	125.7	-23.6	25.8	-49.4
Minerals	45.8	33.4	12.4	9.8	2.6
Coal and coke	111.5	68.9	42.6	18.9	23.7
Total	259.4	228.0	31.4	54.5	-23.1

*No attempt was made to allocate joint costs to passenger categories

In 1958 H.P. Barker produced a far-sighted memorandum 'Long Term Freight Policy' deploring the 'wagon fixation' of many railwaymen and advocated the profitable train-load and freight liners.

The introduction of DMUs reduced, but failed to eliminate, the gap between receipts and costs. Only one of the DMU main line stopping services, Birmingham-Leicester-Nottingham, earned a margin over direct costs, while only one of the DMU suburban services, St Pancras-Bedford, made a positive contribution.

The ER closure in March 1959 of most of the Midland & Great Northern Joint Railway, which duplicated the route from the East Midlands to Norwich and Yarmouth involved the closure of 116 miles, 43 stations, caused 1,063 job losses, but produced an estimated annual saving of £640,000. A bizarre consequence was that coal transferred from Norwich (Thorpe) to the coal depot at

Norwich (City), 2 miles distant by road, was forced to travel a rail distance of more than 60 miles!

An interesting closure in June 1955 was the Lewes-East Grinstead or 'Bluebell Line'. Miss R. E. M. Bessemer, great-grand-daughter of the inventor of the steel converter, cited a clause in the line's original Act of 1878, which forced BR to restore the passenger service in August 1956. The timing of Miss Bessemer's challenge came at an unfortunate time when the Transport Commission was attempting to streamline the process of dealing with unremunerative services. Closed again in March 1958, much of the line has been reopened subsequently as a preserved railway.

Many, if not all, planned closures received opposition. In 1960 the Westerham–Dunton Green branch was used by only about 170 London commuters and train loads varied from 0 to 67 passengers. The Southern Region estimated that closing the line would save £11,600 annually, but objectors put forward an excellent case for using a railbus, produced other suggestions to reduce costs and caused embarrassment by publicising the fact that the track had only recently been relaid. The Central Transport Consultative Committee recommended against closure and the Transport Minister, Ernest Marples, had to give his consent, and closure took place in October 1961.

It was anticipated that by 1962 BR would be making a profit, but by 1960 BR's losses had reached £67 million annually. Steam was to be phased out, so in the ensuing years fewer steam locomotives were built, the last being Class 9F 2-10-0 in 1960, appropriately being named *Evening Star*.

In 1955 there were approximately 19,000 standard gauge BR steam locomotives and it was envisaged that they would be gradually phased out over 30 years but, in the event, due to problems of obtaining staff to work or maintain them, their withdrawal was speeded up and most main lines had lost steam power by 1966. Although the end of steam was announced in 1955, curiously, and perhaps foolishly from the economic aspect, steam locomotives were still being built in 1960.

In 1959 Ernest Marples was made the Minister of Transport and the improvement in the standard of living of many workers, including railwaymen, meant that many could afford cars and as car ownership boomed, the government decided to invest in roads rather than railways. Britain turned its back on railways and it entered the motorway age when the M1 was opened by Marples in 1959.

In 1959, Wyman's bookstalls were taken over by John Menzies & Co, which meant that the Scottish company had stalls at large English stations such as Euston, Birmingham New Street and Liverpool Lime Street. In 1998, W. H. Smith's bought Menzies – and Euston reverted to that firm exactly 150 years after the first branch was opened there.

The multiple-unit concept, first used in Britain for electric trains and then for those powered by diesel, was useful and economic as it meant that there was no need to use time, manpower and track at a terminus, as a driver could simply walk from what had been the front of the train to the rear and was then ready to return. The idea used for stopping trains could also be used for those running longer distances and there first of these was the Blue Pullman, introduced in 1960. These air-conditioned diesel trains, the first time air-conditioning had appeared on BR, had a power car at each end. They were aimed at business travellers and provided an alternative to the growing domestic air market. They ran from St Pancras to Manchester and between Paddington, Birmingham and Swansea. Although a Pullman supplement was charged, luxury was not always experienced in their riding capabilities and drinking tea or soup on the move could be exciting.

The Swiss-designed Schlieren bogie had a well-deserved riding reputation on the Continent and so was adopted for the Blue Pullman, but it was before the days when BR had a comprehensive vehicle testing and research facility and it was not realised that the shorter British bodies and the weight of the traction motors would produce an entirely different ride. With the introduction of air-conditioning and far better riding on the Mk IId ordinary stock, the Blue Pullmans became outdated and were withdrawn in 1973.

Level crossings are of three main types: for public highways, foot crossings and accommodation or occupation crossings, the latter installed when a line was constructed and severed property. In the early days, level crossing gates were kept across the road, but Acts of 1842 and 1845 gave the Board of Trade power to authorise exceptions and with the increase in traffic due to the internal combustion engine, it generally became usual to keep the gates closed across the railway. In the 1950s the usual wooden gates began to be replaced by lifting barriers and in 1961 the first automatic half-barriers were installed, worked by an approaching train. Closed-circuit television cameras ensure a certain amount of safety, but a long, low-hung vehicle can become stranded on a humped crossing. Due to the increased speed and the fact that diesels and electric trains are less visible than a steam locomotive, the trend is to eliminate foot crossings where possible by diverting them or installing footbridges or under-passes.

The principal place for exhibiting locomotives preserved by British Railways was the Museum of British Transport opened at Clapham in 1961, though some went in the same year to the Great Western Railway Museum at Swindon, and others to the Museum of Transport, Glasgow, in 1964. The Great Western Society opened its Didcot Railway Centre in 1967, recreating a GWR steam shed and also short lengths of track to represent main and branch line running and even has some broad gauge track. When the National Railway Museum opened at York in 1972 as part of the Science Museum, many of the exhibits at Clapham were transferred and Clapham closed in 1973. The National Railway Museum is the largest railway museum in the world and owns more than 100 locomotives, 150 carriages and wagons and many artefacts as well as paintings, posters, prints and photographs. Not all the material is displayed, some being loaned to various preservation societies.

In June 1963 the General Post Office diverted much of its East Anglian parcels traffic to road due to the unreliability of the poor railway service, though a new 10-year contract from April 1964 regained this traffic.

The advent of the diesels failed to bring the expected savings, so in 1961 the Minister of Transport, Ernest Marples, a road builder, brought in Dr Richard Beeching, technical director of Imperial Chemical Industries, to be chairman of the British Transport Commission which was ordered to identify railway losses. In April 1961 Beeching carried out a traffic survey during the school holidays when pupils were not using the railway to travel to school. Beeching made no attempt to develop traffic. In 1962 he planned to close 16 out of the 32 railway workshops, which in view of the contraction of British Railways should have been closed before.

It was found that diesel-electric locomotives lacked sufficient braking power for working goods trains without continuous brakes. To solve the problem, 122 brake tenders were built in the early 1960s from redundant carriages, mostly ex-LMS, or LNER. By the early 1980s when all freight trains were air-braked, all the brake tenders were withdrawn.

The first electrification in the Glasgow area was of the former North British lines on the north bank of the Clyde and the Clyde coast lines, this taking place on 5 November 1960. Glaswegians flocked to use the blue trains and traffic rose by 400 per cent. It was pride before a fall because a serious fault in the switchgear forced the splendid new trains to be withdrawn and the steam service reintroduced on 19 December 1960. It was not until 10 months later that the electric trains resumed working. The south side electrification was inaugurated on 29 May 1962. The success of electrification caused the Glasgow Central Railway underground system to be abandoned on 3 October 1964.

On 5 November 1962 British Railways and Glasgow Corporation tried an experiment. Castlemilk, a huge council estate, was not served by a railway so a special bus service was inaugurated from Castlemilk to the electrified King's Park station where a blue train could be caught to the centre of Glasgow. The cost of a through ticket by bus and train was 8*d* compared with the 10*d* charged by a journey by through bus. The journey time by either route was 20 minutes. The prudent Scots thought that the trouble of changing the method of transport on such a short journey was not worth the twopence they could have saved. The service lost money and was withdrawn in May 1964.

In 1962 more than half the network earned insufficient revenue to cover the cost of its track and signalling; half the network carried only about 4 per cent of the passenger-miles travelled and about 5 per cent of the freight ton-miles run; a third of the 4,300 stations handled less than 1 per cent of the total revenue from passengers while the 34 largest stations, less than 1 per cent of the number, took 26 per cent of the passenger revenue. Similarly, on the freight side, half of the 5,000 stations and depots produced less than 3 per cent of the revenue, while 57 of them produced 35 per cent. All traffic requiring shunting or marshalling was of dubious worth and only complete train loads covered direct costs.

On 27 March 1963, Beeching produced a report: *The Re-Shaping of British Railways* and on 16 February 1965, *The Development of the Major Trunk Routes.* The first report, the one for which he is most known, suggested the closure of 2,363 stations, 5,000 miles of track and the withdrawal of 250 train services. Some branch lines receive an income that only covered a tenth of their running costs and there was no social benefit for freight being carried at a loss. It should be noted that Beeching himself did not close stations and lines, he only recommended their closure, which in due course either proceeded or was declined, the matter being considered by consultative committees. Harold Macmillan and the Conservatives were pushed out of office in 1964, but the incoming Labour government did nothing to halt railway cuts.

The Report brought out two points:

i) In the passenger field, stopping trains are by far the worst loss-maker. These trains, which derive little advantage from the speed of rail movement, are known to be very lightly loaded and to run, very largely, on routes which carry very little traffic of any kind.

ii) We should expect the provision of railways to be limited to routes over which it is possible to develop dense flows of traffic, of the kinds which lend themselves to movement in train load quantities and which, in parts at least, benefit from the speed and reliability which the railways are capable of achieving.

Unfortunately, Beeching looked only at the present time and took no account of new techniques such as diesel traction, automatic level crossings, mechanised track maintenance, tokenless block signalling, unmanned bus-stop type stations and conductor-guards, which could cut the cost of running rural railways by more than a half.

The BRB could easily close unremunerative freight stations, but passenger stations were more difficult to close as the public could claim closure would cause hardship. This meant a public inquiry by the Transport Users' Consultative Committee and referral to the Minister of Transport for a final decision. Some of the objections were light-weight – for example in 1966 one objector to the closure of the Waverley line was the South of Scotland Budgerigar & Foreign Bird Society, which claimed that the line's closure would 'spell the death warrant of all bird societies in this area'.

Beeching believed that buses would replace withdrawn trains, but in fact they did not and when the bus services proved unremunerative, they too were cancelled. He also made the mistake of thinking that after closure of a local station, car owners would be willing to drive to the nearest railhead, whereas in the event many decided that they would travel all the way by car. Similarly, industrial firms did not use road transport to carry goods to and from a rail head, but used road for the whole distance.

Beeching's success, or otherwise, can be judged from the fact that BR's loss of £159m in 1962, had only been reduced to £151m in 1968.

With hindsight too many lines were closed, perhaps a third of them should have been kept open and had the development of road transport been foreseen, with overcrowding on roads, it would have been better for the environment had they been available for use today. Some indeed have been re-opened to passenger traffic – a few of the valley lines in South Wales for example, the Waverley line in Scotland and the Oxford to Cambridge line. About 70 closed lines have been re-opened by preservationists. Similarly, some of the main lines were singled as an economy, only for them having to be doubled a few years later.

Not all lines recommended for closure were in fact closed. The Central Wales line from Llanelli to Craven Arms, and the Conway Valley line from Llandudno Junction to Blaneau Ffestiniog, were reprieved due to poor local roads and perhaps due to the fact that they were in marginal constituencies. In Devon, the branch from Plymouth to Gunnislake was threatened but the fact that using road transport was not an option due to narrow lanes and these very far from bee-lines, led to its retention. The Settle to Carlisle Line was threatened, defended by many supporters, and reprieved by the Government in 1989. It has since proved valuable as alternative to the West Coast Line. Scottish lines that escaped the axe through pressure were Inverness to Wick and Thurso; Inverness to the Kyle of Lochalsh and Ayr to Stranraer.

The first of the Beeching proposed closures came under a Conservative government and were strongly criticised by the Labour Party who objected to their trade union members losing their jobs. When Labour came into power in 1964 it viewed the matter from a different perspective and continued closures so that by the mid-'70s more than 4,000 route-miles had been closed and almost 68,000 railway jobs lost.

In January 1963 the British Transport Commission was replaced by the British Railways Board.

By the end of 1973 BR was operating freight with 294,000 vehicles, only 29 per cent of the 1962 figure, yet carrying a traffic volume of 87 per cent of that in 1962.

Full closures June 1963 – December 1973

Year	Mileage closed	Financial saving (£)
1963	8	3,341
1964	847	3,028,622
1965	802	2,158,091
1966	534	2,825,697
1967	251	513,286
1968	247	582,061
1969	242	1,241,026
1970	138	966,439
1971	23	80,366
1972	68	638,500
1973	41	78,900
1963–73	3,201	12,116,599

The first region to abolish steam was the Western Region and this was almost phased out on 31 December 1965. The Somerset & Dorset line between Bath and Bournemouth, which entirely used steam, was to have closed on that date, but due to a delay in providing replacement buses, it was reprieved until 7 March 1966. Another oddity could be found in the Southern Region, an area of England that experienced some of the first electrification. The line between Waterloo and Bournemouth was being electrified using a third rail, but until the work was completed in July 1967 Bulleid's Pacifics continued to work expresses and did so with gusto, drivers reaching 100 mph. On 18 July 1967, the last regular steam-hauled express passenger train on British Railways left Waterloo for the West of England.

East Anglia lost its steam in 1962, but it was still seen in the Eastern Region at Doncaster until May 1966. In the North

Eastern Region, York shed closed to steam in the summer of 1967, and Leeds Holbeck in October 1967, but Royston lasted until November and Normanton closed at the end of December 1967.

In Scotland Gresley's A4 Pacifics worked Glasgow to Aberdeen expresses until September 1966 and steam could be seen at Glasgow Polmadie until May 1967, while Motherwell retained it until June 1967. 1 January 1968 saw only six steam depots on BR, all of them in the London Midland Region in the north-west. By 6 May, Carlisle Kingmoor, Workington and Tebay had closed, leaving only Carnforth, Rose Grove and Lostock Hall. The last standard gauge steam on BR ran on 11 August 1968, when these final sheds closed, meaning that many of Riddle's engines with a planned life of 40 years were withdrawn and scrapped after working only a quarter of that time.

On 11 August 1968 the '15 Guinea Special' was run from Liverpool to Manchester, then over the Settle & Carlisle line to Carlisle before returning to Liverpool by the direct route. It was hauled at various stages by three examples of Stanier's Black Fives and Britannia 4-6-2 No. 70013 *Oliver Cromwell*. It was very appropriate for Black Fives to be used because the class had proved very valuable, capable of work varying from shunting to heading an express. They could be found almost anywhere between Bournemouth and Wick. Designed by W. A. Stanier in 1934, he had worked under C. B. Collett of the GWR and they were, in fact, based on the GWR 4-6-0 Hall class.

Many passengers on the 15 Guinea Special and those by the lineside believed it was really the end for steam on British main lines and certainly it was banned for several years to prove how modern BR had become. In actual fact, it was not quite the end of BR steam because this method of power was still retained on the 1 foot 11½ inch gauge Vale of Rheidol Railway at Aberystwyth.

A key feature to Beeching's revolution was introducing managerial talent from outside the rail industry – he imported men from Shell, ICI, General Electric, English Electric, Lever Brothers, Beaverbrook Newspapers and Jaguar Cars. His vice-chairman, Philip Shirley, was excellent at finance. On a visit to the Scottish Region, Shirley complained about the unnecessary cost of railway fencing where the West Highland line ran alongside a loch where the fence was partly submerged by water. When he asked the general manager

Gordon Stewart 'Now then Stewart, what earthly use is that fencing over there?' the immediate reply was 'It's to prevent the salmon from coming up and nibbling the fishplates.'

Although the steam locomotive generally replaced the horse, these animals continued in railway use being essential for drawing wagons on sharply curved sidings, or sidings whose only access was via a wagon turntable. Horses lasted on British Railways nearly as long as steam engines, the last two horses being withdrawn from Newmarket in 1967. In earlier days, some horses were army reservists – a railway paid £15 a year in respect of horses earmarked for call-up in the event of a national emergency. The coming of the internal-combustion engine of course marked the decline of horse numbers. In January 1921 a North British horse at Kelso was replaced by a petrol shunter, the annual cost of the horse being £1,180, compared with £904 of the petrol shunter, although the company had to spend £121 in easing the curves.

The Great Train Robbery occurred on 8 August 1963. The 18.50 Glasgow-Euston Mail had called at Crewe where driver Jack Mills and second-man David Whitby took over the train of 12 coaches hauled by Class 40 D326. The second vehicle was a High Value Package carriage. The train stopped at the red signal at Sears Crossing and as the second-man walked to the telephone to alert the signalman of the train's presence, he was captured by a gang of thieves.

The gang had covered the lens of the official signals with black leather gloves and replaced them with yellow and red lights powered by batteries. The gang entered the cab and clubbed driver Mills, replacing him with a driver provided by the gang. The locomotive and the first two coaches were detached from the train in order to take them onto Bridego Bridge where the loot could be conveniently removed by road. When the replacement driver provided by the gang tried to start the train, he failed to get it to move – the brake pipe on the end coach had not been secured, so the brakes were leaking. Driver Mills, forced to take over, realised what had happened and opened the large ejector to release the brakes. The sorters in the High Value Package coach were ordered to lie down and close their eyes.

On arrival at Bridego Bridge, the gangsters formed a chain and passed the mailbags down into waiting lorries. Thirty minutes after stopping the train and when most of the mail sacks were stowed in the lorries, the gang handcuffed the driver and second-man in the High Value Package coach and ordered them not to move for 30 minutes.

The gang of 16 had bought Leatherslade Farm, 28 miles from Bridego Bridge and near Oakley, to be used as a hideout before and after the robbery. There they were able to open the packages and count the result of their efforts – £2,595,997 10s 0d – the highest sum ever stolen up to that date. Only 13 per cent of the money was recovered. Driver Mills never really recovered from his injuries and did not live long enough to enjoy the bungalow and pension purchased by money the *Daily Mail* readers had donated. He died in 1970.

It was the usual practice for the High Value Package van containing mail that had been registered and posted by a bank to be the second vehicle. New High Value Package vans had been introduced in 1962 with mechanical bandit-proof doors, locks for High Value Package cupboards, catches on doors and barred windows, but the coach used on 8 August was not a new one.

Mail has been carried by rail since 1830, the first sorting carriages appeared in 1838 and were called Railway Post Offices until 1928 when they were re-named Travelling Post Offices. There were two types of vehicle: sorting vans and sorting tenders, the latter carrying mail bags of sorted mail. Pre-World War II, more than 130 staffed mail trains ran each night, but by 1963 this had been reduced to about 40. What was believed to be the last mail train in Britain ran on 9 January 2004, but then they were soon re-introduced.

The first use of high-visibility clothing on BR was probably by the platelayers on the Pollokshields-Eglinton Street line in June 1964 and the Health & Safety at Work Act of 1974 boosted their use.

The Transport Act of 1968, which received Royal Assent 25 October 1968, meant that from 1 January 1969 the National Freight Corporation was formed and its subsidiaries, National Carriers Limited and Freightliner Limited, took over BR's freight and distribution and thus made a definite distinction between a 'commercial' side, which should make a profit, and the 'social' passenger services, some of which should be subsidised – grants being made to unremunerative passenger services in 1969. Payments of £61 million in 1969 rising to £91million in 1973 maintained a railway net profit for only four years and in 1973 the railway was in deficit again, though the subsidiary businesses – ships, hotels, harbours, hovercraft and workshops – made a small profit.

Beeching's second report proposed substantial investment in the lines remaining after pruning. Some 10 per cent of the investment in the 1955 Modernisation Plan was for building large, mechanised marshalling yards to replace flat yards that required an engine to go backwards and forwards shunting wagons into various sidings for various destinations. Modern yards were of the hump pattern where a locomotive continuously propelled wagons over a hump and gravity took them to the required siding. The cost of these new yards was estimated to be £80 million. Several major yards were opened in 1963: Carlisle Kingmoor; Edinburgh Millerhill; Middlesbrough Tees Yard; Newcastle Tyne Yard and Wakefield Healey Mills.

However, BR wildly overestimated the number of yards required as by the early '60s the trend was away from single wagon loads and customers were encouraged to abandon it for the faster and more reliable Freightliner, or complete train load services, as the latter did not require shunting. Based on the Condor of 1959, intermodal liner trains known as 'Freightliners' began in 1965 and have proved a highly successful innovation. By 1982, only 59 marshalling yards were in use and the large new yards of the 1960s were working well below their capacity. By the end of 1984, all non-air-braked wagon load traffic ceased, which meant the end of all marshalling yards and hump shunting.

As late as 1967 wagon load traffic contributed two-thirds of the total freight revenue. Two of BRB's major customers, chemicals, and iron and steel, took some traffic from rail due to 'slowness and delays' caused through inadequacies of BRB's policy for wagon-load traffic. This resulted in loss of income that could have been made to cover direct costs and earn something towards costs of the whole system. A Planning Department memorandum in February 1968 acknowledged that neither train-load nor Freightliners could entirely replace the wagon-load business. In October 1968 the Freight Plan surprisingly established a commitment to wagon-load in the future. Charges did not exploit bulk traffic in the few remaining areas of quasi-monopoly left, for the coal and iron and steel charges were less than the market could bear, though lower rates had the advantage of encouraging firms to invest in private owners wagons and numbers of these increased in the 1970s. To compensate for the fall of wagon-load coal traffic, partly due to many households changing to central heating, earth and stone traffic increased by a third in 1967–71, while there were also gains in car and waste disposal loads.

Another waste was the building a superfluity of diesel-electric shunters, which were not required due to the reduction in shunting – had this been foreseen some of the steam shunting engines could have been kept in use a little longer. Similarly, some DMUs became redundant when the service for which they had been intended was axed.

Beeching's axe failed to make BR profitable and in 1970 passenger numbers were only a quarter of those carried in 1960.

Although Beeching gets the blame for the severe reduction of British Railways, the blame should really be placed on the shoulders of the Minister of Transport, Ernest Marples. He was greatly biased in the railway/road conflict as he held 80 per cent of the shares of the motorway and construction company Marples Ridgway, so it was obvious which method of transport he would favour. He tried to avoid criticism by selling his shares – to his wife!

Following the Modernisation Report and the Beeching Plan, British Railways was determined to present a new image and so in 1964 commissioned the Design Research Unit to come up with a new logo and house style. In 1965 the name 'British Railways' was changed to the snappier 'British Rail', the double-arrow logo launched and a new typeface, 'Rail Alphabet' appeared. Rolling stock was repainted in blue and light grey. It was a stipulation at privatisation that the double-arrow logo continued to be used. Long-distance expresses were named 'Inter-City', this being painted in white on relevant coaches. In due course it was modernised by omitting the hyphen. West Germany saw how successful the Inter-City brand was, so Deutsche Bundesbahn paid a royalty to BR for using the name. From 1991 ICE 'Intercity-Express' trains operated in Germany.

In the post-Beeching era, potentially profitable services were identified as Interurban, Intercity and Trainload Freight, with loss-making services Urban and Rural. Urban services made a loss due to passengers using the relatively cheap season tickets and travelling at peak hours. Rural services made a loss due to just a few passengers being carried and the expense of a line kept open for a few trains.

A major rationalisation scheme was implemented in Glasgow in 1966 when on 27 June St Enoch station closed and its traffic was transferred to Central; and on 7 December Buchanan Street closed, its traffic using Queen Street.

The electrified Argyle line at Glasgow was opened by the Queen on 1 November 1979, public service starting on 5 November.

1967

On 1 January 1967 the Eastern and North Eastern Regions were combined, while in 1988 the Anglia Region was carved from ER.

A far-reaching development happened in March 1967 with the opening of New Pudsey as a park-and-ride station to enable motorists to board long-distance trains without having to drive into Leeds or Bradford.

BR initially used the 24-hour clock in its summer timetable for 1965, so times such as 8.45 a.m. and 8.45 p.m. became 08.45 and 20.45, though railwaymen had used 8.45 and 8/45 respectively.

The 750-volt DC third rail system opened between Brookwood and Branksome in July 1967. To enable a through service to be worked from Waterloo to Weymouth, a powered four-car electric unit could propel up to eight unpowered coaches. On reaching Bournemouth, a diesel-electric locomotive would be attached to the front of the train, the unpowered coaches detached and these would be hauled to Weymouth. There the diesel-electric would not be uncoupled but would propel the coaches to Bournemouth, the driver remotely controlling the engine from what had become the leading coach. At Bournemouth the locomotive would be uncoupled and the coaches coupled to a powered electric unit.

70 miles of suburban electrification was opened in and around Glasgow in 1967; the Lea Valley in 1969 and the West Coast Electrification Euston to Glasgow completed in May 1974.

With the adoption of air braking on all rolling stock, there was no longer the necessity to have a brake van at the rear of a goods train to assist the driver in braking control. The other important function of a brake van, which was to check that the train was complete and no vehicles had become detached, was covered by the fact that with air braking, any parting would automatically bring both sections to a halt.

In December 1967 a productivity agreement was made between BR and the National Union of Railwaymen whereby brake vans were no longer required on fully fitted freight trains. Goods brake vans had come into general use *circa* 1850, usually four-wheeled and with a verandah at one or both ends; some had side duckets to enable the guard to look forward without actually placing his head outside. Vans were usually ballasted to offer greater adhesion. Some newer vans were equipped with vacuum brakes for working fully-fitted express goods trains.

A goods guard was skilled and had to know when to screw down his brake and when to release it. When a descending gradient was followed by a rise, he had to make sure that there was no sharp snatch when gravity caused buffers, which had hitherto been touching, to move apart when the strain was taken by the three-link couplings. If the snatch was severe, a link could break – thus dividing the train. The use of three-link couplings had the advantage that, when starting, a locomotive did not have to move the whole train at once, but if the links were loose, could move one wagon at a time. A driver needed to be skilful because if he tried to accelerate too rapidly, he might cause a severe snatch, which would break a coupling.

1968

On 29 June 1968 the Keighley & Worth Valley Railway opened as a preserved line. One reopened station, Damems, had closed on 23 May 1949 and with a platform only one coach long, it was reputedly the smallest on the Midland. Legend has it that the building was so small that when a farmer came to collect a hen house, in error he took the station away.

The Victoria Line was the first London tube to be cut since 1907 and was desperately needed to handle traffic to and from King's Cross, St Pancras, Euston and Victoria. Opened from Walthamstow-Highbury on 1 September 1968, to Warren Street 3 November 1968 and to Victoria 7 March 1969, it was extended to Brixton in 1971. The trains were powered and signalled automatically, drivers simply opening the doors. The stations were sufficiently spaced for trains to reach 50 mph. It was the first line without guards. The automatic ticket gates installed on the Victoria Line in 1969 were successful in speeding passenger flow. In May 2017 the line was upgraded to allow trains to pull into stations every 100 seconds, or a world-class 36 trains per hour, enabling 3,000 more passengers to travel every hour during the peak. The improvement has also changed the behaviour of passengers: instead of running for trains and risking being trapped in doors, the regularity of the service means that people know that there is no need to rush because as one train departs, the one behind is less than two minutes away.

The Victoria Line was important because its trains were run automatically, leading to smooth running and faster speeds instead of being subject to the individual characteristics of drivers. The first test of the robot equipment made by the Westinghouse Brake & Signal Company had been made on the District Line between Ealing and South Acton on 21 March 1963. The trains were one-person-operated, having only a driver and no guard. The last guards on the underground were on the Northern Line; they were dispensed with when in 1995 the 1959 stock was replaced.

1970

In 1970 all ships belonging to BR were branded Sealink. When the railways were nationalised, the vessels and ports were operated by the various regions but in 1968, matters were centralised when vessels and ports were transferred to the BR Shipping and International Services Division. By the time Sealink came into being, the fleet had changed from being a mere appendage to the railway system but had become a major ferry operator with ships mostly catering for accompanied cars and roll-on/roll off lorries. Under privatisation it was sold in 1984 to British Ferries Limited and since has had several owners.

From 1970 the 1963 Mk II series of coaches were air-conditioned and electrically heated; the prototype Mk III coaches came into service in 1973.

1971

In 1958 the Glasgow to Edinburgh train service had been dieselised thus overcoming the long-standing problem of Cowlairs Incline.

On 3 May 1971, DMUs were replaced by push-pull operation between Glasgow Queen Street and Edinburgh via Falkirk High, using Class 27 diesel locomotives fitted with multiple-unit control on either end of six Mk IIA coaches. These trains, coupled with track and signalling improvements, allowed the speed limit to be raised to 90 mph and the journey time was cut from 55 to 43 minutes. Reliability problems led to the introduction in 1980 of Class 47/7 locomotives, uprated to 100 mph, propelling, or hauling, Mk 3 coaches, with a Mk 2 drive-end trailer at the opposite end to the locomotive. This rolling stock was eventually needed in East Anglia when London to Norwich trains changed to push-pull operation, thus in the late 1980s Class 156 and then Class 158 engines were brought into use between Glasgow and Edinburgh. These were superseded by Class 170 units in 1998, which continue in use.

The 1970s marked the end of excursion trains, run to carry passengers to such events as the Great Exhibition of 1851, horse races, football matches and Bank Holiday trips. A post-World War II variation of the excursion was the Holiday Express – you would sleep in your own bed but for a very reasonable sum would be taken each day to a resort at some distance. For example, in the first week of August 1964 from stations in the Bristol area the Holiday Express ran on Monday to Weymouth, Exmouth on Tuesday, Portsmouth on Wednesday, Torbay on Thursday and Bognor Regis on Friday. There was no trip on Saturday as the locomotive and train was required as a holiday extra. Excursion trains used rolling stock that would otherwise have lain idle, but by the 1970s there were less carriages and locomotives to spare. Many carriages were scrapped because they were not used every day.

Between 1971 and 1975, BR introduced the Total Operations Processing System (TOPS) a computerised method of keeping track of all locomotives and rolling stock and enabling the best use of them, as well as to be able to provide reliable information to customers on where the goods in transit actually were. This replaced paper documents, the telephone and telegraph. Originally just for freight, it was extended to include coaching stock and locomotives. The database was originally developed for the Southern Pacific Railroad in the USA.

Lineside apparatus for exchanging mail bags at speed was discontinued in 1971 due the fact that diesel power had increased train speeds to such an extent that exchange was becoming dangerous.

1972

Britain's second park-and-ride station, Bristol Parkway, opened in April 1972, was placed close to the M4 and was easily accessible by road. The station offered services to all points of the compass: towards London, South Wales, the south-west and the Midlands. As initially parking was free, it was cheaper and more convenient for passengers from the Bath area, for example to travel by road to Bristol Parkway, rather than to use the local station and change at Temple Meads. As a result, the station soon paid its cost. Building on the successful idea, a third park-and-ride station, Alfreton & Mansfield Parkway, opened near the M1 in 1973. Others followed: Bodmin, Didcot, Haddenham & Thame, Southampton Airport & Parkway and Tiverton.

A curious situation arose on the Yate to Thornbury branch. It had closed to passenger traffic on 19 June 1944, but goods continued until 4 December 1967 when the branch was closed, track lifting starting the following September. In 1972 Amalgamated Roadstone developed its Tytherington Quarry, just short of Thornbury, and wanted a rail link. Fortunately this was no great problem. Six miles of track recovered from the Mangotsfield to Bath branch, which was being lifted in 1972, was relaid between Yate and Tytherington, the 20,000 tons of ballast required being supplied by the quarry. The cost of relaying the branch was approximately £140,000, of which the quarry company paid 40 per cent. The grand official reopening ceremony was performed by the BR Chairman, Richard Marsh, on 3 September 1973, 101 years and one day after the line had first been opened. It is possible that in the long term, Thornbury could be part of the Bristol Metro system.

Something very similar occurred on the Portishead branch just south of Bristol. Passenger services were withdrawn on 7 September 1964 and regular freight on 30 March 1981, though the occasional Freightliner trains were worked after that date. The line was retained out of use by BR in the hope that container traffic from

Portbury, just short of Portishead, would increase. This showed foresight as in 2001 it was decided that most of the branch would be reopened and a short branch laid to the Royal Portbury Dock. It was officially reopened on 21 December 2001, with regular trains, at first of coal, starting on 7 January 2002. Since then, traffic has included road vehicles and biomass.

In October 1972 BR introduced the first high speed scheduled freight service from Bristol to Glasgow, using air-braked wagons; this was later developed into the Speedlink network. Three more Speedlink services were added in 1973–4. In 1974 it was declared that the retention of the wagon-load traffic had produced 'a modest financial success' of £5 million profit over total costs, though by 1976 wagon-load was running at a loss of £30 million annually due to managerial difficulties and problems with industrial relations.

1974

The newly electrified West Coast main line was officially opened on 6 May 1974, though the section between Beattock and Lockerbie was the scene of a new British rail speed record in June 1973 when two electric locomotives reached a maximum of 129 mph. Electrification almost flattened out the Beattock climb with locomotives speeding over the summit at 90 mph.

23

The Advanced Passenger Train and High-speed Train; Rapid Transport Systems Develop

1975

A train ran at speed through Moorgate station and crashed into headwall, causing the underground's worst accident on 28 February 1975. It was the fourth trip of a shuttle run between Drayton Park and Moorgate, the round trip taking about 20 minutes. The journey of about 2¾ miles took 7 minutes, including three intermediate stops. At the time of the accident motorman L. B. Newson had worked for only 1 hour and 50 minutes. It took 13 hours and 19 minutes before the last survivor was rescued and four-and-a-half days before the last body – that of Mr Newson – was recovered. A total of 43 passengers were killed, in addition to the motorman, and 74 passengers received injuries requiring hospital treatment.

The cause of the accident has never been explained. Lt Col I. K. A. McNaughton, chief inspecting officer of the Railway Inspectorate, Department of the Environment stated:

> I must conclude, therefore, that the cause of the accident lay entirely in the behaviour of Motorman Newson during the final minute before the accident occurred. Whether the behaviour was deliberate or whether it was the result of a sudden arising physical condition not revealed as a result of post-mortem examination, there is not sufficient evidence to establish, but I am satisfied that no part of the responsibility for the accident rests with any other

person and that there was no fault or condition of the train, track or signalling that in any way contributed to it.

The high-speed trains introduced into Japan in the 1960s led other countries to try to emulate them. In 1972 Britain offered two answers: the Advanced Passenger Train (APT) and the High Speed Train (HST). The former used new technology and the latter, conventional railway engineering. The APT was fitted with a tilting mechanism, which allowed it to travel round curves on the existing West Coast Main Line at speeds up to 155mph. In 1972 the prototype gas turbine 4-car train was first tested and for four years worked successfully. The next step was the construction of three 14-car electric APT-P train sets with two power cars in the centre and six articulated tilting coaches on either side.

About 1975 BR was at its nadir, but its saviour was thought to be at hand – the APT – the Advanced Passenger Train. Following a decade of research by engineers from the road, motor and aviation industries at the Railway Technical Centre, Derby, this train using ordinary track and could go 40 per cent faster round curves due to its ability to tilt, enabling it to cut almost an hour off the run between London and Glasgow. It was believed no one would consider driving long distances on motorways when they could use the train. In 1979 it achieved the British rail speed record of 162.2 mph. Journalists were invited on the record-breaking London-Glasgow run when it averaged 103.4 mph, but instead of reporting a speed record, they informed readers that it made them sick. Unfortunately on its return run, the tilting mechanism on one car malfunctioned. It began a regular service between Euston and Glasgow Central in December 1981 but problems were experienced with the tilting mechanism and the brakes, so it was withdrawn after just a few days. Following the solution of these problems, the service was re-started in 1984 and operated successfully – but interest was insufficient to warrant building the fleet of APT-S standard trains. The APT-P trains continued running in service until the project was abandoned in 1986 due to the unreliability of the train's hydrokinetic braking system, and failures of the tilt mechanism and gearboxes. Additionally there was the fear of two similar trains approaching each other at speed, one with a faulty tilt mechanism, and them striking each other. The project had cost £37m but had never received the support it needed from civil servants and politicians and it was left to an Italian company to make developments and the tilting Clast 390 Pendolinos brought into service on the West Coast main line in 2004 were built by the French-owened Fiat Ferroviaria.

Fortunately, BRB Engineering had been at work on another new development using conventional technology, the InterCity 125 train, which proved highly satisfactory. It set a world speed record for diesel traction in 1973 achieving 143.2 mph. Designed by Kenneth Grange and introduced initially on the Western Region in 1976, they were smooth-riding. Speeding for long distances at 125 mph between Paddington and Bristol, Cardiff and Swansea, they were a great improvement on the 100 mph limit of previous diesels. Offering a smooth, comfortable ride, inside they were uncannily almost virtually silent. They attracted passengers and extended London's commuter zone. HSTs were introduced to other Western Region main lines and on to other regions from King's Cross to Edinburgh, Aberdeen and Inverness and the Midland main line from St Pancras to Sheffield and Nottingham.

HSTs had innovative features such as automatic internal doors and double glazing, and even second-class had wall-to-wall carpeting. The BR Mark 3 coaches were open saloons, marking the end of the compartments which offered privacy, but on the other hand, open saloons were less likely to be vandalised and passengers less likely to be attacked for robbery or sexually assaulted. More than forty years later, these trains are still in use and have given excellent service.

Initially it was believed that if two HSTs passed in a tunnel at 125 mph, air would be sufficiently compressed to shatter the windows. An experiment was carried out with HSTs approaching a tunnel on the Badminton line at 125 mph and to ensure that they crossed in the tunnel, they were in radio contact with each other. When they emerged, all windows were intact. The first appearance of an HST in Scotland was on 13 June 1977 when the Commonwealth Heads of State, after meeting in Glenshields, were carried back to London.

On 12 March 1978 new colour light signals between Edinburgh and Berwick allowed the speed limit to be raised to 100 mph. In February 1979 five bridges were reconstructed in the East Linton area to give clearance for larger containers.

About this time BR sandwiches were modernised and became the most popular sandwich made from the most popular contemporary ingredients: Mother's Pride bread, Kraft cheese and Anchor butter.

1978

In the last years of the nineteenth and early years of the twentieth century, when gas lighting was common, there were several serious fires following railway accidents, but then for many years, fire was not a hazard.

On 5 July 1978 the 21.30 sleeper left Penzance for Paddington with 12 vehicles. At Plymouth three more coaches were waiting to be added, these had been at the platform from about 22.30 so that if passengers wished, they could go to bed before the arrival of the main train. At Plymouth the sleeping car attendant had locked all the doors on the platform side except the one beside his pantry so that he could check all the passengers in as they arrived. Tragically, he did not unlock these doors before the train left Plymouth.

As it was midsummer, the electric train heating was on but the hot air fan of the pressure ventilation system was switched off in the leading sleeping car and only the cold air fan was working; the convector heater to the leading vestibule was left on.

The train left Plymouth behind Class 47 No. 47498 at 00.30 calling at Newton Abbot and Exeter St David's where a carriage and wagon examiner checked each coach from outside and spotted nothing amiss. Unfortunately linen bags were stacked against the heater in the leading vestibule of the leading sleeping car, the bags contained some soiled linen from the previous night's trip and some clean linen.

As the train passed through Whiteball Tunnel on the Devon/Somerset border, the sleeping car attendant looking after the rear cars smelt burning. He checked his own vehicles first and then went forward and found thick smoke. He returned to his pantry and pulled the alarm before returning to alert passengers, but the smoke was too thick for him to reach the leading car. He found the attendant for the leading car slumped unconscious in the corridor. As the train had now stopped, he helped him out of the train where he recovered.

It was fortunate that the train stopped opposite a lineside telephone so that the driver was able to ring the Taunton station office for assistance. At first the firemen and police were unable to enter the burning leading coach because the doors were locked, but carriage keys were obtained from the sleeping car attendants. Rescuers were driven back by dense smoke while firemen with breathing apparatus were defeated by the intense heat until the coach had been hosed down inside.

Eleven passengers were dead, poisoned by fumes given off by the burning materials and spread through the ventilation system.

In the subsequent investigation by Major Tony King, it was found that although fire retardant materials had been used inside the car for partitions and ceiling panels, some of the laminated panels inside the all-steel body had been replaced during maintenance with material that was not fire retardant. The bedding was not fire retardant and one mattress contained polyurethane foam, which gave off toxic fumes when alight.

Although a similar fire started on a Glasgow to Euston sleeper in 1973 when linen placed against a heater began to smoulder, it had been quickly doused by a fire extinguisher. No warning notices were placed by heaters regarding the dangers caused by obstruction. Although an emergency door from the corridor to the exterior was placed in the centre of the coach and the door could be opened by pulling a tear-off strip at the top and working the release handle, there were no direction signs on this door.

In order to prevent a reoccurrence, immediate precautions were taken that no obstructions were permitted in corridors and that linen bags should be placed in brake vans. Hammers should be available in compartments in order to break windows, the ventilation system should only take air from outside, the central emergency door was to be converted to an ordinary door, a fire precaution notice must be placed in each compartment and exit signs provided, polyurethane mattresses had to be removed and fire retardant bed linen used.

1979

Penmanshiel Tunnel was being relined to allow international containers to run through and on 17 March 1979 it experienced a major collapse, killing two workmen, so all Anglo-Scottish services were run over the West Coast route via Carlisle. As the geological formations were treacherous, it was decided that rather than re-open the tunnel it would be better to have a ½-mile deviation. This was built remarkably rapidly and on 20 August 1979, Penmanshiel Tunnel was formally sealed and consecrated as a grave for the two men whose bodies could not safely be recovered, The new diversion opened on the same day with the East Coast main line using HSTs.

In 1969 the Fleet Line, later renamed the Jubilee Line, had been authorised to run from Charing Cross to Baker Street to relieve pressure on the Bakerloo in the central area and take over its Stanmore service. The line opened in 1979. The Jubilee Line has moving block signalling, a feature which speeds train operation. The government provided three-quarters of the cost, Greater London Council the remainder.

1980

Light Rapid Transport systems, developed on the Continent and elsewhere, were really a cross between a traditional light railway and an electric tramway. Single, light-rail vehicles operated a fast, frequent service serving unmanned stops, often with automatic ticket machines. Britain's first example was the Tyne & Wear Metro, opened in stages from 1980 running on former BR tracks north and south of the Tyne, connected by a new bridge and tunnelling under central Newcastle. To save manpower, stations are under surveillance from a control centre using closed-circuit television. Some of the formation is on the North Eastern Railway's tracks, electrified in 1904, dieselised in 1967 and re-electrified in 1980.

The second system was Manchester Metrolink, opened in 1982. This uses a combination of former BR track and street running using 2-car articulated sets, which can be operated in multiple. The line to Altrincham was shared with BR electric trains. Sheffield followed suit in 1994–1995 with more extensive street running and has gradients as steep as 1 in 10. Other major cities have subsequently opened tramways.

Most rapid transport systems could be classified as tramways rather than railways, but one exception is the Docklands Light Railway. Opened between 1987 and 2011, it has a length of 21 miles and covers the 8½ square miles regenerated by the London Docklands Development Corporation. It is a standard gauge automated system with driverless trains. Using a quite different system from London Transport, through running is not possible. Current is supplied at 750 volts DC by a third rail with underside contact. Some curves are very tight and akin to tramway, rather than railway, practice.

1981

A study in 1981 by the University of Leeds found that BR was not only the cheapest, but after Sweden, the most efficient railway in Europe. So popular were HSTs that for six years the InterCity sector of BR operated without subsidy. They enabled passengers to commute to London from Bristol and York. As the trains ran in sets with a locomotive at each end, they needed little time at a terminus before making a return journey, many travelling more than 1,000 miles a day. An excellent investment, many form the backbone of express services and are still running forty years later. For the electrified East Coast route, the Class 91 Bo-Bo was built with a design speed of 140 mph but limited to 125 mph in service.

1982

British Railways had inherited quite a few up-market hotels from the railway companies but these were privatised in 1982–1983.

Far from making a profit as Beeching had expected, by 1982 BR was making an annual loss of almost £1 billion, so the Government commissioned the Serpell Report, which was published in 1983. One option was to close all lines except the West Coast Main Line to Glasgow; the East Coast Main Line to Newcastle and London to Bristol and Cardiff. The Government believed such wholesale closures were too drastic and the report lay forgotten. Various improvements to BR such as the electrification of the East Coast Main Line to Leeds and Edinburgh, completed in 1991, and the introduction of the Sprinter DMUs, meant more passengers were being carried and losses were decreasing.

1984

When George Stephenson was asked what would happen if a train hit a cow he replied: 'It would be awkward for the coo.' On 30 July 1984, not only was a cow killed but also 13 passengers.

The first diesel-electric working of 100 mph push-pull trains was the Edinburgh-Glasgow service inaugurated in 1979, this type of operation saving the time and trouble of running the locomotive around at the terminus. On 30 July 1984, the 17.30 Edinburgh-Glasgow comprised No. 47707 propelling six coaches, the one at the leading end being a driving trailer brake second. About 1½ miles beyond Polmont, the driver saw a cow standing in the four foot. Unable to stop in time, parts of the cow derailed the leading bogie and the coach was pushed up the side of the cutting. The second coach also derailed, was turned end to end on the opposite line. An engineer estimated that the stored energy in the train travelling at about 85 mph was enough to throw two coaches to the top of the Eiffel tower. Thirteen passengers were killed, and 14 passengers and three railway staff injured, including the driver. In the history of railways this was the first instance of an animal causing the death of a railway passenger.

The tragedy could have been even worse. The 17.30 Glasgow-Edinburgh was approaching, but fortunately the driver spotted a coach somersaulting towards him, made an emergency brake application and stopped just 179 yards from the derailed train.

How had the cow got on the track? Permanent way officials told the inspecting officer that fences in the area were frequently vandalised and although repaired, were again damaged. At the inquiry engineers observed that having a leading driving trailer was not inherently dangerous as it was little different from a diesel or electric multiple unit driving trailer.

24

Privatisation

1986

The Mangotsfield-Bath line, which closed in 1971, was turned into a walkway and cycle track by Sustrans (sustainable transport). It was extended from Mangotsfield to Bristol in 1986 and this 20-km long path was the first major project of its kind in Britain. Although it is good that former railways still remain in use, problems can arise between conflicting interests when it is thought desirable to re-open a line.

Nationalisation had not proved a success as in each year under the British Railways regime, passenger numbers declined. In preparation for privatisation, in 1982 Bob Reid reorganised British Rail and instead of being arranged in regions, it was divided into various business sectors. Five managerial units were created by sector: freight, parcels, InterCity operated express passenger services; the London & South Eastern sector, London commuter services, while Regional Railways ran the remaining passenger services. Regional Railways adopted a livery of white with a blue stripe.

As Regional Railways was a non-profit making concern, being mainly an effort to provide rural areas with rail transport, it received Government subsidies of up to 400 per cent of its annual revenue. Initially, Regional Railways had to tolerate the use of older coaches and first-generation DMUs, but between 1984 and 1987 economical bus-type four-wheeled Class 142 sets named 'Pacers' were introduced on some services. With a riveted steel body and roof, they were built from Leyland National bus parts on Leyland Bus four-wheeled underframes. Class 143 Pacers were of the same design but with aluminium alloy bodies built by W. Alexander on Barclay underframes. Similarly, the Class 144 had Alexander bodies on British Rail Engineering Limited underframes.

The riding of these vehicles has been widely criticised, even in Parliament, but the author enjoys travelling in them, the sensation reminding him of the enjoyable time he had on his galloping horse. Bogie DMUs, with a less exciting ride, were introduced between 1987 and 1989 and known as 'Sprinters'.

On 21 June 1986 the London & South Eastern sector became the snappier Network SouthEast, this being publicised by offering travel anywhere over the system for the very reasonable fare of £3. The author got good value for his money and travelled from Gillingham, Dorset, to Portsmouth; bought a return ticket for the ferry to Ryde; travelled on the Isle of Wight to Shanklin and back; and then on to Bedford before returning to Gillingham. 'South East' was widely interpreted as the network stretched from Cambridge to Exeter. The sector had its corporate livery of red, white and blue.

When BR was split into sectors in 1982, goods traffic was looked after by Railfreight, which adopted a livery of 'Railfreight Grey' relieved with 'Railfreight Red Stripe'. In 1987 the sector was divided into four sectors: Trainload Freight to handle bulk train loads of coal, aggregates and metal; Railfreight Distribution for non-train load freight; Freightliner for intermodal container traffic, and Rail Express Systems for parcels traffic.

The year 1986 brought an interesting development, really a prelude to privatisation, when Foster Yeoman, owners of Merehead Quarry in Somerset, started hauling its own wagons by its own Class 59 General Motors American-built locomotives. Contemporary British locomotives had poor availability, whereas those built by General Motors had 98 per cent – one of the best in the world for a freight locomotive. The best way to get traction is to have a certain amount of slip and the General Motors design was the best for this and had the ability to haul approximately 5,100 tonnes. This was the first time non-BR engines had run over BR since the National Coal Board stopped running over BR in Durham in the 1960s. In October 1993, ARC, another quarry owner in the area, with Foster Yeoman, formed a joint operation, Mendip Rail offering the great advantage that locomotives and rolling stock could be interchanged to match the needs of the respective quarries.

1987

In 1987 the once-threatened Marylebone station was given a boost following the upgrading of the Chiltern Main Line through High Wycombe, Bicester and Banbury, offering an alternative route to Birmingham. Third rail electrification was extended to Hastings and Weymouth and the Midland Main Line electrified between St Pancras and Bedford, while in 1988 dual voltage trains enabled passenger trains to link Bedford and Brighton, offering the 140-mile Thameslink route across London through the re-opened Snow Hill Tunnel. For many years it was a freight-only line and then closed in 1971, being reopened to passenger traffic in 1987. The electric stock used had to be capable of running on both the overhead and third-rail systems.

Fortunately station fires are rare, but an extremely serious one occurred on 18 November 1987 at King's Cross Underground, causing the deaths of 31 people and seriously injuring in excess of 100. At 7.30 p.m. a small fire was spotted on one of the wooden escalators leading to the ticket hall, there was no panic and passengers continued to use the parallel escalator. Then there was a sudden 'whoosh' and the fire raced up at 15 metres a second into the ticket hall, increasing the temperature by several hundred degrees and setting hair and clothes alight. Dense smoke made locating an exit difficult or impossible.

More than 150 fire-fighters were sent, some with breathing apparatus, to search for survivors. Some of these fire-fighters collapsed from heat exhaustion. The next morning at 1.45 a.m., the fire brigade sent a message that the fire had been put out.

What had caused the blaze? Investigators found matches, cigarette stubs, grease, cloth fibres, hair and rubbish under the escalator and it was believed that it had not been cleaned since it had been installed soon after World War II. A lighted match or cigarette thrown on the escalator had set this debris alight.

This fire should not have happened because on 24 November 1984, almost exactly three years previously, there had been a major fire at Oxford Circus station, trapping passengers in smoke-filled tunnels. Soon after, smoking was banned on all Underground stations and trains, but the ban was not fully enforced. Over the years more than 50 fires had been reported relating to wooden escalators.

The report on the investigation into the King's Cross fire was issued on 10 November 1988, criticising the Underground. The report recommended 150 changes to protect passengers, among them a total smoking ban and the substitution of wooden for metal escalators, but it took 27 years before the last wooden one was replaced.

1988

The Class 91 electric locomotives built by British Rail Engineering Limited at Crewe first appeared in this year and were followed in 1989 by the Class 60 diesel-electric locomotives built by Brush Traction. These were the last locomotives to be built in Britain, all subsequent main line locomotives for Britain's railways having been built either in North America or mainland Europe.

On 9 October 1988 the last newspaper train ran. The first nail in the coffin was in 1986 when Rupert Murdoch's group of papers moved from Fleet Street to new high-tech presses at Wapping and used road haulage, the Mirror Group following in 1987. Fifty dedicated newspaper trains had run each weekday, while 75 were required for the heavier Sunday editions. Trains generally consisted of General Utility Vans and a Brake Gangway, while the Western Region used Siphons. Some trains had a seated coach to augment the toilet accommodation found in some vans, and also to allow the staff to relax if work was finished before the end of the journey; it also allowed the public a chance to reach home if working late, or for any other reason. Newspaper vans were returned to their starting point as empty stock, or as part of a parcels train.

In 1988 the Downing Street Policy Unit revealed that the Conservatives were considering privatisation, options included selling BR as a whole, dividing it into a track authority and train operating companies, or breaking it into geographical regions. Something needed to be done because in each of British Rail's 50 years, passenger numbers had continually declined. In 1991 Prime Minister John Major said that to comply with European Community policy, the rail network would be open to any operator. Following his re-election in 1992 privatisation was confirmed and a White Paper on the subject issued in July 1992.

1990s

The Community Rail movement was founded by Professor Paul Salveson in the early 1990s whereby contracts were made between a train operator, the local authority and other stakeholders. Such groups publicise stations and railway routes, tend station gardens and pick up litter. Funding from outside is matched by the train operator. In 2005 the Association of Community Rail Partnerships, funded by the Department of Transport, support more than 30 lines in England and Wales. The partnerships link the railway with the local community with such benefits as organising the maintenance of station buildings, improving bus, cycling and walking routes to stations and organising education projects. The involvement of the local community in the railway has led to greater use of the rail links and passenger numbers have grown significantly.

1993

When the Conservative party under John Major won the General Election in 1992, it did so with the mandate for Britain's railways to pass into private ownership. A new era for railways in Britain started on 5 November 1993 when the Railways Act was passed allowing privatisation, which was far from turning the clock back to the situation before 1947 because the whole set-up was different. Some services on the fringe of BR had already been sold – British Transport Hotels, and Sealink, in 1985. British Rail Engineering Limited was sold in April 1987 to a consortium comprising Asea Brown Boveri (ABB), Trafalgar House, and its own management team. Some workshops previously British Rail Maintenance Limited remained in public ownership until sold with the principal maintenance depots in 1995.

With privatisation, the infrastructure of signalling stations and track was sold to Railtrack, which operated under ten regional zones, while passenger trains were worked by 25 passenger train franchises overseen by the Director of Passenger Rail Franchising – note that lines were only franchised to private enterprise and not owned by them, so re-nationalisation could easily take place by simply not renewing the franchises. The 25 train operating companies did not actually own any hardware. They hired locomotives and rolling stock from Rolling Stock Leasing Companies (ROSCOS), and paid contractors for maintaining them, paid others for providing on-board catering and Railtrack for the use of its lines.

Most stations and maintenance depots were leased by Railtrack to the train operating companies, but some larger stations remained under Railtrack control. The actual privatisation took place on 1 April 1994 when BR locomotives, DMUs and coaches were divided between the three ROSCOS. Today they are Porterbrook, Eversholt Rail Group and Angel Trains.

Although privatisation has generally proved a success, passenger demand having grown exponentially, this has given rise to problems of delays, overcrowding and problems accommodating major infrastructure projects. Although the train operating companies improved their rolling stock, much of the investment came in the early years of a franchise, there being little incentive to invest towards the end of the contract in case that company was unable to renew it. The more profitable franchises also incurred premium payments to the Government, part of which helped to subsidise the less profitable ones. This takes money from the busier lines, thus preventing those companies from cutting fares or investing in a better fleet.

BR operated 249 restaurant cars at the time of privatisation, but since then the number has declined, economics determining that buffets replaced them. Restaurant cars demand that two seats be provided for each passenger: one in an ordinary coach and one in the restaurant car, whereas with a buffet car a passenger just collects food or drink and then returns to his or her seat.

1994

Queen Elizabeth II and President Mitterrand inaugurated the Channel Tunnel on 6 May 1994. Although tunnel companies had been founded in the late 1870s and about a mile of tunnel bored, the British military realised the potential threat of invasion and Parliament ordered that work should be stopped. In 1955 the Ministry of Defence stated that a tunnel would not impair the defence of the realm. Following the publication of a White Paper in 1973, it was realised that a new high speed electrified line using the Continental loading gauge was required between London and the tunnel entrance. A test boring was made in 1973, halted in January 1975 by a change of government, but restarted 10 years later. In 1987 the Treaty of Canterbury gave Eurotunnel, (renamed 'Getlink' in 2017), an Anglo-French company, the concession to construct and work the tunnel.

Three 31-mile-long tunnels link Folkestone and Calais. Two are parallel single track railway tunnels while between them is a service tunnel, which assists in ventilation and, as all three tunnels are linked by cross-passages, doubles as an emergency escape route should passengers need to evacuate a train.

The inaugural Eurostar service from Waterloo International ran on 14 November 1994. The service marked the end of Continental boat trains and the closure of Dover Marine station. The Night Ferry, with its through coaches London-Paris, had already been withdrawn on 31 October 1980 as passengers hitherto using this relatively expensive service preferred to fly. International services through the Channel Tunnel came under a branch of BR, European Passenger Services Limited, and in 1994 became a government-owned company with the intention that it would eventually be absorbed by the company successfully bidding for the contract for the construction and operation of HS1, the high-speed rail link opened in 2007 between St Pancras and the Tunnel, the international platforms at Waterloo being closed and re-converted to domestic use. Today, Eurostar has more London-Paris traffic than all the airlines combined.

During 1994, the freight side of BR – Freightliner, Loadhaul, Mainline, Rail Express Systems, Railfreight Distribution and Transrail – were taken over by the English Welsh & Scottish Railway and Freightliner so, unlike passenger services, freight is fully in the private sector. The Office of the Rail Regulator regulated the entire railway industry. The very last train operated by BR was the 23.15 container service from Dollands Moor-Wembley on 21 November 1997 hauled by No. 92003.

Such a dramatic change in the organisation of the rail industry brought a few problems, which needed solving. In 2000 the Transport Act set up the Strategic Rail Authority, a non-departmental body, to guide the privatised railways. The Railways Act of 2006 saw this body wound up in December 2006 and taken over by the Department for Transport, Network Rail and the Office of Rail Regulation, plus limited powers given to the Greater London Authority, the Scottish Executive and the Welsh Assembly. Had the railways not been privatised it is unlikely that they would have seen the phenomenal growth in traffic that has been experienced over the last five years.

As early as 2004 Lew Adams, general secretary of the Associated Society of Locomotive Engineers and Firemen, said that since privatisation 1,700 more trains were running daily and train frequencies on many lines were more than double those in the BR era. He did not remark on the fact that one advantage of privatisation was that a strike tended to stop traffic of only one operator, rather than across the whole system.

1996

South West Trains ran Britain's first privatised train on 4 February 1996, the 05.10 service from Twickenham to Waterloo. Arguably, South West Trains took over the best constructed infrastructure on BR as its main lines were superbly laid out with flying junctions. It also had a huge commuter/leisure market, split approximately 60/40 per cent, and served some of the Top 10 leisure destinations in the country. About one in eight Conservative MPs lived along, or close to, its routes, so perhaps some politicians had a strong personal drive to privatise the area quickly.

South West Trains was run by the Stagecoach bus company and a review revealed that the drivers' roster showed a poor use of resources and suggested that the company had too many drivers. This resulted in many drivers being allowed to leave on generous redundancy packages – and then it was found that there was a shortage!

About 1996 it again became socially acceptable to travel by rail: it is better for the environment, more restful and avoids traffic hold-ups and parking problems. Young people like trains: they are not always able to afford a car and its insurance, and while travelling by rail can play with their electronic gadgets.

2000

Railtrack proved inefficient and a series of serious accidents ensued. On 5 October 1999 a Down Thames Trains DMU at Ladbroke Grove near Paddington passed a poorly positioned danger signal and collided head-on with an Up InterCity 125. In the ensuing fire, 31 passengers died and 523 were injured. Blame was shared between Thames Trains for poor driver training and Railtrack for placing the signal in a poor position.

The final nail in Railtrack's coffin was on 17 October 2000 when a Down InterCity 125 travelling at more than 110 mph derailed on the approach to Hatfield station, killing 4 passengers and injuring in excess of 70. It was caused by a fractured rail. This caused more than a thousand speed restrictions to be imposed and thousands of miles of track checked for metal fatigue. Compensation and track renewal costs caused the company to become bankrupt and in October 2002, it was taken over by Network Rail, a 'not for dividend' company.

Today, Network Rail has about 34,000 employees and receives income from passenger and freight companies. It owns approximately 20,000 miles of track, 44,000 bridges and tunnels and in excess of 2,500 stations. It owns a fleet of locomotives and rolling stock including DMUs and EMUs for making safety checks on the network.

When the Labour Government created Network Rail in 2002 it was meant to be efficient, dynamic, commercially minded and independent, but in the event, and typical of all state-run enterprises, it suffered from poor cost control and inept planning. Its not-for-profit status and heavy dependence on taxpayer support mean that the incentives for efficiency are weak. Had it been a genuinely private company it would risk bankruptcy if it grossly underestimated costs or delivered appalling customer service, but Network Rail is confident that the Government will continue the subsidies. The Government should allow a return to more efficient 'vertical integration' with the same firms owning the track and operating the trains.

Network Rail has responsibility for a large number of listed structures: of the 2,500 or so stations, more than 380 are listed, of 80 signal boxes, more than 60 are listed, of the 43,000 bridges, tunnels and viaducts more than 600 are listed. Some redundant listed railway buildings have been given a useful new life – for example William Tress's Grade II-listed Etchingham station in West Sussex became a good restaurant and offered community facilities.

2002

Pendolinos were introduced in 2002 to offer high-speed running on ordinary lines. On curves they lean inwards like a motor-cyclist; the carriages necessarily sloping towards the roof to keep within the loading gauge when tilting.

The last Travelling Post Office ran on 9 January 2004, though by Christmas 2004, 16 Class 325 electric multiple units were dedicated to carrying mail between London and Scotland and at the time of writing, 15 are still in operation.

2005

On 7 July 2005 six passengers were murdered at Edgware Road station when a bomb exploded. Two more bombs on the Underground killed a further 32 and injured more than 700.

Modern passenger stock has been equipped with sliding doors controlled by the train staff, which means that passengers can no longer cause accidents by opening doors before the train stops and injuring people standing on the platform and can no longer leap in after the train has left. The final official slam-door train was the 11.35 to Bournemouth on 25 May 2005.

Although England seems to have struggled to make electrification schemes viable, or even achievable without cost overruns and long delay, Scotland has proceeded steadily with a number of schemes. In 2005 Hamilton to Larkhall reopened as an electric route with half-hourly trains integrated into the Argyle Line cross-Glasgow service. In May 2008 Stirling to Alloa reopened to diesel trains with an hourly service to Glasgow and this route will eventually be electrified as part of Stage 2 of the Edinburgh Glasgow Improvement Plan. In December 2010 the Glasgow to Paisley Canal service was electrified, continuing the half-hourly service. In 2014 Springburn to Cumbernauld was electrified as a precursor to the main Edinburgh Glasgow Improvement Plan scheme, providing a half-hourly electric service from Cumbernauld, reversing at Springburn, to Dumbarton Central via Queen Street Low Level.

An hourly service also operates from Cumbernauld by a circuitous route through Coatbridge Central, Motherwell and Hamilton Central to the Argyle Line and Dalmuir. Eventually, as part of the Edinburgh Glasgow Improvement Plan Stage 2, the continuation of the Caledonian Railway route north of Cumbernauld to Greenhill Lower Junction will be electrified. At this point, the hourly Glasgow Queen Street High Level to Falkirk Grahamston via Springburn diesel service will become a half-hourly service, continuing to Polmont and Edinburgh.

In 2014 Rutherglen to Whifflet was electrified, the half-hourly diesel shuttle from Glasgow Central High Level to Whifflet becoming another part of the integrated electric service over the Argyle Line through Central Low Level going on to serve Motherwell and Hamilton.

In December 2017, the first stage of the Edinburgh Glasgow Improvement Plan electrification scheme was completed and offered four trains each hour between these cities over the former North British line. Seven- and eventually eight-car Class 385 EMUs took over the working offering a 45 per cent increase in seating capacity. Eventually, Stirling and Alloa will be added to this electric network, served from both Glasgow and Edinburgh.

Plans are being made to electrify the gap between Holytown and West Calder via Shotts, thus creating another electrified alternative between Glasgow and Edinburgh. Other ideas in the pipeline include electrifying the East Kilbride branch and to Barrhead on the Kilmarnock route, thus further reducing diesel mileage.

There are other less developed plans to upgrade the Edinburgh South Suburban line for electric freight services, but it is unlikely that passenger services will be reintroduced because the route is quite slow and circuitous into Edinburgh and the main line through Waverley and Haymarket is becoming very congested. The cessation of coal traffic over the rebuilt line from Alloa to Longannet power station, which closed in March 2016, means that the line east of Alloa is now disused. There are aspirations to reopen this to passenger trains serving Dunfermline.

Freight, too, has increased. The closure of deep coal mines in Britain has led to a different distribution – from ports where coal has been imported instead of from the collieries. Power stations are changing from burning coal to other fuel such as biomass in the form of wood pellets.

The reopening of a portion of the Waverley Route as the Borders Rail Link on 6 September 2015 was an important event in the history of Scottish railways. Ridership has exceeded expectations, although there have been reliability issues with overheating radiators on the Class 158 DMUs and also a reduction in the planned amount of double track provided. The combination of unreliable trains and limited scope for passing loops meant that delays accumulated. Local campaigners are pressing for the line to reopen to Hawick from Tweedbank and the SNP government has even spoken of extending it to Carlisle, though this may not happen due to the sparse population and the good service offered by the alternative Virgin West Coast and TransPennine trains from Edinburgh to Carlisle via Lockerbie. The opening of the Borders Railway impacted on the demand for bus travel and some bus services became uneconomic and were withdrawn.

When Great Western HSTs are replaced by bimodal units in 2018, it is anticipated that two HST power cars with either four or five Mk 3 coaches updated with power doors and retention toilets will be used on the Edinburgh and Glasgow services to Inverness and Aberdeen.

By 1992 overcrowding was becoming a serious problem on the underground's Central Line. The answer was to introduce more spacious trains to accommodate more passengers and to increase the number of trains by driving them automatically, computers controlling them and drivers just operating the doors and being prepared for an emergency. This method of operation allowed a train to be run every 90 seconds. To speed cleaning at the end of the day, the whole train was driven into a shed where the air was extracted to suck out the dirt. The opening of the Elizabeth Line (*See* below) will relieve some pressure from the Central Line.

With a view to decreasing traffic congestion in London, in 1989 a Paddington to Liverpool Street underground line was proposed, but no funds were available. This Crossrail idea (now named the Elizabeth Line) was not forgotten and after consultation with local authorities and the general public, the plan was extended to run from Maidenhead to Shenfield, with branches serving Heathrow and Abbey Wood, though later it was decided that Reading should be the western terminus. Crossrail is a high-capacity Metro, 85 miles in length, with an estimated cost of £14.8 billion, designed to ease the strain on the existing underground network. It will make a trip to Heathrow just 26 minutes from Oxford Street, London's main shopping district, instead of about 60 minutes. The Crossrail Act was passed in July 2008 and construction started at Canary Wharf on 15 May 2009. With more than 43 kilometres of new tunnel below London, and 10 new underground stations, it was Europe's largest infrastructure project. The workforce peaked at 9,000. Excavated material was taken to Wallasea Island to form a new bird sanctuary. Seven million tonnes of earth were moved and more than 1,000 Olympic-sized swimming pools of concrete was used.

Construction of each station raised different problems: Liverpool Street had to contend with the grounds of Bedlam Hospital involving archaeological examination of 16th- and 17th-century burials. The largest and most expensive station is Farringdon, at a cost of £375m. The original Whitechapel station, built in 1876, was adapted at a cost of £111m to plug Crossrail into the existing services. It was the only place on the system where underground trains passed *over* main line overground trains. In excess of 10,000 archaeological finds were discovered when building Crossrail.

Crossrail is a full-sized line with platforms 250 metres in length, compared with the 125 metres of the Underground. The platform edges have glazed screens to prevent draughts and passengers falling on the tracks. The original specification was for full air-conditioning to get rid of the heat from braking and on-board air conditioning. Initially, extractor fans were planned to be placed below the platforms to suck out hot air from under the trains. Then engineers realised that such fans would also remove the cool air, and ducts would suffice. The passive cooling system works by dragging air down the escalators from outside, along the platform and out through the 'over platform extract' originally designed for smoke removal. This change of plan reduced the number of expensive tunnel ventilation and evacuation shafts from 25 to 5.

In order to avoid settlement, civil engineers reinforced the foundations of old structures with resin grout to strengthen them, pumping it in through tubes. Each section of tunnel has an effigy of St Barbara – the miners' saint. Tunnels are lined with concrete segments, but underground stations have a sprayed concrete lining as the tunnel there is too large a diameter for a boring machine.

Canary Wharf station appears to be floating on water and has a retail centre above it to earn money.

A problem had to be solved at the Barbican Centre. Concert Hall One is two storeys below ground and 17 metres above Crossrail's tunnels. To prevent noise pollution, the track floats on sprung concrete slabs and the springs absorb all the noise and energy before it reaches the concert hall. Special MagnaDense concrete was used at a cost of about 10 times normal concrete but will result in a very low vibration. In 1863, Metropolitan track-laying gangs laid up to 150 metres a day; modern track-laying machinery lays more than 600 metres a day.

Rival bids were received from Spain and Japan, but Bombardier, Derby, won the £1 billion contract supporting in excess of 1,200 jobs. Sixty-six Class 345 sets were built by Bombardier and consist of 9 cars offering a total of 454 seats per train and a capacity of 1,500 passengers. The aluminium car bodies are fully air-conditioned. Each train contains more than 93 miles of cables. As the trains are 200 metres in length and the platform 250 metres, this will allow for trains to be lengthened, should this be desirable. The trains have a maximum speed of 90 mph on the outer sections. Train control is automatic in the tunnel sections, with a driver only taking over in an emergency. The first train was tested in Crossrail's tunnels on 25 February 2018. The train depot with 33 sidings is situated at Old Oak Common, behind that of the Great Western. The 25 KV overhead line is supplied from the National Grid.

An unusual feature was the Crossrail graduate scheme, which had 15 members spread over two intakes and unlike most schemes that offered four-year placements, Crossrail's was done in two years. Research carried out by the graduates was linked to real applications for Crossrail. The scheme was accredited by the Institution of Mechanical Engineers and accounted for up to two-thirds of the way towards C. Eng status.

One new tool being used is Building Information Modelling (BIM). Using a tablet or mobile device, an engineer can visit a site, point the device somewhere and the device reveals what is behind the cladding and the location of the turning or switchgear.

Unlike many railway projects, Crossrail has been delivered on time and on budget, costs being carefully controlled. At Bond Street station, on 23 February 2016, Queen Elizabeth II renamed Crossrail the Elizabeth Line. The first section to be opened was

Shenfield-Liverpool Street on 21 May 2017. On 1 November 2017 the first dynamic testing began, for about two months, with Heathrow-Paddington on 20 May 2018. Tests on the remaining sections are planned for Abbey Wood-Paddington on 9 September 2018; Shenfield and Abbey Wood-Heathrow on 19 May 2019; and the whole line opened on or before December 2019. The value of homes and offices along some parts of the Elizabeth Line has risen 50 per cent since work began.

2012

By the summer of 2012 it was realised that the HSTs of 1976 were becoming dated and preparations should be made for a new design. Agility Trains, a consortium of Hitachi and John Laing, signed an agreement with the Department for Transport to create new rolling stock to replace HSTs on the East Coast and Great Western main lines.

The Great Western Railway and Virgin Trains East Coast would have a mix of 5-car and 9-car units making a total of 866 vehicles, each would be bi-mode and straight electric trains, although the EMUs will have one diesel engine fitted to each set. In 2016 it was announced that due to delays in electrification of the Great Western, the 21 9-car electric Class 801 units for the GWR would be constructed as 21 9-car bi-mode units numbered in the 800/3 series.

The Class 800 bi-mode and Class 801 electric units were based on the Southeastern Class 395 EMUs but with bodies 26m in length rather than 20m.

2015

At a cost of £294m, 35 miles of the Waverley line was re-opened between Edinburgh and Tweedbank on 6 September 2015. It has brought an 8 per cent increase in tourism to the region and a survey showed that 65 per cent of visitors using the line said it had been a factor in their decision to make the trip. It has been estimated that by re-opening the line, 40,000 car journeys have been saved annually. A pressure group hopes to get the remainder of the line open to Hawick and Carlisle.

In 2015 Alstrom introduced the ingenious TrainScanner device, which uses 3D laser-scanning technology and cameras to inspect rolling stock. This produces a highly accurate picture of the health of the train as well as enabling predictive maintenance for wheels, brake pads and the overhead pantograph carbon strips. The technology is superior to manual inspection by a technician underneath the train wearing a head torch. The technology's greatest strength lies in its prognostic capabilities as Alstrom has been able to identify which routes cause trains the greatest wear and the firm can then determine whether the train is the problem or the existing infrastructure.

2016

In 2016 the first British-built 5-car Class 800 IEP was completed at Hitachi Rail Europe's new £82m factory at Newton Aycliffe, situated close to where George Stephenson assembled *Locomotive No. 1*. As many as 1,600 applications were received for the 700 initial staff required at Newton Aycliffe and 2,000 more will be employed by 2019. The company has a full order book for 122 IEP sets, plus 70 Class 385 (AT200) EMUs for ScotRail; 24 AT300 for Hull Trains and TransPennine Express, while the 36 ST300 needed for the GWR will be manufactured in Italy – 70 per cent of the components for the IEP sets will be sourced within a 20-mile radius of Newton Aycliffe.

A large fleet of dual-voltage Class 700 EMUs started to enter traffic in the spring of 2016 and are able to be powered either by the 25 kV AC overhead, or 750 volt DC third rail. The 12-car sets hold the equivalent of 21 London buses. The Class 700 run Cambridge-Brighton and when on the third rail section operate like a Metro with automatic stopping and door-opening. From 2018, a maximum of 24 trains an hour ran through London.

Vivarail carried out an interesting conversion in 2016. The Class 230 D-Train consists of a DEMU rebuilt from former London Underground D78 stock built by Metro-Cammell in the late 1970s and early '80s. The prototype uses the D78 bodyshells, bogies and electric traction motors, but each car is powered by two underfloor Ford Duratorq 3.2 litre diesel engines of 150 kw (200 hp). The controllers incorporate the latest stop-start technology and dynamic braking. Its maximum speed of 60 mph limits its use.

An alternative conversion allows it to operate off 750 volts from either battery, diesel power driving an alternator, straight electric, or a hybrid mix of power types. The electric multiple-unit/battery hybrid will make use of the overhead or third rail for charging the battery during a journey, or the diesel engine charging the battery. A hydrogen fuel cell-powered version is being developed.

On 30 December 2016 a genset providing current ignited and the resultant delay meant that conversion missed the bid for the next West Midlands franchise. It was modified to future-proof the standard framework for gensets or batteries so that when fuel cell technology has developed further, this form of energy could power the units.

2017

At 13.00 on 18 January 2017, the East Wind train arrived at Barking after an 18-day journey from Yiwu, an industrial city 200 miles south of Shanghai. This was the first direct train linking China and Britain. Its 34 containers were transferred from Chinese standard gauge wagons to broad gauge wagons at the border with Kazakhstan, to standard gauge wagons in Poland and in Duisburg, Germany, into DB-operated wagons approved for use in the Channel Tunnel and HS1. The containers were loaded with household goods such as clothes, socks, suitcases, purses and wallets, worth £4 million and which had travelled 7,736 miles, crossing Kazakhstan, Russia, Belarus, Poland, Germany, Belgium and France before passing through the Channel Tunnel and terminating at the London Eurorail freight hub. Its arrival coincided with even greater emphasis being placed on Britain's export business with the wider world following the Brexit vote. The service is one tenth cheaper than air freight, which takes three days, but five times more expensive than going by sea, which takes 36 days. It initially ran weekly to assess demand. The train's name is taken from Chairman Mao's dictum: 'The east wind will prevail over the west wind.' The train returned to Yiwu, leaving London on 10 April 2017.

On 22 January 2017 the first Class 88 bi-modal locomotive was delivered from Stadler, Valencia. Based on the Class 68, it can provide 5,400 hp with electric traction and 950 hp on diesel power.

On 23 February 2017, the HS2 Bill received Royal Assent. The construction of this line should ease passenger and goods traffic on the West Coast Line, which has reached saturation point. Time will tell whether the money spent on building the line was a good investment – it is one of the most expensive infrastructure projects ever planned in the United Kingdom and will be the longest line to be built for more than 100 years. Will the HS2 prove to be superfluous in the future due to developing electronic communication meaning that people no longer need to travel physically? Will technology mean that more people can work from home so that rush-hour commuter travel will become a thing of the past? The places where HS2 integrates with the existing rail network could become pinch points where late-running trains will cause delays to HS2 trains as they transfer from the existing network. It is vital that promoters of HS2, or any other new rail project, consider all scenarios because what may be good now, in this rapidly changing world, may not prove to have been the correct decision.

And then there is the problem of rolling stock. HS2 trains need to be as light as possible on the high-speed line to reduce maintenance costs, but heavier on the conventional network to cope with the greater irregularities and different signalling and control systems. Designing a train suitable for both will result in a compromised vehicle.

The Acton to Euston stretch will cost £1.25 billion a mile, making it one of the most expensive lengths of railway in the world, plus another £3 billion or so for a new Euston with 11 new platforms. This site is in one of London's worst locations as there is no access to the Central and Circle lines or Crossrail. A brand-new integrated transport hub will be created at Old Oak Common, which has connections to the existing Great Western, Crossrail and Heathrow Express services. Old Oak Common will become the Canary Wharf of West London and become an exciting new centre.

Due to the increased threat of terrorism, in May 2017 the British Transport Police confirmed that for the first time armed police will patrol trains across Britain; they had regularly been patrolling on London Underground since December 2016.

London's transport system keeps getting busier, approximately 1.37bn passengers using the capital's stations annually. Although the Elizabeth line will take some of the strain, more capacity will soon be needed and it is anticipated that Crossrail 2 could arrive *circa* 2030. This second cross-London line might run from Wimbledon in the south west, to Tottenham Hale in the north east, with major infrastructure hubs including Clapham Junction, Victoria and Euston. The total cost is estimated at £32bn, with estimates that it could increase by £1.8bn for every year the scheme was delayed. If built, it would increase the capital's rail capacity by 10 per cent.

At the time of writing, locomotive-hauled passenger trains are rare if you discount the power cars of HSTs. Some of the diesel-electric locomotives have had surprisingly long lives. The BR/ English Electric Class 08 shunters introduced in 1952 are still to be seen, while the oldest mainline locomotives are the English Electric Class 20s introduced in 1957. Almost contemporary with these is the Class 31 built by Brush Traction in 1958 and the Birmingham Railway Carriage & Wagon Company's Class 33 and the English Electric Class 33, both of which appeared in 1960. The BR/Brush/ Sulzer Class 40 outshopped between 1963 and 1967 is another long-lived group of engines.

The oldest electric locomotives running are the Class 73 electro-diesels, introduced in 1962 and capable of running on third rail or non-electric routes.

On 19 May 2017 the last Class 121 units were retired: these were the last vacuum-braked trains running on a franchised service.

Domestic Passenger Train Operators 2018
The Caledonian Sleeper franchise operated by Serco, four trains each night between Euston and Scotland.
Chiltern franchise, under trading name Chiltern Railways, operated by Arriva (Deutsche Bahn), Marylebone – Birmingham/ Kidderminster/Stratford-upon-Avon. Marylebone-Oxford.
Cross Country franchise operated by Arriva. Long distance services Scotland-South-west of England. Inter-urban services in the Birmingham area.
Crossrail franchise, under trading name TfL Rail, operated by MTR. Shenfield and Abbey Wood to Reading and Heathrow Airport.
East Coast franchise under trading name Virgin Trains East Coast, operated by Stagecoach/Virgin Trains. Frequent main line services King's Cross-Edinburgh, with less frequent services to Bradford, Harrogate, Skipton, Hull, Lincoln, Glasgow, Aberdeen and Inverness.
East Midlands franchise under trading name East Midlands Trains, operated by the Stagecoach Group. St Pancras-Sheffield and Nottingham, plus some regional services.
East Anglia franchise under trading name Greater Anglia, operated by Abellio (Netherlands Railways)/Mitsui Group. Liverpool Street to Norwich and local services.

Essex Thameside under trading name c2c, operated by Trenitalia. Fenchurch Street-Shoeburyness.

Great Western franchise under trading name Great Western Railway, operated by First Group. Paddington-South West/ South Wales/Hereford and branches in the South West.

London Rail franchise, under trading name London Overground, operated by. Arriva. Various services in the London area.

Merseyrail Electrics franchise operated by. Serco/Abellio under trading name Merseyrail.

Northern Rail franchise, under trading name Northern, operated by Arriva under Northern. Services in the north of England.

ScotRail franchise operated by Abellio under trading name ScotRail. Almost all rail services in Scotland.

South Eastern franchise operated by Govia (Go-Ahead/Keolis) under trading name Southeastern. South east London/Kent/ part of Sussex.

South Western franchise operated by First Group/MTR), under trading name South West Railway. Waterloo-Exeter/Weymouth and the Isle of Wight.

Thameslink, Southern & Great Northern franchise operated by Govia (Go-Ahead/Keolis) under trading name Govia Thameslink Railway. Services in and around the London area.

Trans-Pennine Express franchise operated by First Group under trading name TransPennine Express. Links major cities in the North of England.

Wales & Borders operated by Arriva under trading name Arriva Trains Wales. Services in Wales and the border counties.

West Coast Partnership operated by Virgin Rail Group (Virgin/ Stagecoach Group) under trading name Virgin Trains. Euston-Glasgow/Edinburgh.

West Midlands franchise operated by. Abellio/East Japan Railway Company/Mitsui. Long distance and regional services Euston-Birmingham-Crewe and some local services.

Non-Franchised Services

Heathrow Express operated by Heathrow Airport Holdings. Paddington-Heathrow Airport.

Hull Trains (part of First). King's Cross-Hull.

Grand Central (part of Arriva). King's Cross-Sunderland/Bradford Interchange.

North Yorkshire Moors Railway Enterprises. Pickering-Grosmont-Whitby/Battersby, Sheringham-Cromer.

West Coast Railway Company. Birmingham-Stratford-upon-Avon; Fort William-Mallaig; York-Settle-Carlisle.

Eurostar International; services between United Kingdom and mainland Europe. Established in 2010, jointly owned by SVCF (France), SNCB (Belgium), Patina Rail (Canada and United Kingdom).

Eurotunnel operates service for carrying accompanied road vehicles.

Freight Train Operators

Colas Rail: permanent way machines; freight.

DB Cargo (UK). The largest freight operator. Was the English, Welsh & Scottish Railway until purchased by Deutsche Bahn when it was initially called DB Schenker. Some of its locomotives have been transferred to its operations in France and Poland.

Devon & Cornwall Railways: short-term freight contracts.

Direct Rail Services: originally for transporting nuclear flasks between power stations and the reprocessing plant at Sellafield, has diversified.

Freightliner: intermodal container trains and aggregates, cement and coal.

GB Railfreight, owned by the Hector Rail group: intermodal and infrastructure duties; also operates some excursion trains.

Rail Operations Group: movement of rolling stock; operates a small number of excursion trains.

West Coast Railway Company although it holds freight licence it does not operate any freight: operates empty stock movements and locomotives used on excursions.

About 70 per cent of British privatised train companies are owned by foreign governments and the profits used for supporting Dutch, French and German railways.

Today's railway network lacks style and character: there are few named trains and those that are, seem to be thought shameful and just peep out from under the carpet. Rolling stock too leaves much to be desired – compartments were much more friendly than today's open saloons, and the air-line type seating with high backs and very little knee-room prevent passengers from observing much of what is outside the window, as to do window frames that often fail to coincide well with the seats. It is pleasing that East Midlands Trains still operate HST sets, which have never had the type of seating altered, retaining lower-back seats with a good view ahead; they are mainly found on the St Pancras-Nottingham service. Multiple-unit trains, whether diesel or electric, should be designed like the first-generation DMUs so that passengers can enjoy a forward view such as the driver can enjoy.

Despite airline competition, diesel locomotives continue to haul sleepers between London and Penzance, while the Caledonian sleepers are electrically hauled between London and Edinburgh/ Glasgow with diesel haulage onwards to Aberdeen, Inverness and Fort William.

It is possible that the traditional form of railway will become redundant for longer distances. The Hyperloop system has been developed by the US billionaire Elon Musk. Hyperloops are made up of transport pods that float using magnetic levitation and travel in a vacuum through a tube at speeds of almost 700 mph due to the low air resistance; this could cut a 400-mile non-stop trip from London to Edinburgh to 50 minutes, compared to 1 hour and 20 minutes by air. The cost of the system is prohibitively high, between £7bn and £121bn per mile. Three Hyperloop systems have been proposed for Britain: a 660-mile route from Cardiff to Edinburgh and Glasgow via London; 414 miles from London, Birmingham, Manchester and Glasgow and a 339-mile northern arc covering Liverpool, Manchester, Leeds, Newcastle, Edinburgh and Glasgow. Britain was a leader in maglev technology in the 1960s, but no commercial line has been built in Britain. In October 2017 it was announced that Sir Richard Branson had invested in Hyperloop One and that the company will be renamed Virgin Hyperloop One.

Passenger journeys have more than doubled since privatisation, from 735 million in 1994 to 1.7 billion in 2016, almost trebling since the 1982 post-war slump, in fact, more people are carried by rail today than ever before. Regarding passenger numbers, Britain has the fastest growing railway system in Europe.

The summer of 2017 marks the 25th anniversary of the policy that led to privatisation and reversed the railway's decline. Passenger journeys on the network have more than doubled since privatisation from 735 million in 1994 to 1.7 billion in

2016, almost trebling since 1982. John Major's privatisation plan pledged to deliver 'more competition, greater efficiency and a wider choice of services more closely tailored to what customers want' but most passengers are unable to enjoy competition, having to deal with a monopoly. King's Cross is the exception, where Virgin Trains East Coast faces competition from Hull Trains and Grand Central, they also record the highest passenger satisfaction ratings in Britain: Hull Trains coming top with 97 per cent, Grand Central with 94 per cent and Virgin Trains East Coast with 91 per cent. Grand Central and Hull Trains also come top on value for money, reliability, punctuality and obtaining a seat. Competition also limits fare increases. The Great Western franchise covering an area with little competition suffers one of the lowest satisfaction scores, only 48 per cent of passengers thinking it offers value for money. Similarly in the Greater Anglia monopoly just 42 per cent of the passengers believe they are getting value for money. Britain's busiest station, Waterloo, used by almost 100 million passengers in 2016, is used by just one train operator and that has a score of 40 per cent.

Where there is a lack of competition, such as on the Great Western out of Paddington, there is lack of satisfaction and the franchise scored only 48 per cent of passengers believing that the price of tickets offered value for money, whereas 78 per cent of Grand Central passengers thought the train offered value for the fare. The message is obvious: when passengers have a real choice, companies compete on price and comfort to win passengers.

The government should bring out a new rail policy ensuring that all main lines have competing services – only this will fulfil the Conservatives' rail pledges made a generation ago.

A football fan from Newcastle planned to take his girlfriend to watch his team play at Oxford. To save money, he decided that rather than buy return tickets, he would purchase a sequence of discounted tickets for stages of the journey. He bought 56. He used the same trains from Newcastle-Oxford and Oxford-Newcastle as passengers with normal return tickets but had paid less – the only drawback was that he had to carry a pile of tickets thicker than a pack of playing cards.

At the time of writing, the government is in favour of bi-mode trains, claiming that they will offer improvement 'without the disruption of electrification work' – but bi-modes are more expensive to build, more complex to maintain, less reliable, and more sluggish when using diesel power compared with the diesel trains they replace.

It seems curious that although the Government will ban diesel cars in the future, they have halted electrification of the Midland Main Line to Sheffield and on sections of the Great Western. Bi-model trains, when in the diesel mode, cannot accelerate as quickly as when in the electric mode and thus there is less opportunity to slot in stopping trains between expresses, so line capacity is reduced.

Regarding the present problem of overcrowding in standard class carriages on commuter trains, an Institute of Economic Affairs report suggested that matters could be eased by creating a new 'economy class' with a few carriages on each train set aside for standing passengers only, who would be suitably compensated for their relative discomfort with an offer of a fare discount of 20 per cent.

Driverless operation, which has worked on the Docklands Light Railway for the past 30 years, has been successful and safe and the idea will be copied elsewhere. Automation and digitisation do not destroy jobs – they create new ones and increase the skills of existing roles. The 21st-century railway workforce will be digitally literate, using new signalling, ticketing and traffic management systems producing continuous flows of data. Maintenance technicians will interpret data sets of diagnostic information instead of inspecting track in the rain, and signalling engineers will write code and algorithms instead of pulling levers.

By the beginning of the 21st century, railway revival was in full swing, the number of passenger journeys had passed the post-war peak to reach 1.65 billion by 2015. The Channel Tunnel had been built, the Elizabeth line links East and West London and HST2 is planned. Trains are certainly back in fashion.

There are about 2,560 stations today on the national network, and some are architectural treasures and are now appreciated, and unlike in the days of steam when they tended to become grubby, can be seen in all their beauty. Paddington was renovated in 1999, followed by St Pancras in 2007, both real gems. Some new stations are well designed, such as Canary Wharf, opened in 1999 on

Docklands Light Railway, while the 2015 rebuild of Birmingham New Street is a vast improvement on the hideous 1967 structure.

Regarding signalling, in the 1960s power boxes replaced most mechanical boxes; today Rail Operating Centres cover a much larger area but eventually all lineside signalling will disappear as cab signalling is introduced.

British railway engineers are still at the forefront of development and on 6 November 2017 the Ordsall Chord opened, 300 metres of new track including the world's first asymmetric railway bridge. The line connects Manchester's three main railway stations: Piccadilly, Victoria and Oxford Road and also reveals Stephenson's Liverpool & Manchester Railway Bridge.

Railways were a vital part of our past and the beating heart of our present and future. Britain's railways carry more people than ever before – 1.67 billion annually – and this figure is likely to be doubled by the middle of the twenty-first century.

Ordsall Chord under construction in April 2017. (Courtesy of delusion23 under Creative Commons 4.0)

Bibliography

Allen, C. J., *Titled Trains of Great Britain* (London: Ian Allan, 1953)

Carter, E., *An Historical Geography of the Railways of the British Isles* (London: Cassell, 1959)

Christiansen, R., *A Regional History of the Railways of Great Britain Volume 7 The West Midlands* (Newton Abbot: David & Charles, 1991)

Coleman, T., *The Railway Navvies* (London: Hutchinson, 1965)

Cummings, J., *Railway Motor Buses and Bus Services in the British Isles 1902-1933* (Oxford: Oxford Publishing Co, 1978/1980)

Ellis, Hamilton, *British Railway History 1830-1876* (London: George Allen & Unwin, 1969)

Ellis, Hamilton, *British Railway History 1877-1947* (London: George Allen & Unwin, 1960)

Gourvish, T. R., *British Railways 1948 73* (Cambridge: Cambridge University Press, 1986)

Hylton, S., *What The Railways Did For Us* (Stroud: Amberley 2015)

James, L., *A Chronology of the Construction of Britain's Railways 1778-1855* (Shepperton: Ian Allan, 1983)

Joy, D., *A Regional History of the Railways of Great Britain Volume 8 South and West Yorkshire* (Newton Abbot: David & Charles, 1984)

Kidner, R. W., *The Light Railway Handbook* (Lingfield: Oakwood Press, no date)

McKenna, F., *The Railway Workers 1840-1970* (London: Faber & Faber, 1980)

Nock, O. S., *British Steam Railways* (London: Adam & Charles Black, 1961)

Nock, O. S., *Historic Railway Disasters* (Shepperton, Ian Allan, 1983)

Nock, O.S., *The Railway Enthusiasts' Encyclopedia* (London: Arrow Books, 1971)

Nock, O. S., *The Railways of Britain Past and Present* (London: Batsford, 1949)

Poultney, E. C., *British Express Locomotive Development 1896-1948* (London: George Allen & Unwin, 1952)

Robbins T. M., *The Railway Age* (London: Routledge & Kegan Paul, 1962)

Rolt, L. T. C., *George and Robert Stephenson* (Stroud: Amberley 2016)

Rolt, L T. C., *Red for Danger* (London: Pan Books, 1960)

Simmons, J., *The Railways of Britain* (London: Routledge & Kegan Paul, 1962)

Simmons, J. & Biddle, G., editors, *The Oxford Companion to British Railway History* (Oxford: OUP, 1997)

Simmons, J., *The Victorian Railway* (London: Thames & Hudson, 1991)

Thomas, D. St J., *A Regional History of the Railways of Great Britain Volume 1 The West Country* (Newton Abbot: David & Charles, 1981)

Thomas, J., (revised A. J .S. Paterson), *A Regional History of the Railways of Great Britain Volume 6 Scotland, the Lowlands & the Borders* (Newton Abbot: David & Charles, 1984)

Thomas, J. & Turnock, D., *A Regional History of the Railways of Great Britain Volume 16 North of Scotland* (Newton Abbot: David & Charles, 1989)

Thornhill, P., *Railways for Britain* (London: Methuen, 1954)

White, H. P., *A Regional History of the Railways of Great Britain Volume 2 Southern England* (Newton Abbot: David & Charles 1970)

White, H. P., *A Regional History of the Railways of Great Britain Volume 3 Greater London* (Newton Abbot; David & Charles, 1971

Principal Railways Opened in Britain 1801–1830

Year of Incorporation	Year of Opening	Railway	Length in Miles
1801	1803	Surrey Iron Railway	9¾
1802	1804	Carmarthenshire Railway	16
1802	1805	Sirhowey Railway	28
1803	1805	Croydon, Merstham & Godstone	8½
1804	1806	Oystermouth Railway	6
1808	1812	Kilmarnock & Troon	9¾
1809	1811	Gloucester & Cheltenham Railway	9
1809	1812	Bullo Pill (Forest of Dean) Railway	7½
1809	1812	Lydney & Lydbrook Railway	26
1810	1817	Monmouth Railway	8
1811	1816	Hay Railway	14
1811	1813	Llanfihangel Railway	6½
1812	1814	Grosmont Railway	7
1817	1819	Mansfield & Pinxton Railway	8¼
1818	1820	Kington Railway	14
1819	1823	Plymouth & Dartmoor Railway	30
1821	1825	Stockton & Darlington Railway	54
1821	1826	Stratford & Moreton Railway	17
1824	1826	Monkland & Kirkintilloch Railway	10
1824	1826	Redruth & Chacewater Railway	14¼
1825	1826	Portland Railway	2
1825	1828	Nantlle Railway	9¼
1825	1828	Liskeard & Looe Railway	7

1825	1828	Bolton & Leigh Railway	9
1825	1829	Duffryn-Llynvi & Porthcawl Railway	16¾
1825	1829	Rumney Railway	21¾
1825	1830	Canterbury & Whitstable Railway	6¼
1825	1830	Cromford & High Peak Railway	33

The Numbers & Classification of Persons Employed on Railways in Britain 1 May 1848

Job	On Lines Open	On Lines Not Open
Secretaries	81	102
Managers	30	93
Treasurers	29	21
Engineers	95	405
Superintendents	343	1,897
Storekeepers	125	243
Accountants	70	145
Cashiers	48	88
Draughtsmen	106	306
Clerks	4,360	887
Artificers	10,814	29,087
Labourers	14,297	147,325
Inspectors	-	119
Land Surveyors	-	26
Miners	-	6,250
Foremen	1,010	685
Policemen	2,475	71
Porters	7,559	10
Platelayers	4,391	256
Drivers (carters)	-	45
Engine Drivers	1,752	-
Firemen	1,809	-

Switchmen	1,058	-
Gatekeepers	401	-
Waggoners	141	-
Brakesmen	32	-
Guards	1,464	-
Miscellaneous	197	116
Total	52,687	188,177

On 1 May 1848 4,253 miles of railway were open with 1,321 stations.

Excursion Fares from London by the Cheapest Class 1850

London to:	Return fare		Miles per penny
	S	d	
Croydon	1	0	20
Liverpool	21	0	21
Glasgow	37	6	22
Tunbridge Wells	4	0	23
Windsor	2	0	26
Maidstone	4	0	28
Brighton	3	6	29
Cambridge	4	0	29
Dover	6	0	29
Hampton Court	1	0	30
Kew		8	30
Hastings	5	0	30
Rochester	2	0	31
Gravesend	1	6	32
Guildford	2	6	34
Ramsgate	6	0	34
Oxford	3	6	36
Bristol	6	0	39
Woolwich	6		40
Cheltenham	6	0	41
Bath	5	0	43
Portsmouth	4	0	47
New Forest	4	0	48
Southampton	3	0	53
Salisbury	3	6	55

Constituent Companies of the 'Big Four' Formed in 1923

GREAT WESTERN RAILWAY

Great Western Railway
Barry Railway 1922
Cambrian Railways 1922
Cardiff Railway
Rhymney Railway 1922
Taff Vale Railway 1922
Alexandra Docks & Railway 1922
Brecon & Merthyr Railway 1922
Vale of Rheidol Railway 1922
Burry Port & Gwendraeth Valley Railway 1922
Cleobury Mortimer & Dittons Prior Light Railway 1922
Llanelly & Mynydd Mawr Railway
Welshpool & Llanfair Light Railway
Swansea Harbour Trust Railways
Neath & Brecon Railway 1922
Gwendraeth Valleys Railway
Midland & South Western Junction Railway
Powlesland & Mason, Swansea Docks 1924
Corris Railway
Port Talbot Railway & Docks Co 1922
Rhondda & Swansea Bay Railway 1922
South Wales Mineral Railway

LONDON, MIDLAND & SCOTTISH RAILWAY

Caledonian Railway
Furness Railway
Glasgow & South Western Railway
Highland Railway
Lancashire & Yorkshire Railway (Taken over by LNWR 1922)
London & North Western Railway
London, Tilbury & Southend Railway (Taken over by the MR 1912)
Maryport & Carlisle Railway
Midland Railway
Somerset & Dorset Joint Railway
Cleator & Workington Junction Railway
Glasgow & Paisley Joint Line
Knott End Railway
Leek & Manifold Light Railway
Stratford-on-Avon & Midland Junction Railway
North Staffordshire Railway
Wirral Railway
North London Railway (Taken over by the LNWR 1922)

LONDON & NORTH EASTERN RAILWAY

Great Northern Railway
North Eastern Railway
Great Eastern Railway
Great Central Railway
Hull & Barnsley Railway (Taken over by the NER 1922)
North British Railway
Great North of Scotland Railway
Midland & Great Northern Joint Railway

SOUTHERN RAILWAY

London & South Western Railway
London, Brighton & South Coast Railway
South Eastern & Chatham Railway
Lynton & Barnstaple Railway
Freshwater, Yarmouth & Newport Railway
Isle of Wight Railway
Isle of Wight Central Railway

Index